Theatres

Architectural Press Library of Planning and Design

THEATRES

Planning Guidance for Design and Adaptation

Roderick Ham

The Architectural Press: London

Van Nostrand Reinhold Company: New York

First published in 1972 as *Theatre Planning*
by the Architectural Press, 9 Queen Anne's
Gate, London SW1H 9BY
This edition published 1987

© Association of British Theatre
Technicians, 1987

ISBN 0-442-20497-3

Published in the U.S. and Canada by Van
Nostrand Reinhold Company Inc.
115 Fifth Avenue
New York, New York 10003

Distributed in Canada by
Macmillan of Canada
Division of Canada Publishing Corporation
164 Commander Boulevard
Agincourt, Ontario M1S 3C7, Canada

16 15 14 13 12 11 10 9 8 7 6 5 4 3 2 1

Printed and bound in Great Britain at the
University Press, Cambridge.

Contents

Preface

Since the original publication of this data in the *Architects' Journal* and its enlargement in 1972 into the standard work on the subject (*Theatre Planning*, Architectural Press), the world has experienced a theatre building boom. Inevitably the large complexes are the ones that attract the limelight: in New York the Lincoln Center; in Berlin the Philharmonie; in London the South Bank complex and the Barbican Centre. All the more important to take a close look at the whole range of buildings covered by the word "theatre", especially in Britain at this time when the word conjures up in some minds a type of new building which we either cannot, or at any rate ought not to, afford.

A theatre is by original definition "a place for viewing" and an auditorium "a place for hearing". Put the two together, and any auditorium either is or can become a theatre. The range covered is therefore enormous, but all such buildings will have certain principles in common. The most obvious are that the audience must be got in and out safely and with the minimum of fuss, supervision and direction; and when inside they must be able to see and hear the show well enough to relax and enjoy it. Once that show or any part of it is live, provision has to be made for its easy get-in and get-out of the building; and some of the components may have to be "stored" before they are seen by the audience. This obviously applies to the actors or musicians (hence dressing rooms and green room); what is less obvious is that it also applies to scenery, even when the current show does not need a change of scene. The best economic use of an auditorium may well mean that it should not be tied up to a particular production. Since most live entertainment takes place in the evening, storage to allow clearance of at least part of the stage so that it can be used as a platform for other purposes during the day is a must, even in the most dedicated of theatres.

Similarly, out in the auditorium some flexibility in arrangements, and even the possibility of removing the seats, is useful. Such flexibility must apply not only in plan but also in section; in other words it is a three-dimensional exercise, in order to ensure that the sightlines from audience to show are not impaired. In the past decade great advances have been made in the provision as standard units of comfortable seating blocks which retract for storage. Whatever the form of removable seating, provision for its storage or the storage of other items which may be deployed in the auditorium is of course essential. Some thought at the planning stage can make all the difference. A change of level can turn a simple shove into a herculean heave; just one step or angle in the wrong place is all that is required to triple the task and the time to carry it out.

Multi-purpose flexibility in theatre buildings has a long history behind it. The stalls level in even the grandest of opera houses, for example Vienna, could be floored over level with the stage for the most glittering of state balls – no mere tawdry makeshift these occasions. Indeed our own Royal Opera House in Covent Garden, London, owes its very survival to the fact that for the major part of each year in the twenties and thirties it readily converted to and was used as a dance hall.

If a theatre may find it desirable that it can convert to other uses, it applies with even more force that concert and other assembly halls will play the role of a theatre. As already pointed out, that great bugbear of the assembly halls of the past – the flat floor – need no longer be with us. But the integration of such systems into new buildings needs careful planning, and the conversion of existing buildings to take such things can demand a touch of genius only born of experience on the part of the architect or his consultant. Inevitably, a decision has to be made on which form has the highest priority and this may not always depend on possible frequency of use, and in consequence some compromise may have to be accepted. A common problem would be the occasional need for large audiences for concerts and musicals, whose seating then remains empty to haunt even the most successful of intimate drama. Nevertheless, quite apart from the technical means now available to separate off empty areas and to adjust the acoustics, it can well be that experienced planning of a new auditorium or redecoration and/or some readjustment of seating areas can make an existing place appear half-full rather than half-empty!

Frederick Bentham

Introduction to the new edition

This new book on theatres appears at a time when in Britain there is great reluctance on the part of central and local government to provide any support for the performing arts, and funds for capital investment have been mercilessly axed. A society which lays claim to being civilised must, by definition, allot a proportion of its resources to patronage of the arts. Even in hard times, during the Second World War, for instance, the need for people to assemble and enjoy live drama, music and dancing was recognised, encouraged and supported. It is ironical that in a far more prosperous era, when people have much more leisure time, there is a reaction against such support. The performing arts will nevertheless survive impoverishment in the face of official neglect until their importance to the community as a whole is once again realised and policy is changed.

The planning principles, information and advice in this book, which supersedes *Theatre Planning*, published in 1972, apply to all scales of building for live performances, from the grand new multi-auditoria complexes to conversions and refurbishment of the old.

In the fifteen years since *Theatre Planning* there have been rapid advances in some areas of theatre technology; but the general principles of theatre design have changed little, if at all, and much of what appeared in that book remains as true today as it ever was. In the intervening years we have seen a number of interesting new buildings, and London has acquired two multi-auditoria complexes: the National Theatre and the Barbican Centre. It has at last caught up with the Joneses of the USA, Canada, Australia and Germany, not to mention numerous small nouveaux riches countries and even the Third World. Briefly in the UK the state, nationally and locally, recognised its responsibility towards the performing arts and put some capital investment into new buildings. It seems it was only a short-lived and reluctant interlude, because funds are rapidly drying up and the small boom in theatre building which has lasted nearly twenty years is apparently over, in Britain at least.

The controversy over forms of audience-to-actor relationship which took up much of people's time in the sixties and seventies no longer assumes so much importance. It was once easy to put everyone into a category, from right-wing-equals-proscenium-theatre through to left-wing-equals-theatre-in-the-round. The greater the degree of encirclement, the more avant-garde you were considered. Such a simplistic analysis was never very close to the truth and only survives among students whose library has not been recently updated. It is no longer obligatory to subscribe unquestioningly to the theatre-in-the-round lobby to be considered progressive. Much of the best work is done in proscenium theatres, though now they are seldom used in the old fourth-wall, picture-frame manner. One practice that has become widely established is to make as little use as possible of the stage curtains, so that the stage and auditorium are perceived by the audience as one space. Most theatre companies working in medium-sized theatres work both in their main auditorium and in a smaller studio, which may take many different forms of actor-to-audience relationship. The various forms co-exist quite comfortably, each with its own advantages and disadvantages. There is a parallel with the Modern Movement in architecture, where the theoretical certainties of Le Corbusier, Gropius and Mies van der Rohe are no longer accepted without question.

In this edition less emphasis has been placed in Chapter 2 on the plan diagrams showing the various forms of actor-to-audience relationship. Instead actual examples, ancient and modern, have been added to illustrate each kind of theatre. Historical precedents have continually inspired new approaches to drama, as in all forms of human expression. The diagrams are inclined to convey an over-simplified, two-dimensional, mechanistic view of theatre forms. They are an analytical device which is in danger of diverting attention from the subtleties of the arts of drama and architecture.

The preoccupation with ingenious mechanicals still remains among the designers of theatres, but the rude mechanicals who have to operate them are less enchanted. In the last fifteen years there have been some notable failures of elaborate mechanical stages and claims for the success of others which are hard to substantiate. While there has been disillusion with permanent mechanical installations there has on the other hand been much use of machinery to animate stage sets. A series of shows, mostly musicals in the West End of London, have used specially built machinery to spectacular effect: *Starlight Express*, *Time*, *Mutiny* and *Chess* all depended heavily on displays of mechanical ingenuity. When intended to aid the stage technical staff, machinery is often less than successful, but when used to astonish an audience it seems to fare much better.

In the first edition we deliberately avoided discussion of multi-purpose halls on the grounds that we were concerned with defining the best conditions for performances and that falling short of these definitions could not be excused by the building having to be used for other purposes. It is still our opinion that, however multi-purpose the hall, it should meet the standards for live performances outlined in this book. The usual image of the multi-purpose hall is one of woeful inadequacy for whatever use it is put to, summed up in the oft-quoted phrase "multi-everything, good for nothing". This is unfortunately true of many halls, but it is of course an unfair generalisation, and we have gone some way to making amends in this edition. There are many buildings which can perform a range of functions quite satisfactorily, or at least with acceptable compromises. Probably the most successful are those that do not attempt to do absolutely everything that is known or could be expected in the future, but limit their ambition to a few carefully considered applications. Sometimes all that is required is foresight by the clients and their designers and the necessary technical equipment, as in the case of a concert auditorium which can be used for conferences. Starting off with a conference auditorium and then trying to make it serve for orchestral concerts does not necessarily work. In general the demands of live performances, both visual and acoustic, are more exacting than for any other likely use of the building.

There has been rapid technical advance in the fields of stage lighting and stage sound. In lighting, the control systems are now virtually all computer-memory-controlled, and there have been improvements in light sources and to some extent in the luminaires. Experience has prompted a more generous provision of space in the lighting bridges and slots in the redrawn diagrams, and no doubt all those publications which have copied them from the first edition will amend them to conform to the new recommended standard.

Sound equipment has developed and proliferated vastly in the last ten years and is still expanding at a dizzy pace. Communications systems have become far more sophisticated. In these areas, where electronics make the going, there have been significant changes, but in the more steam-age realm of stage machinery, lifts and flying equipment have hardly altered. Over-ambitious attempts to extend the scope of traditional stage machinery have not met with much success. The one innovation which has proved itself particularly useful is the pneumatic castor.

New technical developments in the performing arts are likely to be spin-offs from other industries rather than the result of direct research into projects of a purely theatrical nature. In developing a new car, an aircraft or an engine of war, a great deal of expensive building of prototypes has to be undertaken, but such an investment of time and money would be quite out of proportion to the limited resources of most of the entertainment industry. Without a prototype everything has to work first time, and the risk of failure cannot often be afforded by enterprises funded from the hard-won proceeds of a public appeal or from the vigilantly husbanded local authority rates. The best hope for new technology in the theatre lies in the imaginative application of devices and ideas already developed for other purposes.

In general this book follows the pattern of *Theatre Planning* but for greater clarity there have been some rearrangements in the treatment of the technical services. All electrical wiring for stage lighting, sound and the general provision for lighting and power in the building has been taken into the chapter on electrical and mechanical services (Chapter 21). The control rooms for lighting, sound and stage management, which have much in common, now have a chapter to themselves (Chapter 15), and sound and communications have been separated from each other (Chapters 12 and 13).

Provision for video projection and slide projection has become increasingly important not only in cinemas but especially for conference uses, and this has been added to the chapter on film projection (Chapter 14). The chapter on administration (20) has been revised and expanded to cover both small and large enterprises. Chapters have been added on arts centres and studio theatres (22) and conference facilities (23).

As the building of new theatres has waned, interest in restoring some of the old ones has waxed, and Chapter 24 discusses the special problems involved in preserving them and making them suitable for today's theatregoers.

The chapter on the comparison of theatres (26) includes a wider range of buildings, many of which have opened since the first edition was published. They include the National Theatre and the Barbican Centre in London, the Sydney Opera House and the Adelaide Festival Theatre in Australia, and several concert halls. All theatre plans and sections in Chapters 2 and 26 are at the same scale of 1:1000.

Acknowledgements

I have been assisted in writing this book by a substantial grant from Glantre Engineering under their Managing Director, Derek Gilbert, which attracted a further grant from the Minister for the Arts' Business Sponsorship Scheme, administered by the Association of Business Sponsorship for the Arts, and a grant for the purpose from the Arts Council of Great Britain to the Association of British Theatre Technicians.

As with *Theatre Planning*, members of the ABTT technical committees have contributed their expertise and practical knowledge.

The chapter on acoustics was vetted by Richard Cowell of Arup Acoustics; those on safety, exits and means of escape, seating layout and safety regulations, and legislation were updated by R. G. Cullington (late of the GLC), stage planning by Peter Angier, stage lighting by Bob Anderson, sound installations by Bill Graham and the ABTT Sound Committee, communications by Martin Carr, film projection by Charles Beddow of the British Film Institute, administration by Richard York, electrical and mechanical services by Derek Gilbert and Gareth Davies, conference facilities by Derek Gilbert.

Throughout the editing process Derek Gilbert has given invaluable advice, particularly on technical matters, and Frederick Bentham, besides writing the preface to this edition, has contributed an overall critical view of the text. Others who have offered advice are Roger Fox, Kim Little, Nigel Jarvis and John Downman.

Stephen Brandes has drawn all the theatre plans and revised the diagrams, and Hedwina Bilton has handled the typing and duplication.

Introduction to the first edition

The Association of British Theatre Technicians was formed in March 1961 by a group of enthusiasts, all professionally connected with the theatre, who believed that it was time to improve technical standards.

There had scarcely been any theatre building in Britain for twenty years, continuity was broken, and it was no longer just a question of starting again from where the matter had been left in the 1930s. The war had accelerated the changes in society; technology was advancing rapidly; and a re-assessment of the problems of theatre planning and design was clearly necessary before a new generation of building arose. It was already apparent that mistakes were being made out of ignorance of the needs of the performing arts, and the ABTT saw that probably its most important task was to examine these needs and make recommendations based upon the wide experience of its members in every branch of the theatre. The association was a forum where ideas were exchanged and tested in discussion. Specialist committees were formed dealing with architecture and planning, materials, publications, safety, sound and stage lighting. Each of these committees embarked on technical studies, and when the *Architects' Journal* proposed to publish a series of articles on theatres in its programme of design guides and information sheets, the ABTT took on the task of preparing the texts and diagrams. The first supplements were published at weekly intervals in the *Architects' Journal* in 1964, and a later series followed in 1967. Two thousand additional sets of articles were bound into paperback volumes and published as *Theatre Planning* and *Theatre Planning II*. The subject had not been covered as comprehensively before and there is little doubt that the work had a profound influence on those concerned with projects for new theatres. The original issues are now out of print, and the ABTT decided that a new and completely revised edition should be prepared for publication in book form. The Arts Council was approached by Norman Marshall, the ABTT's chairman, and contributed a generous grant towards the cost of research and rewriting of the text, and the Architectural Press undertook to publish the book.

The shortcomings of the original publications were mostly due to the magazine form they had to follow. There was no index and a good deal of repetition was inevitable. Some of the articles were only of passing interest and others have been superseded. Much of the basic information in the original work remains the same but all of it has been carefully scrutinised and much of it rewritten. The book sets out to describe the principles and practical considerations which influence the design of the layout and equipment of buildings to house live performances. The information has been gathered from the experience of those who have to work in such buildings and who have to try to use them

efficiently. As more is known about the workings of the proscenium theatre than about open forms it is inevitable that there are more references to it than to the less orthodox types of theatre, but this does not indicate an editorial bias in favour of the proscenium. We have described what there is to describe, and many of the problems examined are common to all forms of theatre. There remain entertainments and dramatic activities, from tattoos to television, which neither need nor ask for the kind of facilities here examined.

One subject not covered in this book is the multi-purpose hall. We have been concerned throughout to describe the optimum conditions for housing live performances, and these remain the same whether the building is labelled "theatre" or "multi-purpose hall". If the process of making a hall multi-purpose forces compromises and prevents proper conditions from being obtained, that is not a valid excuse for applying lower standards. A great deal of ingenuity has been lavished on schemes of adaptability and much time and sometimes money spent on mechanical methods of achieving them. The fascination of the gadgetry should not be allowed to obscure the shortcomings of the results. In any one conformation or arrangement an objective assessment of the result usually shows that it is less satisfactory than a building specially designed to serve that particular purpose.

Flexibility of use remains an important virtue in any scheme, but it is not synonymous with machinery, as some would have us think. While it is very simple to phrase a brief which calls for a building to house banquets, dances, professional theatre, amateur operatics, film shows and jumble sales all in the same space, if not at the same time, it is virtually impossible to translate such words into a satisfactory solution in terms of building. It has never yet been done successfully, though the quest has been as obsessive as for the philosopher's stone or the elixir of life.

Another school of thought which has ample coverage elsewhere, especially in architectural magazines, is the one which demands a covered space and a kit of parts which in theory enable it to keep its options open until the last moment. Schemes of this nature usually rely heavily on rather speculative technological solutions to the problems encountered along the way, and it would not be possible to do justice to them in a book of this nature.

In a work devoted to the study of the design of buildings for housing the performing arts it is well to sound a note of humility and remember that it is people and not buildings which make theatre. Dramatic magic can be created in the most unlikely places and in utterly unpromising surroundings. Nevertheless, good buildings can give full rein to the creativity of those who use them and can enhance the experience of those who come to watch and listen.

Acknowledgements

The original *Architects' Journal* series was edited by Leslie Fairweather, the principal authors were Peter Moro, Ian Appleton, Peter Jay and the present editor, and this work has provided a sound foundation for the present volume. The editor is indebted to Peter Moro and Frederick Bentham for their continual advice and encouragement on matters both technical and syntactical during the two years over which the task of compiling and editing has been spread.

The chapter on acoustics was originally written by Henry Humphreys; safety, regulations and legislation are largely the work of Eric Jordan, who also contributed the section on the comparison of theatres and all the drawings in that chapter. Stage scenery is adapted from the study by the ABTT Materials Committee first published by the *Architects' Journal*. The members of the committee of which the editor was chairman were: Ian Albery, Dorothea Alexander, Alan Cohen, Frederick Crooke, Richard Greenough, Bertram Harrison, Joseph McDougall, Harry Pegg and Edward Tietjen.

The Materials Committee, joined by Peter Angier, Ethel Langstreth, Ken Smalley, Peter White-Gaze and Peter Woodham, gave invaluable assistance with the chapter on stage planning and with the glossary. Richard Brett contributed a note on powered flying. The ABTT Lighting Committee drew up the original recommendations for stage lighting installations, published in the *Architects' Journal*. The members at that time were: Eric Baker, Frederick Bentham, Charles Bristow, Bill Bruce, John Bury, Martin Carr, Peter Coe, Elidir Davies, Joe Davis, David Furse, Barry Griffiths, Cyril Griffiths, Robert Hall, Margaret Harris, Edward Hitchman, Peter Jay, Brian Legge, Robert Ornbo, Richard Pilbrow, Francis Reid, Peter Rice and John Wyckham.

That document has been completely revised by the committee, now joined by: Brian Benn, Bill Besant, E. E. Faraday, Robert Fox and R. G. S. Anderson, who contributed the section on providing for television broadcasts from theatres, and Derek Gilbert, whose notes on memory systems have been included. Requirements for control rooms were taken from the ABTT Information Sheet on the subject by Martin Carr. Sound installation and communications is adapted from the ABTT Sound Committee's studies on permanent equipment for theatres, permanent wiring for theatres and stage management by sound control. The members of the committee were: David Ayliff, who, in conjunction with the West End Stage Management Association, prepared the material on prompt corners, Bernard Bibby, Sylvia Carter, David Collison, Barry Griffiths, Shirley Matthews, Peter Moore, Roger Spence, Dorothy Tenham and Colin Wootton.

The basis of the chapter on film projection was the series of articles by Leslie Knopp and Anthony Wylson which appeared in the *Architects' Journal* in March, April and May 1967, and the section on heating and ventilating is adapted from an Information Sheet by Paul Hanson published in the *Architects' Journal*'s first series of design guides on theatres.

The editor is very conscious of how much he has learned from taking part in the deliberations of the ABTT Architecture and Planning Committee, chaired by Peter Moro, which over the last ten years has examined over a hundred schemes for new theatres or for the improvement of old ones.

The other members of the Architecture and Planning Committee were: Ian Albery, David Ayliff, Frederick Bentham, John Bury, Martin Carr, Douglas Cornelisson, Elidir Davies, Tony Easterbrook, John English, Michael Elliott, Eric Jordan, Iain Mackintosh, Richard Pilbrow, Ken Smalley and John Wyckham. In the editor's office, Ronald Bayliss, George Finch and David Hancock assisted with research, the text and the drawings, and Sheila Brenchley handled mountains of typing and duplicating.

1

Type and size of theatre

The word theatre has a diversity of meanings for different people, and while it is neither possible nor even desirable to fit all theatre buildings into rigid categories, it will help to consider the various types of building at present existing and the way in which they differ from or are similar to one another. In this chapter we are mainly concerned with purpose-built theatres designed for live performances. Factors affecting multi-purpose halls and conference centres are dealt with elsewhere.

Seating capacity

Usually the first characteristic which comes to mind is the seating capacity, especially in relation to the economics of the building.

It is misleading to relate the capital cost of a theatre to the number of seats without taking into account the many different standards of space, technical equipment and amenity which different buildings require for their particular purpose. For purely economic reasons it would seem that the maximum capacity possible should be aimed at, but for every form of audience to stage relationship, there is a limit to the distance of the furthest seat from the action beyond which appreciation of the performance begins to deteriorate. People will no longer be prepared to buy seats from which they cannot see or hear enough to enjoy what is going on. When live theatre was the only form of mass entertainment the public would put up with discomfort and a poor view for want of an alternative, but in these days of television and films this is no longer true.

The capacity should be derived from the visual and acoustic limits for a particular kind of performance and the form of auditorium to stage relationship. These factors will be discussed later in more detail. There will be times when demand for seats outstrips the capacity, for instance on Saturday evenings. It would be a mistake, however, to provide a couple of hundred seats for these occasions if they remain empty on most other days. Both capital and running costs would be increased, and empty seats have a depressing effect on both performers and audience. Full houses and difficulty in getting tickets are the best possible advertisement and are an incentive for the public to choose the less popular days.

It has been suggested that seating capacity should be related to the size of the town or catchment area in which the theatre is to be situated, but this is an unreliable guide. The success of a particular enterprise depends far more on the vigour of the management than the statistics of possible theatregoers. Some large towns have the greatest difficulty in filling a theatre whereas other quite small ones do so very successfully. Management policy plays the greatest part in the success or failure of a theatre, but there are many cases where, however good the management, a shabby old building or a new one with an unwelcoming atmosphere will deter the public from coming at all.

In the case of teaching theatres and drama studios, seating capacity is of secondary importance. The main purpose is to provide the drama student with the feeling of an audience, and seating for betweeen 100 and 300 is usually sufficient.

The universities have built theatres which may be connected with a drama department, but are more often used for amateur productions by students. Professional companies may visit the theatre if it has suitable facilities, in which case a capacity of 400 or 500 would be appropriate. Schemes for university theatres vary a great deal owing partly to the many purposes they have to serve, but also to a vagueness of intent leading to ill-considered briefs for their architects.

When a theatre is for amateur use, the seating capacity should be considered from a slightly different point of view. Most amateur groups can count on a limited audience of friends, relations and others who share their interest in amateur dramatics. If the total potential audience is, say, 900 (way above the average for most amateur societies), it will be of little satisfaction to amateurs to go to all the trouble of rehearsing and preparing a play for one solitary performance. They would be much happier to fill a 300-seat theatre for three performances or even a 150-seater for six.

The situation of amateur opera is rather different. There is much greater expense involved in hiring scenery and costumes, and few amateur societies can operate without engaging some professional orchestral players and principal singers. With a following which is often more numerous than that for straight drama (perhaps because the larger cast, the chorus and musicians have more relations and friends), amateur opera companies look for a large-capacity auditorium, because the cost and organisation of a series of performances are prohibitive. Their needs are difficult to meet, and they are often obliged to play in very unsuitable premises. The danger is that their insistence on a larger capacity, which will be used perhaps three or four times a year, will distort the brief for a building which will be used all the rest of the time for straight drama.

There are rare occasions when the total audience is known within fairly close limits, such as in a school or similar institution, but usually the number of people who can be persuaded to come is a matter of intelligent guesswork and hope.

The seating capacity is not the only measure of the size of a theatre. The size of the stage, the production facilities to support it and the scale on which the public areas are provided may have more effect. As a rough guide and to define terms used elsewhere in this book, the following definitions are adopted.

— *Very large* 1500 or more seats
— *Large* 900–1500 seats
— *Medium* 500–900 seats
— *Small* under 500 seats

Types of production

There is a wide range of types of production which may have to be provided for in a theatre. The brief may call for many different activities to be housed within the same space, and a measure of flexibility will be essential. However, there is a limit to the degree of adaptability which is possible without seriously compromising the success of the primary purpose of the building. A list of priorities of use will have to be made at an early stage. The detailed recommendations for the provision of accommodation for the cast for the various types of performance are given in Chapter 16.

Drama

From a single performer to a large-scale epic such as a Shakespeare history. The average straight play seldom has a cast of more than twelve, but it can be up to twenty, occasionally many more.

Grand opera, full-scale ballet, musicals, pantomime

These activities often involve singers, dancers and chorus. The style of production and scenery is usually spectacular. For the standard classical repertoire of operas and ballets a proscenium stage form is usually implied, but new productions, of musicals in particular, are often played on open stages.

Chamber opera, chamber ballet, music hall and variety, cabaret, plays with music

The cast is not likely to be more numerous than for straight drama, but proper arrangements must be made for musicians.

Concerts

A symphony orchestra averages about 90 players, but may be 120 or more.
Chamber concerts including jazz, pop and folk music will normally be limited to ten or twelve musicians, but occasionally they may number forty or fifty.
The smallest scale of musical performance is recitals, where solo singers and instrumentalists with an accompanist are concerned. The number of performers is seldom more than four or five.
Choral concerts may require space for 200–400 singers, or even more on special occasions, in addition to a large orchestra.

Size of orchestra

Most theatres should make provision for a small orchestra of about ten to twelve players, though when the principal use is for drama, there will seldom be more than two or three musicians.
A medium orchestra would be up to about forty players, which would be sufficient for most operas and ballets. A full orchestra may number 120, which is needed for some operas (e.g. Wagner).

Films

Most theatres should make proper provision for projecting films. A building designed first and foremost as a cinema will not be suitable for live performances, but films can be shown successfully in buildings whose main purpose is to provide for live performances.

Other uses – conferences

The larger conferences need a purpose-designed building and special business services which are not easy to provide on an occasional basis. For smaller gatherings, theatres may be able to offer a competitive service.

Pattern of use

Having decided the range of activities to be housed, the next factor to be considered is the pattern of use. The more intensive this is, the more space will be required.

Multiple use

This occurs when more than one company has to be accommodated simultaneously, for example a children's matinee in the afternoon, a play in the evening followed by a late-night review. There is an increasing tendency for theatres to be used in this way, interspersing plays with films and concerts. It is economically sound to make full use of the building and where the theatre serves a community it is socially sound to provide a wide range of activities.

Repertoire

Theatres used by a company which maintains a repertoire of several productions which it may change every night and between matinee and evening performances. Almost all opera houses and other major enterprises, such as the National Theatre and the Royal Shakespeare Company, play in this way. Such theatres initiate their own productions and should have their own production organisation, preferably on the same site. They need space to store the sets for the repertoire and mechanical aids to help move them about.

Repertory

The so-called "repertory" theatres present a new production at frequent intervals, usually three-weekly, and rarely revive a production. They require production facilities for making sets, properties and costumes. Note the distinction between *repertory* and *repertoire*.

Touring theatres

These theatres take in touring productions at weekly or sometimes longer intervals, but only rarely initiate a production. The pattern of touring has changed very much in recent years. There is still a need for theatres to house the metropolitan-based national opera, ballet and theatre companies, but the viability of commercial tours of plays has declined.

Long run

Shows run for as long as box-office takings permit, which may be for several months or even years. This is the characteristic of the West End theatre in London and Broadway in New York. Like touring theatres, such buildings do not usually require elaborate production facilities on site. If they operate profitably, their workshops are idle most of the time.

Intermittent use

Some university theatres and theatres belonging to amateurs are used only intermittently. In this case it is unlikely that skilled theatre technicians will be employed, and the equipment must necessarily be simple to use and maintain. There should at least be a resident engineer to guide the part-time voluntary staff.

Fringe theatres

In Britain there has been a proliferation of small theatre groups working in improvised premises such as upstairs rooms in pubs (the Bush at Shepherds Bush and the King's Head in Islington, London) or old churches and chapels. In the United States there are the Off-Broadway and Off-Off-Broadway theatres, and Scotland has the Edinburgh Fringe. The work of such groups is often of a high standard and its significance spreads far beyond the small circle making up their audience. New writing, performing, designing and directing talent has an opportunity to try out ideas which eventually fertilise the wider field of mainstream theatre, films and television. The architectural input in these fringe theatre premises may be negligible; on the other hand, many of the regional repertory theatres have studios where work of a similar nature can be produced, and these have been designed for the purpose.

Concert halls

For both acoustic and economic reasons, concert halls where large-scale orchestral works are performed need to have a much greater capacity than theatres. Audiences of at least 1500 to 2500 are appropriate. The original brief may well be to provide a hall purely for orchestral and choral works, but after it is built, or too late in the building process, it is often decided that some stage performances of opera or ballet are to be included in the programme. The result is a series of unsatisfactory makeshift fit-ups which do justice neither to the performers nor to the building. It is vital to clarify the use of the hall at the briefing stage.

Recital halls

Smaller concert halls or recital halls are better suited to chamber music, piano recitals, or other solo instruments and small groups of musicians, singers etc. Recital rooms may be adjuncts of a main concert hall or they may be independent entities with their own programmes of works.

Arts centres

There has been a growth in the provision of arts centres where the visual arts and crafts are catered for in the same building or group of buildings as the performing arts. They can take many different forms with the emphasis on various activities, sometimes more exhibition or workshop oriented and sometimes more concerned with drama or music. The social aspects of a place to meet to share the experience of the arts and to participate in the creative process are the particular concern of the arts centres.

Multi-purpose halls – sports halls

The typical multi-purpose hall is the church hall with a flat floor where jumble sales are held, and a small platform at one end where the band sits for the Saturday night hop and which is occasionally used by the local amateur drama group. More sophisticated versions introduce equipment to improve sightlines with seating on rostra or bleachers, control of daylight and some stage lighting, sound equipment, a larger stage with means of suspending lighting and scenery above it, an orchestra pit and so on.

The crucial problem at the centre of the multi-purpose hall concept is how to treat the floor. To be truly multi-purpose it must be possible to have a flat floor, but for most performances it is essential to have a raked or stepped floor to provide proper sightlines for an audience. There comes a point when it may be better and cheaper to build two halls, one with a raked floor equipped for performances of various kinds, and one with a flat floor for the many activities for which that is more appropriate.

In Britain, many more new sports halls than theatres and concert halls have been built in recent years, and it is not uncommon for them to be used for performances. They have little to recommend them for this purpose; perhaps the most important of their many disadvantages is their acoustical quality both in the matter of reverberation and in the lack of insulation from surrounding noise.

Conference centres

The arrival of specially built conference centres in the last few years has introduced a new type of assembly building with an auditorium of sorts within it. These centres are primarily designed for the business of conferences, but as they have at least a superficial resemblance to an auditorium for performances, they are sometimes used for that purpose. There is usually no need for a properly equipped stage, and if companies are asked to put on a show of some sort they at once find themselves in difficulties. The often quite large auditorium with a platform at the end is physically more akin to a concert hall, but the acoustical requirements of conferences and concert halls are very different.

Conversions of churches and other old buildings

There are many old buildings of historical or architectural interest which have outlasted their original use and are suitable for conversion to recital halls. In fact the supply of redundant churches is far greater than could be absorbed by the demand for concert and recital halls.

2

Design of auditorium

The maximum distance from the effective centre of the acting area to the furthest seat in the auditorium has visual and acoustic limits. It varies according to the kind of activity and differs for concerts, ballet, opera, plays, etc.

Visual limits

Given a full view of the performers, there is still a limit to the distance they can project their performances and "hold" their audience. This depends partly on their skill and partly upon the eyesight and acuteness of hearing of the audience. For most plays, it is essential for the audience to be close enough to discern facial expressions. The usually accepted maximum is 20 m (66 ft) from the geometrical centre for an open stage or from the setting line of a proscenium stage. For musicals and opera, in which facial expressions are less important, the distance can be increased up to 30 m (100 ft). If it is necessary most of the time for performers to be seen against a background of special scenery, as in the conventional proscenium theatre, the sightlines and maximum distance from the performer restrict the size of audience it is possible to fit in. The number of people required to be accommodated in the auditorium should not be the sole criterion for selecting the width of proscenium opening. Looked at in this way it may be tempting for the architect to widen the acting area or the proscenium opening in order to get more people close to the edge of the stage without considering the effect this would have on the productions. The settings cannot just expand to fill up the space, and in any case the actors will remain the same size. The performer tends to be overwhelmed by the scale of the stage if it is enlarged too far in order to fit more spectators into the auditorium.

Acoustic limits

The acoustic characteristics of a space, in simplified terms, are dependent upon the behaviour of sound reflections and on the period of reverberation. The period of reverberation must be short for clarity of speech; it is usually preferred longer for music, and longer still for choral singing. It depends mainly upon two factors: the amount of sound absorbed and reflected by the surfaces of the auditorium and the volume of the auditorium and stage. Design of reflecting and absorbing surfaces can assist acoustics, but there is a limit to the size of a space in which sufficient clarity of unaided speech can be maintained. For different functions acoustic characteristics can to a limited extent be altered physically by covering or uncovering sound-absorbing surfaces and by use of sound reflectors.

Artificial amplification of the sound is possible, but not usually desirable. Acoustics are discussed in more detail in Chapter 4.

Forms of auditorium to stage relationship

During the twentieth century there has been a reaction against the established form of theatre which flourished in the Victorian era. The performance had been pushed back behind the proscenium arch, and in some theatres the opening was literally designed as a large moulded and gilded picture frame continuing along the stage riser. This was the fourth wall removed for an audience of voyeurs. There has been a quest for new actor to audience relationships, or rather a revival of past forms.

Essentially the aim has been to bring auditorium and acting area into the same architectural space and to get the closest possible relation between the action of the play and the spectators watching it. The focus of the audience's attention is on the centre of the drama, and members of that audience tend to group themselves round this focus. Controversy arises over how far round they should stretch, or in other words what degree of encirclement of the stage is desirable.

The term "open stage" is used for an arrangement in which performance and audience are contained within the same space. This is to distinguish it from the proscenium or picture-frame stage, where the whole or a substantial part of the acting area is in a space separated from the audience by a wall with an opening, the proscenium, through which the performance is seen. These terms are not as mutually exclusive as they at first appear. The quality of an open-stage performance can be obtained within a theatre which, nevertheless, has the means to shut off the acting area, or part of it, from the audience for the purpose of deploying scenery.

The forms we shall describe do not cover every possible variation of auditorium to stage relationship. So many terms have been applied and misapplied to them that we have decided to classify them firstly by the degree of encirclement of the stage by the audience. This is inclined to emphasise a two-dimensional characteristic, whereas the subject is essentially a three-dimensional one. We shall illustrate each type with examples both ancient and modern.

360° encirclement

The acting area is surrounded on all sides by the audience. This form is also called theatre-in-the-round, island stage, arena or centre stage.

Entrances are made through the audience or from under the stage. There is no scenic background to the acting area and no problem of horizontal sightlines.

Perhaps the most typical 360° encircled performance is the circus, which carries its own big top and arena around, setting up its temporary auditorium wherever it gives a show. In Britain there

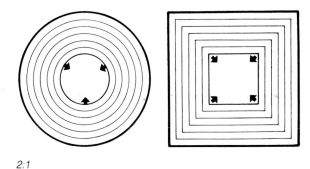

2:1

no longer be discerned is about 20 m (66 ft), but in that case it is assumed that the actor is facing the audience. With his back to the audience the distance is much less, say 10 m (33 ft). For theatre-in-the-round, that distance should be from the far side of the acting area to the rearmost seat. It follows that six or seven rows is the maximum depth of seating for successful theatre-in-the-round. If that is on one level, then the seating capacity will be not more than 300–400; to get more people within the right range of the stage it is essential to put the audience on more than one level.

Promenade performances

is at least one permanent building specifically designed for a circus (under Blackpool Tower), and they are to be found in other countries.

Most sports stadia are in the 360° encircled form, and multi-purpose halls may need to make provision for this arrangement, though more for boxing, wrestling or snooker than for any theatrical activity.

The successful theatres in this form are mostly quite small. The actors have their backs to part of the audience all the time, and this limits the distance at which their performance can be adequately appreciated. In the end stage, the distance beyond which the subtleties of a performance can

This is probably the place to mention the style of production derived from medieval plays where the action takes place within and amongst the audience, with scenes played in many different places and the audience following the action around. The National Theatre in Britain produced *The Mysteries*, taken from the English medieval mystery plays, in this style at its studio theatre, the Cottesloe, and later set it up at the Lyceum Theatre in its flat-floored ballroom format (1985). In the 1970s Luca Ronconi pioneered this type of production with his *Orlando Furioso*, which was presented in various

2:2. The New Victoria Theatre, Stoke-on-Trent (1986). Architects: Hollins, Jones, Oldacre and Partners

2:3. The Royal Exchange Theatre, Manchester (1976). Architects: Levitt Bernstein with Richard Negri

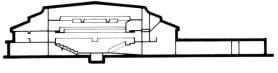

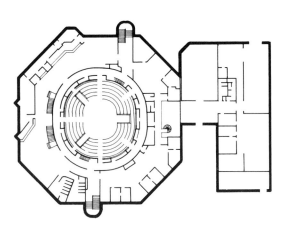

2:2

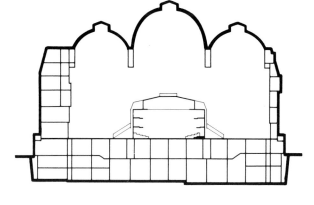

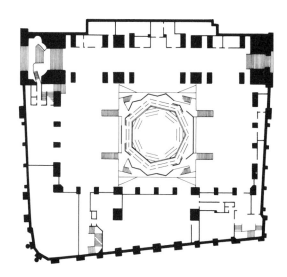

2:3

flat-floored halls in Europe, including an ice rink in Edinburgh. Essentially this is a manner of performance which adapts itself to the place and is not likely to be codified in architectural terms. It needs a large flat-floored area with means for hanging lights and stage properties above it and 5–6 m (16–20 ft) clear height. Even the lighting grid may be a temporary fit-up brought in for the occasion.

Transverse stage

The historical precedent for this form in England was in the performances set up in halls in the sixteenth and seventeenth centuries until the Commonwealth. The audience sat on two opposite sides and faced each other across the stage. It appears that which side you sat on depended upon your social status.

It was an improvised form of staging, and its use at the present day would also be improvised, as it is most unlikely to be required as a permanent form of staging for a theatre. It is, on the other hand, the form of the House of Commons in the Westminster Parliament.

The transverse stage auditorium of the Mannheim National Theatre is a rare example (rarely used) of this form permanently built in to a modern theatre.

2:4

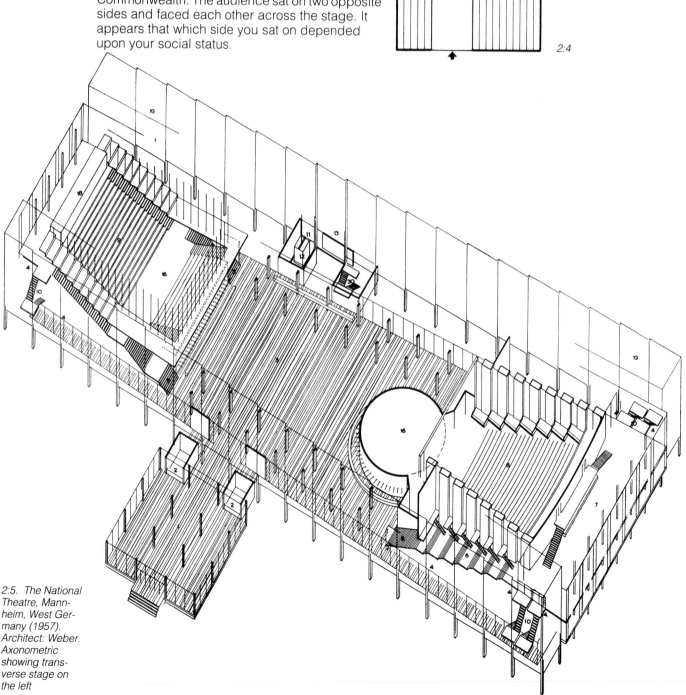

2:5. The National Theatre, Mannheim, West Germany (1957). Architect: Weber. Axonometric showing transverse stage on the left

2:6. The trans-
verse stage in use
at Mannheim

It was usually carved out of a hillside, often making use of a natural amphitheatre. The best-preserved example is the theatre at Epidauros in the Peloponnese, dating from the fourth century BC. Its acoustics are famed, and it is still used in the tourist season for concerts and other entertainments.

Thrust stages

The closest modern equivalent of the classical Greek theatre is the series of what we now call "thrust" stages designed under the influence of Sir Tyrone Guthrie at Stratford Ontario, Minneapolis, Chichester and Sheffield. The Crucible at Sheffield was the last of this type to be built in Britain. The seating capacity of theatres in this family had already shrunk from 2250 at Stratford Ontario to 1350 at the Chichester Festival Theatre and then to 1000 at the Crucible. The encirclement of the acting area of over 180°, with the audience evenly distributed around it, has not been repeated on the scale of these earlier theatres. Any further reduction of seating capacity would make this type of theatre no longer comparable with the Guthrie

210°–220° encirclement

The classical Greek and Hellenistic theatres were of this type. Entrances to the acting area can be made from a vertical wall or platform on the open side, but the principal acting area is at the focus of the seating. The essential feature of the original Greek theatre was that it was always in the open air.

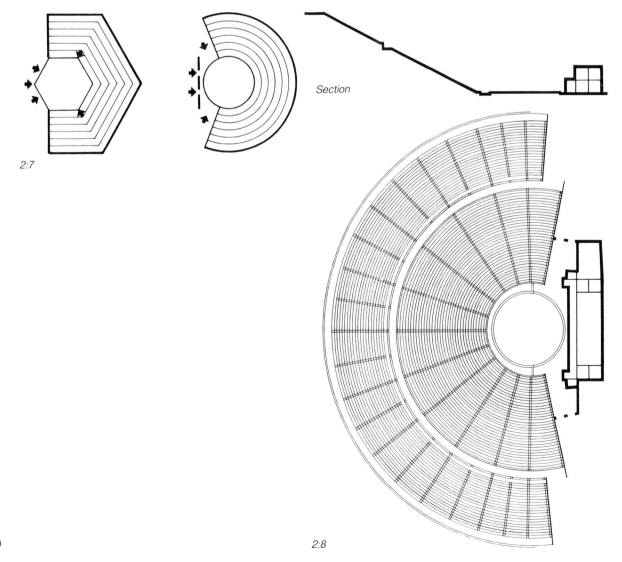

2:7

Section

2:8. The theatre
at Epidauros
(fourth century BC)

2:8

2:9. The Chichester Festival Theatre (1962). Architects: Powell & Moya

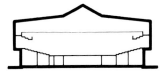

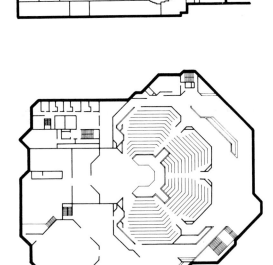

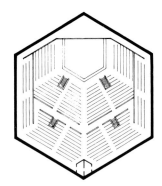

2:9

2.10. The Crucible Theatre, Sheffield (1971). Architects: Renton Howard Wood

2:10

model of thrust stage, which has an epic quality suitable for large audiences.

Stages like the Olivier auditorium at the National Theatre in London are often described as thrust stages because there is a considerable wrap-around of the acting area, but they differ from the Guthrie type in having the bulk of the audience ranged about the centre line, with relatively few seats at the sides. Some schemes have an adapt-able thrust which consists of adding some side seats to a forestage. However, the number of seats is small in proportion to the total and may not make a significant change from the normal end stage. If these side seats are not properly integrated with the rest of the seating, members of the audience in them may feel isolated from the rest. The thrust becomes a mere gesture in the direction of the avant-garde.

2:11. The thrust stage at the Crucible Theatre, Sheffield

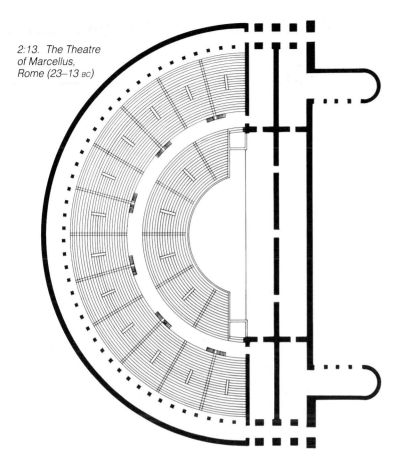

2:13. The Theatre of Marcellus, Rome (23–13 BC)

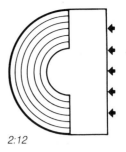
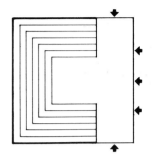

2:12

180° encirclement

The Roman theatre was of this type. Like the Greek theatre, it was open to the elements, but there was an enclosure round it, giving it an urban character. It was usually built up from a flat site on a series of semicircular arches and vaults, with entrances to the very steep amphitheatre through vomitories. Though the audience is focused on the semicircular orchestra, the emphasis has moved to a "proscenium", which is a strip of stage running across the back of the semicircle, and behind this an elaborate permanent set or *frons scaenae*, consisting of a two-storey composition of stone columns, arches and entablatures.

Remains of these theatres can still be found wherever the Romans penetrated. An example which is remarkably intact is the theatre at Bosra in Syria, which dates from the second century AD. One of the first Renaissance theatres, the Teatro Olympico at Vicenza, designed by Palladio and finished after his death in 1580 by Scamozzi, was a scaled-down version of a Roman theatre with a roof added.

2:14. The theatre at Bosra, Syria (second century AD)

2:15. The Teatro Olympico, Vicenza (1580)

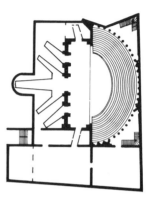

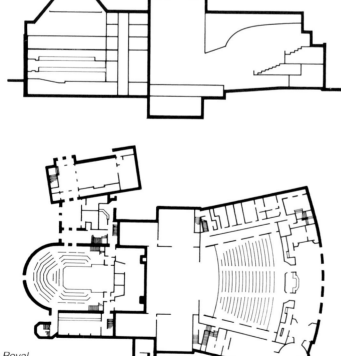

2:16 The Royal Shakespeare Theatre, Stratford-upon-Avon (1932; architects: Scott Chesterton Shepherd), showing the Swan Theatre added in 1986 (architect: Michael Reardon)

Elizabethan theatre

The theatres of the English Renaissance began to appear in London at about the same time as the Teatro Olympico in Italy and were mostly in the 180° to 220° encirclement form. They had galleries round a raised stage thrusting out into the centre of the auditorium. In 1576 James Burbage built a public theatre in Finsbury Fields, London, and it was followed by a series of buildings designed to house the extraordinary flowering of drama in the English Renaissance. These public theatres, the most renowned of which was the Globe, where Shakespeare's plays were first performed, were open to the sky. The Civil War and the Commonwealth interrupted this development when the theatres were closed down in 1645; all of them disappeared leaving no tangible trace. The oft sifted documentary evidence is meagre and contradictory, but this has not deterred alleged replicas from being proposed or built in many places. It is a favourite project for scholars to engage in academic speculation.

The detailed design of the Elizabethan public theatre may remain conjecture, but we are sure of its main lines. The thrust stage was surrounded on three sides by the audience seated in two or three galleries and standing at ground level. Behind the stage the galleries continued round to form a permanent setting, and the whole was open to the sky. In the English climate it is miraculous that they persisted successfully as long as they did. There were also indoor theatres flourishing at the same time, but about these we know even less.

There is an essential difference between the Elizabethan and the ancient classical theatre in the

2:17. Auditorium in the Elizabethan manner at the Swan Theatre, Stratford-upon-Avon

2:18. The Opera House, Bayreuth

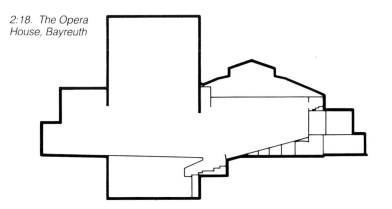

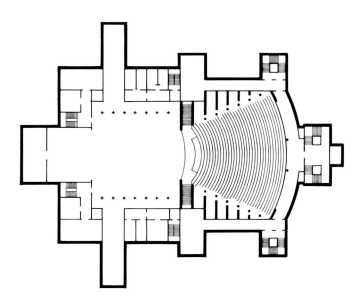

form of the auditorium. The audience being arranged in galleries and boxes is much closer to the action, and the contact between them and the actors is much more concentrated.

From the sixteenth century onwards theatre buildings developed the multi-tiered auditorium, and it was not until the twentieth century that there was a return to the single-tier steeply raked auditorium. The reasons for the change were more philosophical than practical. A very influential forerunner of this type was Wagner's Opera House in Bayreuth, designed by Otto Brückwald in 1872–6.

135° encirclement

This *wide fan* form derives from the "point of command" theory of Sir Peter Hall and John Bury. There is a point on the stage, about 2.5 m (8 ft) back from its edge, from which an actor can command the attention of the whole audience within an arc of vision of 135° without having to turn his head. This is quite a wide fan and is at the limit of what could still be called an end stage. It is the basis of the new Barbican Theatre auditorium for the Royal Shakespeare Company in London. The Olivier auditorium at the National Theatre, London, is closer to a 90° fan. In each case the stage is backed up by large areas of working space in which to deploy scenery, but the emphasis has been on the play taking place in the same space as the audience and not in a separate box with the fourth wall removed.

The very wide fan of one-and-a-half right angles suggested by Sir Peter Hall does make it possible for an actor to take in the whole audience at the roll

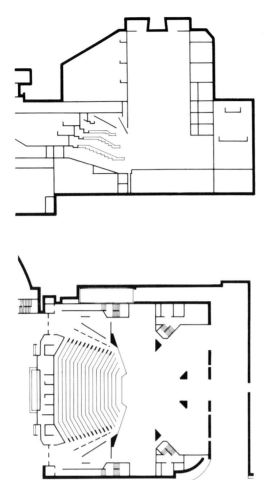

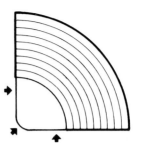

2:20

Up to about a 90° fan, the layout still has the character of an end stage. Most of the small theatres of this type have one steeply raked tier which provides good sightlines for an audience of up to 600. Above that number, the scale of the auditorium begins to be too large and it is time to think about putting some of the audience on another tier or tiers. Even for smaller numbers it is worthwhile considering the introduction of galleries, because they can add a great deal to the character and atmosphere of an auditorium.

Zero encirclement

End stage, as this is usually called, is only an open stage in as much as the acting area and the audience are within the same space. It is not sightlines which limit the use of scenery but the physical limitations of the enclosing structure. The end stage condition comes about because of the restrictions imposed by an existing shell or by a consciously chosen structure. It is basically a proscenium theatre without a proscenium arch and without the working areas needed to deploy scenery.

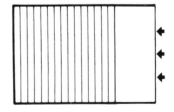

2:21

Courtyard theatre

The end stage is a rather crude and improvised form, but a more subtle arrangement of this actor-to-audience relation is in the "courtyard theatre" which has been developed in the last few years. It draws its inspiration directly or indirectly from a historical precedent, the English eighteenth-century playhouse: the theatre of Garrick.

In essence this was a stage about which rows of galleries were ranged on three sides but with the bulk of the audience in front. It was a rectangular

of an eye, but much of the action of a play is still bound to take place while actors have their backs to at least part of the audience. The extreme sightlines from the edge of the fan limit the area of setting which can be seen by the whole audience. These factors affect the kind of production which can be staged, and the result is more akin to a thrust stage than an end stage. With a true thrust stage, those seated at the sides see much of the action against a background of other members of the audience.

90° encirclement

This *wide fan* arrangement allows most of the action to be seen against stage walls or a scenic background rather than against members of the audience. It is a form with many possible variations, allowing more extensive use of scenery than on thrust stages, but still limited by the extreme sightlines. The technique of performance does not differ radically from that of the proscenium theatre.

version of the European horseshoe-shaped, multi-tiered auditorium. Behind the stage was a scenic background consisting of a number of portals made of painted canvas on wooden frames, in the form of legs and borders suspended from a grid above or sliding in slots in the stage floor. The action of the play took place on what we would now call the forestage or apron, terms suggesting something tacked on to the main stage. In Garrick's day that *was* the stage; if anything was tacked on, it was the scenic area at the back. The acting area had boxes flanking either side and rows of galleries facing it, with the pit audience on benches at the lower level.

The relation between actors and audience was very close, and this form of theatre had a long and stable existence. The Theatre Royal, Drury Lane, London, was built at the end of the seventeenth century, and though alterations were inevitably made, the layout remained essentially the same throughout the eighteenth century. The front part of the stage, with doors on either side for the actors to enter, was the focus of attention; the proscenium behind was to mask the incidental scenic changes.

The modern version has a stage with some scenic provisions at one end, and shallow raked stalls with galleries around it on one or two levels. The galleries are shallow with one, two or sometimes three rows of spectators. For promenade performances there should be some method of rendering the stalls flat and clearing away the seats.

The effects of the choice of the degree of encirclement

The advantages claimed by advocates of the open stage forms are that there is a much closer involve-ment of the audience in the action and a greater emphasis on the three-dimensional qualities of a live performance than can be achieved in traditional proscenium theatres. The essential differences between live performances and the two-dimensional media of film and television are thereby exploited.

With degrees of encirclement over about 120°, performers mask each other and are often seen against the background of members of the audience on the other side of the stage. Voices and musical instruments are partly directional and so are facial expressions and gestures. Their effect is, therefore, different for each spectator, according to the part of the auditorium they are seen or heard from. Unless scenery and props are kept to a minimum, they will obstruct lines of sight. Lighting the actors without at the same time illuminating or causing discomfort to the audience becomes increasingly difficult. Entrances for actors are not easy to manage, and provision must be made for access to the stage through the audience or from below the stage. If these entrances are also used by the public, confusion can arise, and some authorities may not even allow them. Actors' entrances should preferably be at acting area level, and steps should be avoided.

Those who work on the more surrounded types of stage believe that skilful production techniques overcome these limitations and that the closeness of the audience-to-performer relation intensifies the dramatic experience. The audience does not see the actors against pictorial scenery but bathed in light against a background of dimly lit rows of people similarly concentrating on the action. From the artistic point of view, the distinction between a performance on a surrounded stage and one on a confrontation type is probably more important than

2:22. The Tricycle Theatre, Kilburn, London (1980). Architect: Tim Foster

2:23. Courtyard theatre auditorium of the Tricycle Theatre, Kilburn

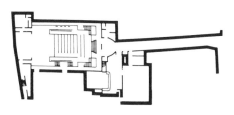

that between a closed and an open stage. The latter distinction is more the product of safety regulations. Scenery is a fire hazard and the necessary protection of a safety curtain imposes physical restrictions on the building which are difficult to comply with in open stages. Without the orthodox protective devices, licensing authorities are likely to place severe restrictions on the amount and kind of materials for construction of scenery on open stages.

The proscenium or picture-frame stage

In discussing the various open stage forms, the essentials of the proscenium type have already been described. In its most clearly expressed form there is an actual picture frame all round the proscenium opening. Used in this manner, it is the embodiment of the "fourth wall" convention (where the action takes place within a room from which the fourth wall has been removed).

What we in Britain call the proscenium theatre is in Europe usually called the Italian type of theatre, because of its origin in the baroque theatres of that country, where splendid buildings dating from the seventeenth, eighteenth and nineteenth centuries still stand. Many have in recent years been lovingly restored to their former magnificence. The main

advantage of the form remains its ability to present elaborate scenic effects and transformations (provided that enough space and facilities are allowed) whose mechanics can be concealed from the audience. Because of the geometry of sightlines, it is difficult to arrange large audiences close to a picture-frame stage; the width of the auditorium is largely determined by the width of the proscenium opening.

Stage scale

The question of scale within the auditorium is very important and affects the quality of production that can be staged. A very large stage tends to overpower and diminish the human figure. This may not matter in a grand epic, but many plays have an intimate human scale, and it is the designer's responsibility to provide a setting which gives the actors something to relate to. Without it the players may seem to be floundering in a scaleless void. Much can be done with lighting, but the theory that sets are unnecessary because all the effects can be achieved with lighting does not hold up in practice. Audiences soon become bored with having to watch the action in a pool of light surrounded by gloom. This can even have a physiological effect by dazzling them and giving them headaches.

2:24. A fine example of an Italian opera house: La Scala, Milan (1778). Architect: Luigi Piermarini; seats 2309

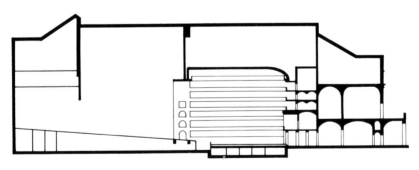

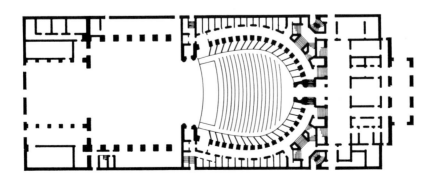

Once in a while the pool of light can be used to dramatic effect, but total reliance on lighting is impractical.

The director and designer will want to create settings to frame the action, but, if the volume of the stage is vast, the physical and financial problems of filling it with scenery may become an enormous burden. Only companies with heavy budget subsidies can cope with large stages. If costs have to be cut, the result is often huge areas of black masking – a rather dreary prospect for the audience.

Forestage and apron stage

Scenery cannot be brought right to the back surface of the proscenium wall or it would foul the safety curtain and the house curtain. The line beyond which scenery cannot be set is called the setting line and is usually about 1 m (3 ft) back from the face of the proscenium.

That part of the stage between the setting line and the stage riser, or edge of the stage if there is no riser, is called the forestage. When it is extended right out into the auditorium it is called an apron stage, and it can give an open-stage effect by bringing the acting area into the same space as the audience. It is difficult to get satisfactory sightlines for both the apron and the area behind the pro-

scenium arch, especially from balconies. Any scenery used in front of the safety curtain may have to be incombustible. The apron can be fixed or movable, and it is often lowered to form an orchestra pit.

Performers' entrances

In the picture-frame theatre almost all performers' entrances are made behind the proscenium. In Restoration and Georgian plays it was common practice to enter the forestage by doors on either side of the proscenium arch, and this method of entry is again in use not only for productions in past styles but also for new plays. Regulations require fireproof doors and a fire check lobby.

Adaptability

Adaptability of one kind or another is often part of the brief for an auditorium. The most commonly required adaptability is in the orchestra pit/forestage area, where it is useful to be able to adjust from the demands of a play without music to an opera which needs a pit for the orchestra. This is described in more detail in Chapter 9 (Stage planning).

Another kind of adaptability is in the capacity of the auditorium. Some performances are suitable for, or will only attract, smaller audiences than the full capacity of the house, and it is useful to be able to reduce the size of the auditorium in a convincing manner. This is very difficult to achieve in a single-tier auditorium. Moving walls or curtaining off the rear of the auditorium is not very satisfactory because the audience usually have to approach through the curtained-off area and the whole contrivance has a makeshift air. With a multi-tier auditorium, on the other hand, it is relatively easy to shut off the top tier. Simply not opening the gallery may be sufficient, but a more sophisticated development is to lower the auditorium ceiling to rest on the top balcony front. An example of this is the Plymouth Theatre Royal, where the capacity can be reduced from 1296 to 764.

When the demand is for adaptability from one form of stage-to-auditorium relationship to another (say proscenium to 180° encirclement), or from theatre use to banqueting, involving major alterations to the seating, the problem is much more difficult to solve, and there have been some notable failures. On a small scale, adaptations may be possible with mechanically or manually operated rostra; but beyond four or five rows of seats the problems become immense, both technically and economically, if the auditorium is to remain a satisfactory space in both forms. If entirely incompatible forms are wanted, two separate auditoria should be considered. However, certain theatres which are used for teaching can be given a fairly high degree of adaptability, as they exist primarily for the benefit of the actors and need make few con-

2:25

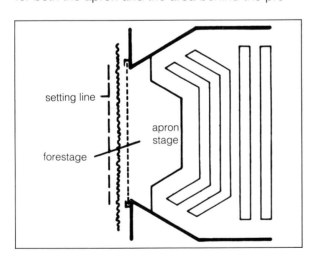

2:26

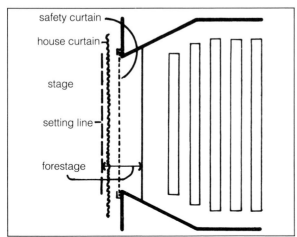

2:27. The Theatre
Royal, Plymouth
(1982). Architects:
Peter Moro and
Partners

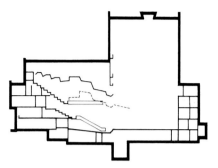

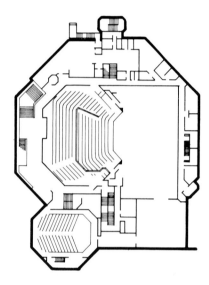

cessions to the comfort and convenience of an
audience. In such theatres, changes which in professional conditions would be mechanised and
therefore extremely expensive can, with far less
capital expenditure, be arranged for manual alteration by making use of the plentiful supply of
unpaid labour.

The demands of adaptability are often purely
theoretical, based on diagrams out of books (perhaps this one) rather than theatrical experience.
The proscenium with its curtain as the fourth wall is
the form that everyone wants to avoid being permanently tied to, since the separation of two
distinct spaces, stage and auditorium, is against
the spirit of most of today's drama practice. When
old proscenium theatres are used by modern companies, the house curtain is often not used at all
throughout the performance; the safety curtain
may have to be brought in at some time but only to
satisfy the licensing authorities. The stage and its
setting are there to be seen as soon as the audience enters the auditorium, and it is the dimming of
the house lights that signals the opening of the
play.

When it comes to planning new theatres, there
are various responses to this desire to emphasise
the unity of stage and auditorium. One is to accept

the basic proscenium form, which has undoubted
advantages in its facilities for deploying scenery,
but to play down its importance and disguise it so
that the auditorium and stage apparently merge
into each other. The feeling of unity can be
increased if the seating is clearly focused on the
stage and does not follow the straight line of the
safety curtain. The safety curtain itself can be
shaped to fit the edge of the stage, but this is not an
easy piece of engineering, considering the weight
of an iron curtain, and it is expensive. Another
approach is to commit the new building to one of
the open forms and try to make it fit that form as well
as possible without compromise.

Adaptability may be multi-form, giving a
changeable relationship of performance to spectator or listener, for example from picture frame to
open stage, or it may be multi-purpose, allowing a
change in the nature of the activities, for instance
from drama to music.

Apart from the initial capital cost the main problems of large-scale adaptability are the manpower
it absorbs even when highly mechanised, the
accelerated wear and tear on all the moving parts,
and the inevitable compromises, which tend to
make each of the various arrangements less satisfactory than it would be if designed specifically for
the purpose. For the same money it would often be
possible to build two different auditoria suitable for
a wider range of activities and to use both simultaneously rather than have to suffer the delay of
changing from one form to another.

Another reason for attempting adaptability is
based on the belief that it is possible to remain
uncommitted to one particular form by literally
reshaping the building with machinery. Keeping
the options open at the planning stage may give an
illusion of freedom, but each piece of machinery
introduced to cope with those options limits the
freedom of use to a few clumsy manoeuvres. The
theoretical possibilities of machinery are used as
an excuse for not making a decision that should be
made at the outset. Machinery is never as reliable
or as easy to use as it appears on paper, and it
often absorbs a great amount of labour and
energy. When it has been used on a few occasions,
and the time and trouble it involves have been
experienced, it usually settles down into one of its
forms and stays there. The end result will not be as
good as it could have been if the decision to settle
for that form had been taken initially, and it will have
been far more expensive to achieve than it ever
need have been.

The auditorium in section

The first objective in auditorium design is to bring
as many people as possible within the optimum
range of distances from the performance area.
One way is to increase the degree of encirclement
in plan, but in the vertical plane more can be
achieved by adding one or more tiers. The action

2:28. The Theatre Royal, Plymouth, with whole auditorium seating 1296

2:29. The Theatre Royal, Plymouth, with the ceiling lowered to reduce the seating to 764

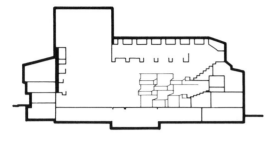

2:30. Derngate, Northampton (1983), a highly adaptable building with a sophisticated system of units moved about on pneumatic castors. Architects: Renton Howard Wood Levin with Theatre Projects

on the stage becomes further enveloped by the spectators, whose appreciation of the three-dimensional quality of the performance is emphasised.

The various levels of the auditorium have been given many different names, e.g. stalls, orchestra stalls, amphitheatre, balcony, pit, circle, dress circle, upper circle, gallery, slips, grand tier – terms which by combinations and qualifications have conveyed many subtle distinctions of luxury and prestige. They had some validity in the past, when at the play or the opera it was just as important to be seen as to see, but such a profusion of nomenclature has little relevance in present-day society. In the opinion of some, the very presence of a circle is an indication of class distinction and therefore suspect; but this doctrinaire approach has had a sad effect on the atmosphere of the auditorium. Privilege apart, it is still not unreasonable to give people the choice of paying more for a better view.

The most important advantage of a multi-tier auditorium is that more seats can be included without unduly increasing their distance from the stage. It also has the effect of surrounding the acting area with audience in section as distinct from extending it in plan, which is achieved by open stage methods. Actors like to feel themselves the focus of the audience in both plan and section, which implies either a multi-level or steeply raked auditorium. One of the disadvantages of a multi-level auditorium is that it is more difficult to get good sightlines. The rake of the stalls has to be reduced so as not to push the gallery too high. The rake of the tiers is limited by safety regulations and by sightlines to the front of the acting area. A tier must not be allowed to interfere with the sightlines from the back row of the level below or with the acoustics of these seats. Several shallow tiers may be easier to handle in these respects than one or two deep ones. Access and escape may be complicated and space-consuming, and may get more so as the number of tiers increases.

The traditional European opera houses consist of a horseshoe of shallow tiers round a slightly raked stalls or parterre. The tiers were originally divided up into separate boxes with partitions between them radiating from the centre of the stage. The boxes would allow no more than two rows of chairs, perhaps with room for someone standing behind. Most of the audience in these tiers could lean on the balcony front, and their view, though often oblique, was not interrupted by other members of the audience. Without the partitions it is possible to put an extra row or two directly opposite the stage, but the low ceiling heights soon get in the way of the sightlines. Originally the pattern of these opera houses was influenced by the way they were financed, which was by the sale of boxes and loges to the more prosperous members of the community. When this was tried in England the lively but unruly theatre-going public objected, and the practice did not become established generally (though the Royal Albert Hall was financed in this way).

It was economic pressures which influenced the development of the auditorium into the familiar pattern of Victorian and Edwardian theatres. In Britain, where there was no tradition of central or local government patronage for the theatre, the buildings had to be commercially viable, with as many paying customers as possible squeezed in. The tiers facing the stage became deeper as sightlines permitted, but at the sides this could not be done, and the boxes and loges with their one or two rows remained. New structural techniques also made it possible to build deeper cantilevered balconies without columns to obstruct the view.

The next development was influenced by the cinema, where oblique side views of the screen are quite unacceptable. Here the auditorium usually became stalls and circle, each one virtually an auditorium in itself. The unity of the audience was no longer important when watching a film.

Auditorium atmosphere

The quality of an individual's response to a live performance depends partly on the fact that it is an
experience shared with others. Audience and performers react upon one another. The audience
becomes a community and its combined reactions
stimulate and intensify the experience of the individual. Auditorium atmosphere is dependent on
the quality of the design, but practical as well as
aesthetic factors are involved. From the actors'
point of view the audience should not be split into
parts visually separated from one another; for
example a large, high balcony may divide an audience into two. There should not be any visual
obstacle or other distracting feature between audience and performance such as might be caused
by a structural projection from the wall near the
stage or by a balcony coming too low over the
lower-level back seats. Materials, textures and
colour have an effect on auditorium atmosphere.
They should help to create a receptive frame of
mind before the performance but not obtrude after
it has started. During the performance a negative
quality is preferable, so that for instance reflections
of light do not distract the attention of spectators. It
should be remembered that the auditorium will
never disappear, however many coats of matt
black paint are applied.

Audience seating

The decision on the practicable degree of comfort
depends on the purpose of the theatre and the
money available. The minimum requirements laid
down by safety regulations afford a very low standard of comfort. On the other hand a close-
packed audience has a better atmosphere than
one that is spread too thinly, and it should be remembered that while comfort is important, seats
too widely spaced may destroy the atmosphere in
an auditorium. These conflicting requirements
have to be balanced and a compromise reached.

Large areas of blank, unpopulated auditorium
wall can spoil auditorium atmosphere. In some
cases this is greatly improved by boxes, loges and
slips, but in proscenium theatres the sightlines
from these are normally poor.

An open stage can have balconies probably
without any sightline problems. One of the
drawbacks of the single-floor auditorium is that it
looks half empty when it is, in fact, half full. A sparse
audience in a multi-tier theatre is less obvious; the
top balcony can be shut off, for instance, and the
audience concentrated in the other levels.

3

Sightlines

The importance of establishing visual limits which are acceptable for various types of performance has already been discussed. Having decided how much of the stage and the back and sides of the acting area must be seen by every member of the audience, it is possible to construct a geometrical volume within which all the sightlines must be contained.

The planning of seating within this volume involves the adjustment of a number of variables, some but not all of them within the designer's power to control. The most important of these variables is one which cannot be regulated: the individual human being.

Anthropometrics

Not only do anthropometric dimensions vary amongst individuals, but the sitting postures adopted by each one are not susceptible to a discipline which would be convenient for mathematicians. In other words, the music-hall joke of the large lady with a hat sitting in front of a small shy gent is still a genuine situation. The key dimensions upon which sightline calculations depend are the height of the eye above the ground in a sitting position and the height of the top of the head above the eyes. If measurements of a sample of the population are taken, these can be plotted on a curve which will show their distribution. From this curve the proportion of the population whose dimensions lie within certain limits can be calculated. Different curves could be plotted for children of certain ages and the data could be further refined by dividing the statistics for males and females and for different races. Thus the proportion of the population whose dimensions lie within certain limits can be determined. In the case of the large person sitting in front of the small one, the probability of this occurring could be worked out mathematically.

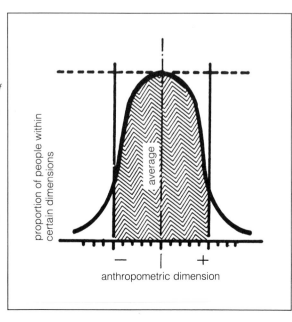

3:1. This is a typical curve obtained when a body dimension of a sample of people is taken and the number of people with similar measurements is plotted against the varying dimension.
The proportion of people included within certain dimensional limits can be assessed, and conversely the percentage of people excluded by a dimensional limitation can be estimated

Seat spacing

The architect does have control over the design of the seats and their spacing within limits laid down by safety regulations. His concern will be for comfort and the circulation of the audience to and from each seat. For comfort, wide spacing of rows is desirable, but this may reduce the capacity of the auditorium to an uneconomic extent or push the rear rows beyond the acceptable distance from the stage. In a live theatre over-generous seat spacing may also spoil the atmosphere of concentration which intensifies the theatrical experience. While the seating should be comfortable enough for a two- or three-hour session, it should help to keep the theatregoers alert rather than lull them to sleep. In cinemas the situation is not quite the same, because the audience cannot play any positive part in the proceedings. The film reels on whatever the reactions of the watchers individually or collectively. Cinema managements are often more concerned with the effect of seat spacing on the sale of ice-cream in the interval than on the dramatic atmosphere of the auditorium.

Design of chairs

The quoting of row spacing without considering the detail design of the seats is very misleading. It is at least unwise to attempt to design an auditorium without first deciding the individual chair that is to be used. Most people's instinctive notion of comfort is judged by depth of upholstery, but a bulky and grossly padded chair may, in fact, be less comfortable than an apparently spartan one, because it reduces the leg-room between rows. It is also important for the seat to allow people to sit easily in a position which is natural for seeing the stage. In the live theatre the spectators are generally looking down on the stage, while in the cinema they look up and naturally take a more reclining position.

With this data assembled and the critical dimensions assumed, the vertical sightlines can be worked out graphically by the following method and a satisfactory floor profile arrived at.

The lowest and nearest point which the whole audience should be able to see clearly must be decided (P). If this is the edge of a horizontal stage, the nearest eye level should be above the horizontal plane. Verticals are then drawn through the eye positions for each row of seats. The point X, 100 mm (4 in.) above A on the first vertical, represents the top of the head of the person in the first row. When PX is produced through X, the point B at which it cuts the second vertical gives the eye position for the second row. 100 mm (4 in.) above B lies the point Y through which the next sightline is produced to cut the next vertical, and so on. When the eye positions for every row of seats have been determined, the floor line can be found by measuring 1120 mm (44 in.) below each on the

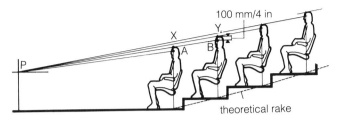

3:2. Method of calculating sightline with low P

theoretical rake

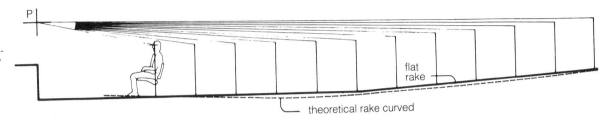

3:3. Theoretical rake curved. Maximum gradient of aisles without steps 1 in 12

flat rake

theoretical rake curved

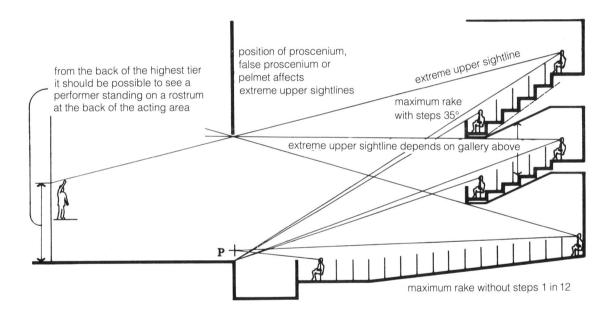

3:4. Vertical sightlines

from the back of the highest tier it should be possible to see a performer standing on a rostrum at the back of the acting area

position of proscenium, false proscenium or pelmet affects extreme upper sightlines

extreme upper sightline

maximum rake with steps 35°

extreme upper sightline depends on gallery above

maximum rake without steps 1 in 12

verticals: this theoretical line is a shallow curve. (For these calculations 1120 mm (44 in.) is a reasonable floor-to-eye height, but a more accurate figure can be obtained by using anthropometric data related to the actual seat chosen.)

It should be noted that where this method of establishing the floor slope is strictly applied, the rake will usually be very steep. If the audience is to be on one level only, this may not matter, especially with an open stage where the encirclement of the stage allows for a large audience. With a proscenium stage, however, the width of the audience is limited by horizontal sightlines, and in order to get more spectators into a given width it is necessary to introduce another tier or tiers, which may lead to a compromise on vertical sightlines. The rake must be reduced to make room for another level. Point P is taken 600 mm or 900 mm (2 or 3 ft) above the edge of the stage, on the assumption that the actual edge may be seen between heads

only and an unrestricted view of the performers from the knees upwards is all that is necessary.

The situation is improved by staggering seats. The arbitrary choice of a position for point P and the variations in the dimensions of the individual members of the audience do not justify the refinement of a subtly curved rake. A varying rake may also introduce the complication of different heights of risers, which are uncomfortable and sometimes dangerous to the public. The maximum gradient for an aisle without steps is 1 in 12, and the maximum slope for stepped seating is 35° (GLC).

Vertical sightlines must be checked on several sections as well as the centre line through stage and auditorium.

The section through stage and auditorium at any point is dictated by vertical sightlines, which will be affected by the following factors:

— Maximum distance desirable for the specta-

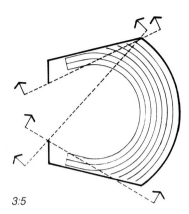

3:5

tor farthest from the performance.
— Depth of acting area and the vertical height above it essential to the type of performance.
— Nearest and lowest part of the stage which must be within the unrestricted view of all spectators.
— Highest point in acting area which must be visible to the spectators farthest from the stage. Balcony fronts, or soffits, proscenium or false proscenium, pelmet or border must not obstruct sightlines through these extreme points.

Vertical sightlines from tiers

The following is an approximate method of determining the slope of a tier. It does not replace the more meticulous method described above, which can be applied to tiers as well as to main banks of seating.

First fix the eye position for the front row of seats (A) and the depth (L) to the eye position of the back row. Vertically above A find point X so

that $AX = \dfrac{L}{10}$. Next draw a line from P (on stage)

through X to cut the vertical through the eye position of the back row at O.

The rake of the tier will then be parallel to AO, but 1120 mm (44 in.) below (see the note above on the eye height of a seated person).

Note that the maximum slope with steps is 35° (GLC).

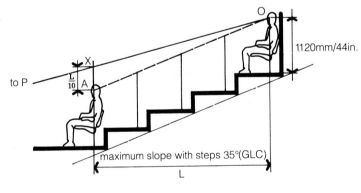

3:6. Graphical method for finding balcony rake

to P

$\dfrac{L}{10}$ A X

O

1120mm/44in.

maximum slope with steps 35°(GLC)

L

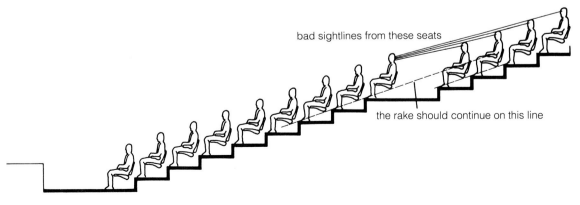

3:7. The line of the auditorium rake must be continuous over cross aisles. To start the rake again after the cross aisle, as shown here, results in bad sightlines for the seats immediately behind the aisle

bad sightlines from these seats

the rake should continue on this line

3:8

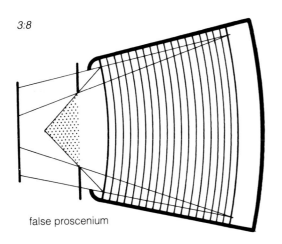

false proscenium

Horizontal sightlines

Horizontal sightlines are most critical in theatres with a proscenium stage. Given a desired acting area, sightlines will limit the width of seating which can be provided in the auditorium.

Note that sightlines from side seats restrict the amount of the stage that can be used as acting area. The addition of a false proscenium will limit the acting area still further.

Staggered seating

In the calculations for determining vertical sightlines described above, it is assumed that it is necessary for the spectators in each row to see

over the heads of the people in the row immediately in front of them. This is the ideal situation, but it is not always possible. One solution is to stagger the rows of seats. It is then possible to calculate sightlines based on each spectator seeing over the head of the person two rows in front. But it must be remembered that the heads of spectators in the row immediately in front will restrict the width of uninterrupted stage that can be seen.

For a given row spacing (x) and seat spacing (y), the unrestricted width of view of the stage (a) seen from any seat is proportional to the distance (d) of the seat from the stage, i.e. $a = kd$ where k

is a constant $\dfrac{y-t}{y}$, t being the thickness of one head:

e.g. if $x = 900$, $y = 500$ and $t = 200$
  then $k = 0.33$
thus at 9 m (about 30 ft) from the front of the stage:
  $a = 0.33 \times 9$
  $= 3$ m (10 ft)

i.e. 3 m (10 ft) width of the stage can be seen without interruption, which is one-third of the average 9 m (30 ft) proscenium opening.

The value of staggering becomes progressively less, the more oblique is the seat to the line of sight through the focus of the stage. If rows are straight, heads in front will be more obstructive and it is uncomfortable to sit for any length of time at an angle to the focus of attention.

3:9. Staggered seating method of calculating view

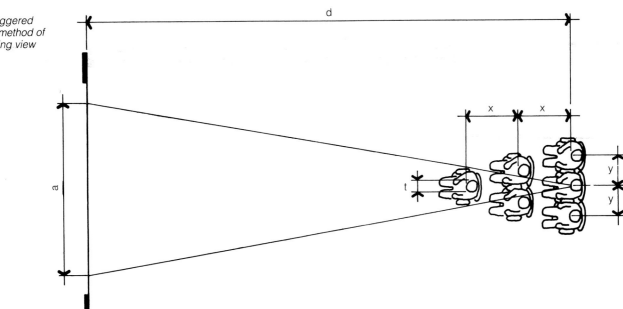

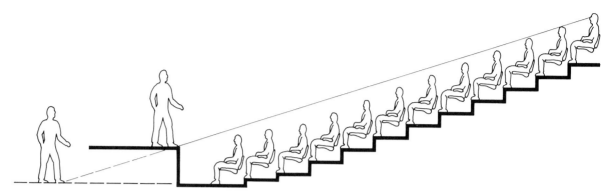

3:10. The performer has a closer relation to the audience if the front rows of seats are below stage level

Viewing is more comfortable if the seat is on the line of sight through the focus of the stage. This can be achieved by curving the rows or setting side banks at an angle. Using the constant *k* the uninterrupted view can be found for any seat in the auditorium, assuming that seats are directly facing the focus of attention.

Level of front row of seats

3:11. Staggered seating may obscure a vital part of the stage

There are occasions when it would be very convenient to build a stepped bank of seating on a flat floor, leaving the original floor to form the stage. This occurs when bleacher seating is extended, in a gymnasium for instance, resulting in the front row of chairs being at stage level. There are even those who consider it some kind of moral principle that there should be no raised stage. The effect on the sightlines is to distance the performers from the audience. To be wholly visible they have to keep back from the front row of seats by about 4 m (13 ft), which can destroy the intimacy of their relationship with the audience.

This problem, which crops up whenever the front row of seats is at stage level, can be overcome in various ways. The seating tiers can be very steep, but this will only work for four or five rows. Or a raised platform can be introduced for the stage, though this may create further problems of having to adjust levels of the floor round the stage to provide access to it.

A better method is to arrange for a trough to be formed in the floor, either manually, by lifting out rostra, or mechanically by an elevator. The first few rows can then be put in the trough, and row three, four or five, say, will be at stage level.

Other methods of determining sightlines

As it is possible to work out the mathematical relationships of the variables involved in determining floor profiles, it follows that it is possible to programme a computer to produce either a series of levels or a direct visual representation. Computer-generated sightline diagrams and perspective views from any position in the auditorium can be programmed, although the economic viability of such a process is questionable.

4

Acoustics

The acoustics of an auditorium will affect every production in it. Because of the extreme difficulty of making substantial change in the acoustic conditions by adjustments to the building itself (apart from some unavoidable variation resulting from the size of the audience), the architect in effect decides its acoustic characteristics at the outset.

Natural versus artificial acoustics

The first requirement in theatres and opera houses is still for satisfactory natural acoustics without any artificial amplification. In recent years more and more microphones have been creeping into live entertainments as the equipment becomes more sophisticated, but opera singers and actors still expect to make themselves heard without these artificial aids.

At the other end of the scale the rock concert relies entirely on amplification and to a great extent on the sound operator who balances the various instrumental and vocal inputs by the musicians. Natural sound could never reach the vast audiences at pop concerts, and in any case the taste of that kind of audience seems to be much influenced by what it hears on its hi-fi set or personal stereo when it has control of the volume knob. The record industry has conditioned an expectation of a quality of carefully manipulated electronically conditioned sound which could not be produced by natural acoustical methods. The volume of sound often reaches levels that in an industrial process would be considered a health hazard and frowned on by a factory inspector.

Pop music apart, amplification is commonplace in musicals, where cordless radio microphones make it less obvious. The problem is that one amplified voice has such a volumetric advantage over the other natural voices that very soon there are demands from other singers for the same assistance, lest their own contribution be submerged. Microphones introduced into the orchestra pit have a similar tendency to multiply until virtually the whole of the sound comes through loudspeakers.

Sometimes pre-recorded music is mimed to by dancers, and as the difference in quality of the artificially reproduced sounds is noticeable, all the sound, even of the live musicians, is channelled through the loudspeaker system for the sake of consistency. Although many shows are well controlled, very often quality is sacrificed to quantity, sensitivity sacrificed to crude volume. The technicalities of sound reinforcement installations are discussed in Chapter 12.

In general the technology has advanced further than the discrimination and taste of the average sound operator.

Manipulation of the sound, if not of the acoustics, by modern amplification systems may go some but not all of the way towards creating good hearing conditions for every one of the many different kinds of programme material which may be presented. Compromise appears inevitable; it is impossible for one auditorium to be equally suitable acoustically for a drawing-room comedy, a string quartet, a Wagner opera or a Mahler symphony.

Loudspeakers have been used to extend the range of acoustic response of some halls. These are discussed briefly on page 36.

The art of acoustics

Acoustics is more an art than a science. The very word seems to strike terror into the hearts of many architects, who feel it is an arcane science that only the initiated can understand.

Designing spaces, particularly auditoria, is a difficult process and needs more than mere competence. Using a few figures and half truths gleaned from an acoustic textbook to produce a shape on paper is no way to create a three-dimensional space with some architectural character. There is no mathematical formula automatically solving acoustical problems to hide behind. There is no substitute for an understanding by the designer of the acoustical environment implied by his design and choice of materials. This sense is acquired by observation and experience. It is as important for an architect to keep his ears open as his eyes.

Acoustic background

A theatre has to be protected from all external noise and must have mechanical plant designed so that the total background noise level does not exceed certain criteria. The larger the auditorium, the lower these criteria should be. For theatres with up to 500 seats a noise criterion of NR 30 should not be exceeded, and for theatres with more than 500 seats, this should be reduced to NR 25 or less.

Lower figures were quoted in the first edition of *Theatre Planning*, but they are very difficult to achieve and the slightly higher figures are perhaps acceptable. However, for those with no previous experience of auditorium design it is hard to realise how distracting even the slightest background noise can be at moments of dramatic tension. Scenes have been spoiled by noise from flushing lavatories, talking in dressing rooms, control room chatter and rattling of cups in bars. These embarrassments can be avoided by thoughtful planning.

It is not always the measured volume of noise which is the trouble but its "distraction factor", which for instance is greater from a rattling ventilation grille than from an aeroplane passing overhead. The distraction factor is a subjective concept, but it does seem to be greater the closer the source of the noise. The ultimate distraction factor is sitting next to a chronic bronchitic, so many of whom seem to be drawn to concert halls.

Curved and concave surfaces

Curves and concave surfaces need not be a problem if their foci are away from the ears of the audience. They must be checked to ensure that, from a sound source on the stage, neither direct nor indirect reflections via plain surfaces focus anywhere at audience head level. The possible focal points should lie in mid-air or outside the auditorium. A concave surface which is likely to give trouble will have to be heavily absorbent if that is the remedy that is proposed. It would probably be better to try and solve the problem by changing the shape of the suspect surface.

Old theatres with elaborate moulded plaster decorations to break up sound reflections stand a much better chance of being acoustically satisfactory than modern auditoria with large areas of plain undecorated wall and ceiling surfaces.

Seating rake and layout

The rake of seating is as important for sound as it is for sight. When sound passes at a low angle of incidence over an audience, it is strongly attenuated because of the audience's highly absorptive properties.

Reinforcement of sound by reflections from the ceiling makes it reasonable to provide a rake rather less steep than in ancient classical open-air theatres, which had rakes of 35° or more. Nevertheless a sightline clearance from one row to the next at any part of the house should never be less than 75 mm (3 in.) and in large theatres 100 mm (4 in.) or more is desirable.

If seats are set out on a circular or part circular plan there is a risk that the concave surface of the risers may cause focusing of sound. The risers are shielded to some extent by the audience and the backs of seats, which reduce the sound reflected from them, but as an added precaution they should be covered with a sound-absorbing material. Concave areas of wall which may be troublesome should be absorbent or have a broken-up surface to be sound-diffusing.

Size and shape

The smaller the average distance between the audience and the actor, the better the acoustical result for normal drama, although for music or musical shows this is not necessarily true. In theatres for up to 200 or 300 people there should be no difficulty, but in larger theatres the acoustic design problems become more intractable. It is difficult to give precisely the largest practical audience size for good acoustics, assuming that sound amplification is not to be used, but it is probably about 1200.

Because of the reduced average distance between stage and audience, open-stage theatres might be acoustically satisfactory with rather larger audiences. But the human voice is directional, not evenly distributed, and at the higher sound frequencies, which are extremely important for intelligibility, the sound behind the speaker's head is at least 10 dB less than in front of his face. Spectators directly behind the speaking actor – and this could mean any member of the audience – are, in terms of the strength of sound, effectively up to three times further away than a member of the audience who is the same actual distance away in the direction the actor faces. This ignores the acoustic gain provided by sound reflections from well-positioned wall or ceiling surfaces, but although there may be some gain from these, the disadvantages of being behind the actor remain considerable.

In proscenium theatres the stage house must be considered as an acoustical disadvantage because it represents a volume of enclosed space in which the sound can be lost. The larger the stage house, the more the waste of acoustic energy and the more difficulty the actor has in projecting his voice through the proscenium opening unless he goes out into the auditorium on to a forestage.

The plan shape of the auditorium will be considerably influenced by the seating layout and for theatres (auditoria with low reverberation) almost any shape resulting from this influence is acoustically acceptable, with the possible exceptions of circular or elliptical auditoria, unless special precautions are taken. Simple plain surfaces, particularly anything approaching a sphere, cube or other regular solid polygon, will be more difficult to handle. Changes of surface level and modelling of the surfaces will provide acoustic diffusion, which is advantageous. Projections with widths and depths of at least 100 mm (4 in.) are necessary to be effective, and they are better arranged in a random pattern.

Balcony overhangs

In auditoria for natural sound, as distinct from cinemas, deeply overhung balconies should be avoided. It is best to restrict the depth from the front of the balcony to the rearmost row of seats under it to not more than twice the dimension from the audience head level (say 1150 mm (45 in.) from the floor) to the balcony soffit, at the front line of the balcony.

Reverberation

Reverberation will improve acoustic conditions for the audience provided it is neither too much nor too little. For speech in auditoria of volumes between 300 m^3 and 12000 m^3 (10600 and 42400 ft^3), the average reverberation time at mid frequencies with an audience present should not be more than 1.2 second, or less than 0.7 second for highest intelligibility. As reverberation is increased, speech

*4:1. The Maltings
Concert Hall,
Snape, Suffolk*

becomes less intelligible, at first slowly, but deteriorating quite rapidly at 1.5 second and above. For music, longer reverberation times are required depending on the type of music. Values between 1 and 2 seconds are satisfactory for much programme material, and thus the acoustics can be good for music without being unduly bad for speech. Choral music needs the longest reverberation time, particularly ecclesiastical music, which sounds best in the cathedrals and churches it was written for.

Reverberation is directly proportional to the volume of the auditorium and inversely proportional to the amount of absorption in it. Allowing for the fact that common materials such as plaster or wood, however hard, will necessarily have some absorption, it is found that a volume of about 3–5 m^3 (106–176 ft^3) per audience seat gives just about the right total absorption (audience plus surfaces) to provide a satisfactory reverberation time for ideal speech conditions. Therefore, if the auditorium can be designed on the basis of this calculation it will be unnecessary to introduce special sound-absorbent materials on the room surfaces. Moreover, as the surfaces will be sound-reflecting, they can be disposed to promote useful reflections on to the audience and help compensate for the normal fall-off of sound with distance from the sound source.

This approach to design is satisfactory for up to 300 seats. If about 0.6 m^2 (6½ ft^2) is taken as the amount of floor area occupied by one person, including some allowance for circulation space, at 3 m^3 (106 ft^3) per seat, a room height of about 5 m (16 ft) is obtained. If the auditorium is a larger one (say exceeding 200 to 300 seats) the proportions will be poor with such a low ceiling height; a volume exceeding 3 m^3 (106 ft^3) per seat therefore becomes unavoidable, and it is then necessary to add absorbents to the room surfaces to obtain the optimum reverberation time.

In contrast to this, auditoria used primarily for music must be designed with a very much larger volume per seat – preferably over 8 m^3 (282 ft^3) – or it will be impossible to obtain long enough reverberation time, however hard the surfaces. The closer together an audience can be seated, the shorter will be the average distance to the stage and the easier it is to keep the volume per seat down to a low value. The densely packed audience in old theatres probably accounts for the reputation for acoustic excellence which many of them earned. However, modern regard for comfort has led to much more generous seat spacing than was common in the past. Continental seating, in which the row-to-row dimension is made large enough for people to pass along a row without forcing those already seated to stand, reduces the number of gangways, but it rarely produces a higher density of audience, and tends slightly to increase the amount of absorption of each person because

owing to their wider spacing they (or their clothes) are more exposed to the sound waves.

Reflectors

When the auditorium is large and the maximum distance to an audience seat is over 18 m (60 ft), ceiling reflectors can make an improvement. They should be designed so that the reflections are concentrated more on the most distant seats. In designing reflectors it is necessary to decide on the positions of the sound sources, which will vary, particularly in a theatre with an adjustable stage. The aid provided by reflectors will be most necessary to an actor speaking from far upstage, as in this position the stage house and the proscenium arch have the greatest disabling effect. Other patterns of sound reflection resulting from sound sources in other positions must also be studied to ensure a generally satisfactory distribution of sound. Materials for reflectors must be smooth and non-porous and should weigh not less than 5 kg/m^2 (1 lb./ft^2) for speech only, or 40 kg/m^2 (8 lb./ft^2) for music.

The same principles should be applied to an open-stage theatre, but the provision of a reflecting surface which will direct sound back over the actor's head from wherever he happens to be on the stage is very difficult to achieve, one complication being that such reflectors will conflict with lighting positions.

Music

Music in a theatre adds to the design problems. The need may vary from an orchestra in a pit for musical shows or incidental music to that of presenting an orchestral or musical programme from the stage itself. The ideal acoustics for light music, opera and symphonic music are all somewhat different, and unless some means can be found to make a major change in the acoustic conditions of the auditorium, a compromise is unavoidable. The main need is to increase the reverberation time, but this may be detrimental to intelligibility of speech and must therefore be done with caution. Possible solutions may be some form of electronic control of reverberation (assisted resonance) or physical variation by adjustment of the room surfaces or of the total volume.

Orchestra pit

The orchestra pit for a large opera house may need to accommodate up to 120 players, while for other theatres not more than ten or twelve may be needed. To avoid encroaching too much on auditorium seating area, the orchestra pit sometimes extends under the front edge of the stage. This is not necessarily an acoustic disadvantage, especially with large orchestras, as it helps to improve the

balance between orchestral sound and voices from the stage.

Methods of adjusting acoustics

There are various methods of adjusting the acoustics of an auditorium where they need to be varied for different types of performance. They tend to fall into two categories – physical changes and electronic. Physical changes may sometimes be on a grand scale, such as moving walls and ceilings (inclined to be very expensive) or altering the absorption in the room, which is usually done by introducing absorbent materials to cover up reflective surfaces. Hinged panels with one side hard and the other soft are folded over to increase or decrease the absorption. Another system is to have a gap at the back and sides of the circle or circles in which a curtain or "acoustic banner" can be pulled out when the auditorium is to be used for drama. With this stowed out of the way, the hard surface and the gap behind the balconies improves the conditions for music. Unfortunately these systems are limited in effect because the bulk of the absorption (about 60%) remains in the audience and seating. Any such physical adjustments can at best only affect the reverberation time by 40%.

Electronic systems include assisted resonance and developed ambiophony, both systems using a large number of multiple sound channels. In principle, sound is gathered by microphones and delivered back to the auditorium through loudspeakers to extend the reverberant response of the space. Such systems, although not as expensive as building two buildings, are costly. Simpler systems, relying on careful reinforcement of specific reflections, are now emerging.

Over the last twenty years many attempts have been made, with varying degrees of success and failure, to introduce this electronic architecture. Undesirable side effects, called "colouration", can be caused by the presence of the system itself. As the technology develops, no doubt the installations will continue to improve.

All these methods rely on the buildings' users knowing how to use them properly.

Concert halls

An auditorium mainly intended for the enjoyment of orchestral music needs a reverberation time of over two seconds and therefore requires a larger volume than is desirable for speech. The number of performers will average about 80 and may often be 120 or, with a choir, 250. Normally a programme is only performed once or twice, and for economic as well as acoustic reasons the seating capacity should probably start at 1500, and will often be in the 2000 to 2500 bracket. The acoustics of concert and recital halls are the first criterion by which their success or failure is judged, and the expert advice of an acoustic consultant is essential. This does not absolve the architect from all responsibility for the acoustics. If the acoustician is brought in to make the architect's design work after it has been fixed, or if the design of the auditorium is left entirely to the acoustics consultant, to be fitted into the rest of the building afterwards, the results are unlikely to be satisfactory. The ideal arrangement is for the architect and acoustician to work together to develop the design.

Recital halls

Performances by small groups of musicians playing chamber music or smaller orchestral works with perhaps fifteen players are more appropriately housed in an auditorium seating up to, say, 600 seats. Such a hall is suitable for piano recitals, lieder, trios, quartets etc. which may be lost in a large concert hall. They are often built as an adjunct to the main auditorium bearing a similar relation to it as the studio theatre does to the main theatre auditorium. There have also been successful conversions of old buildings, such as the Maltings at Snape (Figure 4:1) and several redundant churches. While small-scale music can be heard reasonably satisfactorily in a theatre auditorium, it gains much from being experienced in a hall whose acoustics have been designed for it.

5

Safety

Theatre licensing in Great Britain was originally intended as a measure to preserve public order. As a result of several disastrous theatre fires round the turn of the century, the grant of a theatre licence became dependent upon compliance with safety requirements, and this legal basis explains why the procedure for obtaining local authority approval for a place of public entertainment differs from that for other types of building.

There is a temptation for architects and theatre management to regard safety regulations as an irksome burden imposed from outside by uncomprehending officials. Unfortunately, there have been quite enough tragic experiences to prove that safety precautions dare not be neglected. However, since the introduction of safety regulations there have been remarkably few serious disasters in theatres in modern times, particularly in Britain, and those that have occurred can usually be traced to the neglect of their responsibility by somebody who should have known better.

The architect and the management of the theatre should understand the principles of a safe building and work together to achieve it. The technical staff of the local authority whose duty it is to administer the regulations should, on the other hand, have some appreciation of the workings of the theatre. Regulations can only be framed to deal with known building types. They cannot be expected to anticipate new ideas or forms of construction. Rigid application of the letter of the law may appear the easiest way out for an authority which wishes to relieve itself of any further moral responsibility, but this can bring the law into disrepute, especially if a deviation from the written text is clearly as safe as the literal interpretation of it. Perhaps the best guarantee of public safety is the efficiency and integrity of the day-to-day management of the theatre, and this can be encouraged if those concerned have confidence and understanding of the safety arrangements. These should evolve in consultation between the architect and the authority's technical staff in such a way that, while providing adequate protection, they are strictly related to the particular premises in question, and enforceable in practice by management and authority alike.

Hazards and safeguards

In the orthodox proscenium type of theatre, the greatest hazards arise from fire on the stage. Even with the utmost care the possibility of fire cannot be entirely eliminated when canvas and timber are used in scenic construction. It is not commonly understood that the so-called fire-proofing of scenic canvas does not make it non-combustible; it merely makes it less easy to ignite. Once it has caught alight it burns readily, giving off a great deal of pungent smoke. An obvious danger is the use of candles, flaming torches or other naked flames on the stage as part of a production. In such cases there will usually be someone standing by with fire-fighting equipment to cope with an accident, but most fires arise from less predictable causes such as accidental contact between scenery or drapes and stage lighting equipment.

Although a conflagration of scenery on stage will probably do a great deal of damage to the building it need not have disastrous consequences for the occupants provided panic is avoided. The strategy for dealing with an outbreak of fire on the stage is to confine it within the four walls of the stage tower and to use the powerful upward draught created by the chimney effect of the tower to draw heat and smoke away from the audience. The following arrangements, now generally in use all over the world, have been evolved from lessons learned in a number of theatre disasters in the past.

The proscenium wall

The proscenium wall is made to provide fire and smoke separation between the stage and the auditorium. The number of openings in it is restricted to essential pass doors and orchestra pit access, and each of these should be carefully detailed to provide the necessary fire and smoke cut-off. The largest opening is the proscenium itself, which is provided with a safety curtain. The origins of the safety curtain are obscure, but at least one was in existence long before the advent of regulations. In 1794 a safety curtain was provided at London's Drury Lane Theatre after its reconstruction. On the opening night this curtain, heralded by a verse oration, was lowered in the sight of the audience and its solidity demonstrated by blows with a hammer. It was then raised so that the audience could see cascades of water from a primitive drencher, fed by tanks in the roof, falling into an artificial lake, complete with boats and boatmen. Fourteen years later the theatre was again burned down and, as might be expected in this pre-regulation era, the tanks were empty. Brick proscenium walls and a safety curtain were first required by regulations towards the end of the nineteenth century.

Auditorium ventilation

Ventilation of the auditorium is designed to maintain a flow of air towards the stage at all times. There should be a system of lobbies to prevent the sudden rush of air through exits from the stage. There is a prohibition on high-level natural ventilation over the gallery which is a complete reversal of earlier requirements. It was introduced after the fire at the Iroquois Theatre, Chicago, in 1903, when nearly 600 persons were killed. After scenery had caught fire, the safety curtain failed to complete its descent, smoke and flames were blown under it by opening of the stage exits, and only a quarter of the people seated in the gallery survived. The heavy death toll in other parts of the theatre was due largely to panic aggravated by serious breaches of regulations.

The stage lantern

The automatic smoke vent or stage lantern is a most important fire safeguard introduced largely as a result of researches by Austrian engineers after the disastrous fire in 1881 at the Ring Theatre, Vienna, when 450 persons were killed.

If a fire breaks out on the stage the stage lantern is opened either by manual release, automatic means (such as a temperature-sensitive link), or in the last resort by the shattering under heat of the specially thin glazing. The safety curtain is lowered and the drencher turned on to prevent it buckling under the heat. Automatic sprinklers above the stage also come into operation to reduce the scale of the fire as much as possible. When such a thing happens, artists and backstage staff have only a very short time in which to make their escape and this should be borne in mind when planning the exits from the stage area, including the flys, the grid and the stage basement. The layout and equipment of all the backstage areas must be designed to avoid the outbreak of fire and to make certain that if one does occur it is isolated so that no sign can reach the stage itself, where a single puff of smoke could precipitate a panic. The individual dressing rooms, access corridors, property stores, offices, workshops, and other backstage areas not directly concerned with the actual performance on stage should be separated from one another and from the stage.

All such compartments should be ventilated directly or by individual fire-resisting trunking to the open air. The dressing-room block and parts of the building where stage staff are employed should have alternative exit routes equipped with secondary lighting, appropriate door fastenings and signs. Such requirements are usually given in some detail in the licensing regulations, and they will also apply to some of the technical areas situated in the front of house, such as follow spot boxes and projection rooms. The safety problem in each case is that of the very rapid evacuation of a relatively small number of people from premises with which they are familiar. Staff should have taken part in regular fire drill, and the risk of panic is likely to be small. There may be cases where staff could suffer badly burned hands or damage to eyesight from potentially dangerous equipment. A person temporarily maimed in this way cannot easily negotiate ladders and catwalks, and the exit doors from them should be fitted with panic bolts only. There should be alternative means of escape from all catwalks and technicians' galleries likely to be used regularly during performances or rehearsals.

The stage is the special hazard, but there are potential dangers for an audience both in the auditorium and in the other parts of the building accessible to the public. These may be considered under two related but distinct headings: fire and panic. Fire, used in the strict sense of actual burns or injuries by falling debris, is not a serious risk in the public portion of a modern theatre, if care is taken in the choice of materials. Precautions must be taken against the very rapid spread of flame; in some circumstances this can reach almost explosive proportions. A disaster of this type occurred in Liège during the early part of 1955. The auditorium of a cinema was lined with compressed paper acoustic material fixed on battens, leaving an air space behind. The material was ignited by an unknown cause near the screen, and flames spread with great rapidity over the whole auditorium; the ceiling collapsed "within a few moments"; and 49 out of 135 persons present died, all – or almost all – from asphyxiation. The use of highly flammable materials and substances which produce large volumes of smoke for wall and ceiling linings, curtains and light fittings must be avoided, and sound-absorbent materials, resonant panelling and other acoustic treatments must have a satisfactory degree of flame-resistance.

Open stages

If no proscenium separation is provided, the standard required on the stage or platform should be the same as for the rest of the auditorium. All scenery and properties must be non-combustible or at least of low flammability, and restrictions are usually imposed on the use of a naked flame or other potentially dangerous stage effects.

Panic

Panic in the audience is by far the most dangerous circumstance which can occur in any place of public entertainment. It is probably true to say that over 90% of the many thousands killed in theatre disasters died from this cause and this cause alone. It is sudden and unpredictable and can happen in a wide variety of places, to many types of audience and at many kinds of performance. It has often arisen without any real physical danger being present. On more than one occasion in the early history of London's Old Vic, before the introduction of safety regulations, the desperately overcrowded gallery was evacuated under near panic conditions. It has been pointed out that on these occasions, outright panic was averted by the social instincts of a local audience largely drawn from the criminal classes, and among the few casualties which did occur, no women or children were included. Similar conditions prevailed in many old music halls, and parallels drawn from other fields (shipwrecks and air-raid incidents, for example) indicate that liability to panic is least common among groups of people having a common social background and an accepted position within it, however insignificant.

Other psychological factors may contribute, such as emotional tension created in audiences and the hypnotic, disorientating or frightening effect of some lighting and sound effects.

The borderline between a rapid but orderly evacuation and a disastrous panic is dangerously narrow, and every detail, however insignificant, may be important. Both the architect and the management should bear in mind that the problem is as much a psychological as a physical one. The actual form and layout of the premises are as vital as the presence of mind of staff or performers. Presence of mind is illustrated in the anecdote about Arthur Roberts, who reacted to a cry of "Fire!" in the old Surrey Theatre by standing calmly on the stage and telling his audience "Stop where you are. There's no danger. Dammit – do you think I'd be here if there was?"

Once a crowd of people is in the grip of panic it is doubtful whether any sort of control could ever be regained. Public safety therefore depends upon taking precautions to prevent its outbreak. All possible causes of alarm – fire, smoke or fumes, unusual sounds such as fire alarms and bells, photoflashes or the appearance of undue haste on the part of the staff – must be avoided or reduced to the minimum. Measures which inspire confidence must be considered in every detail, such as maintained safety lighting, the regular lowering of the safety curtain, and a clear view of exits and exit notices from all parts of the house. The staff must be trained to cope with emergencies in a calm and efficient manner.

Although the safety curtain as a fire and smoke barrier may well become obsolete, it would be unwise to disregard its psychological value. Audiences have grown used to its regular descent and the well-worn quotation "For thine especial safety." (Collins' Music Hall preferred *Hamlet* – "What – has this thing appeared again tonight?" – but it probably reassured the audience and, by a rather different association, the performers as well!)

Fire-fighting appliances

The fire authority should be consulted on the scale of provision of fire appliances and where they should be placed in the building. Compliance with these requirements is a condition of the grant of an entertainment licence.

Fire-fighting equipment in the auditorium and public areas generally consists of permanently installed hydraulic hose reels. Stages, in addition to sprinkler systems, would have hydrants, hose reels and sand buckets. To deal with a performer's costume catching fire, the stage and dressing-room areas should have blankets of heavy wool or mineral fibre strategically sited. The backstage areas will have water-type hand extinguishers. These are often placed in corridors, where, if their presence has not been anticipated, they can be a dangerous obstruction. A fire extinguisher protruding from the wall can effectively reduce the width of a corridor and may even catch the costume of a performer hastening by. Recesses should be designed for extinguishers, buckets, blankets and for hose reels wherever there is a chance of these obstructing circulation space.

Different types of extinguisher are needed for particular hazards, for instance carbon dioxide for electrical fires and foam for oil-fired boiler rooms.

Sprinkler systems and smoke detectors

Fly towers should be equipped with a sprinkler system both above and below the grid. Sometimes it has been required to install sprinklers under the stage, but this interferes with the use of traps and machinery and should be avoided. The sprinkler system is often extended to the side stages, the scene dock and the workshops, but never to the public areas, where it could cause panic. There is a more widespread use of smoke detectors in recent years, and it is likely that fire authorities will require a smoke-detection system to be installed in all those vulnerable areas which for one reason or another cannot be covered by sprinklers.

Management responsibility

If the premises have to be evacuated, the morale and training of the staff are vital; they must have confidence that proper safety measures are maintained at all times. The knowledge that some particular requirement is never enforced or that some piece of safety equipment, however small, is not in working order could lead to disaster.

The management's problems of running the completed theatre must be considered. Periodic surveys and inspections should be made to check that the fabric and equipment is maintained in a safe condition.* From time to time alterations are bound to be necessary in the light of experience or to meet changing trends in entertainment, and they must be carried out to the same exacting standards as the original work. A theatre is old only because it has been a long time on the same site. The Old Vic, for example, was built at the end of the Napoleonic Wars, but it has been so altered, refitted and maintained that nothing beyond the massive brickwork of the main structure is recognisable as the original building.

---

*The ABTT Information Sheet No. 5, *Safety Check Lists for Theatre Managements*, has been published to assist managements in drawing up their own list of duties and in allocating responsibility for carrying them out to various members of their staff.

Exits and means of escape

Amongst any audience there are bound to be some people visiting the building for the first time, and many others may not be particularly familiar with it. If an emergency arises and the premises have to be evacuated, much depends upon the clarity of layout of the building. The alternatives open to members of the public should avoid creating a sense of uncertainty and indecision. For this reason the usual "means of escape" principles which are applied to most other buildings, or indeed to the staff portions of the theatre, do not strictly apply.

Escape routes

At least two exits should be provided from each tier or floor, and they should be independent and remote from one another. Two exits close together would in some circumstances not provide an alternative means of escape, nor would they provide an alternative if they both joined into one common space such as a foyer. Exits from the auditorium must be distributed with safety in mind, but they should also be related to the normal circulation of the public. In an emergency it is easier for people to make their way out of the building in an orderly fashion if the route is already familiar to them; it is better to avoid special emergency exit routes if possible. If the building has to be evacuated because of an outbreak of fire on the stage, the public would not naturally go in the direction of the fire, even if the safety curtain had shut it off, and it is therefore inadvisable to place the only exits close to the proscenium. Another reason why it is better to have exits at the back of the auditorium is that in an emergency it is less dangerous to travel up steps than down. However, there are also hazards in the foyer area, especially as these now often contain restaurants and coffee bars where cooking is done. The possibility of an emergency arising in this area will probably justify some exits near the front of the auditorium.

Table 6:1 Minimum number of exits from a room or storey

SR = The Building Standards (Scotland) (Consolidation) Regulations, 1970

CSR = The Cinematograph Safety Regulations, for 1955, 1958 and 1965 (shortly to be updated, but no significant alterations are expected)

HO = The *Manual of Safety Requirements in Theatres and Other Places of Public Entertainment*, issued by the Home Office (to be superseded shortly by British Standard Specification 5588: Part 6, Places of Assembly)

GLC = GLC Places of Public Entertainment, Technical Regulations

Minimum number of persons	SR	CSR	Minimum number of persons	HO	GLC
1–60	1	1			
61–600	2	2	Up to 500	2	2
			Up to 750	3	3
601–1000	3	3	Up to 1000		4
1001–1400	4	4	Up to 1250	4	5
1401–1700	5	5	Up to 1500	5	6
			Up to 1750		7
1701–2000	6	6	Up to 2000	6	8
2001–2250	7	7	Up to 2250		9
2251–2500	8	8	Up to 2500	7	10
2501	9	9			
2701–2750	10			Up to 2750	8	11
2751–3600	12		Up to 3600		15

In the case of the Home Office *Manual*, the number and width of exits is calculated from a formula with a number of variables, including the fire resistance of the construction and the height above ground level. Values have been assumed in order to arrive at the figures in the tables. Regulations are at

Table 6:2 Minimum total exit widths required (assuming a minimum of two exits)

Number of persons	SR		HO		GLC Means of Escape Code of Practice	
		metres		metres		metres
Up to 200	7'0"	2.134	7'4"	2.236	7'2"	2.2
201–300	7'0"	2.134	7'4"	2.236	7'10"	2.4
301–400	7'0"	2.134	7'4"	2.236	9'2"	2.8
401–500	8'9"	2.667	9'2"	2.794	10'6"	3.2
501–750	13'3"	4.024	14'8"	4.470	15'9"	4.8
1000	17'6"	5.334	18'4"	5.588	21'0"	6.4
2000	35'0"	10.668	36'8"	11.176	47'3"	14.4
3000	52'6"	16.002	55'0"	16.764	68'3"	20.8

Minimum width per exit: SR: 2'6" to 3'6" (0.762 to 1.067 m); HO: 3'8" (1.118 m)

present all in imperial measures, which are here converted into metres. New regulations will be in metric but are not known at the date of writing.

Exit widths

The widths of exits should be related to their use. Some licensing and other authorities have fixed minimum widths. A recommendation given in Ministry of Works Post-War Building Study No. 20 is to allow for a rate of movement in cinemas and theatres of 45 persons per minute per unit width of 520–530 mm (20½–21 in.). In new buildings, exit doorways should not be narrower than two such units, 1070 mm (42 in.); but in existing buildings not less than 960 mm (38 in.) in width is at present tolerated.

The number of exits and their widths should be such as to permit an audience to leave the auditorium in two and a half minutes. All exits should be through doorways or openings which are clearly indicated by notices illuminated by two systems of lighting and which are in themselves readily distinguishable from doors leading to bars, cloakrooms, etc. (Self-luminous signs are not accepted by all authorities.) The whole of the exit route to the street must be properly lit from two independent systems and should where necessary be provided with cut-off doors and smoke extract ventilation. Doors in escape routes should all open in the direction of exit. Door handles and other fittings should not project into the exit way more than 75 mm (3 in.). Exit routes wherever possible should be separate from those serving other tiers and lead as directly as possible to a place of safety. They should be enclosed by adequate fire-resisting construction, and their possible use under panic conditions must be considered carefully. Bottlenecks, irregular surfaces or steppings, and doors opening from the side into the line of exit should be avoided.

6:1. Escape stairs. Arrows in the plan show the direction of escape

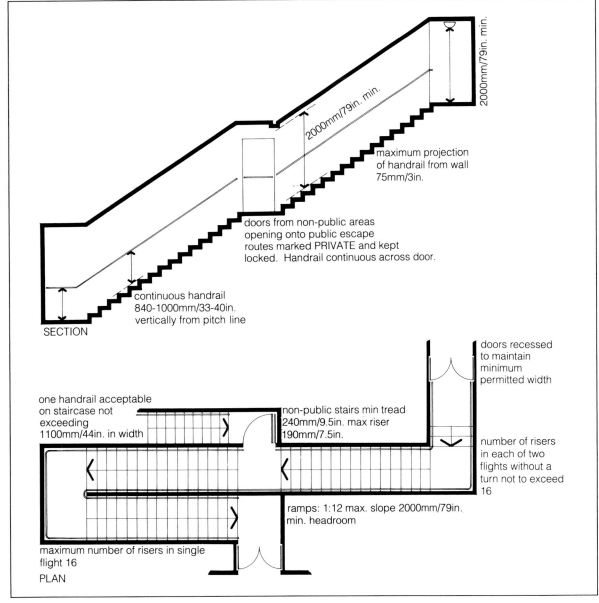

2000mm/79in. min.

2000mm/79in. min.

2000mm/79in. min.

maximum projection of handrail from wall 75mm/3in.

doors from non-public areas opening onto public escape routes marked PRIVATE and kept locked. Handrail continuous across door.

continuous handrail 840-1000mm/33-40in. vertically from pitch line

SECTION

doors recessed to maintain minimum permitted width

one handrail acceptable on staircase not exceeding 1100mm/44in. in width

non-public stairs min tread 240mm/9.5in. max riser 190mm/7.5in.

number of risers in each of two flights without a turn not to exceed 16

ramps: 1:12 max. slope 2000mm/79in. min. headroom

maximum number of risers in single flight 16

PLAN

6:2. Section through escape stairs for the public

280mm/11in. minimum

280mm/11in. minimum

180mm/7in. maximum

180mm/7in. maximum

6:3. Escape staircase

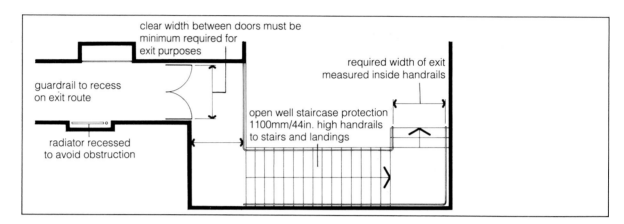

clear width between doors must be minimum required for exit purposes

guardrail to recess on exit route

radiator recessed to avoid obstruction

required width of exit measured inside handrails

open well staircase protection 1100mm/44in. high handrails to stairs and landings

6:4. Scissors escape stairs are an economic planning device which makes it possible to fit two completely independent, fire-separated staircases into one tower by using the maximum number of sixteen permitted risers in each flight

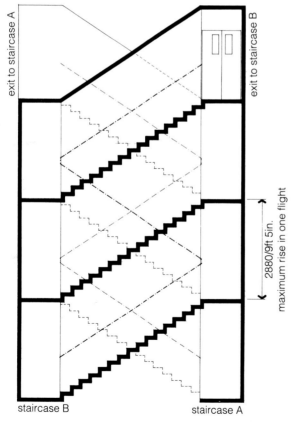

exit to staircase A

exit to staircase B

2880/9ft 5in. maximum rise in one flight

staircase B

staircase A

The National Building Regulations 1985, Part K, have eased the restrictions on staircases in places of assembly. The minimum going of 280 mm (11 in.) remains, but the maximum height of riser has been increased from 150 to 180 mm (6–7 in.). This makes it easier to rise a storey height in a single flight of sixteen risers. It also has an effect on the rake of auditorium seating, which can be that much steeper without having to introduce additional steps. However, it should still be remembered that for safety the height of risers should be consistent throughout the publicly used areas of the building.

7

Seating layout and safety regulations

The minimum dimensions and gangway requirements which follow are based on those of the former Greater London Council. These dimensions are likely to be incorporated in the new British Standard 5588: Part 6, Places of Assembly, which at the time of writing is in draft form. It is intended as a replacement for the Home Office *Manual of Safety Requirements in Theatres and Other Places of Public Entertainment* of 1934. Licensing authorities may still adopt their own regulations, which may differ from these considerably, but the issue of the British Standard should do much to harmonise locally administered regulations.

Minimum dimensions are shown in Table 7:1 and in the diagrams.

Table 7:1 shows the distance of seats from gangways. It should be noted that the width of individual seats is taken as 500 mm, the old standard dimension being 1 ft 8 in. Specialist theatre seating manufacturers can vary the width of their seats to suit the layout. 500 mm is about the minimum for a seat with arms, but 525 mm (21 in.) is more comfortable, and 550 mm (22 in.) is often used. It is probably best, therefore, to use this larger dimension for preliminary planning purposes, but exact sizes of seats will have to be checked with manufacturers.

Minimum dimensions

A   Back-to-back distance between rows of seats with backs 760 mm (30 in.) (minimum)
B   Back-to-back distance between rows of seats without backs 600 mm (24 in.) (minimum)
C   Width of seats with arms 500 mm (20 in.) (minimum)
D   Width of seat without arms 450 mm (18 in.) (minimum)
E   Unobstructed vertical space between rows (seatway) 300 mm (12 in.). See Table 7:1
F   For normal maximum distance of seat from gangway, see Table 7:1. However, rows with more than twenty-two seats, so-called "continental seating", are possible (see below)
G   Minimum width of gangway 1100 mm (44 in.)

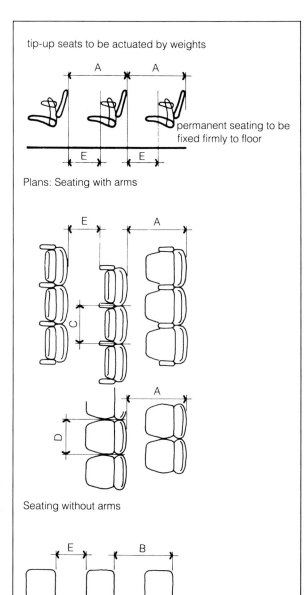

tip-up seats to be actuated by weights

permanent seating to be fixed firmly to floor

Plans: Seating with arms

Seating without arms

Seating without backs

Table 7:1   Distance of seats from gangways

Minimum seatway (measured between perpendiculars)	Maximum distance of seat from gangway (500-mm (20-in.) seats)	Maximum number of 500-mm (20-in.) wide seats per row	
		Gangway both sides	Gangway one side
E	F		
300 mm (12″)	3000 mm (10′)	14	7
325 mm (13″)	3500 mm (11′6″)	16	8
350 mm (14″)	4000 mm (13′)	18	9
375 mm (15″)	4500 mm (14′9″)	20	10
400 mm (16″)	5000 mm (16′6″)	22	11

7:2. Part plan of auditorium

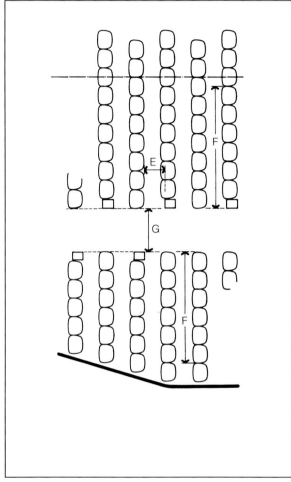

7:2

Balcony fronts

The top of the balcony front, the so-called "rester", must not be used as a resting place for small articles such as binoculars and handbags and should be designed to discourage such behaviour and to lessen the chance of anything falling on people below. If the rester is too narrow some patrons may feel giddy; about 250 mm (10 in.) is an acceptable width. A guardrail must be provided opposite the full width of the end of each gangway.

Continental seating

The term continental seating is now generally used to describe seating where each row extends virtually the full width of the auditorium without any intersecting gangways, i.e. rows in which there are more than twenty-two seats. It has been used in many theatres on the mainland of Europe, particularly in Germany, but only more recently has it been permitted by some English licensing authorities. The distance F in Table 7:1 determines the length of rows which were permitted for normal seating in the GLC area, and other authorities have similar regulations. However, continental seating has now become acceptable in Britain, including the GLC area. Its acceptance depends upon various other safety factors, such as the travel distance to an exit, and may mean an increase in the number of exits from the auditorium and wider gangways where they do occur.

The GLC Code of Practice for Means of Escape in Case of Fire required continental seating to comply with the following, which are additional requirements to those for normal seating detailed previously in this chapter:

1. No seat should be more than 15 m (50 ft) from the exit measured along the line of travel.

2. Gangways or exits should be provided at each end of a row of seats. Where gangways are provided, the position of the exits and seating should be arranged so that the streams of persons leaving the seatway move in the gangways in a direction away from the stage or platform (see Figure 7:5).

3. The clear seatway should be not less than 400 mm (1 ft 4 in.) and not more than 500 mm (1 ft 8 in.).

The great advantage of continental seating is that none of the best viewing positions is lost to gangways, and from the actor's point of view the audience is undivided. As the space between the rows has to be wider, the audience has the added bonus of better knee-room, and nobody has to pop up like a jack-in-the-box when anyone else passes along the row. Seats are gained where gangways

7:3. Section through balcony front

7:4. Section through balcony front opposite gangway

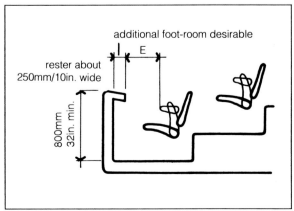

7:3

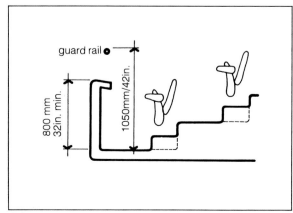

7:4

7:5. A method of providing acceptable means of escape for continental seating. The furthest distance of travel from any seat to an exit is 15 m (50 ft). The restriction of movement between blocks within the auditorium is a disadvantage in normal daily management, but may assist in rapid and unconfused emergency evacuation

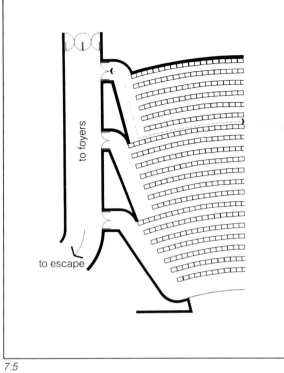

7:5

7:6. Continental seating at the Wolsey Theatre, Ipswich

would have been, but others are lost because of the wider spacing of rows. Continental layouts are not a means of getting more seats into a space than with conventional gangways; in fact the opposite may occur. The critical dimension is the unobstructed seatway, dimension E in Table 7:1. The row spacing depends upon this dimension and another variable, the front-to-back dimension of the seat. The design of the seat is therefore of the first importance in the chain of decisions which have to be taken in the process of designing an auditorium. With a tip-up seat, the arm rest would probably have the furthest projection when the seat is up. If the back of the seat rakes back it may overhang the seatway behind and reduce its width. The back row in the auditorium must therefore be made wider to allow for this overhang and to avoid the rest of the seats being pushed forward closer to the risers of the stepped rows. The gap caused may be dangerous or at least uncomfortable by restricting the space for feet to stretch. These problems can only be resolved by drawing a section of the seats in relation to the various rakes or steppings of the auditorium.

The row spacing is wide enough for members of

7:6

the audience to walk in and out quite easily, but not wide enough for more than single file. This in itself imposes a discipline on them, and audience behaviour shows that they reach the exits from the auditorium more rapidly than with orthodox gangway layouts.

The regulations, by putting a maximum distance of travel to an exit, limit the number of seats it is possible to put in one row to about fifty, but there are other factors which affect the choice. Some people feel uneasy and even claustrophobic in the middle of very long rows, and even if it is not necessary for anyone to stand up to allow one to pass it is nevertheless embarrassing to have to thread one's way over twenty or more pairs of knees.

Stepped aisles

Some authorities find it difficult to accept the detailed design of stepped aisles in an auditorium. Normal staircase regulations cannot be applied without negating the purpose of the aisle. For instance staircases are usually required to have handrails on both sides, and while a side aisle can have a handrail on the wall side, an intermediate aisle with seats on either side cannot have a hand-rail at all. It is very important that members of the audience using the aisles in dim light should have the steps clearly marked by a contrasting tone of nosing or by safety lighting at low level. It is also important that all risers should be the same height because people do not visually judge the height of each riser, but having climbed one step adopt a rhythm which assumes that each subsequent riser is the same height. They are only likely to trip if a higher or a lower step has been introduced without warning.

Another normal requirement is that all treads should be equal, but this is sometimes at odds with the safety of an aisle. If the height difference between rows is one riser there is no difficulty, but if, as is common, it is two risers and the treads are equalised you have an uncomfortable ratio of tread to riser and you create a hazard for people to trip over as they come out of each row into the aisle. Entering the aisle from each row is a bottle-neck in the smooth evacuation of an auditorium, and this is one of the worst positions to place an obstacle. The end of a single step of normal going is covered by the auditorium chair in its tip-up position.

When there are three risers between rows it is still important to provide extra space at the level of each row and the step that projects beyond the seat should be chamfered back to widen the access point from row to aisle. In general members of the audience perceive the auditorium as a series of rows with steps connecting them, rather than as a staircase with rows of seats on either side.

Legislation

The legislation mentioned in this chapter is current in the United Kingdom at the time of writing. It is based on British experience in theatres, which is considerable, and many countries in the world now base their requirements on, for example, the GLC regulations.

Places of public entertainment in the United Kingdom are controlled under various enactments, some general and some locally applied. Under the Theatres Act, 1968, every house or other place of public resort kept for the public performance of stage plays must have either the authority of letters patent or a licence. Patent theatres were granted a royal charter by Charles II. They are the Theatre Royal, Drury Lane, the Royal Opera House, Covent Garden, and the Theatre Royal, Haymarket, all of them in London.

Licensing authorities

The county or county borough council has the authority to grant licences within its area, except that, by virtue of the Local Government Act, 1985, the entertainment licensing functions of the Greater London Council were transferred to the London borough councils and the Common Council (City of London), and those of metropolitan county councils were transferred to the metropolitan district councils.

A county council, other than those last mentioned, may delegate these powers to a district council.

Film exhibitions

Under the Cinemas Act of 1985 a licence is required for all film exhibitions other than private film exhibitions. A licence is required whatever type of film is used, whether non-flammable or flammable, or video or other television equipment other than for normal BBC or ITA broadcasts.

If the premises are used only occasionally and exceptionally for showing films to a paying public (which means not more than on six days in a year) a licence is not needed, but the occupier must comply with the Secretary of State's regulations, which are the Cinematograph Regulations of 1955 and 1958 (shortly to be updated). He must also give the local licensing authority at least seven days' notice before the film show is due to take place and must comply with any conditions they may impose under cinematograph regulations.

No licence is required if members of the public are not admitted or if they are allowed in free. Institutions and non-profit-making organisations can ask the public to pay to see an occasional film without a licence for the premises. They can obtain exemption from the Secretary of State, but only if the premises have not been used on more than three of the preceding seven days for a similar exhibition.

The use of premises for music, dancing, singing, boxing and wrestling

These forms of public entertainment are controlled by authorities in a similar manner but not all under the same legislation. The Greater London Council had its own regulations, as do certain parts of the Home Counties. The rest of England and Wales is different again.

Technical requirements, regulations and rules of management

The licensing authorities have power to make regulations affecting the construction and equipment of buildings used for public entertainment, particularly on matters of protection from fire. They may also make rules and conditions which must be observed by the occupiers to ensure that the premises are maintained in a safe condition. Some authorities issue their regulations and rules of management separately, while others combine them in one document.

The Home Office *Manual*

The Secretary of State makes regulations for cinemas but not for other places of public entertainment. The Home Office *Manual of Safety Requirements in Theatres and Other Places of Public Entertainment* was issued in 1934 as a model code of requirements and conditions for the guidance of licensing authorities who would then make their own rules. Though it is rather out of date it still makes interesting reading and explains some of the background experience which led to the safety measures it recommends. It will be superseded by British Standard 5588: Part 6, Places of Assembly, which at the time of writing is in draft form.

The Greater London Council regulations and rules

Up to the time of its abolition in 1986 the GLC had many more theatres within its area than any other licensing authority in the United Kingdom and its regulations for places of public entertainment in London were comprehensive, covering the site, general arrangements, construction, electrical and mechanical services, lighting, heating and ventilation. It had a department with much experience of administering the regulations, and it was sufficiently flexible to take account of new techniques, materials, methods of construction and of changing trends within the theatre such as the desire for open stages. The GLC issued separate Rules of Management. The GLC, and before it the London County Council, the LCC, were widely respected for the way in which they administered the licensing of theatres and their standards have been adopted elsewhere in the UK and in other countries. London is in for a time of great change, and it remains to be seen what effect the passing of responsibility for licensing control to the London boroughs has on London's Theatreland.

Other authorities

Many authorities have based their regulations and rules on the Home Office *Manual*, while others use those of the GLC as a basis. This variation from place to place makes it essential to find out the particular local authority's requirements at an early stage in the design of any place of public entertainment.

The Fire Precautions Act, 1971

This Act will apply to theatres and various other places of assembly and resort, but the necessary designation order for this purpose has not yet been made. Its purpose is to strengthen and rationalise the law relating to fire precautions in these places and in hotels, boarding houses and similar residential premises and offices, shops, railway premises and factories, including "factories" in theatres. It was also designed to control some places which had so far escaped the net, such as club theatres. Occupiers of premises used for such purposes will, upon designation, have to obtain a certificate of approval of means of escape from the fire authority, to whom they will have to submit full particulars of the premises and its uses, including plans. The building will be inspected where necessary and any work which must be carried out will be notified. This will have to be completed before a fire certificate is issued. The requirements may include conditions about providing and maintaining means of escape, employing enough staff, and training them in what to do in case of fire. Records of fire drill and any incidents may have to be kept ready for inspection. If for a particular premises it is physically impossible to comply with the requirements, then the fire authority may for instance limit the number of people who may be accommodated.

Any offices, shops and "factories" (such as the workshop and backstage areas of some theatres) in places of entertainment are already designated under the Fire Precautions Act by virtue of the Fire Precautions (Factories, Offices, Shops and Railway Premises) Order, 1976, and fire certificates as described above may therefore be necessary in some cases. The fire authority will see that there are proper means of escape for the staff.

Building and other regulations about fire precautions

The fire certificate under the Fire Precautions Act, 1971, is needed by the occupiers of some existing buildings so that the fire authority can keep a check on their use. When it comes to new buildings, the Department of the Environment has made building regulations concerning means of escape under the Building Act, 1984, and the Secretary of State has powers to amend local Acts such as the London Building Acts. He can make regulations to control means of escape, the internal construction of the building, and the other matters which are dealt with during the life of the building by the fire certificate.

The Fire Precautions Act does not introduce any additional regulations to the provisions of the Cinemas Act, 1985, but this legislation comes under its wing and amendments may eventually be made.

Other general legislation

Theatres and other places of public entertainment are also subject to the various Acts which apply to most other types of building, such as: the Town and Country Planning Acts; the National Building Regulations, 1985, for England and Wales, which apply also to the Inner London Boroughs by virtue of the Secretary of State's regulations. In addition, in the Inner London Boroughs, the London Building Acts, 1930–1939, as amended by the Secretary of State's regulations, will apply.

The Health and Safety at Work Act, 1974, is equivalent to entertainment licensing regulations but applies at all times.

Access for the Disabled

It should be noted that the National Building Regulations, 1985, require proper provision for disabled people. Buildings must comply with Regulation 4, Schedule 2, Facilities for Disabled People. This matter is discussed in Chapter 19 (Public areas).

9

Stage planning

The audience-to-actor relationship is the starting point round which the planning of a theatre evolves. For many reasons it is convenient in this chapter to consider the stage as a separate entity, but the complexity of technical requirements must never be allowed to interfere with the vital relation of the auditorium to the acting area.

Provision for orchestra

Continuous musical accompaniment for singers (typically opera) is hard to accommodate satisfactorily. This is an area of compromise; conflicting requirements to be resolved are:

— a musical balance between singers and orchestra as perceived from the auditorium;
— enough space for musicians to play and be able to see the conductor;
— singers must hear the orchestra and see the conductor, the conductor must see both, and may want to be seen clearly by the audience;
— the musicians must not be deafened;
— any orchestral moat separating stage from audience must be minimised; the orchestra must be within the vision of the audience but not too dominant;
— flexibility in size for different orchestras.

As a result the usual position for the orchestra is in a pit between audience and stage. Musicians can be placed in various alternative positions, usually above the main stage level, in the centre or at either side of the stage. This is practicable only for smaller groups of players and where it is not essential for the conductor to have control of singers or other parts of the performance. A musicians' gallery can be incorporated in the permanent structure of the building, for example in a box at the side of the stage, but the needs of particular productions will differ and it is very unlikely that this will suit all purposes. It would be wrong to make permanent arrangements which could later become an unwanted obstruction.

By using closed-circuit television it is now possible for the conductor to control the performance from a remote position. He may conduct the orchestra at the side of the stage while a camera trained on him relays his image to monitor screens in the traditional prompt-box position or strategically placed in the wings to suit the production. Similarly, he can watch the progress of the performance on another screen relaying the show from a camera placed in the auditorium. However, closed-circuit television is usually only favoured for use with subsidiary elements, for example a stage band, and conductors generally prefer the traditional position, which gives them direct contact with the performers.

Size of orchestra

Orchestras vary greatly in size and in the space they require. Space demands have increased recently, particularly from musicians used to concert platform work, to the detriment of musical balance.

Suggested space allowances are:

— 1–1.1 m² (11–12 ft²) per player
— 1.4–1.5 m² (15–16 ft²) per player when under a stage overhang
— 5 m² (54 ft²) for a piano
— 5–6 m² (54–65 ft²) for the timpani

String players can usually share desks, but woodwind will probably each have different parts and must, therefore, have individual music stands, taking up more room. Some modern works have a large percussion section, which again demands more space. If the orchestra pit extends too far back under the stage, the sound will be muffled unless special precautions are taken. The soffit of the covered portion should be designed to reflect sound out towards the audience. In opera houses where the works of Wagner or Richard Strauss are frequently performed, the orchestra has to be very large, up to 120 players, and unless the singers are to be unacceptably remote from the audience, the pit will have to extend some way under the stage. For other operas and musicals, provision should be made for about forty players and their instruments. Excessive stage overhang is undesirable, 1.5–2 m (5–6 ft) being the usual maximum, but this is influenced by pit depth. The level of the floor of the orchestra pit should be adjustable between 2 and 3 m (6 and 10 ft) below stage to allow for the preferences of different directors and musicians. The walls of the orchestra pit should be dark and non-reflective to avoid picking up the inevitable light scatter.

Pit convertible to forestage

In most theatres whose use is mainly for drama a permanent orchestra pit can damage the audience-to-stage relation by leaving a gap between the two. The pit should be partly under the stage, but if it extends back more than about 2 m (6 ft) it will interfere with traps in the stage. It is, therefore, common practice to cover over the orchestra pit and use it as a forestage. This can be done manually by assembling panels and framework, but the labour and time involved may well be an expensive embarrassment to the management, and it is normally a great advantage to be able to make the change from orchestra pit to forestage mechanically by installing a lift or lifts. Even in quite small projects a lift in this position is one of the first pieces of mechanical stage equipment that should be provided.

The most usual provision is a single lift which can be stopped at various levels to act either as an orchestra pit, an extension to the auditorium seating or a forestage. The arrangements can be made more flexible by putting in two lifts, which

9:2. A two-section orchestra pit lift on screw jacks

themselves could be further sub-divided. There is also the possibility of putting seats on the lift when no pit or forestage is required.

When the orchestra pit lift is down, an orchestra pit rail must be provided for safety. This is usually a matter of manually inserting the uprights in sockets along the edge of the pit, but it is possible to mechanise the operation.

Mechanical aspects of orchestra lifts

The most common method of operation is by electrical screw jack, which must be accommodated below the level of the pit. If, as is usual, the pit is at or below ground level, watertight boreholes must be provided to take the screw jacks when the lift is lowered.

9:2

Screw jacks are usually both cheapest and most reliable in operation. Alternative methods are many, and include rack and pinion and hydraulic cylinders. Where boreholes cannot be accommodated, a scissors mechanism is usually necessary. Scissors lifts are normally more expensive, more prone to creep, less rigid and require greater depth for the platform structure than a lift using boreholes. Some lift structures are stable without side support, but generally side guides will be needed. The location of the guides and their details require careful attention if the use of the lift at low levels is not to be obstructed.

A double-deck lift structure is desirable, since it allows access to traps when the lift is at stage level, but it is much more expensive because of the additional excavation and space needed to accommodate it.

Health and safety requirements, in the absence of any known accident record, can allow safety officers free rein for their imaginations. Safe edges, safe light beams, enclosing side blinds, interlocking operating pushes for second operators, warning bells and lights etc. have all been installed recently. The main requirement is for keyswitch access, to restrict operation to experienced staff. The control button should be located where the operator has a full view of the lift and should have to be kept depressed throughout the time the lift is in motion.

The design of the front of the stage and of the covering of the lift will have to be carefully worked out to include any electrical points, microphone outlets and traps. There may also have to be a float trap for footlights and a carpet cut.

Where fire separation of the stage risk is required, the two-hour separation between auditorium and stage must be maintained, and openings other than the main proscenium opening with its safety curtain must be protected by a fire-check lobby with self-closing doors at each end. This applies to the entries to the orchestra pit under the stage and to doors on to the forestage.

9:1. Orchestra pit lift

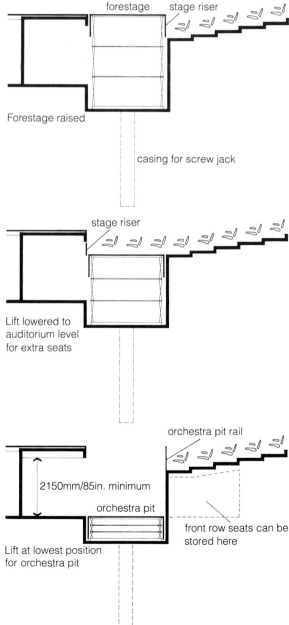

forestage   stage riser

Forestage raised

casing for screw jack

stage riser

Lift lowered to auditorium level for extra seats

orchestra pit rail

2150mm/85in. minimum

orchestra pit

front row seats can be stored here

Lift at lowest position for orchestra pit

Position of safety curtain

Normally the orchestra pit lift is placed on the audience side of the safety curtain. Some theatres have brought the safety curtain forward to come down on the orchestra pit rail, the pit itself being taken out of the stage area. The advantage of this is that the auditorium seating remains unchanged and there is no question of removing seats to accommodate the orchestra. It seems more logical to maintain the capacity of the audience when a large-scale opera production is being staged rather than reduce it by removing seats to make way for the orchestra.

The vital audience-to-acting-area relation is maintained for the straight drama, and scenery can be set right down towards the front of the stage. For the large musical production it is inevitable that there will be an orchestral area between audience and singers, and the relationship between stage and auditorium is no different, even if the acting area does have to be pushed back to accommodate the musicians. This arrangement does imply a larger stage area than would normally be allowed for a small theatre mainly intended for straight drama. It also implies greater width and flexibility in the arrangement of the proscenium.

There are disadvantages in taking the orchestra pit out of the stage, and these are:

— working stage depth is reduced to a minimum just when it is most needed (e.g. for grand opera);
— the position of the crucial proscenium zone on the stage with spotbar, tabs, masking, has to shift upstage, or be duplicated, to allow for the change of focus when the pit is open;
— the possibility of a flexible zone between actor and audience is much reduced by the permanent presence of the safety curtain;
— a shaped safety curtain with its associated supporting structure and fire walls is expensive and may be less reliable than a conventional straight line.

Prompting

In the dramatic theatre, prompting is one of the duties of the stage manager or whoever is running the show from the control point, the "prompt corner". (It should not be imagined that because this is most commonly called the prompt corner its main purpose is actually prompting.)

The full use and arrangement of the prompt corner are dealt with in Chapter 13 (Communications). In a basically proscenium stage condition no special facilities are required, but in the case of thrust stages and theatre-in-the-round prompting as such is sometimes a difficult problem. One solution which has been tried is the use of amplified prompting using a narrow-beam directional loudspeaker.

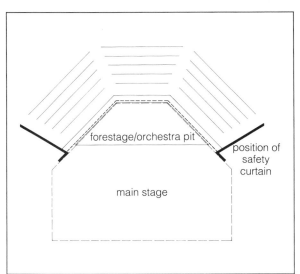

9:3

9:4

With smaller open stages, prompting can usually be done from behind or from a vomitory.

In the opera house the standard method of prompting is from a prompt box: a small enclosure covered on the audience side and open to the stage, sited on the front edge of the stage. The prompter sits in this box with his head just above stage level, with sufficient space around him to place his score on a sloping desk and raise his arms to stage level.

It is essential for the prompter to be able to see the conductor behind him, and for this a mirror system is employed, arranged so that the image can be seen slightly above the prompter's normal eye level. Provision should also be made for a

9:5. Section
through the
prompter's box at
the Royal Opera
House, Covent
Garden, London

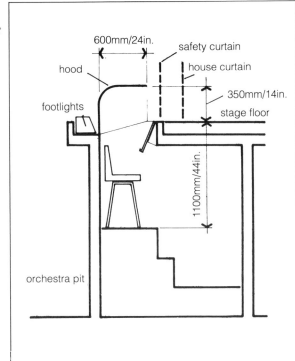

9:6. Plan at stage
level

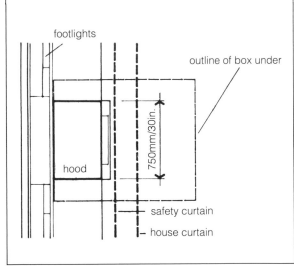

9:5 – 9:6

closed-circuit television monitor.

The hood covering the box should be kept as small as possible while still permitting the prompter some freedom of movement. Too large a box will obstruct the sightlines from the front row of seats and be a disfiguring element in any stage design. The hood must be painted matt black on the outside to avoid reflection, but internally should be white so that the light is reflected on the face of the prompter, whose visual expressions are valuable to the singers.

Some form of directional lighting, preferably low-voltage, must be built in to illuminate the score without spilling light over the stage. A miniature spot is suitable and it should be possible for it to be dimmed and switched off remotely from the stage lighting control position when the needs of the performance demand a complete blackout.

Height of proscenium

The minimum height of the proscenium opening is determined by sightlines from the highest seat in the auditorium. This is illustrated in Chapter 3, Figure 3:4, p. 27.

An auditorium with more than one tier or with a very steep rake will need a higher proscenium than one with seating on a single tier with a gentle rake.

As there could be occasions when for some theatrical purpose a higher proscenium is needed, the building is more flexible if the structural proscenium is raised close to the height of the auditorium ceiling, or even above it in some cases, allowing the incorporation of a lighting bridge on the auditorium side of the proscenium. Pelmets, the house tabs or the safety curtain can then be used to mask the upper part of the opening as required. It should be remembered that the higher the opening, the higher the fly tower will have to be.

To use the safety curtain for masking, the mechanism of the buffer may have to be adjusted.

Proscenium arch

The tendency now in the theatre is to play down the picture frame and make the transition from stage to auditorium inconspicuous. Although there will be many productions which rely on the picture frame there will be others where it is essential to avoid any emphasis on the proscenium arch.

There is often a false proscenium of lighter construction introduced behind the house curtain to limit the size of the permanent opening (see below and Figure 9:19, p. 70).

Entrances to the stage

There must be entrances for performers from the dressing-room area to either side of the stage. It should be possible to reach either side without crossing the actual stage area. Performers crossing behind the set often cause backcloths or cycloramas to shake, either by actually touching them or by setting up a draught. This is very distracting to the audience and can be avoided if there is a passageway outside the stage area. Nevertheless it is wrong to conclude that circulation space is not needed behind the acting and setting area, because there are many occasions when an entrance for actors is required at the back of the set. All entrances to the stage should have lobbies with soundproofed doors at either end to insulate the performance from any backstage noise and to provide the necessary fire separation of the stage.

Escape from stage

Safety regulations will require that there is at least one fire-protected exit from the stage which has no other fastening but panic bolts. With larger stages an additional means of escape may be required by the authorities.

Fire hazard of stage scenery

Some sort of scenery and methods of changing it will be needed for almost all live performances. Even on open stages, where sightlines prevent the use of orthodox sets, there is a tendency to load what space there is with scenery. The traditional materials used to make it are wood and canvas, because they are cheap and easy to handle, but their great disadvantage is the ease with which they catch fire. Theatres burned down so regularly in the nineteenth century that stringent safety regulations had to be imposed to protect audiences.

Traditionally constructed scenery is an obvious fire risk and most licensing authorities will not allow its use unless it is possible in case of emergency to seal it off from the audience with a fire barrier. In the proscenium theatre with a fly tower, this is done by the use of a safety curtain and drencher. But in other open-stage forms of theatre it is difficult, though not necessarily impossible, to arrange for some corresponding device.

If there is no means of shutting off the stage from the audience, the licensing authorities will probably impose restrictions on the materials that may be used for scenery. If it has to be non-combustible, cost is increased and the designer's scope reduced.

The full safety equipment for a stage may also include an automatic smoke vent, sprinklers, hose reels, fire buckets, extinguishers, smoke detectors and so on, but the safety curtain is the most important, because of the limitations it imposes on planning.

Safety curtain

There are various kinds of safety curtain. Maximum protection is given by the rigid type, which is normally suspended in one piece. Two- and even three-piece rigid safety curtains have been installed where flying height is limited.

In the past, roller and festoon asbestos curtains have been used. Asbestos cloth is no longer acceptable because of the possible health risk. An asbestos substitute based on ceramic material is available, but roller and festoon curtains provide little real protection beyond the important creation of an apparent barrier, which may prevent panic.

The heaviest form of rigid curtain, which has earned the name of "the iron", as it is often called by people in the theatre, traditionally consists of a steel frame of angles or channels faced on the stage side in steel sheet not less than 16 SWG

(14 AWG) thick and on the audience side in mineral fibre cloth with wire reinforcement woven in or another sheet of steel.

This runs in steel guides which cover the edges of the curtain and are set back from the proscenium to give an overlap of at least 450 mm (18 in.) at each side. There should also be a 450-mm (18-in.) overlap at the top of the curtain when it is down. It is suspended on steel wire rope and counter-weighted so that when released it will still be heavy enough to fall under its own weight. It is best to have two counterweight cradles, one each side.

As it reaches the end of its travel it is slowed down by a buffer (air or hydraulic) which prevents it from crashing into the stage. When it is down, it completely seals the proscenium opening. At its bottom edge it is provided with a pad, and at the top the seal is formed by another pad between projecting plates and wall angle, or a steel channel and sand trough. The curtain should descend to seal the opening completely within 30 seconds.

Typically, a curtain should be able to resist an air pressure of 0.28 kN/sq. m (40 lb./sq. in.) from either side when falling and when down.

The curtain can be raised by a hand winch or more usually by an electric or hydraulic hoist. The licensing authority's rules of management usually insist that it should be lowered in the presence of the audience at every performance, and, of course, no obstruction must be allowed to interfere with its action.

The construction does not always have to be quite so heavy. Fabric stretched on a steel frame is sometimes acceptable, but the rest of the devices still have to be provided. Roller and heavy wool curtains are often allowed for smaller buildings without full flying facilities. These must have emergency release arrangements and a drencher.

The drencher when operated releases jets of water to keep a steel curtain cool, allowing it to fall without buckling or jamming in its guides. The water will also add weight to ceramic and wool curtains and prevent them from billowing.

The releases for the safety curtain and the drencher are located on the working side of the stage near the prompt corner. A duplicate release for each is also required outside the stage area fire risk, readily accessible to firemen.

Automatic smoke vents

These are often called "haystack lanterns" because the original and still the commonest kind were haystack-shape.

Some kind of automatic smoke vent may be required over any stage in a theatre seating more than about 400 (the number varies according to the authority), whether there is a proper fly tower or not. If there is a stage which has to have a safety curtain, an automatic smoke vent is certain to be required.

If a fire should occur on the stage, the purpose of the vent is to draw the smoke and fumes rapidly up, and ensure that all air movement is away from the auditorium. The stage is effectively turned into a chimney which confines the fire and so gives the audience time to escape.

The principle is that light panels are held leaning out so that when the fastening is released they will fall open under gravity.

A quick-release mechanism is operated by hand from the prompt corner and there is a fusible link which can release the panels automatically. If these means fail the panels should quickly shatter under the action of heat. Thin glass sheets in metal frames behave in this manner, and it is for this reason, and not to let in daylight, that glass is used. The glass is painted black to exclude light.

Regulations require the cross-sectional area of the vent to be a proportion of the floor area of the stage. The figure varies from one authority to another, and in cases where no specific requirement exists the old GLC proportion of one tenth would be a suitable basis to work on. An automatic smoke vent may be required in a scenery store within the building.

The stage floor

The floor of the stage is itself an important scenic element which can best be exploited when there is a stage basement solely for use in connection with a performance extending under the whole of the principal acting area. This basement should have at least headroom and preferably 2400 mm (8 ft) clear height. An alternative means of escape has to be provided. The basement is considered part of the stage fire risk area, with no fire separation between it and the stage itself.

The stage floor must have some flexibility in its construction. The most rigid and intractable form of

9:7. The underside of a stage showing two traps. The timber parts can be easily modified, and if necessary the steelwork can be dismantled

construction is a reinforced concrete slab, and this must be avoided. Timber, on the other hand, supported by bolted steel supports, can easily be adapted. Traps can be cut in the floor wherever they are wanted, and if necessary the whole stage surface can be removed over the basement area.

A further step towards increasing adaptability is to make the whole stage in sections which can be removed separately. Still greater sophistication can be achieved by mechanising the stage with lifts.

If this sort of installation is contemplated, the depth of the basement will have to be increased, and if it is intended to bring sets or large pieces of scenery from below, it may be necessary to have a clear height of 80–90% of the proscenium height and to extend the basement under the whole stage area or beyond. Such an installation is usually only appropriate on the largest scale, such as an opera house working in repertoire.

Raked stage

Stage lifts are discussed in more detail later, but a word should be said here about raked stages, which were once an accepted feature of our old theatres and still have strong supporters in the theatrical profession. The original purpose of a raked stage was to improve the perspective effects of scenery painted in the traditional manner on a series of wing flats all parallel to the proscenium. It also gives some improvement in sightlines, and in some old multi-tier auditoria may be vital to them. Some performers feel that the raked stage assists their performance, whereas to others, particularly dancers, it is a hindrance. The great disadvantages are that scenery, other than a series of parallel flats, becomes much more complicated to make and handle and to take on tour. Solid three-dimensional scenery cannot easily be moved about, because verticals will not remain plumb. If the seating is properly designed the sightlines should be good without a rake on the stage. If a rake is wanted for a particular production it can be built on top of a flat stage, or the entire acting area can be tilted mechanically. Stages, therefore, should preferably be flat, with revolves and trucks provided on a temporary basis on top as part of a production.

Stage floor material

The selection of material for the stage floor is governed by conflicting factors which cannot easily be reconciled. Fire resistance is important, for although the floor does not usually fire-separate the basement, it must nevertheless remain stable while performers escape in an emergency. Timber is therefore usually required to be a minimum of 32 mm (1¼ in.) finished thickness, but without distinction being made between soft or hardwood.

Other properties sought in a boarded floor are that it should not warp or shrink badly as a result of heat or moisture changes; it should be reasonably easy to screw into and should recover well after a screw has been removed; it should not tend to splinter or be brittle.

It is not easy to find either softwoods or hardwoods with these characteristics, but hardwoods have a much longer life and this is most often the deciding factor in Britain. Where straight drama is played, the floor is often an important element in the scene design and for much of the time it is covered with a stage cloth or other material, but this is not usual for dancing. Dancers always prefer the resilience of softwood, and where the main use is for ballet, it will probably be necessary to accept the higher maintenance costs and a life of only five years which are the consequences of choosing softwood.

Permanent dance floors should have in-built resilience, and this is difficult to provide in a general-purpose stage floor, which may need to have traps cut in it and withstand high point loads.

There are problems in the choice of finish for the floor. The timber should be stained to a dark colour to avoid unwanted reflections of stage lighting. It should not be slippery, which would be dangerous, particularly for dancers. Even matt sealers are unpopular with dancers, but it is very difficult to keep a floor clean if it is not sealed in some way.

There are many temporary coverings that can be laid on stage floors for special purposes or to provide a working surface, but it is not appropriate here to discuss them at length. Mention ought to be made of linoleum which, provided it is well laid and thick enough (6 mm; ¼ in.), has proved to be a useful semi-permanent stage finish. It recovers quite well from being screwed into, is quiet, wears well and remains stable. Cleaning is not difficult, but the lino should neither be highly polished nor scrubbed with strong detergent, which will remove the linseed oil and make it start to crack.

Another finish often used is oil-tempered hardboard, which can be used as a wearing surface and then renewed without too much expense. 6-mm (¼-in.) hardboard, shiny side up, combined with 25-mm (1-in.) flameproof ply can be used very effectively for a permanent floor with replaceable surface. Portable plastic sheet dance flooring is extensively used by touring dance companies.

The ballet makes great demands on the physique of dancers, who are prone to strains and injuries at the best of times. One source of these problems is the nature of the surface they have to dance on. The worst conditions are when the floor is concrete or some equally rigid construction. The usual answer is to have a sprung timber floor with the boards of some suitable timber, such as maple, on joists or battens which may themselves be on rubber pads. This too may have its problems if it is

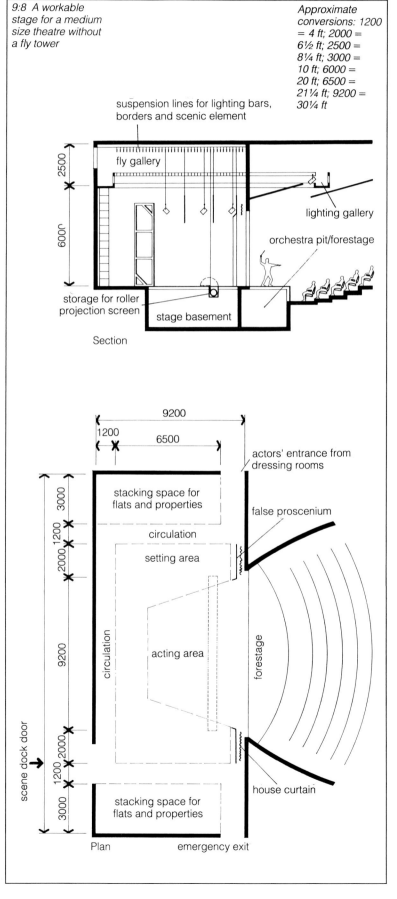

9:8 A workable
stage for a medium
size theatre without
a fly tower

Approximate
conversions: 1200
= 4 ft; 2000 =
6½ ft; 2500 =
8¼ ft; 3000 =
10 ft; 6000 =
20 ft; 6500 =
21¼ ft; 9200 =
30¼ ft

suspension lines for lighting bars,
borders and scenic element

2500

6000

fly gallery

lighting gallery

orchestra pit/forestage

storage for roller
projection screen

stage basement

Section

9200

1200

6500

actors' entrance from
dressing rooms

3000

2000 1200

9200

1200 2000

3000

stacking space for
flats and properties

circulation

setting area

circulation

acting area

false proscenium

forestage

scene dock door

stacking space for
flats and properties

house curtain

Plan

emergency exit

too springy and can give rise to characteristic
types of injury. Other finishes have been devised
taking account of floors designed for indoor sports.
One such includes a pvc sheet surface on layers of
solid polyurethane on a layer of foam rubber on a
solid base. The overall thickness is about 50 mm
(2 in.), and its degree of resilience depends on the
proportion and density of the layers.

Changing scenery

The stage must be designed for rapid changing of
scenery during a performance. Lack of space will
create difficulties and will limit the scope of
productions.

Figure 9:8 shows the requirements for a stage
where sets are assembled and dismantled for each
change. More width and more depth would be
desirable, but the dimensions shown are acceptable for a 400–500-seat theatre not working in
repertoire and without a heavy touring
commitment.

Stacking space for flats and storage space for
properties and rostra could be provided along the
back wall if the depth were increased, but this is
much less convenient than storage in the wings.
The depth should not be increased at the expense
of wing space. If there is not enough room to provide even this amount of working space for a
picture-frame stage, the question of whether it
would be better to have some kind of open stage
should be considered.

Figure 9:8 also includes a section through the
stage without a fly tower but with a system of
suspension lines and a gallery from which to operate them and to give access to an auditorium lighting bridge. It has been assumed that with an audience of less than 500 and no tower a rigid safety
curtain will not be required.

Methods of changing scenery

The elaboration of the methods of changing
scenery depends upon the prospective use of the
building. The more frequent the changes of production are likely to be, the more extensive should
be the provision of facilities and space for handling
scenery.

Mechanical aids to scene-changing have two
main purposes. The first is to permit the scope of
productions to be varied while making them
economical to run by saving time and manpower.
When each set has to be assembled piece by
piece, changes are virtually confined to intervals. If
complete sets are ready to roll into position, the
minimum of time and manpower is needed to
change them and there is no need for a break in the
continuity of a performance.

Second, in theatres and opera houses with a
repertoire it is useful to have sets for more than one
production built so that performances of different

shows can be given on the same day and rehearsals can continue without interfering with the current production.

Some or all of the following methods can be used singly or in various combinations. Those that demand least space in plan are most commonly used, but in general, extra space is more valuable than elaborate machinery. Scenery can be moved in and out of the view of the audience vertically above by using a flying system and vertically below by using lifts. It can be moved horizontally to the sides and the rear on movable stage sections or rotated on revolves.

Flying

Vertical movement by means of a flying system has the great advantage that scenery can be moved in or out very quickly and does not take up valuable floor space when it is stored in the fly tower. Even if for various reasons it is not possible to have a fly tower, it is still essential to be able to suspend things over the stage such as stage-lighting equipment, curtains, pelmets, legs and borders. All these can be suspended from tracks or pulley blocks attached to the structure of the roof.

In its earlier form all the suspension cables were ropes made from natural fibres such as hemp and manilla. Most suspension is now by steel wire rope, but "hemps", as they are called, are still used for some purposes. A special piece of scenery which cannot be conveniently handled by the counterweight system could have a set of hemps fitted up to take it. Hemp lines are hauled up by the muscle power of flymen and tied off on cleats on the fly rail. They may have a sand bag or shot bag tied to them to act as an improvised counterweight.

If an efficient method of changing scenery is required a proper fly tower is necessary, high enough for the tallest flats and backcloths to be taken right up out of sight of the audience. This is the factor which has most bearing on the height of the grid, which is the working platform of steel slats over the stage where alteration and maintenance of the fly system is carried out and temporary rigging and cabling to chandeliers, for example, is installed.

Calculation of grid height cannot be made arbitrarily without careful reference to the design of the auditorium, in particular the vertical audience sightlines from the extreme ends of the front rows. As a general guide it may be said that a desirable height for this grid is three times the height of the proscenium, and the minimum for proper functioning is two-and-a-half times this height.

The proscenium in this case is the working proscenium. The structural proscenium may be too high to mask sets of a reasonable height. Figure 9:9 shows how the sightlines from the lowest and closest seats in the auditorium affect the height of the grid. We have already seen how the furthest and highest seats in the auditorium determine the

minimum height of the proscenium. The view of the flys from the front seats can be hidden by borders suspended from the grid. If these are too low or too many, the spacious effect of a setting with a cyclorama or a large backcloth is lost. The higher the grid, the less likely this is to happen.

9:9. Section, showing effect of front-row sightlines on proscenium dimensions and masking

9:9

9:10. Plan

9:10

9:11. Head blocks. Each set of lines has four wire ropes for a four-point suspension. The hemp rope is for the hand operation of the set of lines. In this illustration there are also power-operated sets behind the hand-operated lines, and the head blocks for these can be seen sitting on the steel beam above the other blocks

The width of the area covered by the flying system should overlap the proscenium opening (W) by 2 m (6 ft) on either side. This width should not be interrupted for the full height of the tower to the grid. The width of the fly tower itself is determined by adding a further 2 m (6 ft) to one side to allow for counterweights and the fly gallery from which they are operated. It is usual to add a further 1½–2 m (4¼–6 ft) to the other side of the stage for another gallery, generally used for socket boxes and cabling to overstage lighting bars.

The minimum internal width of the fly tower should, therefore, be W + 8 m (26 ft).

Counterweights

In a counterweight system, scenery is suspended on steel cables which pass over pulley blocks on or above the grid and on the side wall of the fly tower and is balanced against counterweights which run in cradles up and down this wall.

The pieces of scenery are attached to a suspension barrel, which must be capable of travelling from the stage floor to the underside of the grid. The distance of travel of the counterweights is equal to the height of the grid above the stage, and a continuous vertical well must be provided for the counterweight guides, allowing extra height for the blocks at the top and bottom and for the length of the weight cradle. This system is the simplest and easiest to operate and is called a single-purchase counterweight system.

For the actual operation of flying systems the total width between side walls of W + 8 m (24 ft) is sufficient, but if counterweight guides come down to stage level they will take up about 750 mm (30 in.) including guardrails. This reduces the wing space of the counterweight side to 3250 mm (10 ft 8 in.), which is rather cramped. If the flys were operated from the stage floor, as they sometimes are, instead of from a fly gallery, yet more space would be taken up, reducing the wings still further to about 2 m (6 ft). Usually, more wing space than this is necessary, and with single-purchase flying the whole fly tower must be widened. This is reasonable up to a point, but with deep wing spaces needed the fly tower can become uneconomically large.

9:12. Fly gallery, showing rope lock being operated. This is a single-purchase counterweight installation

9:13. Loading gallery, with a counterweight cradle being loaded

9:14. The grid with the suspension blocks attached to the roof structure beams, leaving the grid clear for fitting up additional spot lines or other suspensions

9:15. Looking up at the grid and the suspension lines. The suspension barrels are trussed in this case to avoid deflection. The fly gallery and loading gallery can be seen on the far wall

9:16. Over the grid showing the single-sheave blocks attached to the bottom flange of the roof structure beams. The heavy block near the proscenium wall is part of the safety curtain suspension mechanism

9:17. Section through stage with single-purchase counterweight system

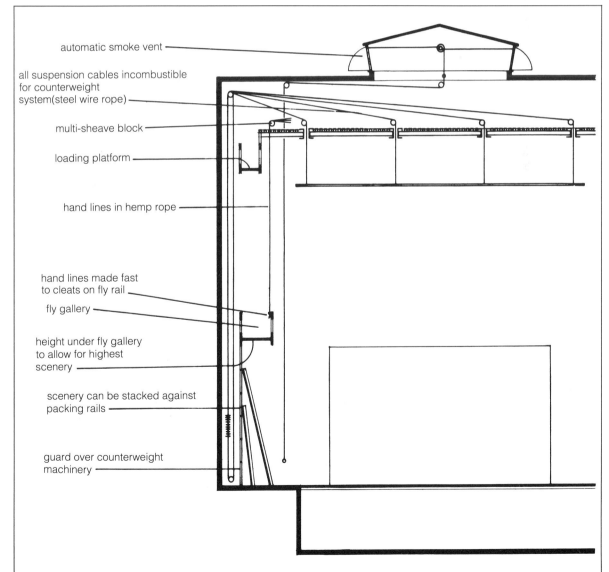

automatic smoke vent

all suspension cables incombustible for counterweight system (steel wire rope)

multi-sheave block

loading platform

hand lines in hemp rope

hand lines made fast to cleats on fly rail

fly gallery

height under fly gallery to allow for highest scenery

scenery can be stacked against packing rails

guard over counterweight machinery

9:17

Double-purchase counterweights

The alternative is to free the stage floor of counterweights and raise them so that the wings can be continued underneath the walls of the fly tower. If single-purchase counterweights were used, the same vertical height of wall would be required and the fly tower would become that much higher. In other words, if the counterweights were taken 7 m (23 ft) above the stage floor a further 7 m (23 ft) of height would have to be added to the fly tower above the grid, which is clearly impracticable. A solution is to use double-purchase counterweights, where, by introducing two extra blocks, the length of travel of the weights is halved in relation to the suspended scenery. This correspondingly reduces the height of the wall required.

The disadvantage is that, while the weights travel half as far, they have to be twice as heavy, which increases the labour of loading and unloading, lengthens the cradle required to hold the weights, and increases the friction and inertia in the system which have to be overcome. It is also less easy than with a single-purchase system to gauge the exact height to which a piece of scenery is raised or lowered. As the counterweight cradle is longer it is difficult to reach all of it from one level, and an extra loading gallery should be provided beneath the main loading gallery. The handling ropes should also be double-purchase. It is understandable that single-purchase systems are greatly preferred in the theatre, because they are so much easier to work.

One method of providing plenty of wing space without introducing double-purchase counterweights is to concentrate the wing space on the opposite side of the stage from the counterweight wall. If, as they usually do, economics curb the amount of space which can be allotted to the stage, it may well be better to concentrate a large area on one side rather than distribute half shares on either side.

Positions for operating flys

There is no mechanical reason why flys should not be operated from anywhere along the travel of the counterweights. In double-purchase systems the operator must, in any case, be on a gallery above the stage.

In single-purchase systems the operator can be on the stage floor. This takes up 1 m (3¼ ft) of valuable wing space and is a method of working which would be used only in smaller theatres, where there is no separate fly operator and the job has to be done by someone who has other duties at stage level. The normal operating position is from a fly gallery above the stage, but it is possible to have a choice of positions by moving the rope lock. No line should have more than one rope lock actually fitted if confusion is to be avoided.

Flying loads

The fly tower should usually extend for the full depth of the stage, but if this is very deep the flying system can be curtailed and the stage continued at lower height in the same manner as over the wings on either side. An indication of the extent of the stage which it is desirable to cover with the flying system is at least 3 m (10 ft) from the back of the acting area or one-and-a-third times the proscenium width back from the safety curtain.

Typical counterweight capacities (distributed bar loads) are:

— Small theatre 250 kg/set (550 lb./set)
— Medium theatre 400 kg/set (880 lb./set)
— Large theatre 600 kg/set (1320 lb./set)

Manual operation of loads greater than this is slow. With very high grids, above 28 m (92 ft) or so, transfer of suspension cable weight from bar to cradle and vice versa at the extremes of travel produces an out-of-balance load large enough to create some difficulty.

Spacing of counterweight lines

Although spacings as close as 75 mm (3 in.) have been used, the recommended minimum is 150 mm (6 in.), and 200–250 mm (8–10 in.) is common. This minimum is dictated not only by the multi-sheave head blocks, but also by the practical use of the flys. If cloths or flats are suspended too close together there is a danger of their fouling one another as they are moved. Closely spaced lines allow more flexibility in positioning the scenery, but if they are so close that it is dangerous to hang pieces on adjacent lines the advantage of flexibility is lost. Nevertheless, many pieces do not have to be moved once they are suspended, and, given intelligent use, close lines are of great value. The system should not be planned round the space needed for spotbars, and the chosen line spacing should be maintained without variation or gaps.

Proscenium details

The position of the first line behind the safety curtain is dependent on the depth taken up by the safety curtain and the drencher. The house curtain immediately behind these must be far enough back to avoid the danger of its fouling the safety curtain mechanism. Figure 9:19 shows an arrangement just behind the proscenium which is only one of many possible.

Some directors will not want a false proscenium at all; others may prefer to have more lighting between the house curtains and the first border. The diagrams in Figure 9:19 show a return on the false proscenium to give the appearance of thickness, but some will prefer not to have this on the grounds that it can interfere with lighting or that

*9:18. Diagrams
showing the
layout of a stage
equipped with a
double-purchase
flying system and
wagon stages*

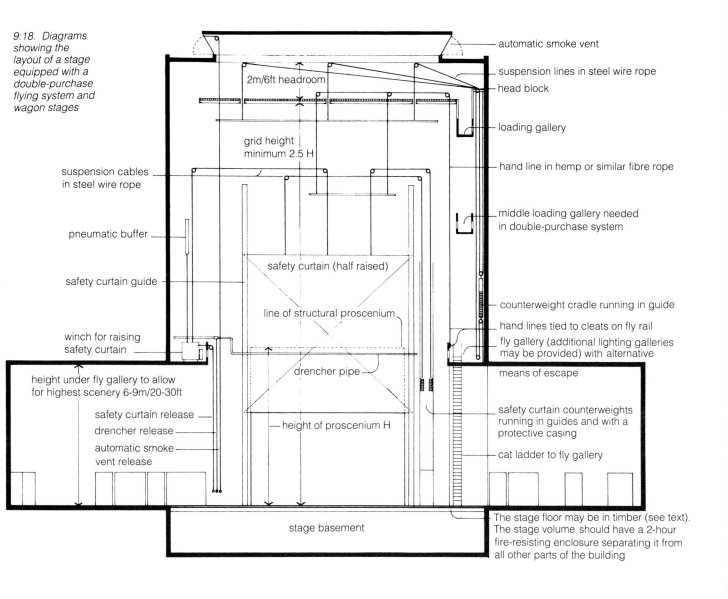

automatic smoke vent

suspension lines in steel wire rope

head block

2m/6ft headroom

loading gallery

grid height
minimum 2.5 H

hand line in hemp or similar fibre rope

suspension cables
in steel wire rope

middle loading gallery needed
in double-purchase system

pneumatic buffer

safety curtain guide

safety curtain (half raised)

line of structural proscenium

counterweight cradle running in guide

hand lines tied to cleats on fly rail

fly gallery (additional lighting galleries
may be provided) with alternative

winch for raising
safety curtain

drencher pipe

means of escape

height under fly gallery to allow
for highest scenery 6-9m/20-30ft

safety curtain release

drencher release

automatic smoke
vent release

height of proscenium H

safety curtain counterweights
running in guides and with a
protective casing

cat ladder to fly gallery

stage basement

The stage floor may be in timber (see text).
The stage volume should have a 2-hour
fire-resisting enclosure separating it from
all other parts of the building

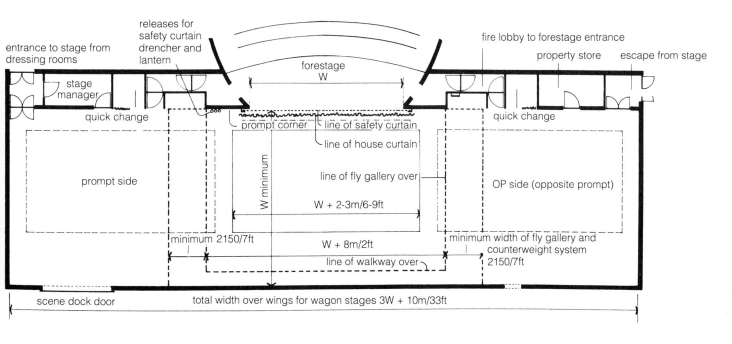

releases for
safety curtain
drencher and
lantern

fire lobby to forestage entrance

entrance to stage from
dressing rooms

property store   escape from stage

forestage
W

stage
manager

quick change

prompt corner

line of safety curtain

line of house curtain

quick change

prompt side

W minimum

line of fly gallery over

OP side (opposite prompt)

W + 2-3m/6-9ft

minimum 2150/7ft

W + 8m/2ft

minimum width of fly gallery and
counterweight system
2150/7ft

line of walkway over

scene dock door   total width over wings for wagon stages 3W + 10m/33ft

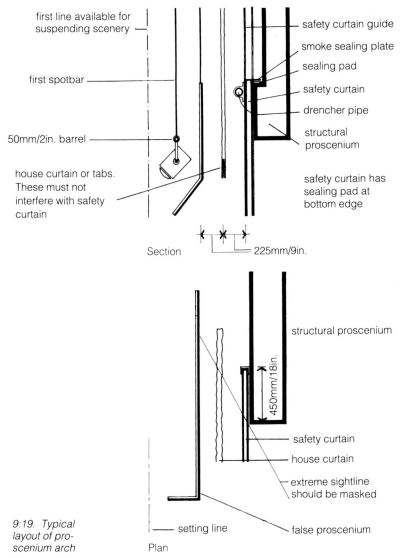

first line available for suspending scenery

first spotbar

50mm/2in. barrel

house curtain or tabs. These must not interfere with safety curtain

Section

225mm/9in.

safety curtain guide

smoke sealing plate

sealing pad

safety curtain

drencher pipe

structural proscenium

safety curtain has sealing pad at bottom edge

structural proscenium

450mm/18in.

safety curtain

house curtain

extreme sightline should be masked

false proscenium

setting line

Plan

9:19. Typical layout of proscenium arch

it tends to push the setting too far upstage away from the audience.

Loftblocks and flybars

When loftblocks for the counterweight lines are suspended from beams above the grid, the grid itself is left clear for working. It is then easier to fix spot lines and sets of hand lines where they are wanted on the grid.

Spacing of lines on flying bars must take account of bar load. Bar span should not normally exceed 4 m (13 ft), and this will determine the number of lines per bar. On wide stages, six or even eight lines per set have been used. Standardisation of 50 mm OD (1 29/32 in.) bar for stage lighting suspension makes it desirable to use the same diameter for flying bars. This comparatively small diameter may bend with high local loads, even with closely spaced suspension lines. Consideration should be given to truss-type bars in these circumstances.

Bridles are undesirable, since they restrict flying height.

Power flying

Despite repeated claims that power flying will eventually supersede traditional systems (as intimated in the first edition of *Theatre Planning*!), there is little sign of this happening. Apart from high first and maintenance costs, an important factor is the superiority of human sensitivity and responsiveness over machines, particularly when something goes wrong.

Much of the expense lies in the sensitivity demanded of the mechanical system. If a flyman feels some unexpected resistance he can make an instant correction and avoid an accident, but a machine, if it cannot sense that something is wrong, may continue and cause a trail of damage before it is stopped. The motors must have a wide range of speeds, up to about 2 m (6 ft) per second, and must stop at predetermined positions with great accuracy. A piece of scenery must not hit the stage floor with a crash. The motors have to be very quiet, and hydraulic noises must be eliminated. It is clear that the specification is very demanding, and although most of the performance criteria can be met by mechanical engineers, the problem is the expense of doing so.

Power suspension has a place, particularly in very large repertoire houses, to avoid the labour of repeated loading and unloading of counterweights, but it is prudent to plan systems which retain complete manual facilities as well. With care, comparatively simple and cheap power flying for heavy loads which mostly do not move in audience view can be combined with manual sets for the occasions when synchronisation with music or other careful timing is needed.

Power flying of a sort has been used in Germany for a long time, but when seen in use it is very obviously "mechanical". Modern control systems can remove much of the crudity of operation, but they are expensive, and usually require expensive maintenance staff. There is no hard evidence that running costs have ever been reduced as a result of installing power systems.

Power systems can be divided into various kinds. The most fundamental division is between power-assisted counterweights and straight-powered suspension.

Power-assisted counterweights rely on balancing out half the rated load, so that the motor has only to drive half the full capacity. The advantages are cost savings and comparatively easy reversion to manual operation. The drawback is the need to provide space for counterweight travel. Power can be provided electrically or hydraulically.

Straight-power suspension without counterweight can use electrically powered winches coupled to conventional or pile wind drums, or hydraulical rams with two or more times mechanical advantage to reduce ram stroke. The theatre is generally suspicious of hydraulic flying systems, not least because of the chance of leaks. This scepticism has been justified in the past.

Variable speed and position control systems are available with different degrees of sophistication; cyclo converters and standard AC motors are now favoured less than DC drives. These can be applied either to standard flying bars or to point hoists. Where point hoists are movable, or where pulleys can be re-positioned on the grid, great care must be taken in resetting the travel limits.

In a theatre with a conventional counterweight-type flying system, it is often useful to supply a limited number of powered lines for applications such as house tabs and a cinema screen.

9:20. Motor room for powered fly lines, situated in this case under the stage

Overload and slack line detectors should be incorporated as standard, but it is difficult to devise a system of such sensitivity that it can detect the resistance of a snagged gauze before it rips.

With full power systems, manual wind can sometimes be provided for emergency use, but this is slow in operating and therefore does not provide an operational alternative.

Stage lifts

These are expensive devices, usually only justified in very large theatres or opera houses working in repertoire, where they can earn their keep. They are a mixed blessing, often imposing a certain stereotyped rigidity on the presentation of productions, and making the stage floor uneven and unpleasant to work on after a few years.

Lifts, bridges or elevators in the stage itself have various uses, which come within the following categories:

1. Multi-level stage

For raising, sinking or tilting parts of the stage to provide rostra, traps, ramps or to give a rake to part or the whole of the acting area. There is a well-established tradition of massive sets on several levels for opera, and the action of many plays can be made much more interesting if the geography of the acting area can be altered in three dimensions. Lifts are not essential for this, but an extensive system of rostra entails a great deal of carpentry and materials. For a long-run play this may not matter, but in a repertoire the problem of finding storage for several sets with rostra may become acute. Lifts can help to solve the problem, and in particular they can save on the labour of changing from one multi-level set to another.

2. Special effects

Lifts are used for special effects of scenery or performers rising from or sinking below the stage. These effects are likely to be needed for the more spectacular entertainments such as opera, ballet and pantomime.

3. Moving scenery

Lifts can be used for moving pieces of scenery or whole sets from below the stage. It must be remembered that scene changes that depend on lifts will not be as rapid as those depending on flown scenery. Lifts move more slowly and, for safety reasons, should not be operated in the dark. With the exception of special effects during performances, lifts would normally be operated between shows or in intervals.

Safety of lifts

Some of the mechanical problems of lift design have been mentioned in connection with adaptable orchestra pits and forestages (pp. 56–7). It is not possible to provide complete safeguards in the use of lifts without rendering them useless from a practical point of view. This is one reason why they are designed to move rather slowly. Even so, great care has to be exercised in their operation.

Safety nets are sometimes placed between lifts when, for instance, they are used to provide an entrance from beneath the stage.

It may be necessary to install automatically rising safety barriers round the edge of the aperture left in the stage when the lifts descend.

Blue lights set into the floor round lift openings in the stage which flash when the lift has moved from stage level can also be used. In general flashing lights and warning notices combined with good staff discipline are more effective than restrictions such as door interlocks, which are usually circumvented after a time.

Lift examples

The extensive system of lifts shown in Figure 9:21 could be used in various ways. The first diagram shows the system used to make a concert orchestra platform. Acoustics are not likely to be good unless the wings and the fly tower are masked. This could be done by suspending reflectors from the grid, or by introducing a band shell, which is the practice in the United States.

The second diagram in Figure 9:21 shows the lifts used to form different levels on the stage, including a rake. The forestage is lowered to form an orchestra pit. This sort of arrangement would be typical for operas. A cyclorama or backcloth with masking borders and wings would be suspended from the grid.

The third diagram illustrates how lifts may be used to bring a complete set on a wagon from beneath the stage. Used in conjunction with a wagon system at stage level it would be possible to have four or five complete sets in existence at one time.

This sort of elaborate mechanisation has scarcely been attempted in the United Kingdom. Experience of large-scale mechanical stages is mostly confined to the heavily subsidised state theatres in Germany. Lifts and wagons used in this way are rather cumbersome and slow. There are other operations that would have to be carried out at the same time, such as rolling and unrolling the cyclorama and masking with borders and wings. To make full use of the wagons, sets would probably be designed to carry their own masking, and for this reason wagons should be wider than the proscenium opening.

Another factor has been that stage-lighting systems probably cannot accommodate more than two complete production lighting rigs because of the sheer physical difficulty of finding room for the number of lanterns unless the necessary discipline of standard lantern settings is accepted. A single production with two or three scene changes may make big demands on the total available lighting equipment. When it is one of a repertoire of elaborate productions the time taken to change the lighting, redirect lanterns and change colour filters may well be the limiting factor. However, now that the accurate remote control of lantern position, focus, beam shape and colour has become a practical reality, this may not be so in the future. The existing systems are at present expensive, and the choice once again boils down to economics.

Sectional lifts

If the lifts can be broken down into a number of different sections which can be operated separately the system is much more flexible, particularly for forming rostra. The danger of providing a system of stage lifts is that their use may be very

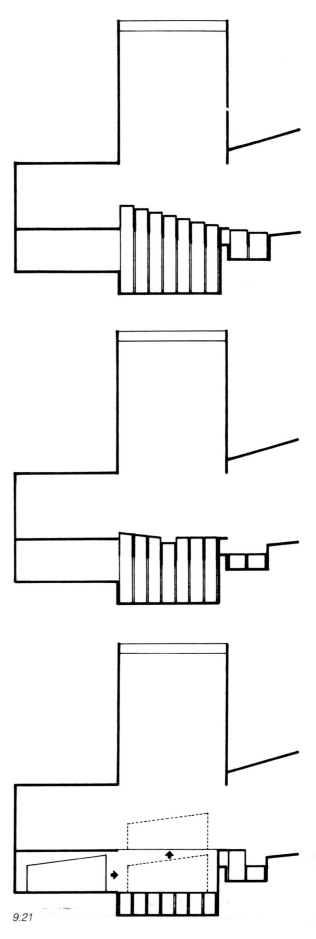

9:21

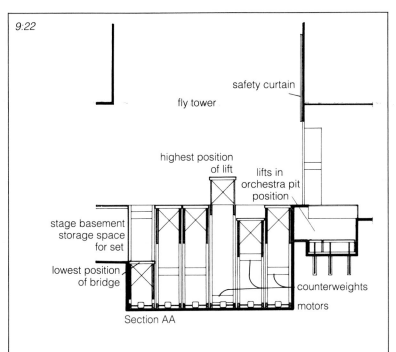

Section AA

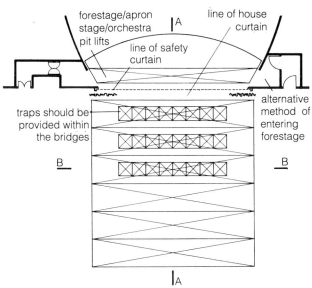

Plan of stage with a system of bridges

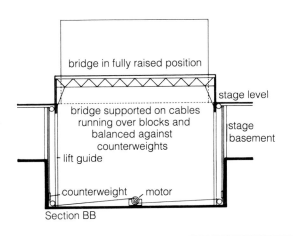

Section BB

limited in relation to their cost. For this reason the system should be as flexible as possible within the budget allowed. However, it should be remembered that the greater the flexibility, the greater will be the cost.

The distance of travel of a lift will probably be from 6 m (20 ft) below the stage to 3.5 m (11 ft 6 in.) above. It would be a great advantage if the lift area could be broken up into a number of independent platforms rising the full height without the interruption of guides, counterweights, etc. Telescopic lifts of this kind can be made, but their use is limited to cases where the vertical travel is small in relation to the horizontal dimensions, as in orchestra pit lifts. With the long travel usually required for stage lifts, the mechanical problem of accurately aligning the various sections of floor becomes extremely difficult, and safety becomes a greater consideration. It is more usual to find the arrangement shown in Figure 9:22, where the lifts are in the form of a series of bridges spanning right across the acting area. Sectionalisation is achieved by incorporating smaller lifts within each of the larger bridges.

Operation of lifts

Stage lifts can be operated by screw jack, rack and pinion, rope and counterweight, hydraulic ram or combinations of these.

Reliability, silence, speed of operation, accuracy of repeat limits, ability to hold a limit, ability to stop and bear load in any position and load-carrying capacity without deflection are some of the main features required in a lift.

The drive mechanism and the guides needed for the lift platform will affect the amount of clear space around the lift well. This is an important consideration when the lifts are used to move scenery to lower levels. In particular when loaded wagons have to be moved to basement storage areas, large clear spans are required over the wagon path, which must not be obstructed by guides, counterweight travel or racks.

Very long travels and the need to carry heavy loads do not suit screw jacks. Hydraulic systems tend to be slow and creep from position unless locked mechanically. Counterweight systems are fast, but the mechanism takes up space.

A large guiding column with rack drive on the side combines the advantages of various types and has been used successfully.

When used to transport whole sets on wagons the lift may be required to carry tens of tonnes over perhaps 10 m (33 ft) or more. Massive construction and considerable expense are inevitable.

Revolving stage

Three or four complete sets can be built on the revolve, and scene changes can be effected smoothly without it being necessary to drop the curtain. The revolve cannot project beyond the house curtain unless a complicated and expensive curved safety curtain is used.

The revolve can be put to theatrical use for special moving effects, but the novelty of this will wear off very quickly. It is rare for a "built-in" revolve to get much use after its first few seasons because it becomes "old hat". Since the mechanism of a permanent revolve obstructs other stage uses it is better on the small and medium scale to leave the provision of a revolve as a temporary measure for the particular production for which it is designed.

On the very large scale it may be possible to provide a special wagon with a revolve built into it. For complete scene changes, the larger the diameter of revolve, and therefore the shallower the curve at the edge, the better.

A combination of revolves can be used, as shown in Figure 9:24, but such arrangements are scenic devices which have no place in a permanent installation.

Wagon stages

Complete sets are built on shallow platforms which can be rolled into position. A full wagon system demands a great deal of space. Each wagon must be larger than the proscenium opening and deeper than the acting area required, so that there is room for the supporting structure of the set which is built upon it, and there must be sufficient space left round it for circulation. Conventional wagons can be rolled to each side of the stage and upstage, giving three complete set changes. The change is not as rapid as it first appears when the time taken to rearrange masking and lights has been taken into account. The system is best suited to repertoire working on a large scale, and where rehearsal provision must be made during the day with change back at night. It is not the golden answer to "instant" scene changes, as often claimed in press releases, and there is a danger the productions may become secondary to the mechanics of presentation.

The wagon space can be extended to the sides of the rear stage, giving five complete wagon positions. In addition, basement storage areas can provide more spaces on the very largest scale. There is a tendency on this scale to leave elaborate scenes assembled on a wagon, which then becomes an obstruction, and much time is spent shunting.

Wagons can be sub-divided into smaller elements; where provided, it is conventional to make these elements the size of the stage lifts.

Permanent wagons must have a depth of about 300 mm (12 in.). This step is best dealt with by sinking the current wagon to stage level by lowering the stage lifts 300 mm (12 in.).

To avoid a step in the wagon storage areas, compensating elevators are provided in the most

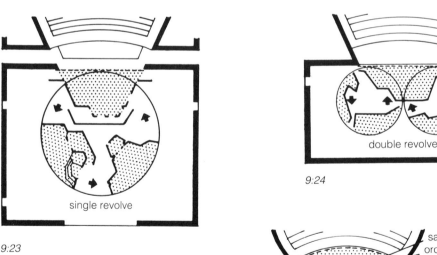

9:23

single revolve

double revolve

dock door

9:24

9:25. The T-shaped stage with one wagon at the back is the standard layout of many German theatres. Another variation is split wagons, where each set is divided into two, one half being carried on each wagon

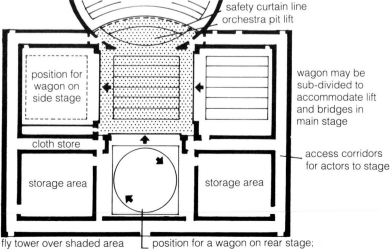

safety curtain line
orchestra pit lift

position for wagon on side stage

wagon may be sub-divided to accommodate lift and bridges in main stage

cloth store

access corridors for actors to stage

storage area

storage area

fly tower over shaded area

position for a wagon on rear stage; wagon includes a built-in revolve

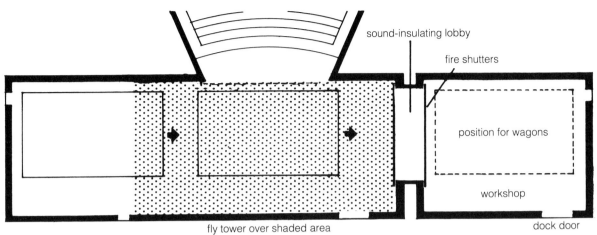

9:26. This diagram shows the workshop used to house one of the wagons. Changes are slowed up by the opening and closing of the shutter between the workshop and the stage; this has to be fire-resisting, sound-proof and noiseless

sound-insulating lobby

fire shutters

position for wagons

workshop

fly tower over shaded area

dock door

comprehensive installations which will lower the wagons flush in these locations as well.

The use of lifts with wagons requires very precise drive and locating mechanisms, and also complex operating interlocks.

Wagons can be rail-guided, which is very accurate, but the rails make for an unpleasant stage floor. Alternative free drives rely on vertically driven locating pins in the stage floor. Where wagons have to move in two directions, two sets of drive wheels are needed, at right angles, with a change-over which lowers one set and raises the other.

Power for wagon drives can be electrical or hydraulic, and the drives are usually wagon-mounted. In this case the wagon must have a removable umbilical connection. Alternative drive methods use endless chains under the floor, which are linked to the wagon with drive pins running in floor slots.

Where there is no provision for lowering the wagon into the acting area floor, auditorium sightlines must take the raised stage level into account.

9:27. Air pallet in use at Derngate, Northampton

Air pallets

A recent development has been the application of air pallets to stage use. These devices are load-bearing units which when fed with compressed air create an air bearing under themselves with load-carrying capacity and virtually no friction.

Their great advantage is that they allow very heavy loads to be positioned with accuracy, without any of the difficulties associated with swivel castors. It is a revelation to move several tons with ease to an exact location, only having to overcome the inertia of the load.

Inevitably air pallets have drawbacks. They are not particularly cheap, they are rather vulnerable, they will not ride over gaps larger than about 8 mm (⅝ in.), and they are not silent.

Uneven stage floors can be made suitable by laying down sheet steel or hardboard to make a path; and gap-bridging ability can be created by overproviding the number of pads.

An air line is needed, and compressor plant elsewhere, preferably in a sound-insulated enclosure. Allowance must be made for easy access to pads for replacement, since a large item, or wagon, becomes very immobile when a pad has been torn. On a small scale a combination of pads and castors can be useful, with the pads just lifting the castors clear when they are pressurised, but retaining normal wheels for emergency.

Most likely future applications would appear to be in flexible auditoria, moving large seating units or structures as part of setting up, and also on stages, moving special trucks with heavy or awkward loads which have to be positioned precisely.

10

Stage scenery

Not all types of performance need scenery. At concerts and recitals the performance is purely aural and no visual make-believe is involved. For plays, opera and ballet, on the other hand, the audience are expected, according to convention, to suspend their disbelief of what they are told or what they see. However naturalistic the setting, everyone present knows that it is all a pretence, and enters into the spirit of the deception.

It is often said that an illusion is created in the theatre, but this is true only in the sense that it is willingly connived at by each member of the audience. They all know they are sitting in a theatre seat and, if they are reasonable beings, no amount of naturalism and verisimilitude can convince them they are looking at the real world. They consciously accept the theatrical convention and allow their imaginations to be led by the imaginative creations of the stage designers just as they do for the other contributors to the production.

The unwritten rules are very flexible, and there is nothing immutable about the conventions which are acceptable at any point in time. At the ballet we accept that a dancer is a princess bewitched and changed into a swan, while at the theatre we can accept that we are eavesdropping on a scene lifted out of everyday life. In both cases the setting is equally unreal.

The theatre is a place of fantasy which relies on the imaginative co-operation of the audience. For it to live and flourish, it cannot be tied down by a too literally defined set of conventions.

Functions of stage scenery

The stage setting assists visual expression of the dramatic performance by providing a geography for the actor within the stage space, assisting the action, contributing to the atmosphere of the play, and clarifying the time and place of the scene. It also serves to screen other visual distractions from the audience.

The stage setting is made up of scenery, properties and costume. There are three kinds of properties: hand properties, which are things worn or handled by the actors, such as a sword or a fan; purely decorative properties which may be virtually part of the scenery, a vase of flowers or a picture on a wall; and large pieces, such as tables, chairs, bedsteads or other items used in the action, which are known as "stage properties" or "props". Often the dividing line between properties and scenery is hard to define. The stage setting is more than mere decoration or illustration; it is an integral part of a production. It should both present a visual stimulus to the imagination and emphasise the mood of the play.

History

In the classical Greek, Roman, early Spanish and Elizabethan public theatres the audience surrounded the greater part of the stage; there was usually a permanent architectural background to the stage and a permanent arrangement of different acting levels. In such theatres the plays themselves indicated the time and place of the action, and little or no scenery was needed. Assistance to the action and the geography for the actor were provided by "practical pieces".

It was in late Renaissance Italy, where artists and architects were preoccupied by the newly discovered laws of perspective, that elaborate scenery began to be developed. It was an extension of the building itself, developing from the solid permanent architectural background of the Roman theatre, as interpreted by Palladio, for instance, in the Teatro Olympico at Vicenza (see Chapter 2, pp. 13–14). The solid construction of permanent architectural settings gave way to flimsy timber frames covered with canvas. The greatest flights of baroque architectural imagination were not realised in masonry, but on painted cloth in the theatre. Very often the architects of the buildings were the designers of the sets as well. The Bibiena family in Italy in the seventeenth and eighteenth centuries were splendid examples of this versatility. Such scenery was often more lavish and important than the play itself. It became the convention in the eighteenth and nineteenth century and still lingers on in traditional pantomime. Pollock's toy theatres, first produced in the Victorian era and still on sale today, illustrate the system very well.

Running parallel to the proscenium were wings which could be slid in and out to form sides of a setting; above were suspended borders to complete the top of the frame. The back of the scenic picture was filled in with a painted cloth. A scene change was made by sliding out one set of wings and sliding in another, raising and lowering the appropriate borders and dropping in a new backcloth.

Even the classical Greek theatre used stage machinery, such as derricks for the *deus ex machina*, and scenic effects have been used at all periods of history since.

It was in the latter part of the nineteenth century that, in order to meet the needs of the domestic scenes of the realistic drama, it became common to close in the sides of the acting area by turning the flats forming the wings to an angle of about 60°. Thus was created the three-sided box set with its seemingly right-angled walls, a form with which we are familiar today. To simplify construction of scenery at an angle to the proscenium and to accommodate heavier furnishings, stage floors began to be made flat, although many raked stages have remained and are still in use.

The beginning of the twentieth century brought new philosophical, historical and aesthetic considerations into theatrical thought. In a reaction against the excesses of archaeological realism in commercial Shakespeare productions of the time, William Poel had in 1879 introduced a plain curtain

10:1. *Illustrations of stage machinery taken from D'Alembert and Diderot's* Encyclopédie ou Dictionnaire Raisonné des Sciences, des Arts et Métiers *(1751–6)*

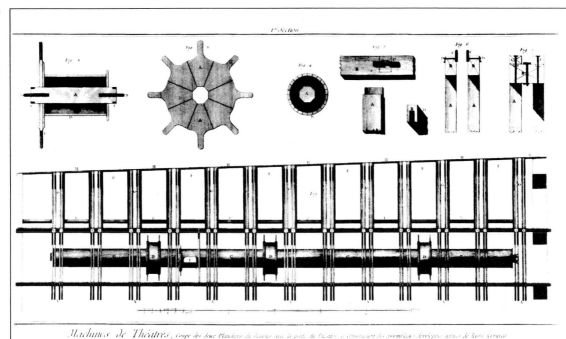

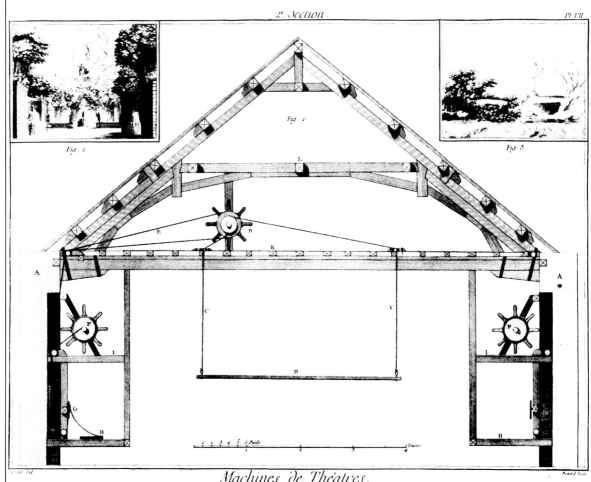

set for his productions, which he based on the original uncorrupted scripts. The discovery of the 1596 drawing of the Swan Theatre in London prompted many attempts to reproduce the original Elizabethan form of staging, which still occupies the thoughts of academics today. Poel's example of the plain curtain set is still followed as a cheap way to furnish a stage but is visually limited.

One technological advance had a very powerful influence on scenic design, and that was the use of electricity for lighting. The first to realise the revolutionary effect that precise control of lighting would make were Adolphe Appia and Gordon Craig. The sculptured shapes of the actors and their setting could be exploited. Until the potential of electric lighting in the theatre was fully understood, there was very little use of real shadows and directional lighting to emphasise the solidity of actors and scenery. Stage lighting was a matter of even, overall illumination which could be raised or lowered in general intensity, changed in colour rather crudely and sometimes augmented by follow spots. The light and shade in the setting was all supplied by the scene painters. Architraves and cornice mouldings were painted on a flat surface with fixed shadows. In the present day such details are more likely to be made in three dimensions. It is quite easy to reproduce them by, for instance, using techniques of blow-moulding plastic sheet. The change in lighting methods has also had its effect on stage make-up. With the old-fashioned shadowless lighting, shadows on faces had also to be painted on. Actors now need to wear far less make-up than they used to.

The stage floor as an element in the design became more important. Scenery became more solid to cast real shadows, and large set pieces made scene changes difficult, but many apparent changes could easily be effected by lighting. This opened new possibilities for the "permanent" set.

All the various "isms" of art have been reflected in scenic design, sometimes profoundly, often superficially. In this century Cubism, Expressionism, Surrealism and Constructivism have all had their effect. Many purists reject the use of scenery altogether, because it is associated with the proscenium arch and "bourgeois theatre", but in the open and thrust stages in use today there is very little sign of any diminution in the volume of scenery used.

At the present time, the wing set, the box set, the curtain set, the permanent set and the open set, and their various intermediate forms can all be found in our theatres as policy or the whim of management, designer or director may demand.

Considerations affecting stage setting

Whether a production is to be spectacular or intimate, lavish or simple, the designer will be faced with financial restraints. No doubt first thoughts are directed towards the interpretation of the play or opera but stage settings must also be appropriate to the limitations of the particular stage on which they will appear. Considerations must be given to:

1. Requirements of the licensing authority.
2. Size and form of the stage/auditorium.
3. What stage machinery, if any, is available.
4. The possibilities for stage lighting.

Requirements of licensing authorities

Where public performances are given, one of the principal factors which determine the quantity and nature of the scenery to be used in a production is the requirements of the licensing authorities. They will not usually permit the unrestricted use of stage scenery unless the premises are equipped with a safety curtain and other fire-protection apparatus, such as an automatic smoke vent and sprinklers over the stage. In premises without these safeguards, restrictions are normally placed either on the quantity of scenery to be kept and used on the premises, or on the materials from which the scenery may be constructed, or sometimes on both. Even in premises equipped with a safety curtain, there is usually a licensing condition requiring the scenery materials to be rendered and maintained non-flammable.

The licensing authorities arrange for periodic inspections and on-site testing of scenery, drapes, etc. to ensure that their conditions are properly complied with, and it is probably due to this practice as much as to the increasing fire-consciousness of theatre technicians that in Great Britain in the last fifty years there has been no fire during a performance in a theatre approaching the scale of the theatre tragedies of the last century. In London, in premises without a safety curtain, the main house curtain is normally required to be of inherently non-flammable material, that is, material not requiring treatment to render it non-flammable. Most licensing authorities will permit the use of scenery and stage drapes made from incombustible or inherently non-flammable materials in premises without a safety curtain, and those forms of stage where there is no proscenium or other separation between acting area and audiences.

We are still awaiting legislation to replace the old Home Office *Manual of Safety Requirements in Theatres and Other Places of Public Entertainment*, published in 1934. The principles will doubtless remain the same, and it is to be hoped that some account will be taken of the unorthodox methods of staging which have become more popular since then. Regulations are, by definition, framed to regulate the situation that exists at the time; they can only deal with the status quo and cannot be expected to anticipate what will happen in the future. It is, therefore, important that they should not be so rigid that they prevent innovations and frustrate new means of artistic expression. The regulations are drawn up to protect firstly persons and secondly property, not for the convenience of the administration whose job it is to enforce them.

Size and form of stage

Attempting to reproduce or imitate a stage setting designed for one kind and dimension of stage on a quite different one gives rise to many difficulties. A setting originally designed for, and artistically satisfying when used on, a large stage will almost certainly look out of scale and ineffective if reproduced in a cut-down form on a small stage. All the settings should credibly suggest an environment that is appropriate in a theatrical sense.

"Suggest" is the keyword – realism is not essential. The form of actor-audience relation is a fundamental factor controlling the design of scenery. "Adaptable" theatres, where the physical form of the stage can be altered at will to suit the producer's concept of a play, add to the problems of both designer and builder of the scenery.

In most theatres the form of stage is fixed and can be modified only within very narrow limits, so that the settings have to be tailored to the stage. Obviously, where the whole or a substantial part of the acting area is behind a proscenium opening, scenery can be in the the form of painted flats and/or cloths which provide a background and surroundings for the action. This type of scenery can also be used in a much more limited way, on an open stage which has at least one side against a wall, although it becomes more difficult to merge the scenic setting into the decor of the auditorium. But flats and cloths cannot be used on the projecting portion of a thrust stage, nor upon an in-the-round stage, across which spectators need to have a virtually unobstructed view. In such open-stage settings, any scenery must be kept low or "transparent".

Stage machinery

Another factor that will affect the scenery is the amount of stage machinery available. It may be either part of the permanent equipment or installed for the particular production. It can have two functions:

1. Suspending and changing scenery.
2. Creating illusions and special effects.

Most professional theatres with picture-frame stages have provision for flying scenery etc., either with or without a counterweight system and/or motorised handling equipment, but there is scope for certain items of flown scenery even on a completely open stage.

Other stage machinery may include revolves, trucks and lifts and mechanical devices for special effects, such as vertical rollers for traversing a long backcloth to give the illusion of linear movement (e.g. along a street) or rockers to simulate the motion of a boat.

10:2. John Bury's set for the National Theatre production of Grand Manoeuvres *by A. E. Ellis at the Old Vic, London (1974)*

10:3. Ralph Koltai's set for Billy, *directed by Patrick Garland, at the Theatre Royal, Drury Lane, London (1974)*

10:4. The set for Benjamin Britten's opera The Turn of the Screw, *designed by Patrick Robertson for the English National Opera production by Jonathan Miller at the Coliseum, London (1979). Much use was made of projected scenery*

10:5. The set for Andrew Lloyd Webber's Starlight Express, *designed by John Napier, under construction at the specially adapted Apollo Victoria, London (1984)*

Stage lighting

The appearance of scenery on a stage depends very largely upon lighting, and it is hardly possible to design a set now without considering how it is to be lit. Optical projection is often an essential part of a setting and can be the sole scenic device.

General requirements for scenery

Apart from any licensing requirements about non-flammability, there are six practical requirements which stage scenery must fulfil:

1. It must be economical, and materials must be carefully chosen to keep down costs and avoid waste.

2. It must be of the simplest and most efficient construction consistent with its purpose.
3. It must be strong enough to stand handling in the course of scene changes and in transport from one theatre to another.
4. It must be easy to store in the minimum space.
5. It must be suitable for quick and quiet scene changing by the minimum number of stage hands.
6. It must be easily assembled on stage when changes of setting are necessary during a performance.

Forms of scenery

Although there are almost unlimited possibilities of modification to suit the needs of a particular production and the inspiration of the designer, the arrangements and devices described below are commonly used in both professional and amateur productions.

House curtains

These are used to close off from the view of the audience the whole of the acting area except for any forestage or apron designed to project beyond them. They are placed immediately behind the proscenium and safety curtain (if there is one). They may be either draw curtains, suspended from sliding or rolling carriers running in an overhead track and opened by being drawn off to the sides; or drop curtains, hung on a set of lines and closed by lowering vertically; or festoon curtains, fixed at the top and raised by drawing the meeting edges up to the top corners of the proscenium arch, so that the fabric is gathered upwards and to the side in swags; or they may be combinations or variations of these basic arrangements. All these types are weighted at the bottom with lengths of chain inserted in the hem. House curtains are also known as "house tabs". The fabric they are made of must be carefully chosen to be strong enough to withstand its own weight without stretching and distorting, and its response to the auditorium lighting is also important.

Cyclorama

One of the main types of settings used in the theatre depends upon the use of a cyclorama. This is basically a large plain surface used as a background to a setting. By varying the intensity and colour of light upon it, many different effects can be obtained. If there is no mark on the surface on which the eye can focus, an illusion of great depth can be created. Ideally the cyclorama should be self-masking, extending out of sight behind the proscenium. It should close round the sides of the acting area and eliminate the necessity for wings or legs to mask the sides. It should also stretch as high as possible to reduce the need for masking by borders hung above the stage. A permanent plaster cyclorama can be built into the back wall of the stage, but although very effective it takes up a great deal of room and limits the use of the rear stage area. An alternative is to have the back wall of the stage plastered and painted white. Although this might be a good idea in some circumstances it is very difficult to prevent the back wall from becoming damaged and collecting dirty marks. There are many occasions when scenery and props will be stacked against it.

The more usual arrangement is a stretched fabric cyclorama which is erected for a particular performance. In its most common form it is a large cloth attached at top and bottom to bars with curved or angled ends and stretched taut. To function properly the cyclorama must be very high (see Figure 9:9). This usually means that it cannot be flown out of sight. A variation of the fabric cyclorama is the type that is rolled on and off a cone at the side of the stage and is suspended on a track round the acting area. This type allows much more scope for changing scenery than the fixed variety. It is more likely to be used in a large theatre or opera house, where it will be big enough and far enough away from the audience for the inevitable wrinkles not to spoil the cyclorama effect of infinite depth. On a smaller stage the effect would be lost and it would be more accurately described as a curtain surround.

The usual colour of a cyclorama is off-white towards blue, which is commonly used for sky effects and projection, but other colours and textures can be used for special purposes. Black velvet or velour can be used for dark nights or other special effects implying vast distances.

Permanent masking

This is placed just behind the proscenium arch to mask the offstage edges of pieces of scenery set further away from the audience, and comprises the tormentors and teaser, or false proscenium, or show portal. Frequently, other permanent maskings are placed at intervals between a false proscenium and a cyclorama; these are known as portals and together they provide a permanent masking so that offstage areas cannot be seen from any seat in the auditorium.

Other cloths, flown pieces and built sets can be set between the permanent maskings, and this is the frequent practice in revues and musicals.

Backcloth-and-wing sets

A backcloth, or backdrop, is a large sheet of canvas, usually somewhat larger than the proscenium opening, battened at top and bottom and suspended on the upstage side of the acting area to form a general background to the setting; it is frequently painted to represent the sky or a distant view. It is made so as to be rolled up for storage; if it is large, a special roller is provided. Cut-cloths are cloths with voids cut in them to reveal another cloth

set behind; frequently more than one is used, as in a woodland scene. In the sense used here, 'wings' are painted and usually profiled flats of canvas on battens, which are set to stand out from the sides of the acting area approximately parallel to the proscenium, to add atmosphere to the setting, to cut off the spectators' view of the ends of the backcloth and to mask the offstage spaces at the sides of the acting area, the wings. They are normally used in pairs, one to "stage right" and the other to "stage left", and the offstage edges of each pair are masked by the pair in front or by the tormentors just behind the proscenium opening. Borders are similar to backcloths, but very much shorter from top to bottom, and are used above the acting area to mask the scenery suspension lines, lighting battens, etc. They may be painted to represent, for example, sky or overhead foliage. The border furthest upstage masks the top edge of the backcloth, and the top edge of each border is masked by the one in front; the top edge of the foremost border is masked by the teaser just behind the proscenium arch.

Box sets

A box set is composed of a series of canvas flats arranged in a more or less continuous line around three sides of the acting area; it is normally used for interior settings. Specially constructed flats, incorporating doors, windows, dummy fireplaces or other features, are inserted where required, and the view beyond "practical" openings is masked by backings, which may be single flats, a series of flats, drops or borders.

The top of a box set may be closed in by suitably painted borders, as used in backcloth-and-wing sets; or by a ceiling piece, which is a large horizontal canvas-covered frame hung on two sets of lines, with the downstage edge higher than the upstage edge; or by a series of teasers, small ceiling pieces comprising rigid borders with horizontal extensions at the bottom. The last two methods leave gaps between adjacent units through which light may be projected. Recently, however, it has become the practice in some productions to leave the top of the set open and let the light source be seen.

Other scenery units

Other units, which can be used with any of the settings described above, include rostra, steps, groundrows, rocks and built-up ground, columns and trees (see the Glossary below).

Curtains

In addition to the house curtains already described, fabric curtains may be used as part of stage settings. Curtains used to dress window openings etc. in the scenery are included under the heading of stage properties.

Traverse curtains – known as "tabs" – are usually placed upstage of the false proscenium or tormentors and suspended on a tab-track, which is normally manually operated; their purpose is to provide a backing for front scenes. They may be made from canvas, hessian, gauze or other scenic material, or from plain-coloured fabrics such as velour. They are frequently used in revues and similar presentations where front scenes alternate with full-stage scenes; they may also be used in a half-way position, when they are known as "half-way tabs".

Setting and changing scenery

Backcloth-and-wing sets of almost any form can be suspended from above, and, where height and equipment are provided for flying scenery, the scene can be changed by pulling one setting up out of sight and letting another down in its place. Even where provision is not made for flying, this type of setting is convenient to erect and strike and therefore can be changed easily. Where the wings cannot be suspended from above, they can stand on the stage floor and be held upright by braces; cloths can be rolled or tripped when not in use.

With the backcloth-and-wing settings, however, the representation of any particular place involves considerable stylisation, especially interior scenes. An appearance of solidity at the sides can be obtained by substituting book flats for the ordinary wing pieces, but these are much heavier and more difficult to handle. For transformation scenes, common in pantomime and classical ballet, the change of setting can be made in sight of the audience by using gauzes, which, when suitably lit, enable one setting to become visible through another. Striking effects can be achieved in this way.

Box sets, normally used for naturalistic interior settings, cannot be changed so easily. They have to be stylised to reconcile the size of the proscenium with the relatively small dimensions of a domestic interior. On a large stage, walls and windows have to be distorted in shape and size even when the intention is to convey an impression of realism. Box sets are normally built up flat by flat on the stage floor, which effectively limits major scene changes to the intervals of the performance unless they are made behind a cloth or curtain drawn downstage during the playing of a front scene. Neither of these types of setting is suited to fast-moving productions in which the scene changes rapidly. For productions of this kind, and particularly for Shakespeare, solid built-up settings are more often employed, which, with the addition of easily changed properties, can be made to represent any one of a number of different localities. In some cases, settings may consist of several large pieces which can be moved about and turned round to represent different objects; in other cases,

the setting is permanent and may even be used for several different productions in the company's repertoire. In opera, there is an established tradition of massive sets, with the playing area on several levels.

Large rostra, ramps and steps are even more difficult to change than the pieces forming a box set, and this has led to the use of large revolves, stage elevators and systems of wagons. Recently the use of air pallets (described in Chapter 9) has provided a new way of moving unwieldy and heavy pieces of scenery about.

Materials for scenery

The general requirements for scenery materials may be summarised as follows. They must be relatively inexpensive, readily available, light in weight, easy to work with and durable. For flats and similar pieces, framing materials must have sufficient rigidity and should be easily jointed. Covering materials must be capable of being made taut on the frames and must have a surface that will take scenic paint. All scenery materials should be flame-resistant. In this respect, materials may be grouped under five headings.

1. *Non-combustible*: In normal circumstances these cannot be made to burn. Examples: glass and plaster.
2. *Inherently non-flammable*: These will burn away in a fire, but are difficult to ignite and do not continue burning unless kept in a flame. Example: heavy woollen fabric.
3. *Self-extinguishing*: These take flame from a small source of ignition, but quickly cease burning when the source of ignition is removed or when the material immediately around that source has been consumed. Some plastics are of this type.
4. *Treated*: These take flame from a small source of ignition and would continue burning but for the fact that they have been subjected to treatment to make them flame-resistant.
5. *Flammable*: These have not been and perhaps cannot be rendered flame-resistant by treatment; they can be easily ignited by, and will continue burning after, contact with a small flame.

Most of the painted scenery used in the theatre, whether framed or unframed, is made from stout canvas or ply, but other materials may be used. The canvas is commonly made from flax, but there are cheaper substitutes.

Frames for scenery are almost universally made from timber which is soft enough for easy working, light enough for easy handling, yet strong enough to stand the stresses and strains to which scenery is subjected in use. The timber must be straight-grained, free from serious faults and well seasoned so as not to warp. Where an irregular profile is required, stout plywood is normally used. All these materials are of course combustible, and indeed they are flammable in their natural state and need treatment to render them flame-resistant.

It is, of course, possible to construct scenery from non-combustible and/or inherently non-flammable materials, such as ceramic fibre reinforced board on light metal framing; but such scenery does not accord with the general requirements set out above and is resorted to only as an expedient to comply with the requirements of licensing authorities in certain premises where the more usual types of scenery cannot be permitted. That is not to say that they cannot be used for special effects by some designers. John Napier's set for *Starlight Express* was almost entirely made of a welded steel framework.

In recent years there has been an increasing use of plastics in the construction of scenery. All these are combustible and some are flammable. Only the flame-resistant or self-extinguishing grades of plastics should be used for scenery. Examples of these materials which have been used successfully include lightweight expanded polystyrene, unplasticised polyvinyl chloride, special cellulose acetate and polyester resin/glass fibre laminates.

Curtains and other draperies on a fully equipped stage may be of almost any fabric, treated, if necessary, to render it flame-resistant, but where a stage is not equipped with the usual safeguards the local licensing authority may insist that any curtains be of either non-combustible or inherently non-flammable materials. Until recently, these latter materials were limited to fabrics of natural mineral fibres, such as glass cloth, or to fabrics of natural animal fibres, such as heavy woollen cloth. Advances, however, are being made with inherently non-flammable and self-extinguishing synthetic fibres, which should increase the range of fabrics available. All fabrics of vegetable fibres, e.g. cotton, flax, jute, etc., and many of the synthetic materials are flammable in their natural state, but most of them are responsive to treatment to remove the danger.

Mention should perhaps be made of the fabric known as "silk noile", which has been used successfully for both curtains and painted scenery in premises where the licensing authority would not permit the use of treated materials. Among the synthetics, the guaranteed "flare-free" nylon net should be borne in mind.

Experience and fire records indicate that the principal fire hazard in a properly constructed theatre is that associated with traditional canvas scenery, especially when used in conjunction with a naked flame on the stage or unguarded or insufficiently guarded high-powered lighting units. Hence the requirement that canvas scenery should be treated to render it flame-resistant,* but it is accepted that the treatment does little more than render the scenery more difficult to ignite than if it were not treated. Nothing can make timber and flax canvas non-combustible, and such treated scenery will, in fact, burn if involved in a fire. There are various well-recognised methods of treating timber and fabrics to render them flame-resistant

and, except in very exceptional circumstances, it is strongly advised that even where there is no licensing requirement to compel it, all scenery and hangings used on a stage should be so treated. Timber, including plywood and hardboard, can best be rendered flame-resistant by thorough impregnation with a flame-retardant salt by an approved process, such as Oxylene or Pyrolith. A measure of protection can also be obtained by coating it with a flame-retardant paint, but this method is not acceptable to all licensing authorities. In recent years intumescent paints have been introduced which have a high degree of fire-resistance. Generally speaking, the authorities do not require any particular method to be adopted to render scenery and curtain fabrics non-flammable so long as the fabrics have, in fact, been rendered satisfactorily flame-resistant. It must be remembered that most of the flame-retardant treatments are water-borne and consequently can be removed by any form of wet cleaning, but some will stand a limited amount of dry cleaning. It follows, therefore, that treated materials which have been washed or cleaned must be re-treated before they are used again. However, during recent years some flame-resistant finishes have been developed which are durable and not affected by washing or cleaning. Among these are the Proban and Timonox processes.

Construction of scenery and painting

Flats and similar pieces are timber frames covered with tightly stretched canvas. Each frame is constructed from lengths of selected 75 mm × 25 mm

*Both the following solutions have been found suitable for scenery and for the coarser fabrics, and solution 2 has been found suitable for the more delicate fabrics:

Solution 1

Boracic acid	15 oz. (450 grams)
Sodium phosphate	10 oz. (300 grams)
Water	1 gal. (5 litres)

Solution 2

Borax	10 oz. (300 grams)
Boracic acid	8 oz. (240 grams)
Water	1 gal. (5 litres)

It is advisable to experiment with a small portion of the fabric before treating the whole, as the texture and colours of some materials are detrimentally affected. The fabrics should be dried without rinsing or wringing, but may be mangled or ironed when dry.

A simple test for flame-resistance may be made thus: A strip of the fabric, 25 mm (1 in.) wide and not less than 150 mm (6 in.) long, should be hung vertically in a draught-free position. A lighted match should then be applied for five seconds at the centre of the bottom edge. If less than 25 mm (1 in.) square in area has been consumed by the flame at the end of one minute, the material may be regarded as satisfactorily flame-resistant. If the fabric has been claimed to be inherently non-flammable, it should be well washed in plain hot water and thoroughly dried before being tested. Where appropriate it is advisable to confer with the local licensing authority regarding methods of treatment and tests, as requirements may vary from place to place.

(3 in. × 1 in.) prepared timber such as yellow deal. Sometimes 100 mm × 25 mm (4 in. × 1 in.) timber is used. The vertical members are called stiles and the horizontal members rails, as in ordinary joinery. The frame must be perfectly square and rigid.

For jointing the members, various methods may be used. These fall into two categories: fixed and temporary. Fixed joints are made at corners, traditionally by mortise-and-tenon, and dowelled or glued and screwed. Contrary to normal joinery practice, the mortise is cut in the rail and the tenon on the stile. This gives a very strong connection, but the time taken and the expense incurred in making the joints often dictates the use of simpler and quicker methods, such as glued and screwed half-lap joints and butt joints, both square and mitred. These later joints are usually strengthened by adding corner plates of either thin plywood or hardboard, or even thin sheet metal; the reinforcing plates are fixed to the rear surface of the flats only and are kept clear of the outer edges of the frame. If necessary, the glue can be omitted. Connections can also be made with special metal fittings requiring only screws for fixing, or, to a more limited degree, with coachbolts. The rigidity of a frame is sometimes increased by fixing a bracing member at 45° across each corner. The in-between rails, known as toggle rails, are preferably fitted into the frames by temporary joints, each end being tenoned into a short piece of similar timber to form a T which can be attached to the inside edge of the stile with woodscrews; these members can be positioned as necessary to suit the attachment of other pieces of scenery.

The outer edges of stiles must be straight and true, so as to avoid any possibility of gaps when flats are fitted together. The canvas, which should be on one side of the frame only, is cut slightly smaller than the overall frame size, and is stretched across the frame by tacking with large-headed tacks to the wide surface of the outer frame members and then glued, but not to toggle rails or corner braces. The canvas must not be carried round the outer edges of the frame, as the fabric would wear and its tautness would be lost; furthermore the fabric would prevent the flats from fitting closely together.

Canvasing is a job which requires care and skill; a well-canvased flat has a smooth even surface without sagging or wrinkles. Unless the canvas is stretched tightly and evenly on the frame it will never give the illusion of solidity, however well it may be painted.

Other frame units are constructed in a similar manner. Door flats, window flats and fireplace flats have appropriate openings into which the door frames, window frames and fireplace surrounds can be fitted. These will not be the heavy sort of thing used in normal building construction. For realism, and to increase the illusion of solidity of the scenery, door and window openings are frequently formed with reveals of timber or other materials attached to the edges of the openings in the flats. Practical doors are made as light as possible consistent with realism; sometimes they have to be double-faced, constructed with plywood instead of canvas to retain solidity. Windows and "glazed" doors are normally without glass to save weight and to avoid dazzle from reflected stage lighting. Real glass is never used, but where an infilling is necessary gauze or plastic material may be employed. After canvasing, the canvas is primed with a mixture of glue size and whiting. This gives the final tightening to the canvas as well as preparing the surface for scenic painting.

Cloths, borders etc. are formed with similar canvas, the lengths being stitched together with flat seams where necessary; they do not have frames, but stout timber battens are fixed along their top and bottom edges. They are similarly prepared for painting.

Scenic paint is traditionally made up by mixing dry powder colour into a thick paste with cold water and then mixing in a hot solution of glue size until the required consistency for working is achieved. Whiting is often added to give body to the colour. All scenic paint dries much lighter than it appears when wet, and to check that the required tint has been achieved, a small piece of scrap canvas or other material is coated with the mixed paint and quickly dried near a radiator. When the paint/size mixture has cooled it can be applied to the canvas. If it is not allowed to cool down, previously applied colour will lift under the hot mixture. On no account should dry powder colour mixtures be used without adding size; the colour would flake off or rub off on to costumes brushing against it, resulting in the ruin of both sets and costumes.

As an alternative to the traditional scene paint, plastic (pva) emulsion paint may be used for scenic painting, but the two cannot be mixed or used together on the same piece of scenery. No glue size is needed; the paint is thinned, if necessary, with cold water. A wide range of tints is now obtainable in this type of paint. Should the canvas sag with use, a coat of glue size on the back will help to restore its tautness.

Storage of scenery

Scenic flats need to be stored in pairs, face to face, resting on the bottom rail to prevent warping. Their size depends upon the scale of the stage, but average dimensions would be 1.2 m × 5 m (4 ft × 16 ft). Flats are best stored in packs – the number of flats required for one setting – and racks should be provided for each pack. These racks should be situated in the scenery store adjacent to the stage or workshop or both. It is desirable that the temperature of the store be approximately that of the stage itself. Backcloths and gauzes require long racks, as they are usually stored rolled on their respective battens. One useful position for storing them is in a long trough at the rear of the stage

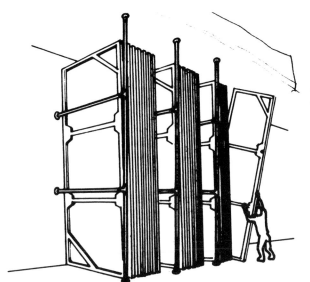

10:6. Method of storing flats

which can also be used as a pit for lighting a cyclorama. Drapes require dustproof cupboards with plenty of slatted shelves to keep them aired.

Set pieces, such as trucks, rostra, etc., need enough room for manoeuvring. These pieces are often three-dimensional, and as they are frequently tall, bulky and heavy, are not easy to transport.

Construction and repair of scenery requires plenty of space within easy reach of the stage, good working conditions with supplies of gas, water and electricity, and the right conditions for storing timber. All storage should be easily accessible from backstage without going through the auditorium.

At the same time, the storage and working space should be separated from the stage by soundproof and fire-resisting construction.

10:7. Backcloth store under the rear of the stage

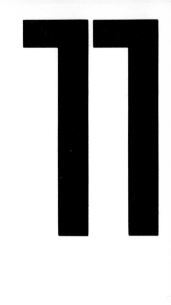

Stage lighting

The first function of stage lighting is illumination of the actor and his setting. The earliest theatres were in the open air, and the source was the sun itself. Dramatists exploited the situation and Euripides, for instance, made references in *Iphigenia in Aulis* to the sunrise, which coincided with the time of day when the play was actually performed.

But when the theatre came inside under cover there had to be artificial light. People made do very well with oil lamps and candles until the nineteenth century, when there was a brief change to gas lighting before electricity took over. Each change made possible a greater measure of control until at the present time stage lighting is capable of achieving much more than mere illumination of the action. It is used as a means of artistic expression and has become a vital component in the drama. As the action unfolds it can draw attention from one character to another or from one area to another, and by changing the direction, intensity or colour of the light, a great variety of atmosphere and moods can be conveyed. This versatility is demanded in all sizes of theatre with all forms of actor-to-audience relationship. The pattern of lighting seldom remains static for long; it changes from production to production, scene to scene and often many times during a scene.

All stage-lighting schemes, whatever the theatre, must begin on a basis of general illumination. In this role, lighting must be seen as the source of the sightline. The actor and his environment are illuminated and the light reflected from them to the eyes of the audience. However good the position of the audience in relation to the stage, the contact is lost if the actor is not properly illuminated.

The lighting process

Before describing the technical provisions that should be made for an effective stage-lighting installation, it will help to have an understanding of the process of setting up the lighting for a production. The director of a play or opera or the choreographer of a ballet is concerned with the total effect, aural and visual, of the production, and this includes the lighting. In recent years great advances and consequent technical complications in multi-lantern stage lighting have made it very difficult for a director to devote to lighting the time it demands without taking that time from his main task – directing the performers. The work is now usually in the hands of an additional member of the production team: the lighting designer. His contribution is a creative one, but he is part of a team and the measure of his success is in the integration of his lighting with the total conception of a production.

The lighting designer attends early conferences with the director and scene designer so that he is aware of the visual style decisions which are taken. He sees that the model or drawings of the set have allowed for large enough openings through which lighting units can operate without obstruction before they are sent to the workshops for construction to start. The first opportunity the lighting designer will have to try out his scheme will be with the scenery in position on stage. All the other departments will have time to rehearse, improvise and alter before the production reaches the stage, but the lighting can only be set up at the end of the preparation period. Time is limited, and the operation must be carefully planned to avoid, as far as possible, the delays which can be caused by having to rig lanterns more than once. The lighting designer will have prepared a layout plan of the stage showing the position of each lantern, its type, its colour filter and the dimmer circuit to which it is to be connected. Using this layout the lanterns are rigged in position and plugged into the right circuit, and each one is angled and focused on the area of the stage chosen for it. This process of "setting" the lanterns is best done one by one with all the other lights out, a difficult ideal to achieve when all the other departments are pressing to complete their work. At this time the filaments of the lamps are hot and at their most vulnerable as they are moved. When they fail, they more often than not blow the fuse in the dimmer room at the same time. An emergency like this shows how important it is for the lighting positions and the dimmer room to be easily accessible.

With all the lanterns set, the lighting designer will sit in the auditorium with the director and the scene designer and build up each picture by calling the circuit numbers out on the intercom to the operator of the stage-lighting control desk and deciding the intensity of the light on each one. Alternatively, the designer may choose to operate the control desk directly. This is best done by using a portable console which can be plugged into an extension socket located in the stalls.

Each picture must flow into the next with the right timing. The lighting plot is recorded so that it can be reproduced on cue at the right moment in the script. This recording used to be done in longhand and was a tedious chore, especially when it was decided that alterations had to be made. The process has been greatly simplified by introducing computer memory devices which allow every effect to be instantly recorded and instantly recalled with total reliability whenever desired.

The procedure just described is followed for a new production which has exclusive use of the stage. The situation is different when the production is to slot into a repertoire of productions which may be changing every day. The time available both for rehearsal and for adjusting lighting between performances is even further curtailed, and compromises have to be made.

It is possible to have an entirely different set of lanterns for each production, but for several shows this would become extravagant and there may not be room to hang so many units. In special cases, remotely controlled colour changers can be of use, and full remote control for focus and direction is available, though at considerable cost which may be difficult to justify. For most theatres the solution is to decide that certain basic lanterns will have to remain in position for all productions, and alterations and redirection of the rest must be reduced to bare essentials. Where other activities such as concerts or conferences are held, this basic rig should be capable of providing the "open white" coverage needed for general illumination. When the policy is to play in repertoire, accessibility of the lighting equipment is vital and sophisticated control systems show their value.

Light sources

Illumination of the acting area (as distinct from backcloths etc.) is rarely achieved by using sources throwing a wide angle beam of light. The task is to build up a pattern of illumination from a number of localised lighting units, each fed from its own electrical circuit. The pattern can then be altered by increasing or reducing the intensity of light from the appropriate units, and the principal instrument for this purpose is a centralised lighting console from which all circuits are controlled.

The general task of providing illumination has to be integrated with lighting to achieve specific dramatic or decorative effects, or a suggestion of the origin of the illumination – sunlight, moonlight, etc. – sometimes known as "motivating lighting". These results may be achieved in a variety of ways, using colour, direction and intensity in a manner characteristic of each individual designer. A wide choice of lanterns will be required, with beams capable of being expanded and contracted and in many cases of being shaped. Light must not stray outside these intended beams; it must fall only on the specific area of the stage desired at the time. Accurate delineation of beam edge is particularly important in open staging, where the audience is often very close to the glare. Such equipment, designed for the purpose, is available from specialist stage lighting companies. Other equipment designed for domestic, commercial or industrial use is not suitable for this type of work.

11:1. Spotlight directed straight at actor

11:2. Spotlight crossing on actor

Stage-lighting installation

The electrical installation to supply the stage-lighting instruments – lanterns – must combine electrical safety with convenience and flexibility of use. The electrical specification must include the provision of power for foreseeable maximum load requirements connected to a general provision of dimmers and subcircuits, all terminating in theatre standard sockets. Equally essential is the provision of lighting positions integrated into the building design and equipped with proper means of access and lantern suspension points.

As lanterns are portable items, decisions on types and quantities are often best left to the end of

the project, when resident staff have been appointed and can contribute to the choice, provided sufficient money is reserved for this purpose. The same argument may sometimes apply to the choice of lighting control desk, though this can be complicated by the need to match to the dimmers and the difficulty of commissioning the power installation before the control is available.

Lighting positions

Proscenium or end stage

To meet the demands upon it, the stage-lighting installation must make provision for lighting any part of the stage from as wide a range of angles as possible. There are basic lighting positions which are essential if the performance and setting are to be seen with clarity. But when these have been provided still other angles and directions of light may be required to build up an effective composition.

Some light must come from the general direction of the audience. When the actor is downstage close to the audience, it follows that some lighting positions must be in the auditorium. The basic positions for lighting from the direction of the audience should be arranged so that light strikes the actor's face at about 45° above horizontal. If the angle is much steeper it will produce dark unflattering shadows under the brows, and if it is at a shallow angle there is the danger of unwanted shadows on the set or on other actors.

11:1

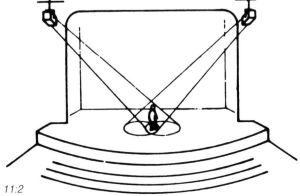

11:2

Spotlights are rarely directed straight at actors, but are usually crossed. The preferred elevation of 45° cannot, therefore, be used to locate the lighting positions on a section drawn on the centre line of the auditorium, but if these positions are sited at an angle of elevation of about 55° to the actor's face, the light will strike at approximately 45° after crossing diagonally.

If the forestage is deep, additional front-of-house lighting positions will be required, as explained in Figure 11:3. Spotlights at A will light an actor at the edge of the stage at 55° in section, and about 45° to 50° after crossing; but as the actor moves in from the edge the angle will decrease. At Q it is only 40° in section, about 35° after crossing, and this is the minimum. It is, therefore, necessary to provide another lighting position, B, which will cover the area Q to R within the same range of angles, and then positions C and D, lighting areas R to S and S to T. Where, as with proscenium and end stages, the audience sit only on one side, A, B, C and D will be preferred positions for overhead lighting.

In proscenium theatres, A and B correspond to the front-of-house lighting positions and C and D to numbers 1 and 2 spotbars. More bars may be required if the theoretical angles of coverage shown in the Figure are obstructed by the scenery.

Figure 11:3 also shows the effect of height on the layout of the lighting. Where the lighting grid is only half the stage depth above the eye level, four bars are required, but where the height is the same as the stage depth, only two, A1 and B1, will give the same coverage. The factors determining the height on proscenium stages will be the dimensions of the effective openings and the borders, which may lead to several bars being required. Positions C and D and onstage low-level positions can be contrived as part of the scenery. Front-of-house positions in the form of lighting bridges must be incorporated in the building design from the outset.

These overhead positions should be supplemented by side positions, often vertical bars or ladders, in the stage wings and on the side walls of the auditorium in lighting slots. The side lighting provides coverage from a much wider range of angles than can be shown in Figure 11:3.

Arena and thrust stages

The same principles apply when locating the lighting equipment for arena and thrust stages. Here, since the audience surrounds the stage on three or all sides, to achieve the preferred angles of light with the actor facing in any direction, the lighting positions also have to be provided on all sides. A typical arrangement has lighting bars running in two directions at right angles over the stage and audience areas, forming a grid.

In theatre-in-the-round it is not easy to light the face of an actor standing on the edge of the playing area looking inwards without lighting units glaring directly into the eyes of the audience seated behind him. The illumination of a front row of embarrassed knees can be distracting. Spectators are sometimes troubled by reflections of incident light from the stage surface. The remedy for this lies in choosing a non-specular floor finish.

When a theatre is intended to be adaptable from one audience-to-stage relationship to another, including thrust stage and theatre-in-the-round, the lighting systems should be designed to suit all forms. Changing the lighting equipment to accommodate a different form of staging may involve a great deal of time and labour costs, some of which can be saved by having an extra number of circuits and additional stocks of equipment. The situation is greatly eased when the acting area is planned to remain in the same position for whatever audience-to-stage form is in use.

Access to lighting positions over the stage

All lighting positions have to be reached so that individual units can be directed and focused, colour filters changed and the fittings maintained. It is most convenient if the electricians can reach the lanterns from permanent walkways or platforms with room to walk without stooping, but this is rarely possible over a conventional stage, where hanging space is in great demand. Only in large opera houses and similar buildings where the productions in a repertoire are changed every day will the saving in electricians' time and labour justify a bridge just inside the proscenium.

Lighting over the proscenium stage is usually suspended from internally wired bars attached to suspension sets forming part of the scenery flying system.

Lighting bridges and wall slots

The objection to lighting bridges over the stage itself has been discussed, but elsewhere over the auditorium they are, without doubt, the best solution. Access to positions in the auditorium ceiling from stepladders or towers is even more perilous and tiresome than reaching the spotbars over the stage. Lighting equipment on bridges can be altered, adjusted and serviced if necessary during

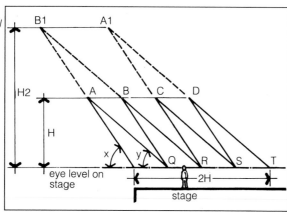

11:3 Method of locating theoretical positions of luminaires

a performance without the electrician having to pass through the auditorium. Side positions in the walls of the auditorium are extremely useful, and it should be possible to reach these too without bringing ladders into the auditorium. If the lighting equipment is put in wall slots, provision can be made for access from outside the auditorium or from catwalks in the ceiling. The absence of slots will not prevent these valuable lighting positions

from being used and bars will soon sprout from the walls if they are forgotten in the first place.

Figures 11:4 and 11:6–7 show the recommended sizes for lighting bridges and for wall slots. The dimensions depend upon the size of lanterns. Within 15 m (50 ft) of the stage, 1 kW lanterns will generally be used, but at greater distances more powerful, and therefore larger, equipment may have to be accommodated.

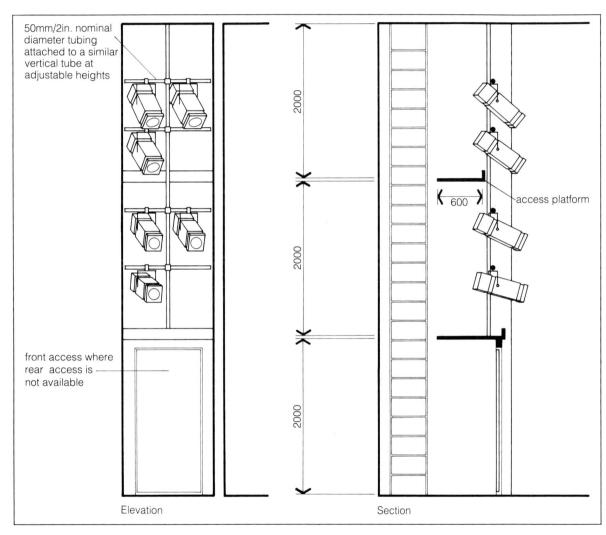

11:4. Auditorium wall slot

50mm/2in. nominal diameter tubing attached to a similar vertical tube at adjustable heights

front access where rear access is not available

2000

2000

2000

600

access platform

Elevation

Section

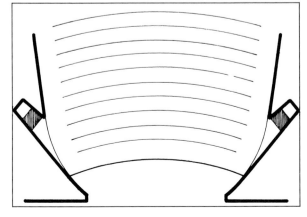

11:5. Typical location of auditorium wall slots

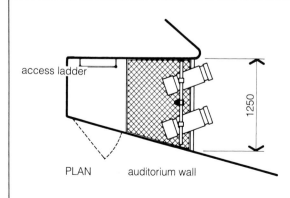

access ladder

1250

PLAN   auditorium wall

11:6. Auditorium lighting bridge (large lanterns)

11:7. Auditorium lighting bridge

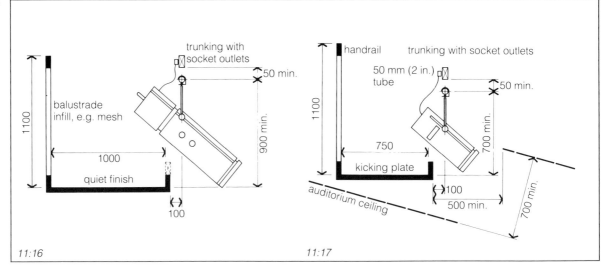

11:16

11:17

Access to the lanterns from bridge and slots should be easy and safe. It may be necessary to kneel down to make some adjustments to the extremities of the lanterns, but this is no reason to expect technicians to reach lighting positions by crawling on all fours. There should be proper headroom of 2 m (6 ft 6 in.) over all access routes, so that people can walk naturally without having to crouch. Platforms and walkways should be finished in a material which is quiet to walk on and reasonably comfortable to kneel on; wood or linoleum are suitable. Kicking plates must be provided at the edges of walkways to prevent small items being knocked off. Where there is a risk of technicians falling through open balustrades in positions where lanterns are not being used, a solution may be to space the uprights at closer than normal centres, or to provide removable wire mesh infill panels.

All the bars mentioned for suspending stage-lighting equipment should be 50-mm (2-in.) outside diameter standard scaffolding tube. Other sizes or square-section tube will not take the standard hook clamp used for attaching lanterns, and are therefore unsuitable.

11:8. Stage-lighting boxes at fly gallery level on the OP side. One has the cover removed

Storage

Storage space and racking for spare lamps, equipment, colours and cables should be available where there is convenient access from both the stage and the auditorium bridges and slots. It is reasonable to provide space for 20% spare lanterns, coils of cable, spare colour frames, tools and accessories. The fitting-out of the space can be left to the users of the building.

Reflecting surfaces

There is inevitably some light spill from lanterns, and to avoid distracting reflections, all those auditorium surfaces near bridges and slots should be of low reflectance. In particular, polished surfaces which give specular reflections should be avoided.

Lighting control room

The subject of control rooms generally is discussed in detail in Chapter 15. Here we are concerned with the control equipment, some of which will be installed in the lighting control room.

Lighting control equipment

The lighting control equipment is the nerve centre of the stage-lighting installation. Instead of the switch and distribution panels of the normal electrical system, the stage-lighting circuits are each controlled by a dimmer specially designed for theatre use and usually supplied in cabinets containing 24 or more. Control of all dimmers is centralised at a remote control desk.

The electrical power handled by the dimmers is considerable. A small theatre may require 100 kW and a very large theatre up to 1 MW. Calculation of normal and maximum demand, heat loads and the number of sub-circuits is best left to experienced theatre consultants.

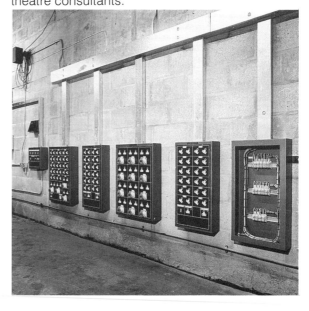

11:9. A dimmer room

11:10. A lighting control board by Strand Lighting. The reflections in the control room window could have been reduced by tilting the glass

Circuits are mostly 2.5 kW (10 amp), though there is sometimes a requirement for 5 kW (25 amp) and occasionally 10 kW (45 amp) for special purposes. It is usual, though not essential, to group all dimmers in a central dimmer room where noise, security and ventilation problems can be handled effectively. Choice of location for the dimmer room must also take account of cable costs and convenient user access. Circuits are fused on the dimmer cabinet and should terminate in the industry standard sockets, preferably un-switched. In the United Kingdom, BS 546, 15 amp is the essential standard socket for 10 amp circuits. BS 4343 (CEE 17) 16 amp, 32 amp and 63 amp designs are used for other ratings. Multiple sockets are often fitted to each radial circuit with the user taking responsibility to limit the overall load connected. Larger dimmer sizes may connect to a full capacity socket and have two or more smaller-size sockets connected in parallel through local protective fuses or circuit breakers.

Type of dimmer

Dimmers are now exclusively thyristor designs. These dimmers have one major disadvantage: they generate electrical interference which can be picked up on audio circuits. In certain cases improved-quality filtering may be employed to reduce this interference, but this is not normally necessary if dimmers designed for theatre use are specified.

Remote control from a centrally positioned control deck is by means of extra-low voltage control circuits (usually about 10 volts) connected by multicore cable. Plug connection at several positions is possible, though at slight risk of unreliability. New systems using multiplexed data on one pair of screened cables instead of the multicores offer reduced cable costs and increased portability.

The lighting control desk

One of the main objectives of stage lighting is a smooth flow from one lighting picture to the next, precisely timed to the action on stage. For this reason the dimmer control desk is usually positioned in a control room giving the operator a good view of the stage. Simple control desks usually provide two control faders per dimmer, with master faders to give overall fades and smooth changes between the two sets of dimmer faders. This type of system, known as "two scene preset", can be satisfactory for up to about 36 dimmers but requires too much space, labour and plotting time for larger installations. Memory controls are now the normal provision for all but the smallest theatre.

Memory lighting control desks use computer techniques to store and process the dimmer-level information required for each scene. Most systems use calculator or telephone keypads for calling up circuit and scene numbers, and most use a TV screen or VDU to display information about the lighting. The facilities offered by rival systems differ widely. The choice should be made after a careful consideration of the needs of the theatre. All should be able to store the rehearsed lighting effects with complete reliability and to carry out various types of change, both in rehearsed order and in random order for rehearsals. Options to store the lighting plots on magnetic disk, portable or duplicate basic controls for use on stage or in the stalls during rehearsal are usually worth having; and a hand-held remote control for use while setting lighting can save time and reduce costs. The final package must also provide for some form of emergency control, basic spares and arrangements for urgent repair if the system fails.

The lighting control room has to be carefully positioned and designed. This subject is discussed in more detail in Chapter 15 (Control rooms).

Independent and non-dim circuits

Traditionally theatres also require a number of independent or non-dim stage-lighting circuits in addition to the main dimmed circuit installation. These are for loads such as effects motors and equipment, which require distortion-free power not possible from a thyristor-type dimmer. Independents may also be used for control of any stage-lighting units such as rehearsal floodlights which may need to be operable when the stage-lighting control desk and dimmers are switched off.

Normal practice is for independent circuits to be contactor-switched from the lighting control room, although direct switching may be provided for the simpler installation.

Some dimmer manufacturers offer non-dim facilities through modification of a thyristor dimmer to incorporate by-pass or step law operation. In this case the circuit loads are controlled through the stage-lighting control system and should be considered as forming part of that system.

Additional controls

A considerable number of controls for ancillary services accumulate in the lighting control room. They should be integrated into a single purpose-designed panel within convenient reach of the operator, either as an extension to the lighting control desk or in a separate housing above the observation window or on a side wall.

Any or all of the following may need to be provided:

Stage lighting
— Independent circuit controls
— Colour change controls
— Curtain dressing and cell lighting controls
— Remotely positioned spotlight controls
— Dimmer room temperature indicators
— Load monitoring ammeters

Ancillary lighting
— Auditorium lighting controls
— Orchestra pit lighting controls
— Stage working light master controls and indicators
— Cleaners' lighting master controls
— Safety/emergency lighting indicators
— Local lighting intensity control

Communications
— Intercom station
— Cue lights, possibly with buzzer
— Show relay loudspeaker
— Clock with sweep second-hand

Certain of the ancillary lighting controls together with the communication section are common to sound and projection rooms and are considered further in Chapters 13 (Communications) and 15 (Control rooms).

Working lights

In all stage areas, including fly galleries, wings, the grid, lighting galleries and on the stage itself, a high level of illumination is needed for setting up and maintenance. This is provided by a system of working lights quite separate from the stage-lighting installation. To minimise running cost, fluorescent lighting is usually used, though tungsten halogen floodlights are useful for the larger spaces.

During a performance a lower level of lighting is required which will not spill on to the stage and interfere with the stage-lighting effects. This performance lighting must be adequate for safety, circulation and all other backstage activities. Low-wattage incandescent lamps are used, mounted in deep cut-off fittings and often sprayed blue. It is desirable that the safety and circulation lighting should be battery-maintained.

Control of working lighting must combine convenience and efficiency with switching, to allow the stage management to override lights that could spoil the production effects. Larger theatres install custom-designed contactor-controlled systems for worklight control. The working light contactors and control equipment can conveniently be mounted in a common rack with the independent circuit contactors.

Stage power

All stage areas should have a generous provision of 13 amp ring main sockets for tools and cleaning equipment. Sockets intended for stage lighting or sound equipment are not suitable for this purpose.

Additionally, power supplies may be needed for the temporary lighting and sound equipment installed by touring productions and for special stage machinery. 60 amp TPN should be a minimum for the onstage temporary supply. In a large theatre, big touring pop lighting rigs will require 400 amp TPN or more. Connection arrangements must be both convenient and safe, with locks and interlocks to prevent casual use and access to live parts. Use of the BS 4343 range of connectors is to be encouraged, but with direct connection to switch output terminals or bus-bars as an option. Local fuses should be easily changed to match the capacity of temporary wiring. Generous provision for earth connections is essential.

Auditorium decorative lighting

The brightness of the auditorium affects the scale of intensity required on the stage, and if the audience has become accustomed to too high a degree of brightness before the play begins, it becomes very difficult to establish the effect, for instance, of strong sunlight. The CIBS Code for Interior Lighting 1984 gives a level of 100 lux for theatre auditoria, and this should be regarded as the upper limit for the light which the audience will need to read their programmes. However, the appearance of the auditorium and the adaptation level of the audience's eyes are determined not so much by the light falling on the programme, or other objects of regard, as by the brightness of the seating, carpets, walls and ceiling.

If the auditorium is to be used regularly for conferences it may be necessary to provide a high level of light for attenders to read and write in comfort, while still allowing the level to be reduced to something more appropriate for performances.

Large polished surfaces should be avoided in the auditorium, as they will pick up reflections from the stage which move as the actors move and can be most distracting. This applies not only to glass and similar materials, but even to polished wooden panelling and marble. Further, there should be no bright glaring sources of light in the auditorium, and where chandeliers are used to add sparkle they should be fitted with low-power lamps. Fluorescent lighting is very difficult to dim effectively without low-level flickering. It cannot match the smooth response to control of incandescent lamps, to say nothing of their warmth and sparkle, and should therefore be avoided.

All lighting in the auditorium should, of course, be controlled through dimmers operated from the same position as the stage lighting itself. In most auditoria several dimmers will be required to cope with the load, and these can be connected to a master control or separately controlled so that the lighting can be faded sequentially to suit the production. The foyers are likely to be strongly lit, either by daylight or artificial light, and it is necessary to ensure that the passages leading from them into the auditorium offer a gentle gradation of brightness from one level to the other. All daylight should be excluded from the auditorium, and it is especially important that there should be means of preventing daylight or artificial light leaking in through the exit doors. Curtains, which for safety reasons should never come right to floor level, are unlikely to be satisfactory, and the fittings and windows immediately outside the exit doors must be placed in such a way as to prevent shafts of light distracting the audience when latecomers or ushers move in and out.

An auditorium requires separate lighting for rehearsal and cleaning purposes. High-efficiency MBIF or SON lamps may be suitable for this purpose. The switches should be located outside the auditorium and readily accessible from it, but not where they could be operated accidentally by members of the public. Some licensing authorities require a "panic switch" under the control of the house or stage manager, allowing him in an emergency to bring lighting on in the auditorium without the need to contact the lighting operator.

Television requirements

Television performances from theatres are now commonplace and can be an important source of additional income. The engineering department of the television company expected to use it should be consulted before provisions are made in a new building.

A mobile control room vehicle will be essential for colour television outside broadcasts from theatres. It will require 14 m × 4 m (46 ft × 13 ft) parking space during rehearsals and performances, and other essential vehicles will need additional space three times this area. There should be 4 m (13 ft) of headroom; the turning circles are approximately 25 m (82 ft) in diameter, and weights are up to 14,000 kg (14 tons). The parking area should be close to the side of the building, with easy routes for personnel both to the auditorium and to the stage. As the broadcast is likely to take place while the public is present, cables and equipment must not interfere with the normal audience flow and means of escape, nor with the light and weather insulation of the building. There is some preference for access to the front-of-house areas, if a choice is necessary, but proximity to the stage door is also valuable.

Cable access

Good cable routes both to the auditorium and to the stage space are essential. The main entry point near where the control vehicle will be parked needs an aperture in the wall of 0.2 m² (1½ sq. ft), about 300 mm (1 ft) above ground level, leading into a corridor or an easily accessible duct. In corridors the cables may be supported in trays or on hooks. They must reach stage-floor level, the stalls, and the first tier if there is one. Where they pass through fire-compartment walls, holes of 300 mm (1 ft) diameter should be provided, which, when not in use, should be sealed with fire-proof caps or shutters. When the cables are in position the broadcasting organisation will plug the gap with fire-proof packing. All the cable ducts should be as short and straight as possible.

Power supply

A mobile control room vehicle may require up to two 100 amp single-phase mains power connections. The television company can take this supply direct from the bus-bars in the main intake switch room, using temporary conductors, but installation of permanent connector sockets at the vehicle parking position should be encouraged if repeated visits are expected. Occasionally the theatre lighting installation will have to be supplemented, but the connections provided for touring companies on stage should be suitable. Where temporary power cables have to be installed, cable routes of approximately 150 cm² (23 sq. in.) should be provided.

Dimmer control

Television technicians prefer to make use of the theatre's own stage-lighting control desk and operator, but there are certain conditions that must be met, mainly that there must be sufficient dimmers and circuits of suitable size connected to locations suitable for TV lighting techniques and sufficient overall power. Nowadays most TV lighting designers will accept 2 kW circuits for the majority of their lighting.

The theatre's lighting control room must have space for a television adviser in addition to the normal house operator. The control room will have to accommodate a colour picture monitor 600 mm × 600 mm × 900 mm (2 ft × 2 ft × 3 ft), weighing 70 kg (150 lb.), and a sound communication panel. Cable routes to the mobile control room are essential, and should have a cross-section area of 25 cm^2 (4 sq. in.). If the control room is designed in accordance with the recommendations given in Chapters 13 (Communications) and 15 (Control rooms), it should satisfy the requirements of television.

If the house board is unsuitable or unavailable for some reason, portable dimmers and a portable control panel will be brought in by the television company. The dimmers will be placed close to the lamp loads at the sides of the stage, the ends of the circle, in the boxes or on the fly floor. The control panels will usually be at the front-of-house and preferably at circle level. So long as the cable routes, including a 25 cm^2 (4 sq. in.) hole through the proscenium wall, are provided, there is seldom any difficulty in setting up this equipment.

When working on a stage with theatrical lighting already rigged, the television equipment is usually supported underneath on spare lines or auxiliary bars hung below the normal lighting bars. The extra load on the suspension gear can be up to twice the weight of the standard equipment, and this should be taken into account at the design stage.

When a forestage is in use, a temporary scaffold grid may have to be hung over and in front of the playing area. Provision should be made for load-bearing connections in or through the ceiling at design stage.

A feature of television lighting is the emphasis on back lighting from upstage bars, which is a factor when considering grid loading.

Camera position

It is not possible to predict exactly how the television cameras will be used. Platforms and tracking rails will be built to suit each production, and it is helpful if seating can be easily removed in the stalls and front circle areas.

Stage sound

Television lighting will probably use thyristor

dimmers, and the temporary lighting wiring may run close to house microphone circuits. A special microphone cable can be obtained which virtually eliminates the risk of interference, but wiring enclosed in ferrous conduit or trunking is equally satisfactory. Balanced cables and careful earthing are, however, essential.

The future

Stage lighting is developing continuously, and technology has already created new devices that can be used in the theatre of tomorrow if the money can be found.

Full remote control of spotlight focus, colour and direction has been convincingly demonstrated in German opera and in pop concert lighting rigs. The most obvious application is for lighting positions where access is difficult; but with memory control, new lighting techniques using moving beams may find applications in theatres devoted to drama as well as in the world of popular music.

There may also be a revolution imminent in dimmer technology. Portable dimmers, either fitted to lanterns or mounted alongside and connected only to power and a looped data circuit, might be more convenient and less expensive than the established dimmer room or multipack portable dimmer rig. With built-in dimmers the higher efficiency of low-voltage light sources can be used to increase the light output from lanterns yet again. Dimmer circuits will change to eliminate the last of the old analogue technology and become drift-free and with no need for time-wasting setting-up controls.

Lasers and fibre optics will remain interesting effects, and perhaps will replace wire for connecting the control computers to the dimmers, but they probably have no potential for actually lighting the stage. The more efficient modern light sources, though offering attractive savings in running costs, will also probably remain unused except for special effects and work lights.

Theatre designers should be highly suspicious of claims made for new techniques, unless, as sometimes happens, the client is ready to pay for prototypes to find out if the ideas really work. There have been many disappointments in the past, and it is unwise to place total reliance on untested techniques without keeping the tried and trusted solutions available as a back-up.

Types of stage lighting equipment

The following list is intended to be a series of definitions only. The symbols are internationally agreed.

Floodlight: A lantern with a beam angle of 100° or more, and with a cut-off not less than 180°.

Special floodlight: Unit with a specified beam angle (less than 100°) and a specified cut-off angle.

Reflector spotlight: Lantern with simple reflector and adjustment of beam angle by relative movement of lamp and mirror.

Sealed beam lamp: Lamp with integral reflector giving an even beam.

Lens spotlight: Lantern with simple lens and with or without reflector and capable of adjustment of beam angle by relative movement of lamp and lens.

Fresnel spotlight: Like a lens spotlight, but with stepped lens providing a soft edge to the beam.

Profile spotlight: Lantern giving hard-edged beam which can be varied in outline by diaphragms, shutters or silhouette cut-out masks.

Effects spotlights: Lantern with optics designed to give an even field of illumination of slides and well-defined projection of detail using suitable objective lenses. The slide can be of the moving-effects type or stationary.

Softlight: A lantern of sufficient area to produce a diffuse light causing indefinite shadow boundaries. For stage-lighting purposes this is taken to cover batten flooding equipment, two such symbols being joined by a line.

Bifocal spotlight: Like a profile spotlight (see above), but fitted with two sets of shutters or other such means at the gate, so that the profile may be composed of either hard or soft edges or a combination of both.

12

Sound installations

Good audio design for an auditorium space begins with the understanding that the audio system is there to aid and enhance the performance or presentation, not to compete with it. The subject of this chapter is dealt with in more detail in ABTT Information Sheet No. 2, *Recommendations for Audio Systems in New or Refurbished Auditoria*, but in this extremely complicated, fast-developing area, books and publications cannot keep pace, and it would be wise to seek the advice of a specialised consultant or an experienced practitioner.

Basic principles

The production audio system collects live sound via microphones and recorded signals from tapes or discs, balances and mixes those signals, and then transmits them to the auditorium via appropriately placed loudspeakers. It must also be capable of recording those signals when required.

The positions of the initial and final elements in the chain, microphones and loudspeakers, need to be extremely flexible if the artificial sounds are to be both acoustically and visually integrated with a performance.

A high standard of engineering is essential in all the components in the chain. Audiences expect sound to be convincingly natural. Although they will accept stylisation of sound to fit the production, they will not accept representational sound of poor quality. The acoustic consultant with specialist knowledge and experience of the various aspects of the subject, from the design of control room space to loudspeaker specification, has an important role to play in the design of the sound installation.

Physical spaces

The sound system and its operation make relatively little demand in terms of physical volume within the main auditorium space. Two areas are, however, of critical importance, the sound control room and the principal loudspeaker system. The control room and the remote sound equipment room are described in Chapter 15 (Control rooms).

Principal or proscenium loudspeaker system

The principal loudspeaker system will be sited on the line of division between the performing and audience areas: at the proscenium or, in an arena or open stage theatre, at an equivalent line.

The number, size, type and position of the principal loudspeakers will depend on the primary use of the auditorium, the size and shape of the space (particularly the number of levels), the general acoustic properties of the finishes and the reverberation characteristic. Where loudspeaker units are built into the structure, considerable volume will have to be allowed for adequate bass reproduction, usually far more than would at first be expected, and it is therefore important that there is early liaison with the architect so that he knows how much to include.

One option is for this system to be located as a single cluster of loudspeakers centrally above and just forward of the proscenium or dividing line, rather than as units placed in a "stereo" position each side. For this to be effective there must be a clear line of sight from that position to every seat in the auditorium.

The specification of these loudspeaker arrays should ensure proper matching of power and dispersion over the audience listening area and must include graphic equalisers* in the input circuits to aid the acoustic alignment of the system, so that the right frequency response can be achieved.

Sound and communication wiring

This subject is dealt with in Chapter 21 (Electrical and mechanical services).

Layout

A block layout of the audio system is shown below in Figure 12:3. Although in the past it was considered necessary to have all the amplifiers in the control room, current design and practice make it more sensible to locate them adjacent to the loudspeakers they serve. Where space in the backstage area is at a premium they can be put in a single position under or behind the stage, but not more than 20 m (66 ft) from the sockets to which the loudspeakers will be connected.

Jackfield

Central to the system is the main jackfield, where the operator will set up the signal paths as he needs them for each production or event. It must therefore be within the main control room. It should be fitted in a standard electronic racking cabinet (IEC 297/BS 5954) and composed of the BBC/IBA broadcast standard three-contact Gauge B jacks. As these have switching circuits on them it is possible to set up "standard" or "normal" paths across those contacts, but when plugs are inserted the contacts open so that the signal is routed elsewhere.

*A *graphic equaliser* is a high-resolution tone control device. It consists of a number of audio filters which can be independently boosted or cut. The controls are generally vertical sliding faders, which indicate the setting graphically. It is used to tailor the frequency response of a sound system to compensate for equipment or room irregularities. Once set during commissioning, it should not again be altered.

A proscenium array seldom needs permanent delay lines, but in some cases it may be necessary to introduce a signal delay into the loudspeakers feeding the upper balcony. If supplementary loudspeakers are located further back in the auditorium, these must be fed via delay lines.

It is unwise to specify a unit system by a particular manufacturer without the advice of an independent acoustic consultant.

Other jackfields sited locally will be necessary, but all lines are brought back to the main position. Jackfields are one particular area where only the best and most reliable components will do. Cheap plastic individual jacks should not be used. With such a number of cables to identify, it is important that each one is numbered with a durable slip-on label.

Facilities panels

All round the building there will be boxes with microphone sockets, output feeds for amplifiers, feeds from amplifiers to loudspeakers, and technical power. Often communications outstations for ring intercom and cue lights, as described in Chapter 13, will be integrated in the same set of boxes. These have become known as "facilities panels" and must be designed to ensure that the three categories of cables, as described in Chapter 21, remain separated and that all the connections are readily accessible. The sound boxes need to be robust and reliable.

A note on connector types appears at the end of the chapter (p. 110).

Cable distribution

A chart of the cable distribution appears in Figure 12:3, which is a minimum specification in modern practice for a small to medium-sized theatre and should not be departed from without professional consultation.

Many of the outstations to which the control room is linked by cable will have no equipment permanently fitted. Units appropriate to a particular production or presentation need only be connected as and when required. Tying them down in specific locations limits the potential of the system. A conventional musical production will require microphones and probably foldback loudspeakers in the orchestra pit, but a more adventurous presentation might need the same or more equipment on a platform at the rear of the stage. To have to trail cables across the floor to reach positions like this may obstruct scenery and fire doors and, above all, it increases the likelihood of line faults, interference and failures of the sound system during performances.

Out of the 300 or more screened pair cables coming into the control room, seldom more than 20% will be in use at any one time. However, it is most unlikely to be the same 20% for any two productions or events. If the lines are not installed at the outset where they are needed, a mess of temporary cables will appear, or finishes will have to be damaged to extend the permanent system. In either case alterations and additions made in a hurry are prone to faults and interference.

In some theatres there may be no orchestra pit or one that is too small to accommodate the required number of musicians, and for some drama and musicals the orchestra in its traditional position may be visually unacceptable. In such cases it is possible to use live musicians in an offstage studio area, which will have structural design criteria similar to a recording or broadcast studio; a specialist in that particular field should be consulted.

Audio tie lines

Input signals from the stage or auditorium (such as microphone lines) and output signals from the control room (such as to amplifiers) are usually referred to as low-level audio signals and are transmitted on identical cables known by the collective title of audio tie lines. The only difference between input and output lines is the sense (i.e. sex) of the connector at the remote end of the line from the control room. Lines can easily be reversed, whatever their initial intended function, thus adding to the flexibility of the system.

The recommended number and positioning of the audio tie lines is based on practical experience and has been assessed to allow for flexibility in diverse circumstances. Varying artistic and commercial circumstances will produce heavy demands on different areas of the system, but it is not possible to predict which areas.

All lines will be terminated at the main control room jackfield. Every cable must be numbered at both ends and at any joint, using a slip-on numbering system.

Input lines are generally placed as close as possible to the points where electronic or acoustic sound sources are likely to be located. Output lines run either to amplifier racks and thence to loudspeakers, or to points at which portable amplifiers, headphones or other return feeds may be required. In certain locations audio tie lines need to be multipurpose, and their connection at the remote end may be to pairs of connectors, one of each sense, or to a local jackfield.

General-purpose tie lines run to areas where they may be used in either direction; these can include the auditorium mixing position and rehearsal room.

All points should be sited where access can be maintained however the building is being used.

Questions of the number and locations of audio tie lines and their termination points are ones where specialist advice should be sought.

Amplifier racks and loudspeaker points

Feeds will be provided by the output-designated audio tie lines from the control room to amplifier racks located around the stage and auditorium area. These will then provide amplified feeds to loudspeaker points for the connection of permanent or portable loudspeakers. Usually these racks will serve loudspeaker points located in more than one area. For example, it might well be practicable to combine a proscenium side

12:1. *Diagram of a medium-sized sound system*

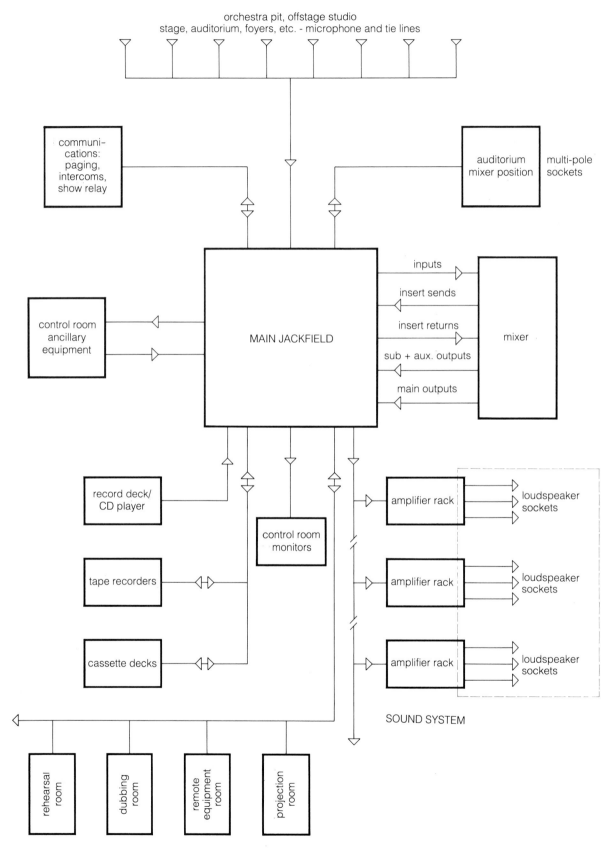

orchestra pit, offstage studio
stage, auditorium, foyers, etc. - microphone and tie lines

communications: paging, intercoms, show relay

auditorium mixer position — multi-pole sockets

control room ancillary equipment

MAIN JACKFIELD

inputs
insert sends
insert returns
sub + aux. outputs
main outputs

mixer

record deck/ CD player

control room monitors

amplifier rack — loudspeaker sockets

tape recorders

amplifier rack — loudspeaker sockets

cassette decks

amplifier rack — loudspeaker sockets

SOUND SYSTEM

rehearsal room

dubbing room

remote equipment room

projection room

amplifier rack with that for the adjacent downstage corner. Alternatively, some amplifiers could be located behind or under the stage area or in a remote equipment room.

Each amplifier rack will need to incorporate some form of input patching on the front of the rack, and in areas which may be dirty, such as the stage and the roof space, it is recommended that this should be in the form of XLR-3 connectors rather than a jackfield, so as to reduce problems of dust penetration. Output patching will also be needed, in this case using standard loudspeaker connectors.

The line between the amplifier and the loudspeaker should operate at *low* impedance, i.e. with the amplifier directly coupled to the loudspeaker. The cable run from amplifiers to loudspeaker connection sockets should not exceed 20 m (66 ft), and this requirement should be borne in mind when deciding the locations of the amplifier racks.

Equipment

The recommended approach is to design the system infrastructure as far as possible without particular reference to the hardware it will interconnect. Although certain items of equipment are regarded as "industry standards", there remains a great deal of choice between both makes and types for most items of loose equipment. Staff achieve the best results with equipment familiar to them, which is a more important factor than the existence of an alternative piece of equipment with marginally better technical specifications. One cause of the problems that have beset new performance audio installations in recent years has been the unfamiliarity and lack of confidence in the system by staff who had not been consulted about the selection of equipment.

Types of equipment favoured by the BBC and other major broadcasting organisations will have been well tested for quality and reliability, and, although probably rather more expensive, will have the compensation of reduced maintenance costs.

Building projects often take two or three years to reach the point where the loose sound equipment is ready to be installed. During that period, prices will have risen and, with the rapid development of the technology of sound, the specification of equipment may be entirely different from what had originally been anticipated. Provisional sums in the contract for sound equipment should be reviewed when it finally becomes necessary to decide what to buy. This allows the scheme to incorporate technological developments (there is no point in installing equipment which is two or three years out of date at commissioning) and means that the knowledge and experience of the staff who will operate the building can be made use of in the selection process.

The outline which follows is primarily intended for budgeting purposes and is based on the requirements of an average (750-seat) repertory theatre with one auditorium. Larger halls will require additional facilities, whose scale and cost will be approximately pro rata to the seating capacities. Smaller halls should aim for a similar level, but appropriate professional advice should be taken.

Microphones

Reinforcement

The most usual method of non-specific reinforcement for musical productions is to place a number of capacitor-type unidirectional microphones on shock-resistant mounts along the front edge of the stage. Sufficient should be provided to allow a maximum spacing of 1.5 m (5 ft) between microphones. On larger stages it is sometimes necessary to suspend additional microphones further upstage above the performance area. These should be of a more directional characteristic, and are sometimes known as "shotgun" or "rifle" microphones.

Modular systems

Several manufacturers make modular capacitor systems with a common pre-amplifier body and interchangeable capsules of varying characteristics. These form a first-class base for a microphone stock, allowing rapid adaptability.

Vocal and general-purpose microphones

At least six microphones will be required for offstage announcements, voices, singers, formal speeches and special effects. If the number is restricted it is better to choose one type of high-quality microphone of extremely robust construction. The types used by pop vocalists have much to recommend them.

Instrumental microphones

Microphones will also be required for the amplification of instruments in concert performances, for offstage musicians in drama and pit musicians in musicals.

Types and techniques vary and are a matter of personal preference and experience. If the staff who will be using them cannot have a say in their selection, then a professional audio engineer with current experience in this field should be consulted. The minimum complement is twelve of varying types.

D I boxes

Modern electronic instruments are normally connected to the mixer via a direct injection box, which is inserted between the instrument and its amplifier. This provides an isolated signal for direct connection to the mixer input without affecting the local amplifier. Four of these are a minimum complement.

Radio microphones

These find increasing use in both musical and non-musical drama. Only units of first-class quality are a worthwhile investment. Cheaper radio microphones will not be able to compete with the large amounts of stray electrical interference and structural steelwork in an auditorium. The types used by the BBC and other broadcasting organisations are the most reliable and are recommended. Radio microphones with fixed batteries cannot be recharged rapidly enough to use the same microphone for a matinee followed by an evening performance, or for a rehearsal followed by a performance. Disposable or exchangeable battery types are preferred.

In Britain a licence is required for the use of radio microphones and should be obtained, before purchase, together with the allocation of frequencies, from:

Department of Trade and Industry
Radio Regulatory Division
Waterloo Bridge House
Waterloo Road
London SE1 8UA
Tel. 01-275 3000

Rising microphones

If the auditorium is to be used for variety, cabaret or pantomime, one or more automatic rising microphones at the front of the stage may prove an asset. These require an understage clearance of at least 2.5 m (8 ft) and easy access for servicing. Controls should be duplicated to the stage manager and the sound control room. There should be an automatic switch in the control circuit to mute the microphone during movement.

Microphone accessories

A comprehensive stock of stands, clips, windshields and other accessories will be required. At least 40% of the cost of the microphones themselves should be added to the budget to cover these items.

Control room equipment

Layout

Different performance situations will require different pieces of equipment to be most readily to hand. It is useful to have tape machines and record decks mounted in mobile units on castors and connected to points on the wall by multicore umbilical cables. They can easily be moved for use else-where in the building or transferred to workshops for maintenance purposes.

Furniture

The bases of the furniture units should be provided with drawers for editing accessories and suitable-sized cupboards for tape and record storage. There should be cable racks in the room, particularly adjacent to the jackfields, and, if possible, a small bench for minor repairs. A sound control room soon lapses into untidiness if the storage space is inadequate.

Decor

All finishes should be dark to avoid reflecting light into the auditorium. Although black is usually suggested, dark shades of blue, brown, green or maroon are normally more comfortable to work in. The floor should have an anti-static carpet. The control room acoustics should be considered: the design and finishing of walls, floor and ceiling should be based on acoustic parameters.

Interconnection and impedances

Much of the equipment as built will have input and/or output impedances appropriate to recording studio or even domestic use. Connectors will vary depending on countries of origin as well as intended markets. It is of the utmost importance that all items of equipment located in the control room area or intended for occasional use as part of the control process should be adapted prior to installation to an identical professional standard of impedances and connectors. This eliminates any matching or earthing problems and ensures compatibility with hired or brought-in equipment. The standard is set out in ABTT Information Sheet No. 2 and is derived from BS 428: Part 10:1979, Chapter II: Section 4; IEC: 268–15: 1978, Chapter II: Section 4; BS 5428: Part 5: Section 5.3: 1981; and IEC: 268–12:1975.

Turntables

There should be a record turntable of transcription quality, with a broadcast standard pick-up arm and cartridge. The control systems for the pick-up arm should be damped and able to be operated manually and accurately.

An active pre-amplifier should be located in the same unit as the turntable to equalise the output and give a nominal 0dBu balanced stereo output. The unbalanced leads from the pick-up to this unit should be kept as short as possible.

Compact disc

Compact discs are finding increasing application because of their superior quality, resistance to dust and ability to be accurately cued. If a CD player is specified it should be of a type able to be cued to specific tracks in a specific order and having 16-bit digital to analogue conversion.

Tape decks

A minimum of two semi-permanent reel-to-reel tape decks, both of which should have recording facilities, must be provided. A third transportable machine able to be used outside the control room for recording, rehearsals, etc. is also essential. Two first-class cassette record/replay machines with noise-reduction facilities should be available. The decks should be removable from their positions for cleaning and maintenance. Standard 483-mm (19-in.) rack mount systems are recommended. Cassette players can be mounted vertically, but reel-to-reel decks, which may be used for tape editing, should be at an angle no greater than 30° to the horizontal.

Tape speeds on all reel-to-reel machines should include 19 cms/sec. (7½ in./sec.). At least one unit should be capable of 38 cms/sec. (15 in./sec.) and one of 9.5 cms/sec. (3¾ in./sec.). The decks should be able to take both ordinary "cine" spools and NAB hub spools up to 265 mm (10½ in.) diameter. In order to control the machines during performances there should be a full set of remote function controls fitted in or adjacent to the main mixing console. The tape decks should have an optical automatic stop mechanism and, most important, an elapsed time counter.

Certain installations, particularly larger drama theatres, will require NAB cartridge-type tape machines. The precise requirements for these will need to be defined by the operating staff.

Mixers

For many years it was thought that the only way to produce a theatre mixer was to "custom-build", but this is no longer necessary. With amplifiers remote from the control room, and no need for loudspeaker switching on the desk itself, more adaptable mixers with better facilities can be found from the ranges made for live music performance or even for recording. The choice depends on the features offered – such as auxiliary outputs and good equalisers – and numbers of outputs. A minimum of eight main outputs, preferably with sub-groups as well, should be sought.

Mixing desk inputs

Each signal source should be routed via the main jackfield to the mixer inputs. All mixer inputs must be balanced, preferably by transformers, and switchable between microphone (−70dBu) and line (0dBu) sensitivity. The input stages should be capable of accepting signals up to at least +20dBu. Phantom power at 48 volts to operate the pre-amplifiers of capacitor microphones should be switchable to all inputs (see IEC: 268–15A: 1982).

A rotary input gain control should be provided: see *Controls and legends*, p. 108.

Equalisation

There should be controls for adjusting the equalisation (tone) in at least three bands on all input channels.

The centre-point of the mid-frequency bands must be continuously variable, and those of the high- and low-frequency bands should be switchable to at least three settings. High-pass and low-pass filters to eliminate rumble and hiss and an equaliser by-pass switch are essential: see *Controls and legends*, p. 108.

Level control

Main level adjustment on input channels, sub-groups and groups should be by flat linear faders of at least 105 mm (4 in.) travel, graduated in dB.

Monitoring

There should be comprehensive aural and visual means of monitoring signals, including pre-fade listen (PFL) on all inputs and after-fade listen (AFL) on all outputs, both of which can be fed to either monitor loudspeakers or to headphones.

It is useful if, in addition to the conventional VU (volume unit) meters, there is an ability to patch in a pair of BBC-specification PPM (peak power) meters. Where the option is available, PPM or bargraph peak reading meters are of more value than the VU meter, as rapid peaks and distortion are easily missed.

Auxiliary outputs

Auxiliary outputs for foldback, reverberation and other effects are necessary if the desk is to be used for the preparation of effects or for live music mixing. All auxiliary outputs should be switchable pre or post fade and accessible from every input and output via independent rotary level controls. Auxiliary master level controls should have a large, clearly indicating on/off switch next to them.

Inserts

When mixing for musical productions or for concerts it is extremely useful to be able to insert additional signal-processing equipment into the circuitry of either inputs or outputs. This is usually achieved by an "insert point" in each unit. Where these can be provided they should be connected via the main jackfield, using separate jacks for send and return signals.

Connections

In addition to the individual input and output connectors which will be fitted as standard, the mixing desk should be connected by multicore cables to a wall-mounted termination box and thence to the main jackfield.

This is essential if the desk is to be transferred to an auditorium position, and an identical termination box will be required at that position.

The choice of multipole connectors is of critical importance. Examination should be made of the current practices for touring concert sound systems with particular emphasis on robust metal shells, large rigid gold or gold-plated connecting surfaces and good shrouds or locating devices. This is not an area for economy or for the use of connectors originally designed for semi-permanent installations.

Transit case

The desk should also be provided with a robust flight case for movement between the two positions, as should its power supply unit(s). Most manufacturers are able to supply these.

Controls and legends

It is important to remember that the operator will often have his eyes on the stage, not on the desk, particularly when mixing live music. Push buttons should, if possible, be illuminated, and non-illuminated switches must give unambiguous indications by touch.

It is helpful if all rotary controls are detented, meaning stepped in tiny notches, rather than continuously variable. This also aids re-setting in repertoire changeovers. A further advantage is to have the centre or null position pointing down the desk towards the operator so that he can easily see the settings without having to stand up and lean forward over the desk, particularly when mixing from the auditorium.

The legends should be engraved rather than silk-screened, and white on a dark background is more legible in dim lighting than black on white.

Script space

Unless the mixer and its accommodation are very large there is unlikely to be any space on the desk to keep the script, plots and cue sheets. One solution is to construct a transparent table which fits over the desk, preferably on rails so it can slide up and down.

Mixer size

In the average-sized theatre of 750 seats with a normal repertory-based policy, the minimum mixer size should be 16 inputs and 8 main outputs, but 24 inputs is preferable, particularly if musicals and concerts feature in the programme. These are standard configurations, readily available from

several manufacturers. The smallest practicable size for even a studio theatre is 12 inputs and 4 main outputs. It is best to allow for expansion when investing in a mixer, for example by buying a large frame with less than a full number of channels fitted.

Amplifiers

Certain amplifiers will be permanently located, such as those for the principal loudspeakers and the positions around the stage area most likely to be required on a regular basis. Further amplifiers should be provided in transit cases to be sited with or close to mobile loudspeakers for particular uses at particular times.

Amplifiers should always have power in reserve. Running amplifiers flat out leads to obtrusive background noise and audible distortion. It is a good idea to have lockable input controls to ensure balances are maintained.

Output control

Some form of patching or routing control will be required between the mixer, the amplifiers and the loudspeakers. In an average or larger installation, the operating staff should be consulted to determine how much loudspeaker patching is necessary for repertoire changeovers. It is now generally accepted that the correct point in the chain to have any switching or routing system is between the mixer outputs and the amplifier inputs. The system should be designed to avoid any re-patching between amplifiers and loudspeakers during a performance. If the mixer has enough inbuilt facilities it may not be necessary at all.

Monitors

The control room will require a pair of first-class loudspeakers driven by an amplifier of equivalent standard. The quality of the monitoring is vital to the success of the system, and BBC-preferred types are recommended. The positioning of the loudspeakers should be part of the acoustic design of the control room.

If a remote amplifier room is used there should be a facility within it to generate test signals (e.g. a cassette deck and an oscillator), plus a system for patching a good-quality monitor loudspeaker to any of the amplifiers.

Quality show relay

If the control room may be used with the window closed, an independent audio relay of high quality should be provided from the auditorium. This should appear at the monitoring controls on the mixer, so that the operator can route it as he requires.

Peripheral equipment

A number of outboard units, signal processors, delay lines, reverberation units, graphic equalisers will also be required in the control room. These units should be mounted in a standard 483-mm (19-in.) rack cabinet and linked to the main jackfield.

If a mixer concert position is provided, this rack should be constructed as a mobile unit able to be taken to that position with the mixer. It will require multicore cables to connect it to the mixer or to the main control room installation. These should be terminated to an integral jackfield which gives access to the inputs and outputs of the units in the rack, the mixer channel insert sends and returns, the mixer output insert sends and returns and any auxiliary or effects inputs on the mixer.

Chairs

It is important to ensure that the mixer and operator are positioned for both comfortable operation and maximum visibility of the performing area. The operator may have to sit at the desk for up to fifteen hours a day without unnecessary fatigue. A first-class draughtsman's chair on castors, adjustable for height, is recommended.

Loudspeakers

The principal or proscenium loudspeaker system has already been discussed (p. 102).

Mobile loudspeakers

A number of mobile loudspeakers will be required for the reproduction of music and effects from onstage and auditorium locations.

At least three distinct types will be required:

1. a large-scale high-power type able to reproduce everything from thunderclaps to high-quality/fidelity orchestral music.
2. a medium-sized unit able to be located among scenery and easily moved, but having the best possible characteristics for its size and weight.
3. a compact unit of very high quality capable of being used in more restricted scenic spaces and in auditorium locations.

The number and proportions of these speakers should be decided as late as possible in the scheme, as the choice will be affected by artistic policy and the type of events presented.

Appropriate units will come from many backgrounds – rock concert systems, hi-fi, studio monitoring etc. The relative importance of robustness, reliability and quality in each application basically depends on how close the unit is to the audience. Speakers marketed as "all-purpose theatre loudspeakers" should be treated with suspicion, as they are usually inadequate compromises.

Auditorium loudspeakers

In major drama theatres and multi-purpose halls, sets of loudspeakers arranged around the perimeter and ceiling are necessary for ambiance effects in drama and subtle speech reinforcement in other uses. Multi-output audio delay lines accessible via the main jackfield should be installed to enable these units to be acoustically synchronised with the principal loudspeaker system when required.

The choice and siting of these units is critical, and the advice of an acoustic consultant should be sought.

Refurbishment schemes

Where loudspeaker systems are to be introduced into an older building undergoing refurbishment, the critical point to remember is that the space will have been designed for a diffuse natural sound, as opposed to the concentrated directional sound produced by loudspeakers. A full acoustic survey should be undertaken prior to the design work, as the acoustically ideal loudspeaker positions are often the least obvious.

Connection of loudspeakers to amplifiers

Amplifiers and loudspeakers can be coupled together by either of two methods – direct coupling at low impedance (4 to 16 ohms) or transformer coupling at high impedance (200 ohms).

The advantages of transformer coupling are most apparent in paging or background music applications, where the relative sizes of the transformers can be adjusted to match accurately the load of a number of loudspeakers to the amplifier, giving maximum efficiency. This also permits adjustment of the relative power delivered by each loudspeaker to gain even coverage.

In terms of the production sound systems, the only advantage of transformer coupling in modern practice is the ability to use smaller-gauge cables between the amplifiers and the loudspeakers and to site them a great distance apart – usually with all the amplifiers in the main control room. Any financial saving on cabling rapidly disappears when the cost of transformers of adequate power and quality is taken into consideration. Modern loudspeaker designs rely on higher wattages to produce smooth frequency response, and the transformers necessary if detrimental effects on the quality are to be avoided are now disproportionately large and costly.

In the interests of both quality and flexibility it is recommended that the production sound system should use direct-coupled amplifiers and loudspeakers operating at low impedance, with the output signals from the main mixing desk being distributed via the jackfield to amplifiers located on or immediately adjacent to the stage area, or next to the individual loudspeakers. Many of these can be portable amplifiers, allowing greater flexibility in usage. Provided there is easy access for maintenance, amplifiers for the principal or proscenium system and any ceiling-mounted units can be mounted in the auditorium ceiling void. The power supply for remotely situated amplifiers should be master-switched from the control room or a central point backstage.

Workshop and other areas

Workshop space

Some form of workshop space will be required for the repair and maintenance of equipment. In contrast to the normal working conditions in the control room, the workshop should have natural light and fresh air if at all possible. A bench twice the size of the largest single piece of equipment is required, together with storage cupboards, tool racks, power points and adequate space to manoeuvre bulky items such as mixers and loudspeakers. This room can also contain the secure store for high-value equipment.

Test equipment

Much time and money can be saved if the building is equipped (and staffed) to carry out its own first-line maintenance. A considerable sum will, however, need to be expended on test equipment, which must be of the best quality if it is to be any real use.

Dubbing and editing room

If the auditorium is a producing theatre for all or a major part of the year, a separate room will be required for the preparation of music and effects tapes without disturbing the use of the control room for the current production.
   Within the room will be required:

— Minimum 12 input, 4 output mixer with full studio facilities
— Minimum of three reel-to-reel tape machines, identical to those in the main control room
— Record turntable and pre-amplifier
— Cassette tape recorder
— Stereo graphic equalisers
— Monitor amplifier and loudspeakers, as fitted in main control room
— Cartridge recording and loading system (if required)
— Large amount of storage space for effects tape/records, materials etc.
— Rack space for signal processors etc.

This room should have its own jackfield which interconnects all the equipment and has a minimum of 24 audio tie lines to the main control room.

Connectors

The recommended connectors for use in performance audio systems are as follows.

Microphones and low-level audio signals

Cannon XLR-3 series (or mating equivalents) with the signal (source) appearing on the PIN (male) connector, and the equipment input (load) being on the SOCKET (female) connector, with connections as follows.

Pin 1: Cable screen (NB. This must *never* be directly connected to case or earth)
Pin 2: In-phase, "hot" or signal
Pin 3: Anti-phase, "cold" or return

Examples:
Microphone chassis connectors – male
Microphone wall sockets – female
Tape or gram outputs – male
Mixer inputs – female
Mixer outputs – male
Tape machine inputs – female
Amplifier inputs – female
Processor inputs – female
Processor outputs – male

Amplifier outputs and loudspeakers

Cannon AXR-PDN series (or mating equivalents) with the signal (amplifier output) appearing on the SOCKET (female) connector, and the input to the loudspeaker being on the PIN (male) connector, with connections as follows.

Pin P: In-phase, "hot" or signal
Pin D: No connection
Pin N: Anti-phase, "cold" or return

Note that this connector should only be used on low-impedance systems. 100-volt line systems for paging or background purposes should be permanently wired in on screw terminal blocks or soldered connections.

13

Communications

With ever-increasing technical complexity on the stage, and the pressure to make efficient use of manpower in all areas, the inclusion of comprehensive communications facilities is essential to any building in which an audience gathers to watch an event. Such systems are no longer confined to technical operations areas, but may include other important management aids for security, public control or emergency announcements, and general dissemination of information around the building; for example, show relay by sound or vision not only to dressing and control rooms, but also to offices and public foyers.

Details of the control rooms for stage lighting, sound, stage management and translators' booths are covered in Chapter 15 (Control rooms).

The term "communications" may cover a variety of independent systems, some related solely to performance control, others to more general uses. To achieve compatibility, it is important to take all aspects of current and potential demand into consideration when planning new installations. The aim should be to avoid unnecessary duplication, and to ensure that the end product will be logical in its controls and thus readily understood by operatives who may either be non-technical or temporary visitors to the building, for example, house management staff and touring stage managers.

Communication systems

During performances and rehearsals, activity centres around the main operations point, the prompt corner, from where the stage manager is in control, and needs to communicate by a variety of means to all areas of the building: by cue light signal, by one-way speech (call system) or in two-way conversation by intercom, talk-back or telephone. Supporting systems will include audio relay of events on stage (show relay) to certain working spaces, such as dressing rooms, control rooms, and senior management offices, and, in a well-equipped building relay by closed-circuit television to a more selective list. Show relay by vision or sound or both may be needed on the stage for blind cues, such as to relay the conductor's beat to an offstage chorus, or in the foyers to keep late-comers and non-ticket-holders informed of performance progress. Television screens in the public areas may also provide a useful means of advertising forthcoming attractions if the appropriate equipment is available.

The stage management performance control system

The ability to communicate quickly and reliably is a key requirement for stage managers, and it is inadvisable to rely entirely on a single system. Most comprehensive SM systems therefore provide a variety of communications channels, some in apparent duplication, but serving different principal functions whilst offering alternative routes in the event of a partial breakdown.

These systems will mainly be controlled from the stage manager's desk, which should be a portable unit on a flexible cable so that it can be placed where it has the best view of the action under different scenic conditions. However, not all controls need to be on this mobile desk; some, such as working and rehearsal lighting selectors and telephones, will be better placed on an adjoining wall where other technicians can reach them.

Traditionally the point of connection for the SM desk is known as the prompt corner, though prompting in itself, whilst occasionally essential, may be the least frequent of its uses. However, on an open stage conventional prompting by the SM may be impossible, and solutions have been attempted which couple the SM microphone into directional overhead speakers. These do not seem to have been entirely successful, since the disembodied voice may prove even more of a distraction to both cast and audience than an actor "drying".

On a proscenium stage the prompt corner will be the area immediately adjoining the structural proscenium opening, designed so that the SM desk and associated control panels can be tucked out of the way of actor and scenery movements, whilst allowing as good a view as possible of the performance, and quick access around the back of the set. Also located in this area will be the release controls for the safety curtain and drencher, whose use must never be impeded.

Though most stage managers dislike being separated from backstage, in a non-proscenium theatre it may be necessary to work from an auditorium box similar to those for sound and lighting control. In some cases the SM may share space with other operators, but this can be distracting, and in a large theatre a separate room is generally preferred. In theatres with an extended forestage, the option of prompt corner or front-of-house operation should be offered by duplicating the wiring and terminating in plug and socket connections.

Though tradition dictates that the prompt corner be on an actor's left side, more critical is the relationship of the SM to overall stage planning such as available wing space, the location of the flying system, prop room, pass door and dressing room access. On a large stage it is normal to have duplicate wiring and fixed performance controls on either side of the proscenium, to allow the SM to take up the best possible position to suit particular production requirements.

Stage manager's desk

This should be a compact unit, but readily portable. The stage manager will either stand or sit on a high stool. The unit must be stable; castors should be lockable and the base should provide a foot rest, and space for storing spare cable, scripts, hand-

13:1. Detail of the prompt corner, showing some of the fixed controls for intercom, cue lights, sound and working lights

13:2. The prompt corner, with stage manager's mobile desk on the right

bags and similar items. The working part will comprise a sloping script space, with flat area above for pencils and a torch, and a near-vertical panel for switches and controls. The top of the unit should provide an additional resting-place for papers and other small items. Overall finish should be matt and dark.

Script space must be large enough to accommodate musical manuscript paper; up to 430 mm × 760 mm (17 in. × 30 in.) may be necessary. Separately adjustable lighting should be provided for the script space and control panels, each with dimmers. Light spill on to the floor or adjacent scenery should be reduced to a minimum.

Operating controls will be mounted on the panel, and should be arranged in a layout that is both logical and easily understood by visiting stage managers. The form and placing of controls should assist accurate identification in times of urgent activity or dim lighting. There are, at the time of writing, no agreed standards on layout or use of colour coding and switch types.

Legends should be clearly engraved with white-filled letters to assist legibility under dim lighting, and different types of switches should be used to identify particular system blocks, for example:

— lever key switches for cue lights
— illuminated push buttons for working lights masters
— other push types for interval bells

Certain controls whose inadvertent operation might spell disaster will require special consideration, and may need hinged covers – for example, auditorium call keys, and effects circuit switches.

Sockets for headsets, microphones, cue masters and effects circuits should be kept away from the main operating panel, and are best placed on recessed panels to the sides of the desk, where their cables will not get in the way.

Cue light systems

With advances in electronics providing sophisticated speech communication at modest cost, cue lights are no longer the only reasonable means of controlling a performance; however, they are silent, reliable and interference-free, and should still form part of all comprehensive stage management installations.

Standard systems provide red "warning" and green "go" lights at specific outstations where technicians or actors require cues. Circuits should be controlled via separate lever keys, each with an indicator light wired in series with the outstation to give bulb-failure indication. Masters can be selected by two-way keys with centre off position. Outstations should be provided with a "reply" push which momentarily interrupts the "warn" circuit to indicate that the operator is ready for the cue. This may not always be seen if the SM is very busy, and on more sophisticated systems flashing lamps are used which turn steady on acknowledgement. The SM may have to move from the desk to obtain a better view for a cue, in which case he will need an alternative master push on an extension lead.

Outstations may comprise in-built lights on fixed equipment such as the lighting console, or portable units connected via flexible cable and a socket outlet. On a long fly gallery more than one set of lights may be required, with special arrangements in the circuitry to maintain the fail-safe principle of series operation.

In a large theatre, provision of operating keys on the SM panel for every circuit, no matter how infrequent its use, may create an unwieldy, oversized panel and add to the difficulties of identifying the right key at critical moments. The number of direct operated circuits should be restricted, with a patch panel allowing selection of less frequently required outstations to a limited group of control channels.

Intercom systems

Nowadays two-way speech (talk-back) is usually achieved through simple devices in which the outstation operator wears a lightweight headset with single earpiece and small boom microphone. This is connected to a belt-pack housing volume and microphone controls, which in turn connects by flexible cable to the fixed wall socket. In rehearsals, when the constraints of permanent attachment via cables may be a nuisance, speaker/microphone units can be plugged into the same termination. In a large theatre two channels are useful, since they allow members of different technical departments – electrics and stage hands – to communicate with one another without mutual interference. The same terminations are common to both channels, and selection is on the belt-pack. Where loudspeaker outstations are used, care must be taken in siting and volume setting, to minimise the risk of disturbance to actors or audience. Induction loop systems, which depend upon an aerial wire running around the relevant sections of the building, are valuable for one-way communication when cues may have to be given to operators who otherwise are out of direct physical touch – for example, to the driver of a mobile scenery unit. However, surrounding steelwork can absorb a high proportion of signal energy, and careful siting of the aerial is essential to achieve reasonable cover. The possibility of breakthrough into sound reinforcement systems has also to be considered. Two-way radios would be ideal for many theatrical operations, but they are expensive and liable to be stolen, they may suffer from interference, and their official use is restricted by licensing authorities.

General cover of the stage by a public-address system of loudspeakers mounted at strategic points is a valuable asset during the normal working day and in fit-ups, when headsets are unlikely to be worn. They also provide a means for the director to talk to actors and technicians from the stalls during rehearsals, but the selector key must be protected from inadvertent use, for obvious reasons.

Calls systems

The SM will need facilities to pass messages and calls to dressing rooms and certain technical spaces or offices, for example workshops and the dimmer room. Each of these spaces will be equipped with a small wall-mounting speaker permanently connected to the appropriate call circuit. To ensure that these speakers cannot be disconnected or otherwise silenced, plugs and sockets should be avoided, and volume set by screwdriver rather than adjustable knob.

Other circuits will provide separate call facilities to public areas and to the auditorium, the number of circuits being a function of the building's scale and mode of operation. Where more than three circuits are provided, a "general call" key may be appropriate, but should never include the auditorium circuit.

Show relay

Dressing rooms will require a constant relay from the stage, so that performers know how far the show has progressed. Similar relay may be useful in certain offices, particularly those associated with technical operations. A microphone suspended just forward of the stage should provide a reasonable signal for this purpose, with its own amplifier feeding into the appropriate call circuits already provided. To ensure that essential calls are not obscured, operation of a call selector key should cut off the show relay on that particular circuit. Individual speakers should be fitted with volume controls to allow local adjustment of the show relay side, but this must not affect the volume of calls.

In control rooms continuous relay of the performance without interruption must be available, so circuits independent of the call system are required. Operators should not have to leave their consoles to adjust levels, so remote volume controls should be provided at appropriate positions.

In lyric theatres, performers, offstage musicians, or the stage manager may need assistance in picking up the orchestral sound for a cue, so there should be a dedicated circuit feeding sockets around the stage into which appropriate show-relay speakers can be connected as necessary; such a relay could be provided through the theatre's sound reinforcement system as conventional foldback, but where the need may be quite frequent it is better to provide the facility automatically in the stage management system.

In foyer areas it may not be appropriate to broadcast sounds from the stage at all times, for example during rehearsals, but on occasions house management may wish to show latecomers what is happening in the auditorium and they should therefore have the option of switching the show-relay source to the foyer speakers. Where there is a closed-circuit television relay from the auditorium, this will need an audio feed from the same show-relay source.

Auxiliary controls

The stage manager may need to operate certain effects himself, rather than by cueing others to do so. These can include telephone and door bells, maroons, flash boxes, or control of practical fittings, and the system should cater for a variety of voltages and a telephone ringing circuit, selectable to remote sockets around the stage through a patch field. Controls for effects circuits must be clearly distinguished, and for safety it may be sensible to provide a master key-operated switch.

Critical controls for stage working lights should also be mounted on the SM desk, and may comprise a single master, or the master plus one or two switches for most frequently used circuits. Illuminated push buttons give a clear state indication, and a similar indicator should show the house lights situation. In a concert hall it may be appropriate to provide the platform manager with direct control over house lights, and selected stage lighting states which will be pre-set on a memory control.

Wall panel

This should house all those controls not essential to the immediate running of the performance, for example rehearsal and pilot lighting, individual working lights switches, telephones, cue light and effects circuits and patch panels. The unit should be mounted where it is within relatively easy reach of the stage manager when at his desk in the standard operating position, but it should be usable also by other technical staff without disturbing the SM.

Telephones

The various systems comprising the stage manager's control panel are to some extent integrated, and may all be put out of action in mid-performance by a sudden power or equipment failure. There will be times also when the system is not switched on during the day for economy or maintenance, or when exchanges have to be confidential and not subject to the publicity inherent in talk-back systems. So it is sensible to provide performance buildings with a simple alternative means of communication between technicians, independent of other systems, and not subject to external influences. This is best achieved by a restricted push-button telephone system linking only the main operating positions, such as SM, lighting and sound controls, fly floors, follow spots, orchestra pit and trap room, and receiving its power supply from a reasonably secure source, unconnected to other systems.

Ringing of telephone bells, other than as a special effect, must be avoided where the sound could be heard by audience or actors, though during the day a bell may still be necessary to attract attention. Such telephones should be provided with alternative bell and light calling facilities, with automatic change-over through operation of the working lights master control.

Warning lights

Warning signs to indicate "performance in progress" may be desirable over stage entrance doors, and should similarly come into operation with the cancellation of the working lights master.

Rehearsal facilities

Previously mentioned is the option of making the stage manager's desk portable so that it can be used in alternative positions on the stage, or in an auditorium control box, as the occasion demands. Another possible position for the desk is in the auditorium, to allow the stage manager to sit with the director during rehearsals and control the action from there. A parallel set of cables to the appropriate position should therefore be included.

A more general application would be for a production desk to be used in the same auditorium position as a means for the director and lighting designer to communicate directly with technicians and operators without interfering with the stage manager. This should be an uncomplicated unit, easily portable and designed to sit on a table top; it should be fitted with adjustable stalk lights on dimmers to illuminate scripts and plots, headset intercom facilities for at least two people, a microphone with selector switches for the stage PA speakers and dressing room calls circuits, a duplicate set of lighting control cue lights, so that the precise timing of those cues can be observed, and a performance telephone. Provision should also be made in the wiring to connect a portable telephone for the building internal system.

General building communications

The calls section of the stage management performance control facilities provides a ready means for general one-way communication throughout the building at any time without need to duplicate equipment, wiring or loudspeakers. Remote input and switching arrangements can be installed at key positions such as the stage door office and the telephone exchange, and in the foyers to allow the house manager to make public announcements. The same amplifiers and speakers may also be used for background music in public areas during the day, or to advertise forthcoming events, for which that particular tape equipment would need to be under the control of the front-of-house staff, rather than of the stage.

Since the main stage management system may not be in use during the day, calling stations must be able to switch on the system power when necessary by remote means, and should be provided with indicator lights to show when the circuits are in use by others. Consideration should be given to the need for the stage manager to have overriding priority in performance, but the one circuit that directs calls into the auditorium must never be available to anyone but the stage manager.

Acknowledging the necessity nowadays to plan for emergency situations, such as bomb scares, in large buildings involving many floor levels, selective use of the call system may be a sensible way of making the relevant announcements for areas outside the auditorium. Specially protected

wiring and an alternative/secure source of power for the amplifiers may be required by the licensing authorities. There is no standard solution to the problem of emergency announcements, and each situation must be discussed with the authorities while communications systems are still in the embryo stage.

Radio paging systems are extremely useful for staff location in large buildings where personnel are mobile. When connected through fire alarm and internal telephone systems this equipment can be very effective for warning key personnel of an emergency before general alarms are activated. Such systems are relatively inexpensive for a whole building, can usually be covered by a single aerial, and will soon repay their capital cost in saved time.

Closed-circuit television

The arrival of small, relatively cheap CCTV cameras has provided opera companies and those involved with "offstage" bands with practical means of transferring the unseen conductor's beat to remote corners of stage or auditorium without involving cutting holes in scenery, or repetiteurs perched upon ladders holding a score in one hand and waving a torch to relay the beat in the other. Many touring companies nowadays carry their own CCTV system for this purpose, but in a well-equipped building, especially one intended for conference use, a comprehensive wiring installation should be considered from the outset. Terminal equipment is expensive, but simple systems can be hired with relative ease, so it may be sensible to limit initial purchases to the basics until the level of real need is established.

In a large permanent installation it may be necessary to distinguish between the CCTV requirement for technical operations at video signal level, and the need for a CCTV radio-frequency distribution system for the rest of the building, for example foyer monitors and "off-air" programme relay to offices and staff rooms. The planning of such a television distribution network is a matter for specialists.

Television screens in public areas offer valuable opportunities for information display and advertising. CCTV systems should allow for the injection of pre-recorded material of this type.

Hearing-aid assistance

Auditoria should be equipped with systems to help those with hearing difficulties. These now fall into two categories, namely
a)   systems which make use of standard hearing-aids;
b)   systems requiring special aids.
The common hearing-aid inductive loop systems allow patrons to use their own receivers provided these are fitted with the proper selector switch. The signal from a dedicated microphone is transmitted

along a loop aerial wire in the auditorium; the path of this loop and the type of wire to be used are matters to be decided by a specialist supplier, and will need early attention if the wire is to be concealed behind finishes; if mechanical protection is required, only plastic can be used. These systems can be quite efficient if planned with extreme care, but conflicts sometimes arise between the technical requirements for positioning the loop and other considerations, such as architectural design, type of seating, and the absorption provided by steelwork in the structure.

Alternative systems involve special hearing devices owned by the theatre which can be borrowed or hired by patrons. These will be quite expensive to buy, and must be cleaned and serviced after each use, so they tend not to be favoured by management, though they are often used for translation purposes in conference halls. The most common system operates through infrared signals, similar in general terms to the remote control for TV and video recorders. The signal is transmitted by small radiator panels which can be built into walls or suspended inconspicuously from ceilings, requiring only a reasonably direct line-of-sight between radiator and user. For those who normally wear a hearing-aid pre-set to overcome a particular hearing problem, the infra-red receiver can be used in conjunction, so that these settings need not be changed.

14

Film projection

This is not intended to be a comprehensive treatise on the design of cinemas, but films are so often shown in places intended primarily for live performances that an outline of the subject is necessary. This also applies to large-screen video projection and slide projection.

An auditorium which has evolved from balancing the acoustics and sightlines required for films will not be the same as one based on the requirements of the live theatre. Even the pre-war cinemas where live shows were a regular feature of the programme were very limited in the sort of performance that could be staged. Sometimes in the more important movie palaces quite elaborate music and dancing acts were put on, and even in the relatively small suburban houses the cinema organist would contribute a live element in the programme. In the design there was a balance between the needs of film projection and the live theatre, though it was heavily weighted in favour of the movies. Most new cinemas no longer make provision for anything but film shows. On the other hand there have been cases in recent years of buildings designed for tactical reasons as theatres which for commercial reasons very soon turned over to the movies. Film shows can be viewed quite comfortably in a theatre, though not from every seat, but the demands of live productions are more extensive and exacting, and if the architect's brief calls for both it is the requirements of the live performance which must take precedence.

Projection systems

The four standard types of film are described by their width – 8 mm, 16 mm, 35 mm, 70 mm – and each has its appropriate type of projection equipment. 8 mm film is for home movies, and at the other end of the scale 70 mm film is used only for very large-screen spectacles and needs special equipment that is most unlikely to find its way into a theatre regularly used for live performances.

Projectors for 16 mm film

16 mm projections are most commonly used for educational, scientific, advertising and entertainment purposes where audiences are rather small. When the light source is a tungsten-halogen lamp the equipment is comparatively simple, compact and portable. The sound-reproduction systems are combined with the projectors. Assuming the screen has a matt white surface, its size should be limited to 2 m × 2.7 m (6 ft × 9 ft). It may be possible to project a larger picture successfully if the stray light from all other sources falling upon the screen does not exceed 1% of the luminance at the centre of the screen.

If it is desired to show 16 mm film on a small scale within an auditorium licensed for cinematograph exhibitions, projectors with tungsten-halogen lamps may be set up in the auditorium provided that no flammable film is used, no repairs are made to the film in the auditorium with a flammable substance, and a clear space of a metre (3 ft 3 in.) round the projector is roped off to keep people away. This sort of temporary arrangement is not at all satisfactory and should be avoided if possible. The projectors make a noise and spill light, and the projectionist causes more distraction as he handles the film cases.

16 mm films can be exhibited on screens up to about 3.5 m × 5 m (11½ ft × 16 ft) using projectors with xenon arc; but in this case they must be treated just like regular 35 mm projectors and have to be housed in a projection room.

Projectors for 35 mm film

Portable or semi-portable 35 mm projectors fitted with tungsten-halogen lamps are often used in lecture theatres and similar places where better picture quality is required than can be obtained with 16 mm film. Because of the larger image, bigger screens can be used. On premises licensed for cinematographic exhibitions, 35 mm projectors must be in a projection room. 35 mm projectors with xenon arc light sources are standard equipment for commercial cinemas throughout the world, and are widely used for high-quality, non-commercial work.

Projectors for dual 35 mm and 16 mm film

In many cases it may be found that the use of dual-gauge 16/35 mm projectors is more efficient than separate 35 mm and 16 mm units, especially if space in the projection room is limited. A common solution is to provide one 35 mm projector and one dual-gauge 16/35 mm projector, as this gives a standard two-projector 35 mm arrangement with changeover for full-length feature films, and the added bonus of a 16 mm projector when required.

Two types of dual-gauge projector are available: common film-path type and separate film-path type. Common film-path projectors, such as the Zeiss Ernemann machine, have the advantage that the same light path is used for both formats and the operational side of the projector is always the same. Separate film-path projectors have a 16 mm mechanism on one side of the projector and a 35 mm mechanism on the other with the light path being deflected through the 16 mm gate.

Reels

Present-day standard spools contain 600 m (2000 ft) of film, which passes through a projector in about twenty minutes. Thus in most cinemas and wherever films lasting longer than this were shown

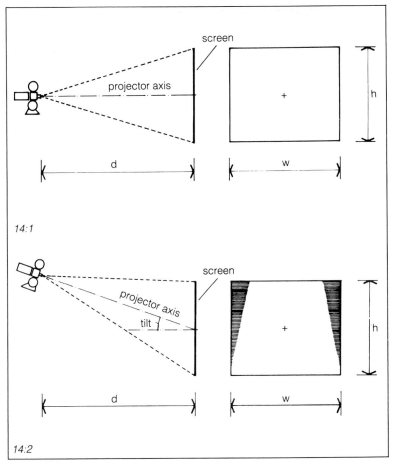

screen

projector axis

d

w

h

+

14:1

screen

projector axis

tilt

d

w

h

+

14:2

Xenon arc lamps

Xenon lamps, like carbon arcs, run on direct current and therefore need rectifiers to convert the AC supply, but they are less adaptable than carbon arcs. They are manufactured in various sizes ranging from 450 W to 5,000 W and cannot be interchanged in any one lamp housing. Their principal advantage is that they require no attention other than replacement and are easily controlled automatically. Light output diminishes with age, and, as the lamps operate under high negative pressure, they are likely to implode if cooled suddenly. Operators must wear goggles and protective gloves when handling them. There are no combustion products, but the arcs can ionize the surrounding atmosphere and produce ozone, to which some operators may be allergic. One remedy is ducted extract ventilation from the lamp housing to the outside air, but this is not necessary now that ozone-free bulbs are standard.

Projection systems

At present three methods may be used for film projection: direct, indirect and back projection. The first is by far the most commonly used. Indirect projection requires mirrors and is used as an expedient where direct projection is impracticable. Rear projection has limited uses, but some advantages in special circumstances.

Direct projection

The ratio of width to height (w:h) is known as the aspect ratio. The standard aspect ratio is 1.375 to 1. It is derived from the standard size of frame on cinematograph film, the screen representing a direct enlargement of it.

In Figure 14:1 the simplest case is shown, with the projector axis horizontal and centred upon a vertical screen. In practice this is not always convenient to arrange, and so the projector axis is put at an angle to the horizontal. This angle is known as the projector rake. If the screen is vertical the projected image is then distorted, as seen in Figure 14:2. Similar distortions occur if the projector axis is tilted up or is set sideways to the screen. Within certain limits these distortions are not important if

14:1. Basic arrangement of projector and screen

14:2. Distortion of projected image caused by tilt of projector axis

it was always necessary to install two projectors if the programme were to be seen without a break. Commercial 35 mm cinema projectors now usually have Standard 1800 m (6000 ft) spool capacity (though a variety of other options is available), which allows the make-up of the film to run for 66 minutes. However, commercial problems relating to running costs and staffing levels have seen the introduction of long-playing systems, such as Towers and Platters (cake stands) which will permit between 2½ to 4 hours running time, the latter being a non-rewind system allowing instant re-threading of a single projector. Extra time is necessary for the make-up and breakdown of the programme.

Specialised theatres having one-off programmes could still find it advantageous to install two 35 mm projectors, which was standard practice for many years.

Light sources

The various types of light source – tungsten-halogen, xenon or carbon arc* – have different requirements for power supply, ventilation and water cooling. The choice must be known in advance so that the right provision can be made.

* *Carbon arcs.* In the UK, carbon arcs are rapidly being replaced by xenon lamps. The advantages of the carbon arc lamp were the constant light output, its almost uniform light distribution and its good results when projecting colour films. The basic problem was that the carbons burned away during the process, and the products of combustion had to be carried away in ventilating ducts to the open air. The attention of a skilled projectionist was needed all the time to adjust the carbons if necessary, a process which did not lend itself easily to automatic control.

the outline of the picture is kept rectangular by placing black masking along its edges. For the standard aspect, ratio limits for deviation of the projector axis from the horizontal are 18° for 16 mm film and 15° for 35 mm. Distortion of the image can be corrected or reduced by tilting the screen from the vertical so that it is at right angles, or nearly so, to the projector axis. It is usual to tilt the screen to an angle equal to one half of the projector rake.

Wide screen

The human field of vision normally extends to a wider arc sideways than vertically. Increasing the magnification to the standard aspect ratio gives less value than enlarging the width of the picture. Thus aspect ratios of between 1.65 to 1 and 1.85 to 1 have been adopted since 1950. British Standard 2784: 1956, Aspect Ratios for 35 mm Motion Picture Films, gives 1.75 to 1 as an optimum for wide screens, but 1.85 to 1 is most commonly used. The proportions chosen will depend upon the structural shape of the particular auditorium and the type of film it is proposed to exhibit; for example, foreign language films usually call for 1.65 to 1 so that subtitles can be shown below the picture.

14:3. Screen aspect ratios

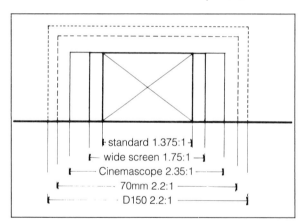

Mirror projection

If provision for film projection is included in the initial brief, it should be possible to include direct projection even if the primary use of the building is for live performances. But when converting an existing building, structural considerations may make ideal cinema conditions impossible. These difficulties have been overcome by using either rear projection or mirror systems or a combination of both. Mirror projection can only work if the light source is powerful enough and if the screen does not exceed 9 m (30 ft) in width. The advice of a specialist consultant should be sought.

Rear projection

Rear projection is not practicable for a large curved screen, but the system has certain advantages in small auditoria and in lecture halls. Direct rear pro-

jection involves a lateral reversal of the screen picture, unless specially adapted projectors and sound heads are used. Mirrors also reverse the picture, and where rear projection is to be used it is often an economy and convenient to introduce mirrors.

Projection suites

Projection suites may include a projection room, rewinding room, a dimmer and switch room, a work room and store, remote control room, a projection staff rest room and a lavatory. Unless automatic control equipment is installed, a projectionist must be on duty in the projection room whenever the projectors are in use.

A convenient size for a projection room containing basic equipment is 3 m × 4 m (10 ft × 13 ft). If additional equipment, such as a slide projector, large-screen video projector or follow spotlight, is included, the minimum size should be 5.5 m × 3.9 m (18 ft × 13 ft). The essential items are two projectors, sound amplifiers and controls. Ancillary equipment may include an effects lantern, video projection control and television monitors, a non-synchronous music desk (cassette player), a rewind bench, rectifiers and screen masking controls. Some of these may be in separate rooms.

Projectors are usually placed 1.5 m (5 ft) apart centre to centre, which leaves the projectionist about a metre (3 ft 3 in.) clear in which to work. Statutory regulations demand enough space round the projector and other equipment for the projectionist to work freely. The minimum clear space is 750 mm (2 ft 6 in.). A typical layout for the projection room is shown Figure 14:4. The follow spot, which may double as an effects lantern, is normally to the right of the projector and adjacent to non-synchronous music equipment and dimmer controls for the auditorium lighting. There should be an observation port close by.

Ports

The wall separating the projection room from the auditorium will have a projection port for each projector, an observation port for each projectionist and a port for an effects lantern. The projection and lantern ports are glazed with optical-quality glass, while the observation ports are fitted with plate or float glass. Cleaning is simplified if the glass is fitted into hinged metal frames. Where flammable films are used, all ports must be provided with fire shutters made from heavy-gauge sheet (3-mm (0.1-in.) steel) in steel guides and designed so that the shutters fall to cover the ports when released. The regulations require that fire shutters can be released both from within the projection room and from a position in the auditorium, usually at the back. Where non-flammable film is used, fire shutters are not required by regulations, but shutters or curtains of some kind should be provided to pre-

14:4. Typical
layout of projec-
tion suite.
Approximate
conversions:
500 = 20 in.;
750 = 30 in.;
1000 = 39 in.;
1200 = 4 ft;
1650 = 5 ft 5 in.,
2400 = 7 ft 11 in.;
4500 = 14 ft 9 in.;
8100 = 26 ft 6 in.

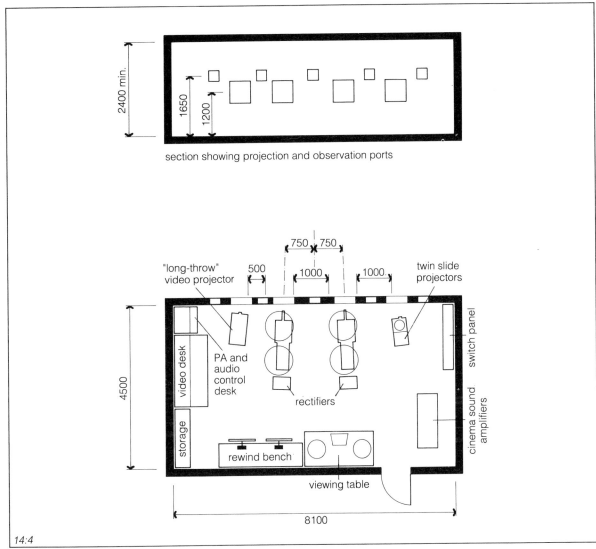

section showing projection and observation ports

14:4

vent stray light reaching the screen through the ports when they are not in use.

Amplifier racks

The position of the amplifier racks themselves is not critical, but the controls and changeover switches must be fitted between the projection ports unless a remote-control system is in use. The racks may be placed against side or rear walls of the projection rooms. Some types have to be pulled forward half a metre (20 in.) to gain access to wiring for maintenance or repairs. Figure 14:4 shows three amplifiers, which would be necessary for stereophonic sound reproduction; monophonic sound only requires one amplifier and a power pack.

Projector power supply

16 mm portable equipment needs only a domestic power socket outlet. For 35 mm equipment with arcs requiring up to 45 amps, a single-phase supply is sufficient; but above this, a three-phase supply is necessary.

Lighting

Lighting in projection rooms has to be arranged with care so that no light is accidentally spilled through the ports. Bracket fittings on the front wall of the room to the right of each projector, or narrow beam spotlights on adjustable arms suspended from the ceiling, are usually considered suitable.

Water supply

The old pulsed discharge lamps and 35 mm projectors with carbon arcs operating at more than 55 amps had to be water-cooled. A 15-mm (½-in.) diameter supply pipe and 20–25-mm (¾–1-in.) drainage pipe were installed, using water at a rate of between 5 and 10 litres (1–2 gallons) a minute, either from the mains or in a closed-circuit system. This required a tank of up to 700 litres (150 gallons) capacity and a circulating pump working at about 2 kg/cm^2 (30 lb./in.^{2}). As a precaution a stand-by pump was usually fitted. This type of equipment is no longer installed, but some old systems may be encountered.

Heating

Where non-flammable film is used, the temperature should not be allowed to fall below 10° C (50° F), especially when film is stored overnight. Electric heaters controlled by a thermostat are often used. A suitable temperature for working is 18° C (64° F), and heating must be provided to maintain it.

Ventilation

Projection rooms, rewinding rooms and lobbies connecting them must have a ventilation system entirely separate from the auditorium. Ventilation can be natural or mechanical, according to circumstances. Where carbon arcs were used, draughts could cause uneven burning and hence changes in light intensity during film projection. The ventilation should provide a steady volume of air at low velocity. Grilles both for input and extract of air must be provided separate from any skylights or windows. Regulations require that there shall be not less than 174 cm² (27 sq. in.) effective clear area per projector installed. The need for additional outlet ventilation for projectors equipped with carbon or xenon arc light sources has already been mentioned. It may connect directly with the open air by ductwork. If the route to the outside air is at all complicated, an extract fan will be needed at the end of the ducting. Access panels should be provided in the ductwork so that it can be cleaned along its full length.

Fire-fighting equipment

No special structural precautions other than those required under the building regulations are necessary where non-flammable film is used. In such cases the Home Office merely recommends that two 2-gallon (10-litre) soda acid or water gas-expelled extinguishers shall be provided. Where flammable film is used, a blanket of heavy wool or mineral fibre is required.

Rewinding room

When a reel of film has been shown it has to be rewound and stored for the next showing. Most 16 mm film projectors incorporate a mechanical rewinding device, but it is nevertheless better to rewind on a bench so that films can be inspected. Only when flammable films are used is a separate rewinding room required; otherwise rewinding space fitted with a bench can be provided within the projection room.

Rewinding benches

These are bench tops, 600 mm (2 ft) wide, at least 1200 mm (4 ft) long, and 600 mm (2 ft) high, with a small frosted glass panel set centrally and illuminated from below. This allows the film to be inspected as it passes between rewind heads fitted at each end of the bench. These are made to accommodate various sizes of spool and have to be suitable for the type of projection system in use. There are seven sizes of standard spools for 16 mm film, of which the largest is 600 mm (2 ft) in diameter, representing 55 minutes of showing time. Larger non-standard spools are sometimes used. Reels for 35 mm commercial showings have been described above (pp. 120–21). Rewind benches are used for splicing together a film which has been broken or torn. Close to the bench or underneath it there should be metal lockers fitted with divisions and spring-loaded, self-closing flaps.

Cinema screens

In the early days of the cinema a small picture was projected on to a flat, matt white screen with an aspect ratio of 1.375 to 1. This is still the usual practice for 8 mm and 16 mm films, but when large and wide screens are used, as with 35 mm and 70 mm, some important factors must be considered. With a large picture on a flat screen, the distance from the optical centre of the lens to the edge of the screen is appreciably greater than the distance from the lens to the screen centre. Either the outer parts of the projected pictures are out of focus when the middle is in focus, or vice versa. To keep the whole of the picture in focus, it becomes necessary to curve a large screen so that its surface is reasonably equidistant from the centre of the lens. The surface of the screen should really be part of a sphere, but that would be difficult and expensive to make. This is another reason why the standard aspect ratio of 1 to 1.375 has not been used for very large screens. A broader aspect ratio permits screens to be curved in one plane only.

Another important consideration is the amount of light available from projection light sources. Twofold to fourfold increases in areas of cinema screens have not been accompanied by equivalent increases in light output from these light sources. If the original type of matt white surface were used in such circumstances, picture luminance would be insufficient. Instead screens have a surface with partial specular reflection characteristics which give an increased luminance within a limited forward sector. It becomes necessary to curve the screen to provide a uniform distribution of the increased luminance, but the required curvature depends upon the reflection characteristics. The actual curvature adopted is a compromise between the needs for picture focus and uniform distribution of luminance in the auditorium seating area. This requires the advice of a specialist consultant.

Screen position

Screens are usually placed on the centre lines of auditoria and normal to them. In the case of curved screens, centre lines are normal to the chord of the screen arc. Screens may be tilted from the vertical plane according to the location of the projector, the type of auditorium and the system of projection. Masking is normally adjustable at the sides and sometimes at the top. This black serge masking contains the picture and obtains the maximum apparent brightness.

In auditoria designed for both stage performances and cinema exhibitions, many compromises are necessary. A flat picture screen up to 6 m (20 ft) long can be fitted in the proscenium opening in front of the safety curtain or main curtain. It can be housed on a roller in a wooden box set into the forestage and can be raised electrically or by hand. In such cases, retractable davits are used to support the top of the screen. Another position for housing the box is under the proscenium arch and hidden from view by a pelmet or valance. The screen is then lowered into position when required.

Variable masking is not practicable for these types of rolled screen. Curved screens, or those more than 6 m (20 ft) wide, have to be fitted on the stage behind the proscenium opening. Probably the best solution is to mount them on a rigid frame attached to one of the theatre's counterweight suspension sets. They tend to take up valuable flying space, especially if they are curved. There must be enough flying height under the grid to get the screen well clear of the proscenium. It is possible to hang a lighting spotbar underneath them, thus making use of hanging space which might otherwise be lost. An alternative is to move them away on castors, which is possible if there is plenty of room to manoeuvre without getting in the way of sets for live performances.

Another method is to use a screen frame traveller, as in Figure 14:6. This has the advantage that the screen is protected from damage when it is stored away, but it does require the whole of the stage to be cleared of scenery, props or furniture before the screen can be brought out.

14:5. Removal of screen by rolling or flying

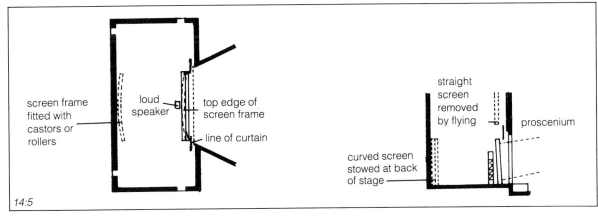

14:6. Removal of screen by screen frame traveller

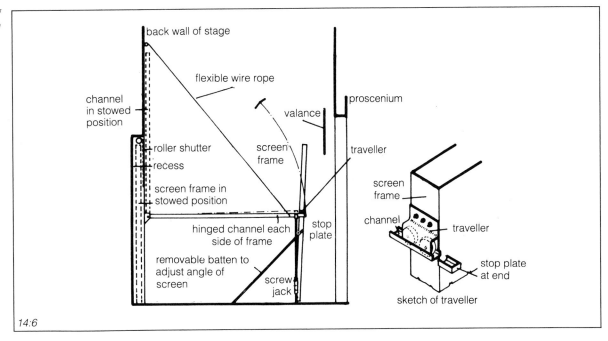

14:7. Construction of screen

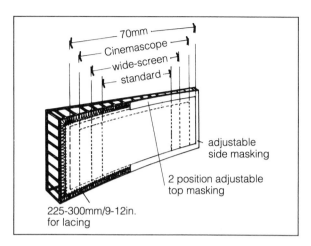

70mm
Cinemascope
wide-screen
standard

adjustable side masking

2 position adjustable top masking

225-300mm/9-12in. for lacing

Screen construction

Screens are generally made from a flame-resistant material such as pvc or metallised fabric, stretched into position by cord lacing to hooks on a special frame, usually made of steel or aluminium lattice construction. Such a screen can be free-standing, but lighter construction is possible when the frame is supported by brackets fixed to the rear wall, ceiling and floor. The size is determined by the largest type of picture that will be shown. To this an allowance must be added all round for fitting eyelets and lacing to prevent localised rucking of fabric when stretched. Screen frames are thus 500 to 1000 mm (20–40 in.) larger overall than the maximum size of picture. A further allowance has to be made when motorised variable masking is provided.

Screen surfaces deteriorate and have to be replaced from time to time. New rolled screens will be delivered in a roll which measures about 1 m (3 ft) in diameter and has a length of about 600 mm (2 ft) more than the height of the screen. These have to be manoeuvred into position without being bent. Masking is usually done with black wool serge fixed along the bottom edge of the screen, but carried on rails attached to the top and sides of the screen and adjusted by cables over pulleys connected to hand or electric controllers.

Screens mounted on stages

Stage screens should have the whole of the back, including the back and sides of loudspeakers, covered with heavy felt or mineral fibre cloth. Fore-stages should be carpeted with black carpet or heavy black felt to prevent reflection of sound or light. The stage should have some background heat to prevent condensation on screen and speakers. This also serves to prevent movement of warm air from the auditorium through the screen, which can cause deterioration.

Cinema auditoria

Satisfactory viewing conditions in a cinema depend upon each spectator having an unobstructed view of the whole of the screen without picture distortion. The size and position of a cinema screen must be related to the shape and rake of the auditorium floor.

Viewing conditions

Figures 14:8 and 14:9 show what are considered satisfactory viewing angles for 16 mm and 35 mm films. One geometrical limit which has already been mentioned is the angle between the centre line of the projector lens and the centre line normal to the screen. Other limitations depend upon the dimensions of the screen itself. The angle between the top of the screen and the eye level of the first spectator should not exceed 30° for 16 mm films. A committee set up by the Illuminating Engineering Society to consider "Eye-strain in Cinemas" recommended that the angle should not exceed 35° for 35 mm film, and this was adopted by the GLC and many other authorities as a condition for the grant of a cinematograph licence.

14:8. 16 mm projection

14:9. 35 mm projection

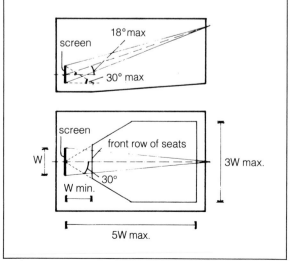

screen
18° max
30° max

screen
front row of seats
W
3W max.
30°
W min.
5W max.

screen
15° max.
35° max.

screen
2W
front row of seats
W
2W
25° min.
3W max.

14:8

14:9

The position of the closest and furthest seats from the screen are fixed in terms of the width of the screen, and the width of the seating area on plan is also limited by the width of the screen. The picture height should be at least one eighth of the viewing distance of the furthest member of the audience from the centre of the screen.

Where 70 mm film and various special wide-screen forms of projection are used, there are other dimensional limitations, but these are matters for a specialist.

Acoustics for films

The sound track of a film is complete in itself, and the ideal conditions for listening to it would be a direct sound untrammelled by any acoustic characteristics of the space in which it is played.

It is common for cinemas to be equipped with quite elaborate stereophonic sound systems, and these do not profit from any extra reverberation in the auditorium itself. The ideal cinema auditorium is acoustically dead. This is not possible to achieve in practice, but the low levels of reverberation that can be achieved give poor conditions for live performances. A theatre auditorium is not, therefore, ideal for showing films, though it probably has the advantage of a lower level of extraneous background noise than is usual in a cinema. The musical sound track of a film is there not only to underline the dramatic mood but also to drown the level of unwanted noise filtering in from outside and caused by the audience coming and going, eating popcorn and crushing plastic cartons.

Loudspeakers

In cinemas loudspeakers are usually housed behind the screen. For monophonic sound, only one speaker unit is required, but for multi-channel and stereophonic sound reproduction from 35 mm film, three units are used, with one on the centre line and the other two spaced equally on either side. Special wide-screen processes such as that produced by Dolby Laboratories can have more elaborate speaker systems, with up to five units behind the screen and others placed round the auditorium.

The typical cinema loudspeaker unit is usually much more powerful than any single unit in a theatre sound system. It comprises one horn or cone with a bass response and one or more responding to higher frequencies. Being both bulky and heavy it presents problems of storage and mobility in theatres where films alternate with stage performances. A space of 1400 mm (4 ft 8 in.) clear between the back surface of the screen and the back wall or any other obstacle on the stage is required. Best results are obtained when the speaker has a solid base such as a brick pier, but this is seldom possible in a movable system. The more massive the base, the less likely are sym-

pathetic vibrations at harmonic frequencies. Probably the best place to store the speaker is in the wings, but it is possible to have a trap in the stage through which the unit can be lowered to a storage place in the stage basement. This imposes a limitation on the use of the stage floor which may not be acceptable to the stage management. It is inconvenient to have to keep a central area of the stage clear of a stage cloth or any other covering.

Video projection

Provision for large-screen video projectors is now often required in theatres, particularly those that are used from time to time for conferences and commercial presentations. While the quality is far inferior to cine projection, the use of video projection is becoming more and more popular because it provides instant replay, can project live programmes from video cameras and can project "off air" from national broadcasting organisations or from cable television.

There are two distinct types of video projection: close range and large screen. The close-range types work on the principle of three electron tubes projecting a picture directly, and are suitable for pictures up to 3 m (10 ft) high. They are designed to be ceiling- or stand-mounted, with the lens level with either the top or the bottom of the screen. The projection distance is from 1.5 to 1.6 times the width of the picture. With such a short throw these projectors are not suitable for housing in projection rooms.

The large-screen-long-range type works on the principle of the oil-film reflective light valve, using conventional xenon light sources and focused optically through lenses. With these projectors the pictures can be up to 5.5 m (18 ft) in height. The Eidophor, General Electric Talaria or Laser Vision are units of this type. As they use high-power xenon light or lasers as their light sources, they should be operated subject to the technical regulations of the local authority. These more powerful types of equipment are best installed in the projection room. They are available with a selection of lenses to enable a suitable picture size to be obtained.

It is possible to programme video projections to eliminate image distortions such as keystoning. Room will be required for the control and back-up equipment for these projectors, consisting of racks to hold the VCR equipment, monitor screens, off-air tuners and other ancillary control units.

Most small lecture theatres or small cinemas can get an acceptable image by the use of the ceiling-mounted Hi-Beam, Barco, Sony or like types of units. All these systems have remote control so that the operation can be carried out from a booth.

Television systems have not yet been standardised throughout the world, and it is therefore important to ensure that all the video equipment is suitable for the standard adopted locally (PAL, SECAM or NTSC) by the national broadcasting organisation and any video tape sources.

Slide presentation

The use of dual-slide projectors with a dissolve unit has raised the potential of the amateur slide show to an art form. There are enthusiasts who devise quite elaborate programmes linked to a sound track on a magnetic tape of pre-recorded music, commentary or dialogue. The process of preparing a show of this nature is very much like editing and dubbing a sound track for a motion picture.

Slide presentations of this kind find commercial applications in advertising, and are used as an educational aid. They are rather more complicated to set up than an audio-visual show encapsulated in a video cassette, but the pictures are of a much higher resolution than can yet be achieved with video tape.

The most common use of slides is in lectures, where they do not need a highly sophisticated programme but do need to be under the remote control of the lecturer. The minimum is a single projector with standard remote control, but for better presentation two projectors with an electronic dissolve unit are recommended.

There are many patterns of slide projector, but the most commonly used is the carousel type, which can be used in either sequential or random-access modes. Smaller systems use projectors with tungsten-halogen lamps which are suitable for pictures up to about 2 m (6 ft 6 in.) in height or width, or up to 3 m (10 ft) if a very complete blackout can be achieved. The maximum throw distance is about 10 m (33 ft). The tungsten-halogen lamps can be dimmed with the normal thyristor dimmers. For larger pictures or longer projection throws, xenon projectors should be used, and they should be housed in a projection room. Dimming for the dissolve in this case has to be by a motorised shutter.

The screen format for slide shows should be square, because the slides may be projected either horizontally or vertically.

15

Control rooms

Demands for front-of-house control room space have steadily increased over the years. In Britain the first notable FOH lighting control position was installed at the London Palladium in 1941. Frederick Bentham's Light Console, an adaptation of a cinema organ keyboard providing remote control of motorised resistance dimmer banks, went into service in December of that year in full view of the audience at the right-hand end of the Palladium's grand tier. Over the following years, as resistance and autotransformer dimmers were replaced, remote lighting control technology developed and freed the operator from direct involvement with the dimming equipment. The question was now to decide the ideal location for the lighting control. A number of early installations experimented with converted auditorium boxes at stalls or circle level, but before long it was accepted that the best position for the lighting control desk is in a purpose-designed control room at the rear of the auditorium. Similarly, as sound mixing and reproduction technology evolved, it became the practice to have a sound control room also in a front-of-house location. In very small theatres the lighting and sound control rooms may sometimes be combined into one, but even in such cases the degree of compromise is generally unsatisfactory.

The third principal element of a control suite, the projection room, had already begun to make its appearance in some theatres from a much earlier date as managements realised the economic benefits of offering film shows on days when the theatre would otherwise be dark.

More recently there has been increased use of theatres and arts centres for conferences and conventions. When such events involve an international audience, simultaneous interpretation facilities become essential. Interpreters require sound-proofed booths with a good view of the speakers; a separate booth must be provided for each language being translated. In multi-purpose theatres equipped for conference use, a sensible provision is for four or six translator booths, although numbers of up to twelve are not unknown. Control room space is also needed for the conference technician who operates the microphone selection and switching keyboard, although interpreters normally key their own microphones in and out.

While on occasions a separate conference control room may be provided, the equipment can usually be accommodated in the sound control room. The systems of communication used in conference centres are discussed in Chapter 23.

Television outside broadcast companies appreciate the provision of one or more dedicated control, commentary or observation rooms, although these would generally be regarded as a luxury rather than an essential. Where provided, the design criteria applicable to translator booths would apply. Front-of-house stage manager control rooms are usually required in theatres with thrust stages and for theatre-in-the-round, and they have also been tried in more orthodox forms.

The architect needs an early decision from the client as to exactly how many control rooms should be allowed. There is a tendency towards excessive demands for space from technicians, and while they should be provided with good working conditions there is a danger of the control rooms becoming out of proportion to the size of the auditorium, which is, after all, where the paying customers are accommodated.

Control room location

In modern multi-usage theatres, control suites are usually sited at the rear of the auditorium and comprise a projection room on the central axis, flanked on one side by a lighting control room and on the other by a sound control room.

In a tiered auditorium, the rear of the stalls is the best location for the control rooms, provided that floor levels are arranged so that the operators' views and projected images are not obstructed by any member of the audience standing or sitting in front or by the structure of the building, such as the overhang of the balcony. If the overhang is deep, this requirement may force too big a gap between stalls and circle, affecting audience sightlines and splitting them into separate parts. To avoid a gap of this kind alternative positions at the rear of the circle or balcony should be considered. The design problem is to strike a balance between the provision of a good view for the technicians and for the audience.

All control rooms must be provided with observation windows allowing an unrestricted and undistorted view of the stage, wing to wing and floor to borders.

Control rooms, projection room and interpreters' booths also need to be provided with access from outside the auditorium, preferably separate from the public circulation. Doors giving direct access to the auditorium can be useful at rehearsal.

The lighting control room

The control room houses the stage-lighting console and the console operator, preferably with space for an assistant or the lighting designer, together with ancillary control panels, surfaces for the script and lighting plans, communications equipment and, if not provided more suitably elsewhere, space for storage and maintenance. Most modern memory lighting control consoles include integral electronic memory storage and data-processing crates containing printed circuit boards and power supplies. Some proprietary systems may require a separate free-standing 500-mm (20-in.) equipment rack, for which additional space must be allowed.

There should be easily accessible connections from the lighting control room to the stage, dimmer room, auditorium lighting bridges and slots, without having to go through the auditorium. The entrance door must be light-trapped to avoid light spill into the auditorium through the observation window and also to avoid disturbing the operator's dark adaptation.

The sound control room

While viewing requirements are identical to those of the lighting control room, listening requirements must also be considered. Although one or more monitor loudspeakers will be provided within the sound control room, it should also be possible for the control room window to be opened to permit the sound operator to hear direct live sound from the auditorium. The window should be a simple lift-out or sash unit but must provide at least 30dBA of acoustic isolation when closed.

The sound control room may require a higher degree of sound-proofing than other control rooms, as it will contain electro-mechanical equipment such as tape machines that are more noisy in operation than electronic controls and keyboards.

Equipment racks which do not require access during performances can better be located in a separate equipment room in the backstage area. This will include such items as paging equipment, communications system and power amplifiers and will reduce the amount of cabling necessary between these units and the loudspeakers they serve.

Auditorium sound mixing position

If the sound control room is off centre, under a low balcony or has only a small opening to the auditorium, then for use during concerts and musical productions, an additional mixing position should be provided at an approximately central position in the auditorium.

This should be located clear of any overhangs and be a distance at least the width of the proscenium or stage front out from the orchestra pit rail, or from the stage itself where there is no pit. It should be a flat area 3 m (10 ft) square, or an area which can be made flat by the installation of a temporary platform. It is an intrusive element, and as far as possible it should be located so that the presence of the equipment and the operator causes the minimum amount of disturbance and distraction to the audience. The correct location of the sound control positions is a vital factor in the sound quality perceived by the operator and therefore by the audience.

The projection room

Where a film projection room is included, the ques-

tion of its relation to the other control rooms must be considered. In general it is better for it to be separate, and fire precautions may make this essential. There are certain controls which will have to be duplicated in this case. The projectionist should, for example, be able to dim the auditorium lights and operate motorised curtain tracks and screen maskings without having to go into another room.

Design and layout of projection rooms are fully treated within Chapter 14 (Film projection), which also covers the subjects of projection angles and ports.

Translators' booths

Booths for a simultaneous interpretation system may be positioned at the rear or sides of an auditorium at stalls or balcony level. The booths should have unobstructed views of speakers, both on the stage and in the auditorium, and of any projection and information display screens; they should be located side by side and provided with small interconnecting windows to permit interpreters of different languages to communicate with one another. Acoustic isolation between booths is also important. Each one will normally accommodate two interpreters who will alternate duty periods, according to normal practice. For short periods during changeover, there may be three interpreters in the booth.

Table surfaces should be provided adjacent to the main observation window for mounting of interpreters' control panels, fitted with microphones, channel selection buttons and indication devices, as well as allowing plenty of space for texts, scripts and note pads. Each booth should also be provided with a loudspeaker with local volume control, although interpreters normally use headphones to listen to the floor language from which they are translating. Where the wiring is not a permanent installation, cable ducts and traps between all the rooms should be provided for the technicians to cable up.

Control room dimensions

The minimum dimensions of lighting and sound control rooms should be not less than 3 m × 2.5 m (10 ft × 8 ft), with ceiling height not less than 2.5 m (8 ft). Overall minimum floor area should not fall below 8 m^2 (85 ft^2), although figures of 10–12 m^2 (100–130 ft^2) are preferable. Projection rooms should be at least 4 m × 3 m (13 ft × 10 ft), or 5.5 m × 4 m (18 ft × 13 ft) if full facilities such as video projection and follow spots are to be included. Square rooms can have undesirable acoustical effects and should be avoided. In deciding control room size, allowance should be made for the amounts of equipment to be housed there; if separate rooms are to be provided for equipment, then control rooms may be smaller.

Minimum dimensions for translators' rooms for simultaneous interpretation should be 2.25 m × 1.7 m (7¼ ft × 5½ ft), with a floor area of say not less than 4 m² (45 ft²) per booth.

The observation window

The size of the control room window should be governed by the sightlines from the operator to the stage and to any equipment which he should be able to see. A typical size for a lighting control room window would be 2000 mm width × 1000 mm height (80 in. × 40 in.), i.e. an area of 2 m² (20 ft²). Sound specialists may insist on a minimum window area of 3 m² (32 ft²) for their control room. For uniformity and symmetry a compromise may have to be struck. During rehearsals the window often has to be open, but during performances it must provide good sound insulation. This can be achieved using 12-mm (0.4-in.) plate glass, or preferably by double-glazing designed for sound insulation, with 50 mm (2 in.) minimum gap between panes. Reflections of the illuminated part of a control board in the window may distract the operator, and on the auditorium side reflections of stage lighting can be a nuisance to performers. These can be eliminated by angling the glass. Tinted or one-way glass which affects the true colour or intensity of the operator's stage picture is entirely unacceptable.

Similar arrangements should apply to windows for translators' booths, except that it is not necessary for these to be openable, and minimum window area can be as low as 1 m² (10 ft²) provided the translator has adequate lines of sight to as much of the auditorium as possible.

Control room lighting and power

For lighting the control room itself, two distinct situations have to be met. During performances, localised illumination of the operational area of the control console is needed. Methods for adjusting the intensity and direction of this lighting must be provided. The placing of the performance lighting should be arranged to avoid reflections of the source in the observation window.

The second system should offer incandescent or fluorescent lighting of suitable intensity for plot writing, cleaning and maintenance.

Electrical power supplies will be needed in every control room for permanent or semi-permanent equipment and for portable maintenance equipment. Main and auxiliary control panels should each have independent radial power supply circuits from the local distribution board, with sufficient points for all the equipment likely to be connected. In the sound control room, separate supplies will be needed for each tape recorder, cassette player or record turntable, in addition to supplies for the main mixing console and equipment rack. Projection and lighting control rooms can also require several separate supplies. At least three general purpose 13 amp power sockets should be provided in each control room for tools and test equipment.

Ventilation

Since daylight must be excluded, control rooms must have silent dust-free ventilation, thermostatically controlled. It must not conduct noise or smells from other rooms or public areas, and must maintain a reasonable working temperature whenever the equipment is in use. There are advantages in providing a ventilation system totally separate from that for the auditorium.

Finishes

The floors, walls and ceiling of control rooms should be dark and non-reflective. A soft floor finish, such as a carpet, both absorbs sound and muffles it at source. The walls should also be lined with sound-absorbing materials.

Flexible cables will need protection. A false floor may simplify the positioning of equipment and improve the accessibility for alterations and maintenance. The manufacturers of lighting, sound and projection equipment will be able to give details of the positions of entry of control cables and access points required for maintenance.

16

Performers' accommodation and rehearsal space

Many of the older theatres were so poorly provided with accommodation for the cast that actors had to put up with near slum conditions which would hardly be tolerated in other industries. Most of the older buildings have been upgraded in recent years, and it is now in the fringe theatres that the most primitive conditions are found. Actors may have to spend long hours in their dressing rooms, not only during and between performances but also during rehearsals.

A distinction should be made between dressing rooms, used by actors and other performers for changing into costume and applying stage make-up, and changing rooms, for musicians and others who, for instance, change from outdoor clothes into evening dress. The scale of provision of dressing and changing room accommodation depends on the type of production and will range from one shared room for men and women to a complex including special rooms for stars, shared rooms for other performers, chorus rooms, musicians' rooms and rooms for conductors and soloists. It will be seen that the status of the performer tends to pro-

duce a hierarchical order in the arrangement of dressing rooms. This can be in conflict with the flexibility which is essential to meet the varying demands of different types of production. It is not economical to provide for the largest possible cast. In a theatre where most plays have an average of about ten actors, occasional large-scale productions may entail temporary dressing room arrangements, for example in a rehearsal room or a committee room.

The tables which follow give dressing room and changing room requirements for various types of production.

Opera house

This schedule is for a resident company producing a full repertoire of large-scale operas. Smaller-scale works can do with less, and if it is understood from the start that the productions cannot comfortably include the more extravagant works of Wagner, Richard Strauss etc., then accommodation can be reduced.

Table 16:1 Opera dressing rooms

Type of performer	Number	Occupancy of room	Remarks
Male principals	3	Single	Should be at stage level. At least one single room for each sex should have a piano, or there should be a performance practice room. These star dressing rooms should be planned to allow for visitors and dressers.
Female principals	3	Single	
Male minor principals	20	Up to 4	These rooms should, if possible, be at stage level. They would be allocated according to the size of cast, and though four occupants could be accommodated they would more usually have two or three.
Female minor principals	20	Up to 4	
Male chorus	36		It is an advantage if these large shared dressing rooms can be subdivided into smaller spaces if required.
Female chorus	36		
Extra chorus	48	Up to 20	
Male ballet dancers	10		
Female ballet dancers	10		
Male supernumeraries and actors	50		Make-up in these cases may be done by specialists in a separate room.
Female supernumeraries and actresses	12		
Children	20		The employment of children is governed by regulations. They have to be separated from other performers and will have to be accompanied by responsible adults. A separate WC must be set aside for their sole use.

Table 16:2 Ballet dressing rooms			
Type of performer	*Number*	*Occupancy of room*	*Remarks*
Male principals	3	Single	Should be at stage level, and it is desirable for them to have their own showers and lavatories. These star dressing rooms should be planned to allow for visitors and dressers.
Female principals	4	Single	
Soloists (male and female)	24	Up to 4	These rooms should, if possible, be at stage level. They would be allocated according to the size of the cast and would more usually have two or three occupants.
Male corps de ballet	25	Shared	The numbers will depend on the kind of company and the size of the stage.
Female corps de ballet	40	Shared	
Male supernumeraries	40	Shared	
Female supernumeraries	12	Shared	
Children	20		Children must be chaperoned, accommodated separately from the rest of the cast and have their own lavatories.

Table 16:3 Changing rooms for opera and ballet			
Type of performer	*Number*	*Occupancy of room*	*Remarks*
Conductors (visiting)	2	Single	The room should be large enough to accommodate a piano and an ensemble of six musicians for rehearsals. These rooms are for use during performances and rehearsals. A resident musical director would have separate accommodation.
Orchestra leader	1	Single	
Section leaders	6	Shared (2–4)	
Musicians	120		The sexes should be segregated, but as the proportions vary large rooms should be capable of subdivision.

Table 16:4 Variety, musicals, spectacles: changing rooms			
Type of performer	*Number*	*Occupancy of room*	*Remarks*
Conductor	1	Single	The room should be large enough to hold auditions.
Musicians	30	Shared	Divisible for male and female musicians, e.g. five rooms to take a maximum of six each.

Table 16:5   Variety, musicals, spectacles: dressing rooms

Type of performer	Number	Occupancy of room	Remarks
Principals	4	Single	Should be adaptable for two occupants.
Minor principals	30	Up to 6 per room	Capacities of rooms can be varied to take a maximum of 3 to 6 performers. As many as possible of the principals' and minor principals' rooms should be at stage level.
Chorus, dancers	60	Shared (up to 20)	The size of cast will vary with the size of the production, but this provision should be sufficient for the average maximum.
Children	Variable	They may be accommodated in one of the chorus rooms	Regulations for child performers require that they be separately accommodated and properly supervised.

Table 16:6   Drama: dressing rooms

Type of performer	Number	Occupancy of room	Remarks
Principals	2–6	Single or occasionally two	The principals and as many minor principals as possible should be at stage level. The allocation of dressing rooms will vary continually according to the scale of the production and they will only be fully occupied for large shows.
Minor principals	16–20	Shared (2, 3, 4, 5 or 6)	
Supporting cast	20–40	Shared (up to 15)	

An opera house taking only touring companies demands less space. The economics of touring large productions force such companies to limit their repertoires and the scale of presentation. The scale of operation of a theatre for drama depends very much upon the policy of the company using it. The figures in Table 16:6 would be adequate for most repertory theatres, but a specialised company like the National Theatre or the Royal Shakespeare Company, running several productions at the same time, would require more accommodation. Theatres mainly for amateurs do not need as much.

Changing rooms are not often needed when a theatre is used mainly for drama, but the programme for most theatres is bound to include the occasional musical production. For instance, most repertory theatres have an annual pantomime. Though this seldom calls for more than three or four musicians, a larger orchestra is occasionally desired, and a reasonable allowance would be a shared changing room for about fifteen musicians. It is preferable to have two rooms or a partition so that the sexes can be segregated, but if musical performances are rare it may be necessary to make temporary arrangements in one of the dressing rooms. Where they are regularly performed, the accommodation should be similar to that recommended for variety, musicals and spectacles in Table 16:4.

Dressing room equipment and layout

The most specialised function of a dressing room is putting on stage make-up, which has to be done in artificial light of similar quality to that used on stage. It does not follow, however, that all daylight must be excluded at all times. Actors often have to spend long hours in their dressing rooms during and between performances or rehearsals, and in addition to natural light and ventilation it is of great benefit psychologically for them to have contact with the outside world through a window. Blinds or curtains will cut out the daylight when they are making up. For applying stage make-up, each performer must be able to see head, shoulders and head-dress in the dressing room mirror while in a sitting position.

Table 16:7 Concerts: changing rooms

Type of performer	Number	Occupancy of room	Remarks
Conductors	2	Single	Piano and room to rehearse an ensemble. Lavatory and shower.
Soloists (instrumental and singers)	4–8	Single or twin	There should be a piano in at least one room. Lavatory and shower; provision for making-up.
Leader of orchestra	1	Single	
Section leaders	8	Shared	
Musicians	120	Shared	As the proportion of male to female musicians varies, there should be flexibility in the changing room provision, say, six holding twenty each.
Choristers	250	Shared	The sexes should be segregated and a flexible system adopted to allow for varied proportions.

Table 16:8 Recitals: changing rooms

Type of performer	Number	Occupancy of room	Remarks
Conductor	1	Single	There should be a piano in at least one room.
Soloists (instrumental)	2	Single	
Soloists (singers)	2	Single	
Musicians	40	Shared	For flexibility it should be possible to sub-divide larger rooms or provide several smaller ones which can be suitably allocated.

Hinged side mirrors are sometimes provided, but these lead to difficulties with the lighting, and most performers will have a hand mirror as part of their make-up kit. The make-up top itself should not project further than 450 mm (18 in.) from the face of the mirror, or the actor will be pushed too far away to see properly.

Dressing room lighting

Traditional dressing room lighting is bare tungsten bulbs ranged round the mirror, and this is still the most usual method. There should be a minimum of four lamps at each position (40 watt to avoid dazzle, but most actors insist on at least 60 watts to make up by). It is important that some light should come from above so that hairdos and wigs can be adjusted. Some special effects may depend on a particular colour of light on a particular colour of make-up, in which case a colour filter can be rigged up. Ordinary fluorescent lighting must not be used.

As an alternative to bare bulbs, or in addition to them, lights on flexible arms can be fitted to either side of the mirror. This has advantages of greater adjustability and helps to avoid glare. The fittings have to be robust to stand up to continuous use. In chorus rooms and where space is very limited a continuous run of mirrors with the bulbs above it may be used. Performers can be more closely spaced, but illumination from above alone is less effective than from all sides.

These dressing-table lights should not be the sole illumination in dressing rooms, and each position should be individually switched. When make-up is complete and actors want to relax it is a great advantage to be able to switch off the more dazzling lights.

Each dressing room should be provided with one long mirror so that performers can check their costume before leaving to make an entrance on the stage. Lighting should be arranged so that they are illuminated when standing in front of the mirror.

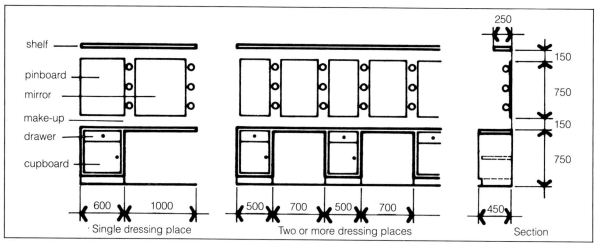

16:1. Approximate conversions:
150 = 6 in.;
250 = 10 in.;
450 = 18 in.;
500 = 20 in.;
600 = 2 ft;
700 = 2 ft 4 in.;
750 = 2 ft 6 in.;
1000 = 3 ft 3 in.

shelf
pinboard
mirror
make-up
drawer
cupboard

600 · 1000 · Single dressing place

500 · 700 · 500 · 700 · Two or more dressing places

250 · 150 · 750 · 150 · 750 · 450 · Section

Power sockets

Shaving sockets should be provided between each pair of dressing room positions.

The authorities have often frowned on ordinary power sockets in dressing rooms, largely because there has been a tendency to misuse them for plugging in electric fires and cooking equipment likely to cause a fire hazard. However, if the dressing rooms are properly heated and there is a green room where hot drinks can be prepared, these abuses are less likely. Power sockets are useful for hair driers and curlers and similar gadgets. They are also needed for vacuum cleaners for cleaning carpets and costumes.

Storage in dressing rooms

A small cupboard underneath the make-up top between each position is useful for personal possessions, and a drawer should also be included. Management policy may be for locks to be provided on these cupboards, but in many theatres there is a continual change-round of cast, and keys are easily lost or taken away by mistake. The stage-door keeper or someone on the stage management staff should have the responsibility for issuing and looking after keys.

Performers have to store their day clothes and any changes of costume for the production they are engaged in at the time. When they are performing in repertoire, they may have to keep costumes for more than one production, but it will be the policy of most wardrobes to store all costumes not currently being used in the wardrobe department or in storage bays off the circulation and not in the dressing rooms. Touring productions travel with costumes hanging on rails, and it should be possible to move these straight into the hanging cupboards in the dressing rooms. The fixed rail should therefore be high enough to clear the portable one. A minimum length of hanging rail of 600 mm (2 ft) should be provided for each performer, but double this where there are likely to be numerous changes and a repertoire of productions. In chorus dressing

16:2. Dressing room for four performers. Area 17.4 m² (187 sq. ft)

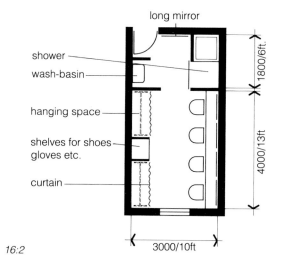

long mirror
shower
wash-basin
hanging space
shelves for shoes gloves etc.
curtain

16:2

1800/6ft.
4000/13ft
3000/10ft

16:3. Single dressing rooms. Area 14.4 m² (155 sq. ft)

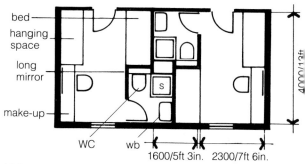

bed
hanging space
long mirror
make-up
WC   wb
1600/5ft 3in.   2300/7ft 6in.
4000/13ft

16:3

16:4. Single dressing room with provision for piano. Area 15.7 m² (169 sq. ft)

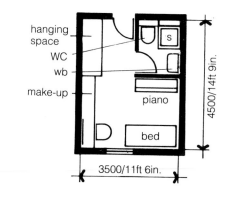

hanging space
WC
wb
make-up
piano
bed
3500/11ft 6in.
4500/14ft 9in.

16:4

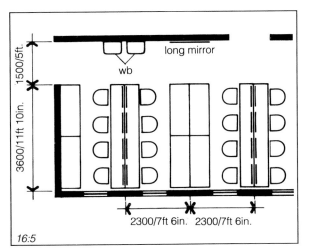

16:5. Communal dressing room. Area 8.3 m² (89 sq. ft) each bay

16:6. Section through hanging space

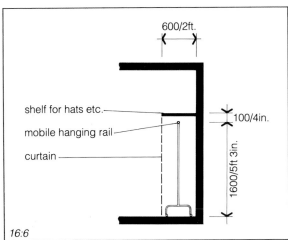

rooms the amount of fixed hanging rail can be reduced to 300 mm (12 in.) each.

A convenient method of temporary storage of costumes is on wheeled racks which can easily be moved to and from the wardrobe. It is best to hang all clothes and costumes on hangers, but for changing rooms coat hooks could be used instead.

Hats and wigs need a shelf, which can be over the dressing-table mirror or over the hanging rails, and boots and shoes should have a rack under the hanging space. Hooks at 1 m (3 ft 3 in.) height are useful for hanging swords and similar costume accessories.

Pinboards are an essential provision in dressing rooms for greetings telegrams and notices, which are very often put alongside make-up mirrors.

Furniture

Most dressing room furniture is built-in, but loose chairs will be needed. The most useful chair is an armless, upholstered, swivelling and adjustable type. It is desirable to make room for a day bed or sofa in some dressing rooms, or at least in the star dressing rooms. If there is no room for a bed, there should be some easy chairs in the other dressing rooms. The floor finish should be soft, for the comfort of bare feet and for quietness. Carpet is best, but soft-backed vinyl or similar materials might be used for economy. Waste-paper baskets are essential in every room, at least one to every two performers.

Washing and bathing

A wash-basin with hot and cold water should be provided in every dressing room holding up to four performers. In larger rooms there should be at least one per four positions. Basins should be large, with a splashback and mirror over and a towel rail within easy reach. They should not be set into the make-up top.

Showers should be provided on a similar scale to wash-basins, and the best arrangement is for these to open off the dressing rooms. However, for reasons of economy it may be preferred to group the showers together, at least for the larger dressing rooms. In this case, access from the dressing rooms must be easy.

Lavatories

Lavatories for the cast will normally be grouped together, but it is desirable to provide some dressing rooms with a private lavatory opening off a lobby. A star dressing room becomes something like an hotel room with its own small bathroom containing shower, wash-basin and WC. The scale of provision of lavatories for performers may be laid down by the local authority, but this minimum is seldom sufficient. As a guide, one WC should be provided for every five males. Each WC compartment should have a coat hook in it. Wash-basins should equal the number of WCs and urinals. There should be lavatories close to the entrance to the stage and for each sex on each level of dressing rooms.

Circulation

The most important circulation link for the dressing rooms is with the entrances to the stage. The best position is at stage level, close to the main entrance to the stage, and at least the principal rooms should be located there. Site limitations and the complications of fitting in many other essential parts of the building close to the stage make it unlikely that all the dressing rooms can be at stage level. Ideally, they should not be more than two floors up or down, and the vertical circulation should be close to the stage entrance. Performers do not usually accept passenger lifts as a means of reaching the stage. This is due to a fear of missing an entrance through being trapped if the lift breaks down. There are situations, particularly on restricted city sites, where valuable space could be saved at ground level and better conditions could be created for performers if the dressing rooms were to be located higher up, even over the fly tower. Passenger lifts would in this case be essential, but they would have to be exclusive to the dressing rooms, and their use would have to be carefully disciplined to ensure that they were never out of action during a performance.

Performers often have to go quickly from dressing room to stage wearing an elaborate costume. The doors through which they pass should not be less than 850 mm (34 in.) wide, and the corridor should not be less than 1500 mm (5 ft) wide to avoid encounters with other performers, similarly attired, going in the opposite direction. Corridors should not be less than 2400 mm (8 ft) high to allow for head-dresses. The designer must take care when choosing the ironmongery to avoid door handles which tend to catch in clothing and other hazards like the unprotected end of a hand-rail or a hose reel projecting from the wall. It is very likely that the corridors will have various pieces of equipment in them such as fire blankets, fire extinguishers and telephones. These must be recessed or situated where they do not encroach on the clear width of the circulation.

Entrances to stage

There should be a lobby between the stage and the route from the dressing rooms, to prevent light straying from one to the other. It should also be remembered that the human eye takes an appreciable time to accommodate from a brightly lit to a dimly lit area, and a sudden transition from one to the other may result in a few moments of temporary blindness. The lighting in the backstage area should, therefore, be contrived to reduce in intensity before the lobby to the stage is reached.

The lobby also acts as a sound lock, preventing noises from the dressing rooms filtering through to the stage. There are occasions when an actor listens for a cue before making an entrance through the door to the stage. This is more likely to occur in open stages where the doors may be in full view of the audience.

A long mirror placed near each stage entrance enables performers to make a last-minute check on their appearance.

There should be at least two entrances to the stage, one on either side, and in large theatres and opera houses there may be three or four. In opera houses a separate entrance for the chorus is sometimes necessary so that there is no danger of the principals getting tangled in the crowd. In the proscenium type of theatre a way round from one side of the stage to the other is essential. A corridor running round the back of the stage, possibly serving the dressing rooms at the same time, is the straightforward answer. Where space is limited, the crossover may have to be on the stage itself behind the set, and in this case the more depth of stage, the better. The disadvantage of the crossover on stage is that performers have to creep round as silently as possible in dim light, avoiding the obstacles such as stage braces and cables which are likely to be lying about. If they are close behind a backcloth or a cyclorama they may set it moving merely by the draught they cause.

In addition to entrances for performers at stage level, there are often others from under the stage through traps and at high level to a Juliet balcony. In open stages, and particularly in theatre-in-the-round, the actors come through the auditorium. They should have entrances segregated from the members of the audience to avoid clashes with latecomers or other straying spectators. These entrances must be on the same level as the stage or with an easy ramp in case props have to be rolled or wheeled on to the set. In any case it is very difficult to make a rapid entrance or exit which entails running up and down steps, and in the dim light often necessary for dramatic purposes, steps are a physical danger.

Specialist make-up room

Professional performers and most experienced amateurs will put on their own stage make-up, but children and novices have to be made up by specialists, who require a room in which to do their work. If this is a rare occurrence, probably one of the dressing rooms will be used, but when it is a regular procedure a room will be needed especially for this purpose. It is basically a dressing room, with mirrors and lighting, but with plenty of room for the make-up expert to move round the subject, rather like a barber round a barber's chair.

Hairdresser

Most elaborate hairstyles will be accomplished by wearing wigs, but there are times when a performer's own hair is used and needs to be dressed in a special way. It is therefore useful to have a room fitted out with hairdressers' equipment. While it will be used occasionally by the whole cast, it will probably serve mostly as an amenity for the female members of the company.

Children's dressing rooms

When there are children in the cast there are strict regulations about how they are to be treated. In the dressing rooms they have to be segregated from the adult members of the cast in separate rooms, where they are looked after by chaperons, and they must have lavatories for their exclusive use. Some managements may include a child supervisor on their staff who will need a small office with a desk, chairs and a filing cabinet.

Changing rooms

Many of the recommendations for dressing rooms apply equally to changing rooms without the emphasis on the arrangements for stage make-up. Single rooms for conductors, soloists and singers need a minimum area of about 10 m^2 (108 ft^2), but if an upright piano is to be accommodated this should be increased to 14 m^2 (150 ft^2). For communal changing rooms, a minimum of 1.5 m^2 (16 ft^2) should be allowed for each person.

Single rooms need a hanging cupboard for street clothes and top coats, a cupboard and drawer for personal possessions, a wash-basin with mirror over, a long mirror, a wide shelf – 600 mm (2 ft) – covered with something resilient like linoleum, for resting musical instruments, a table and chair (armless), a sofa and/or an easy chair. At least one single room in a concert hall or opera house should have a piano and be big enough to hold auditions or ensemble practice.

In shared rooms, each user needs a chair, hanging space and some table space. It may be worth considering lockers for clothes and personal possessions, particularly for resident companies. There should be a long mirror in each room and some other mirrors on a scale of one between two or three persons.

It is preferable for single rooms each to have their own WC and shower, but they may have to be grouped for economy. The shared rooms will have access to lavatories, and if possible to showers, though this is not essential.

Orchestra assembly area

The members of an orchestra should have an assembly area next to their entrance to the orchestra pit or concert platform, connected to it by a sound lobby which will also act as a fire check between the auditorium and backstage areas. It should have benches and a broad shelf for musical instruments.

The circulation of the orchestra musicians and choral singers should be segregated from that of the conductors and soloists. In an opera house, the conductor's changing room will be grouped with the dressing rooms of the principal singers rather than with the musicians, and it should be placed near to the stage.

Instrument store

The storage arrangements for musical instruments depend upon their size. The smaller ones will be looked after by individual musicians who will need in their changing rooms the broad shelves which have already been mentioned. The larger instruments and their cases should be stored near to the musicians' entry to the orchestra pit or concert platform. The route from the loading bay to this store should be direct and if possible without steps. Openings and corridors should be wide enough for a grand piano. If the piano does have to be taken to a different level, there must be a lift to move it. In theatres with a forestage convertible to an orchestra pit, the lift for this can be used, and a piano storeroom provided at basement level.

Green room

The green room is the performers' common room, rest room and canteen, where snacks and drinks can be served. For a small theatre one room of about 20 m^2 (220 ft^2) could serve all these purposes, while in an opera house playing in repertoire with a resident ballet company and orchestra, a separate dining room with a canteen kitchen, a bar, a lounge and a writing room should be provided. The scale of green room facilities depends on the policy of the management. In a repertory theatre the whole company, including performers, stage technicians and workshop staff, might use the same room. In another situation the stage staff would have their own common room and the musicians theirs. If the principals have well-equipped and spacious dressing rooms where they can entertain visitors, they are less likely to use the green room. In an opera house it is sometimes useful to have a separate green room for conductors and soloists.

As it is for the use of the actors during performances and rehearsals, the green room should be near the dressing rooms, the stage and the stage door. It must have daylight, and, if it can be arranged, a pleasant outlook helps to improve the atmosphere of relaxation which it is the main purpose of the green room to provide. The room should be furnished with easy chairs, coffee tables, sofas, some writing tables and chairs, a television set, and the floor should be carpeted. Refreshments should be available served from a counter on a self-service basis. A small kitchen with sink, cooker, refrigerator, and crockery and cutlery storage should be included. If the budget allows for the employment of someone responsible, alcoholic drinks can also be served, and there will have to be a lockable bar and store. In smaller organisations a vending machine for various kinds of hot drinks has the great advantage of saving staff time. In any case there must be some provision for serving hot drinks to the green room, dressing rooms and changing rooms.

The stage-door keeper

The entrance for artists and technicians to the backstage areas is normally supervised by the stage-door keeper, who has a small office strategically placed so that he can check and if necessary stop anyone coming through the stage door. For the artists he will receive mail and post it in a rack of pigeon holes, take messages and look after valuables. He probably keeps the keys on a keyboard, including those of the dressing rooms, rather in the manner of the chief porter at a hotel. He will take care of visitors, both wanted and unwanted. The usual planning arrangement is to have the doorkeeper's office with a counter open to a lobby just inside the stage door. The lobby acts as a sound lock between the outside and the corridor leading to dressing rooms and the stage. It also acts as a reception area, with a table and seats where visitors can wait. A noticeboard will be required in a prominent position just inside the stage door.

The stage doorman will usually receive outside telephone calls for the artists, with whom he is connected by extensions in the dressing rooms and green room.

Not all small theatres can justify the expense of a full-time stage-door keeper, in which case his duties have to be divided amongst the stage management. Outside telephone calls have to be made and received through a coin-operated call box situated in the dressing room area, preferably somewhere near the green room.

Rehearsal spaces

All types of production need space where they can be developed in rehearsal. The stage or platform will at times be used for this purpose, and final dress rehearsals must take place on the stage so that scenery and lighting technicians can practise their contribution to the show. In a busy theatre or opera house there will be great demands on the stage area and it will not be available long enough or at the right times for a continuous programme of rehearsals. Very often companies have to find space away from the theatre, a situation which can be expensive and is certainly inconvenient.

A rehearsal room is what we shall call a place where the whole company can prepare a drama or opera. Rehearsal studio is the term given to a space for the preparation of dance and ballet productions, and, like the rehearsal room, its dimensions must be related to the size of the stage upon which the production will eventually appear.

Spaces for the practice and tuition of speech, movement, music and singing need not be related to the size of the acting area. These we call practice studios.

Rehearsal rooms

For opera and drama the rehearsal room should be as big as the acting area of the stage, plus a margin of about 1 m (3 ft 3 in.) at the back and sides, and space of 2–3 m (6–10 ft) at the front for the director to have a broad view and for the performers to have some space into which they can project their performances. The height of the room should be related to the height above the stage floor which can be used by performers.

The rehearsal room should be close to the dressing rooms, and it is an advantage if it is also close to the stage and workshop. If, for example, a production involves rostra built on the stage, it is very useful if these can be moved into the rehearsal

room so that the actors can practise their moves in conditions closer to those they will find on the stage. For some, nothing short of a replica of the stage and all its equipment will suffice, but it is most unlikely that this can be economically justified.

Flexibility of use

More often than not a rehearsal room will have to serve other purposes. For instance, if it is to be used as a chorus dressing room it should have provision for make-up tops and mirrors in some portable or dual-purpose form. There should be wash-basins within easy reach and portable hanging rails for clothes and costumes. If it serves as a ballet practice room it should have a barre and some wall mirrors, as long as there is some means of covering these or hiding them away when they are not wanted.

A room the size of a rehearsal room has obvious potential for other activities, and it is most likely that it will be used for experimental productions to which the public will be admitted. If this is the case, a separate entrance accessible from outside will be needed, and the circulation of the public should be planned so as to avoid routes used by the actors.

If there is no easy connection with lavatories for the public in the main foyers, provision should be made for both sexes near the entrance to the rehearsal room.

A small stage-lighting system will be needed consisting of some lanterns suspended from a grid of 50 mm (2 in.) diameter tubes hung from the ceiling. The control can be of the simplest kind. A small sound system with speakers, amplifier with inputs for microphone, tape deck and turntable pick-up will normally be sufficient. It is best to house these controls in a cubicle off the main rehearsal room floor, preferably with a view over the heads of an audience. If it is known that the rehearsal room will serve regularly for public performances, the whole planning of the space must be considered in that light. (Small theatres and studios are discussed below in Chapter 22.)

The rehearsal room will be equipped with a piano, probably an upright. Chairs and one or two tables will be needed for the director and other technicians. A good deal of storage space is necessary to house all the equipment, which may otherwise clutter the floor while rehearsals are in progress. The room should be properly heated and ventilated, and noise levels must be kept low.

When the only use is for rehearsals it may be possible to get sufficient natural ventilation through windows, but for performances these have to be blacked out, and artificial ventilation becomes essential.

Orchestra and choir rehearsal

Whereas a rehearsal room for drama or opera

should have a flat floor, one for an orchestra, choir or opera house chorus should have rostra similar to a concert platform so that all musicians and singers have a clear view of the conductor or coach.

The size of an orchestral or choir rehearsal room depends upon the number of members who will be using it. Choir members need about 0.6 m² (6 ft²) each and orchestral players 1.1 m² (12 ft²). A grand piano is essential, and chairs and music stands should be provided.

Rehearsal studios

Rehearsal studios for dance and ballet productions have many requirements similar to those of rehearsal rooms for drama and opera. If anything they need more space round the acting area of the stage, and a height of about 4.5 m (15 ft). A sprung floor is essential. The walls require large areas of mirror up to a height of 2.4 m (8 ft), which can be curtained off on occasions, and a practice barre 300 mm (12 in.) from the wall and at a height of 1.2 m (4 ft). The studio should be furnished with a grand piano, a table and a few chairs.

Practice studios

Individuals or small groups may wish to practise or rehearse without needing the full dimensions of the acting area or the orchestral rostrum. For this purpose, practice studios or practice rooms, sized according to the number likely to use them, should be provided. They would be used for speech and movement practice, singing practice and by musicians, and often act as classrooms.

Finishes and lighting

All rehearsal spaces need good sound insulation to avoid disturbance both of and by rehearsals taking place in them. They should have a floor finish similar to that of the stage, but wall and ceiling finishes may need some sound absorbents to improve the acoustics.

Artificial lighting must give a high, evenly distributed illumination, but daylight should not be excluded. Some windows with a view outside have a psychological advantage, but wall space and a background which does not distract are essential. Most windows should, therefore, be at high level. Where a rehearsal room is used for performances before an audience, it must be possible to exclude all external light with light-proof blinds.

17

Performance organisation

In other chapters, various aspects of the technical working of a stage have been discussed, and many of these come within the "performance organisation", a title which indicates the group of activities which are involved in a live performance as distinct from those which are essentially part of the preparation for a performance.

In general these activities are under the control of the stage manager, and his task can be made easier by careful planning of the areas concerned. During a show, a rehearsed sequence of events is taking place depending on split-second timing not only by the performers themselves, but also by the technicians controlling lights, sound, stage machinery, curtains and scenery. Their duties often have to be performed in near darkness and as silently as possible. All entrances to the stage or technical spaces open to the auditorium must have adequate sound insulation. Doors should have solid cores and be provided with acoustic sealing strips all round. Where there is likely to be much coming and going during a performance, a lobby should be formed with doors at each end. There must be a very thorough sound insulation between any workshop and the stage. Metal roller shutters are inadequate, and purpose-designed sound-reducing doors should be provided.

The performance organisation should function independently without being interrupted by or interrupting the work of general preparation for other presentations. It is unwise, for instance, to put a paint frame on the stage where the scene painters can work only when there is no performance and only under difficulties when there is a rehearsal. For that matter there should be a rehearsal room for most of the early work on a future production, so that the current set need not be disturbed by rehearsals on the stage.

Compromises may be forced by economic restrictions and may be quite acceptable in small-scale schemes and where the main use is for amateurs. But a busy theatre working in repertory or repertoire needs to have its performance organisation independent of all activities not directly concerned with the actual performance.

Scene dock

There are also storage and maintenance spaces which should come within the performance organisation. The scene dock is the place for storage of scenery for the current production or repertoire of productions. The desirable size depends on the scale of productions and on the number of sets likely to be used in repertoire. Its clear height should allow for the highest pieces of scenery plus 500 mm (20 in.), or the same as the height under the fly gallery in theatres where this occurs. Storage space is always in demand, but the scene dock close to the stage is probably in a position where space is at a premium, and it is not sensible to use it for long-term storage. The most

economical use of the scene dock is for the current production or repertoire of productions, and the management should either be ruthless with old sets or, if they must be stored, should find somewhere less important to put them.

The connection between the stage and scene dock should be generously sized, going to the full, clear height, and wide enough for rostra, built pieces and boat trucks to be trundled through. 3 m (10 ft) wide would usually be sufficient, but circumstances may vary this. The fire authority will probably require a fire separation of the scene dock from the stage area and may also require an automatic smoke vent at high level, similar in detail to that over the stage tower.

The dock door

This is the place to mention the "get-in", which is the term used for the process of bringing scenery, lighing equipment, props and costumes on to the stage. There should be a route for all articulated vehicles with 12-m (40-ft) containers to approach the stage end of the building, where they can back up to a loading bay, preferably at tailboard height, and have their cargos discharged under cover. The association of petrol and diesel fuel with lorries may unduly attract the attention of the licensing authority and the fire brigade. In very large schemes it may be possible for lorries to drive right into the building, but it is more likely that loading and unloading will be through the dock door, either directly on to the stage or into the scene dock, whence it will be moved again to the stage. The dock door should be as high as the tallest item that will go into a pantechnicon plus 500 mm (20 in.), and the width should be 2–3 m (6–10 ft). A door such as this, opening straight on to the stage from outside, presents a noise hazard, and it must be carefully detailed to reduce sound penetration. Again, a roller shutter is not satisfactory. It is better to have a solid wood door with acoustic sealing strips all round, and, if the area at the rear is near a road or is likely to be noisy for any reason, some form of lobby, or two sets of doors with a substantial gap between them, should be considered.

Repair workshops

Minor repairs to the set during the run of a show can be carried out in a small workshop opening off the stage or the scene dock. Here the stage carpenter should have a bench and vice and storage space for tools, nails, screws, etc. In a touring theatre or a long-run theatre such as those in London's West End, where scenery is not made on the premises, this workshop has a greater importance and should be large enough to handle the biggest flats or built pieces that may be used. A repair and maintenance bench near the stage is useful in all theatres, but if the main workshops are in a close and convenient relation to the stage it is probably

*17:1. Perform-
ance spaces:
relation of
functions*

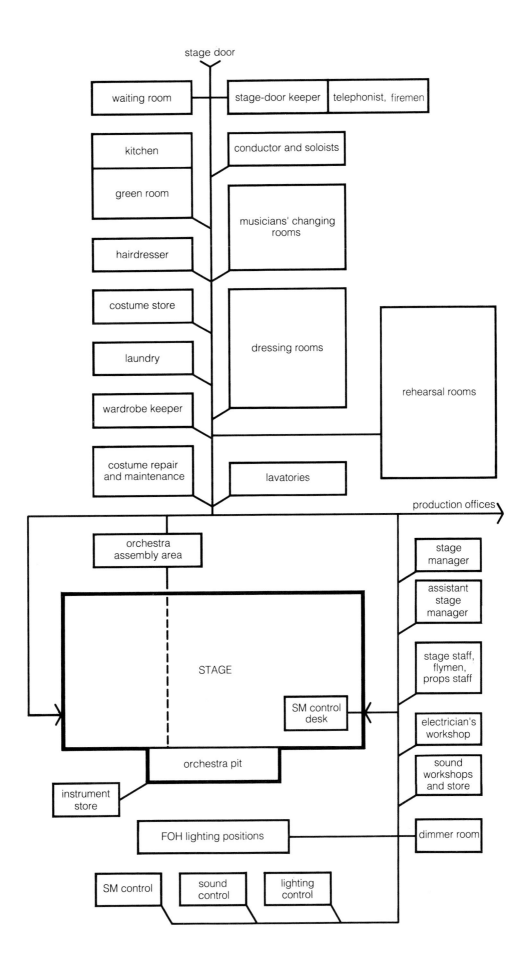

better for large pieces of scenery to be taken there for repairs.

Wardrobe repairs

A similar situation arises with the wardrobe. There should be provision for running repairs and minor alterations to be made to costumes in the current production. This activity comes within the performance organisation; it will be linked closely to the laundry and dressing rooms, and it is essential in all theatre, opera and ballet operations. Where productions are initiated and there is a costume-making workshop, it may at first appear that a separate wardrobe unit for the current show is not needed, but on further examination it may be found that the main workshops are not geared to cope with the sort of emergencies which occur during a performance. They may even be well enough organised for their staff to work from nine till five, rather than uncivilised theatrical hours. The wardrobe mistress should, therefore, have a small workshop with a sewing table, hanging space for costumes in the current production, racks for footwear, hats and accessories, an ironing board and space for the daily dressing of wigs and beards. The laundry should be alongside.

Property store

Properties are of two kinds, those which are part of the set, such as furniture, chairs, lamps, etc., and hand properties which are used by the actors as a part of the action of the play, such as a letter or a tray of food or drink. These are all the responsibility of the stage manager and his team. A property store, either opening directly off the stage near the control point (prompt corner) or close to the main actors' entrance to the stage, will be needed to lay out those hand properties which are essential to the action of the drama. Often food has to be eaten on stage and this will usually be prepared by an ASM, who needs a sink and small cooker either in or close to the property store. Larger pieces of furniture and set dressings will probably be stored in the wings if there is more than one setting in the production. For longer-term storage there should be a furniture and drapery store, but this is not really part of the performance organisation, any more than the property-making workshop and stores would be. In a large theatre there may be staff whose special task it is to look after and lay out props under the supervision of the stage management.

Electrician's workshop

The electrician's workshop is included in the performance organisation because it will be used directly in connection with the current production. Unless it is part of a large complex it is unlikely that there will be any other workshop on the premises

dealing with electrical work, and it must therefore cope with all the general maintenance and repair of lanterns and electrical equipment. It needs a workbench with metalwork vice and storage for tools. The electrician's duties as part of the performance organisation will influence the location of his workshop. It should open directly to the stage area, but not necessarily at floor level, where there is always a great demand for space. The majority of lanterns will be suspended above the floor, many of them on lighting galleries in the auditorium ceiling or in lighting slots reached from above, and it can be an advantage for the electrician's base to be near these. He should also be within easy reach of the dimmer room, where he may urgently need to replace a fuse at short notice. While quick access to these parts of the stage and auditorium complex is essential, the workshop itself ought to have daylight, if possible, and its connection with the quiet area should be well insulated against noise.

Theatres can collect a great many lanterns which begin to clutter up floor space if they are not put away in a store. The best way of keeping them is hanging them on lighting bars, i.e. 50-mm (2-in.) barrels. Another vital commodity which must be stored away, preferably under lock and key, is the stock of lamps or bulbs for all the stage-lighting equipment. The electrician will probably also be responsible for re-lamping the auditorium lights and the light fittings throughout the rest of the building, unless it is large enough to justify the employment of maintenance electricians. This store should have adjustable shelves to deal with all the various sizes of lamps and tubes which may be used. The electrician also needs hooks on which to hang the coils of flexible cable used for extensions to lanterns, and space for stands, clamps and other accessories. It may be useful to have small local stores close to areas where there is a high concentration of lighting equipment to keep lamps, fuses and luminaire accessories.

Smaller items such as the electrician's stock of colour filters should be found a place where they can be stored flat. They need an area 1300 mm × 650 mm (52 in. × 25 in.) of shelf or drawer, and a bench space of a similar area where they can be cut to shape.

The electrician will probably look after the pyrotechnics for theatrical effects, and for this he will need a secure and fire-proof store.

Sound store and workshop

Storage space and a workshop will be needed close to the stage area to keep and maintain speakers, speaker stands, microphones, cables and all the other impedimenta associated with stage sound. Space may also be needed for video equipment if it is used for production purposes. This is often packed in flight cases to protect it, and these too need storage space.

18

Production spaces

Areas for the activities described in the chapter on performance organisation will be needed in all places where live performances involving scenery and costumes are to be presented. Production spaces, on the other hand, are needed only where productions actually originate.

They do not have to be part of the building complex or even on the same site as the rest of the building, though there are obvious advantages when they are. Site conditions or the high cost of land within a city centre may bring economic pressures to bear on the location of what is, in effect, a light industrial activity. The production spaces are workshops manufacturing a range of specialised products. Their industrial nature should be understood, and they should be planned to make the process of manufacture as simple and efficient as possible. This objective is easiest to achieve outside urban areas, where there is plenty of space, rather than on a congested site in the centre of town. Workshops are generators of dust, fumes, noise; they are a fire risk and are subject to the requirements of the Health and Safety at Work Act. Including them within a theatre, where conditions of cleanliness, quiet and the minimum of fire risk are desirable, may be disproportionately difficult to achieve successfully. However, all the advantages of moving out may be outweighed by the cost of transport, the labour of loading and unloading, the need to employ extra staff and the time wasted in traffic delays.

There are some specialised items which will be made elsewhere or sub-contracted out for even the best-endowed companies. For instance, only the biggest organisations will make all their own wigs. The more that can be done under the control of the company's own designers, the more complete is the opportunity for artistic expression. It is very desirable to have the resources of elaborately equipped workshops at command, but it may be difficult to justify on economic grounds. Where an organisation has extensive production workshops, it will from time to time have capacity to spare, and it may be able to take on work for other companies. Very often it is worthwhile setting up a hire department, a useful and lucrative sideline, particularly for the wardrobe, whose stock of costumes will be in demand for amateur productions.

The first priority in the provision of production spaces must go to the workshop for building and painting scenery. Stage sets are often bulky, and they are expensive to move about and to store. Professional companies, and many amateurs, will expect to have a set tailored to their own conception of the show they are presenting and to the stage upon which they will present it. The opportunities of hiring sets which will be really suitable for a particular application are very limited. No serious theatrical enterprise can get along without having its own scenery specially made. There are excellent commercial firms who make scenery for new productions in the West End of London, for instance, though not many undertakings will be able to afford to employ them.

The situation with costumes is less restricting; they are easier to store, and there are theatrical costumiers who both make up to special design and hire out their stock. It is, nevertheless, desirable for a company both to design and make costumes to measure to suit its own actors, but for a short run this may be uneconomical. The demands of a particular production will influence the resources needed to fulfil them; for instance, some classic plays not only have a large cast but need several changes of costume for the principals. A series of such shows in repertoire will need a large wardrobe organisation to cope with the output required. Less ambitious enterprises will develop a pattern where some things are made and some hired.

When the brief for a new project is being drawn up, these are some of the arguments which must be thought out before company policy on the extent of the accommodation for production spaces can be decided. It may be necessary for management and architects to carry out feasibility studies to arrive at a reasonable conclusion.

Carpenters' workshop

The process of manufacture of a set begins when the designer presents his sketches, working drawings and model to the head of the carpenters' shop. The raw materials for the construction will be drawn from stores or ordered as necessary. The most commonly used will be timber framing and scenic canvas, as traditional flats are still the cheapest for stage scenery. Many other kinds of materials may be used provided they are sufficiently flame-proof.

Chapter 10 on scenery describes this in more detail. The frames will be made up on long carpenters' benches, canvas stretched over them and tacked down in the case of flats and plywood fixed to them for rostra. All kinds of special pieces, such as steps, doors and windows, fireplaces, etc., may have to be made in the carpenters' shop.

Assembly area

The various components of the set as they are made will pass, together with any suitable stock items, to an area where a trial assembly can be made. The dimensions of this depend upon the area a large set will occupy on the stage, and there must be sufficient height to clear the tallest flat.

It is useful to be able to fix blocks to the roof structure or even a few three- or four-line hemp or winch suspension sets, so that parts of the set which will be suspended can be dealt with in a similar manner for the trial assembly. The floor, preferably of timber construction, should be carefully levelled to make it easier to align the parts of the set which must fit accurately together.

There must always be an assembly area, but in smaller-scale schemes it may just be one end of the workshop or a clear space in the middle with the workbenches around the walls.

Workshop equipment

Carpenters' benches against the wall have easy access to power sockets for hand tools and wall racks; but for handling larger assemblies a bench with space all round it is more useful. Some of the larger woodworking machines must have a clear area in which to manoeuvre the pieces of timber

which are being shaped. Figures 18:1–4 give an indication of these requirements.

The workshop should be planned to accommodate the following machines, though the list is not exhaustive and special purposes may call for a different selection:

— circular saw; planer; band saw; mortiser; grindstone.

To work efficiently, the machines must be firmly bolted down on non-vibration mountings, and it would be unwise to plan a carpenters' shop on the assumption that they are easily portable.

18:1. Space requirements for woodworking machine

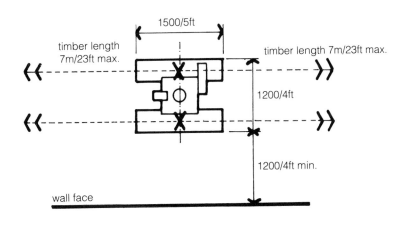

18:2. Space requirements for mortiser

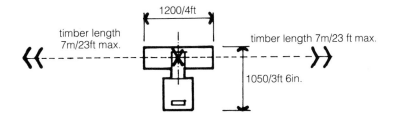

18:3. Space requirements for circular saw

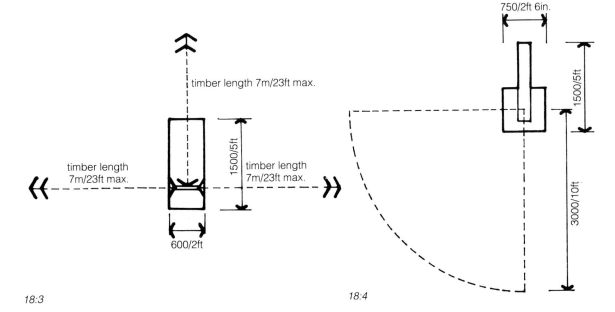

18:4. Space requirements for band saw

18:3   18:4

Electric power must be brought to the wood-working machines, some of which may need three-phase supplies. For most smaller workshops it is probably more economical to power the machinery with electricity, but for a larger workshop there is much to be said for pneumatic equipment. A mortiser, for instance, is much more efficient working on compressed air, because it is not necessary to keep removing the cutting head from the work in order to clear away wood shavings. Pneumatic nailers and staplers are very much quicker and more accurate than a man with a hammer. The canvasing of flats can be done far more rapidly than by traditional hand methods. Another important use for a compressor is paint spraying in the paintshop.

Dust extraction

Sawdust and shavings have to be cleared away, and for a busy workshop a dust-extraction plant should be installed. The system consists of extract points located close to the cutting blades of machines; sawdust will be carried away in metal trunking under the power of an extract fan to a discharge point, where it is collected in bags.

Heating

There is bound to be a certain amount of dust and sawdust in the atmosphere, and for this reason it is not advisable to use a warmed-air system of heating. Probably the most comfortable environment for working in is provided by radiant panels overhead. The workshop has to be high, and when the source is far enough away the unpleasant feeling of heat at head level, sometimes felt with low ceilings employing this form of heating, is avoided. Ordinary hot-water radiators are often used, but they take up valuable wall space. Piping and radiators should be sufficiently robust in positions where they could get knocked about. These remarks apply to cooler and temperate climates; the problems in hot countries will produce quite different answers.

Lighting

The walls of the workshop will sometimes be used to stack timber or pieces of scenery. Windows in them would be vulnerable and their existence restricting to workshop operation. There should be daylight, but it is better for this to come from rooflights or clerestory windows high up out of harm's way. The best light is north light, and if too much direct sunlight is allowed to penetrate there may be overheating problems in summertime. Artificial light should produce the intensity of illumination recommended for woodworking shops by the Chartered Institution of Building Services, which is from 200 to 250 lux. Fluorescent or metal halide fittings will produce this intensity most economically.

Finishes

Finishes in the workshop should be appropriate for industrial use: robust, easily cleaned and cheap. The surface which needs most thought is the floor. The importance of accurate levelling has already been stressed, and this can be achieved in various finishes. Scenery is made for a timber stage floor, and for that reason alone timber is a good choice. It can be made level, is fairly easily cleaned, fixings can be made into it, and it is not particularly tiring to work on. On the other hand it is fairly expensive compared to some industrial finishes such as asphalt, and its life in a workshop is limited.

The workshop should have a large sink with hot and cold water and a bench with a gas ring for heating glue and size. Timber storage may be in the workshop itself, or preferably separate, with easy access for long pieces of timber to the main workshop area.

Timber store

The maximum length of timber is not likely to exceed 7 m (23 ft), and a convenient method of storage is along a wall of this length on 50-mm (2-in.) galvanised tube cantilevered 900 mm (3 ft) from a wall at about 1200 mm (4 ft) centres. Rolls of canvas and other materials need shelves about one metre (3 ft 3 in.) deep. Sheet materials keep their shape better if they are laid flat, but they are easier to select if they are stacked upright; the latter method is more convenient if the turnover of material is fairly rapid. Nails, screws, ironmongery and various odds and ends can go on shelves or in cupboards and drawers. A large workshop may need a storekeeper's office.

Staff room

The workshop staff should have a rest room with space for coat hangers or preferably lockers. There should be lavatories and showers for both sexes. These staff rooms can be shared with other departments if they are not too far away but should not be mixed up with the performance organisation.

Paintshop

The process of preparation now takes the scenery to the paintshop for the scene painters to get to work on it. Other scenic elements such as backcloths and gauzes will be taken direct from a cloth store to the paintshop. The dimensions of the paintshop should be such that the built-up pieces of setting can easily be reached, but the item most critical to its size will be the largest backcloth that is likely to be used on the stage. Painted backcloths are quite common in the proscenium theatre and are an essential element in operas and ballet. Their size is related to the proscenium and to the depth of the stage, and this size in turn determines the dimensions of the paint frame. In Britain, the common practice is to paint backcloths in a vertical position suspended on a paint frame, but this is not the case in the rest of Europe, where it is more usual for painting to be carried out with the cloth laid out on the floor. Designers there, who often do the painting themselves, prefer this method, and it is one that should be considered if there is any likelihood of continental designers being invited to design sets. Paint can be built up more thickly on a horizontal surface and there is no fear of drips running down. However, this method demands a great deal of floor space, and where both budget and site area are restricted, economic factors favour a vertical method.

Paint frame

In a vertical position the problem of letting the painter get to all parts of the canvas, from top to bottom, can be solved in two ways. Either the painter remains on floor level and the frame is moved up and down in a slot in the floor to suit him; or the frame remains stationary and the painter is carried up and down on a bridge. There are advantages and disadvantages in both methods. Where the frame moves, the painter can at any time step back from his work to see the effect he has obtained, which is not recommended on a bridge. There has to be a slot in the floor so that the frame can sink far enough for a painter to reach the top of the backcloth, say 2 m (6½ ft) from the floor. The vertical dimension of the wall against which the paint frame moves must, therefore, be almost twice the height of the maximum size of the backcloth. If this is an outside wall without the rest of the building to brace and buttress it, construction could be expensive.

The pit into which the frame sinks should be accessible for cleaning and should have a drain so that cloths can be washed down.

The paint bridge travelling against a fixed frame is less convenient for painters, but does not involve the structural problems of a pit in the floor. It does have the advantage that high, bulky pieces of scenery which cannot be put on the frame can be painted from the other side of the bridge. One paint frame large enough to take the largest backcloth is sufficient for most operations, but where there is a heavy repertoire, and particularly in opera houses, it may be necessary to have several paint frames, though they would not all have to be full-size. Very often the painter is only concerned with painting flats; these can be done on a much smaller frame.

Paintshop equipment

The paintshop should be equipped with a large sink with hot and cold water for general use and a bench for preparing colours and cleaning tools. Gas rings will be needed, mounted on the bench or possibly in the form of a small cooker hotplate. Some of the paint will be applied with spray guns. If the workshop is already equipped with pneumatic tools, flexible airlines can be taken from the compressor plant to feed the spray guns; if not, small compressors will have to be connected to power sockets. When paint is brush-applied a useful accessory is a mobile palette, a trolley on castors holding colours, brushes, buckets and cloths which can be trundled around the paintshop. Scenery will eventually be seen on the stage under artificial stage lighting, and there should be a few lanterns in the paintshop which can be rigged up to give similar lighting conditions. Most painters, however, prefer to work by daylight when they can. An even north light from above is best, and direct sunlight should be avoided. The staff of the paintshop will share the facilities provided for the workshop. From the paintshop the set goes to the scene dock, and from there on to the stage.

The backcloth will be rolled and taken to the position on stage where it will be attached to suspension lines. A rolled cloth can easily be 15 m (50 ft) long, and it is important that the relation between the paintshop and the stage should be carefully planned to enable an object of this length to be moved on to the stage without it causing too much havoc by being swung about. Paint frames have been put at the back of the stage itself. This can sometimes be justified when there is a very deep stage, but the more usual reason in smaller projects is to economise. A busy stage used for shows and rehearsals, and perhaps cinema shows and recitals in between, will not leave the scene painters very much undisturbed time to do their work. In these situations the poor scenic artist usually has to work in the small hours of the morning.

18:5. Section through paint frame

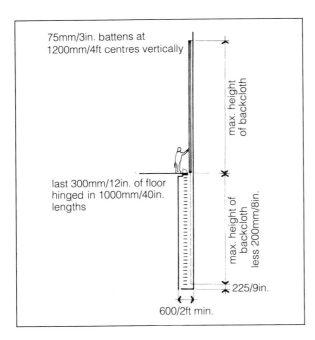

75mm/3in. battens at 1200mm/4ft centres vertically

max. height of backcloth

last 300mm/12in. of floor hinged in 1000mm/40in. lengths

max. height of backcloth less 200mm/8in.

225/9in.

600/2ft min.

It is far better to separate all workshop activities from the performance organisation. The fire authorities will probably insist on a two-hour fire barrier between workshops and stage, and in any case acoustic separation is essential. The workshop staff should be able to work normal hours without fear of interfering with anything happening on the stage.

Property workshop

Properties are defined in Chapter 10 (Scenery), p. 78. They may be made in a wide variety of materials such as wood, metal, plaster, fabrics, papier mâché, rubber and plastics, particularly polystyrene and glass-reinforced plastic (grp).

Properties made of wood can be made in the main workshop, especially where it is equipped with a lathe, band saw, etc. Smaller items do not, however, need the height of the main carpenters' workshop. A room with 3 m (10 ft) head height would be sufficient.

Equipment

Equipment should consist of a sink with hot and cold water, a gas ring and working benches along the walls. These should be 800 mm (32 in.) wide, and each working position should take up 1400 mm (4 ft 8 in.) run of bench. There should be socket outlets for hand tools and storage space on shelves and in drawers. Daylight and artificial light should be as recommended above for the carpenters' shop. If there is going to be a great deal of metal work, it is probably better to have a separate workshop. In recent years plastics have become more and more important, particularly expanded polystyrene, which can be carved into a variety of shapes very easily. Glass-reinforced plastic (grp), particularly in the form of polyester reinforced with fibreglass, has largely replaced metal for such things as helmets and armour. During manufacture this material gives off a vapour with a very unpleasant smell, and it should be given a well-ventilated room to itself.

Other techniques such as blow moulding of polystyrene sheet are also being introduced. The painting of properties will probably be carried out in the property workshop rather than the main paintshop, and it may be worth considering installing spray booths.

Storage of properties

The actual props being used in the current production will be in the property store, which is part of the performance organisation, but there is also a need for longer-term storage of properties, particularly if the company is performing in repertoire. Space must be provided for the following items: furniture, which will include tables, chairs, sofas and desks; carpets and stage cloths, which can be rolled and stored on long shelves cantilevered from the wall; crockery, glass, cutlery and similar small items, which are better put away in a cupboard, and spears, swords and other weapons, which are best hung in racks or from hooks.

A separate store is required for cloths, draperies and curtains, some of which may be quite bulky. Long shelves cantilevered from the wall are probably the best way of dealing with them.

Wardrobe

A distinction was drawn in the previous chapter between a wardrobe repairs workshop, where costume maintenance for the current production is carried out, making it part of the performance organisation, and the main manufacturing wardrobe, which will now be described.

Costume making is a manufacturing process which must be carried out in a proper sequence if it is to be efficient. In addition to cutting, sewing and fitting costumes, facilities should be provided for dyeing and painting cloth, for millinery, for making accessories, and even for making boots and shoes.

The designer's sketches are discussed in the supervisor's office, and a programme of work is decided. The actors' measurements are taken or checked with records, and paper patterns are cut out on a drafting table. This would be about 900 mm × 1800 mm (3 ft × 6 ft), and should have space all round it. The next stage is cutting the cloth, which is done at cutting tables 1200 mm × 1800–2400 mm (4 ft × 6–8 ft). These must have access all round, and there should be an allowance of 12–14 m^2 (130–150 ft^2) per table. During the rest of the process, tailors' dummies are used. These will be mobile, but a person working at one will need about 3–4 m^2 (30–40 ft^2) of floor space. Each sewing machine on its table, with a chair and a space round it, takes up about 1100 mm × 1100 mm (44 in. × 44 in.). It is unlikely that hand or foot-powered sewing machines will be used now, and 13 amp socket outlets should be allowed in a convenient position for each electric machine.

The general lighting should be reasonably bright, but it is a good idea to have adjustable lamps near each sewing machine to give the operator extra light where it is needed. Other tables for sewing and general use should be 750 mm × 1200 mm (2 ft 6 in. × 4 ft). Each of these with a chair needs about 5 or 6 m^2 (54–65 ft^2) of floor space. Ironing tables can be built in, but it is more common to find the portable domestic type. There should be a bench nearby for standing irons and equipment. Each ironing board needs 6 or 7 m^2 (65–75 ft^2). Another useful portable piece of equipment is a wheeled cabinet or trolley with shallow drawers for boxes of pins and needles, cotton reels, etc. The costume shop should have a sink and draining board with both hot and cold water laid on.

Storage

It is probably best to store raw materials for costume making in a separate room. Rolls of dress fabric are usually about 1 m (36 in.) wide, but curtain fabrics are more likely to be about 1300 mm (54 in.) wide. A system of deep pigeon holes or shelves can be used for bolts of cloth, and drawers or boxes on adjustable shelves are suitable for small supplies and haberdashery. Made-up costumes, while they are in the workshop, will be stored on hanging rails, which can be fixed or, more conveniently, mobile. Tubular hanging racks on castors can be used for storing costumes temporarily in the costume shop itself and for taking the completed clothes along to the dressing rooms. If there is a lift nearby, the hanging rails should be designed to go into it. It has been assumed that men's and women's costumes will be made up in the same area, but it may be necessary to have separate fitting rooms. Each of these should have an area of about 10 m^2 (110 ft^2) and be provided with a wall mirror in which a full-length view can be obtained.

Dye shop

A separate area is needed for dyeing and painting cloth for the costume shop. There will be a heated dyeing vat alongside a large sink, plumbed with both hot and cold water. The dyestuffs and acids will be stored on shelves or in cupboards and will be weighed out at a bench traditionally topped with marble. Colours for painting cloth will be mixed at another bench faced with laminated plastic. The colours should be stored nearby on shelves or in cupboards. Painting would be done on a plastic-topped bench or table with working space all round.

Drying room

A drying room should adjoin the dye shop. The wet cloth will here be draped over a drying rack, which can be made of steel tube, galvanised or plastic-covered. The tubes of the rack should be fitted at about head height at ½-m (20-in.) intervals, and each tube should be about 1½ m (5 ft) long. Moisture will drip on to the floor, which should be laid to fall to a floor gulley. A suitable floor finish such as asphalt should be chosen. The speed of drying will depend on a good circulation of warm dry air.

Millinery and accessories

Millinery work will need its own area for making and storage. Though related to the work in the costume shop it should have its own separate accommodation.

Making hats and accessories involves sewing by hand and machine, but other techniques such as grp, more appropriate to the property workshop,

are also employed. The work will usually be done seated at worktops about 750 mm (30 in.) wide, with about 1 m (40 in.) run for each person. Each position should have a drawer for tools and shelves for materials, hat-blocks and wig-blocks. The room should have a sink with hot and cold water and a bench with a gas ring. Each position should have access to a power socket outlet, and, in addition to a good overall illumination from both daylight and artificial light, individual adjustable lamps should be provided for each position. Floor space should be allowed for a sewing machine and ironing board. Cupboards or a small storeroom with adjustable shelves will be needed for fabrics, paints, glue, wire and the accumulation of raw materials which come into use for this work.

Wig maker

Wig making would require similar accommodation. Even if wigs are not made on the premises, there should be a well-ventilated store-room, fitted with 300 mm (12 in.) deep shelves, for storing them in boxes or on wig-blocks. Drying cabinets for damp wigs are also necessary.

Shoemaker

Boots and shoes are an important element in stage costumes, and some production organisations may include a separate shoemaker's workshop. Like the other work rooms it requires a bench, a sink with hot and cold water, good light (both natural and artificial), power sockets, storage drawers and cupboards for tools and materials and racks for the products.

Jeweller

Jewellery for the stage is most often hired from specialist firms, but if it is made by the company it will probably be done in a corner of the property workshop. The proper jeweller's bench is fixed at a height of about 1050 mm (42 in.) and has a semi-circular cut-out of about 450 mm (18 in.) diameter at each work position. Gas is needed for soldering, and there should be a sink and drainer with resistance to the acid which is used.

Armourer

A theatre with a classical repertoire will need a workshop for the manufacture and maintenance of swords, guns and other weapons. It should be equipped with welding, brazing, grinding and polishing machinery. Storage in the armoury should be particularly secure, and it is worth seeking advice on this from the crime prevention officer.

Storage of costumes

When describing the dressing rooms, the necess-

18:6. Production offices

18:7. Production spaces

ity for a place to store costumes for the current production was stressed. When they stay within the building, costumes are best hung on rails, either fixed or of the mobile rack type which has been mentioned already. When they are taken out of the building, to go on tour, for instance, they are traditionally packed in skeps (or skips), which are strong baskets, easily lifted and stacked by two people. Average dimensions are 900 mm × 650 mm × 650 mm (36 in. × 26 in. × 26 in.), and doors and corridors along the route they will take should be wide enough to let them pass. Skeps are usually moved about on trolleys, and if they have to travel between floors there should be a hoist big enough to take them. It is convenient to be able to load them on to lorries from a loading bay at tailboard height.

Dark room

Photography can be used extensively in stage settings, both in its own right and as an aid to scenery production. There is an increasing use of projected scenery as light sources become more efficient and more intense. Slide making will often involve photographic processes.

Publicity too relies to a great extent on photography, and it may be worthwhile setting up a photographic department with a proper dark room to cope with all the various demands that can arise. The extent of the accommodation depends on the scale of the enterprise and on the kind of equipment it is proposed to install. The most important provisions are ventilation, drainage and a plentiful supply of water.

Recording studio

From time to time a theatre company will want to record sound effects or music for use in a production. It may be possible to do this in the auditorium itself which is equipped with microphones and has a sound-control booth, but the acoustic conditions will not be suitable for many types of recording. A company can employ the services of a professional recording studio if the need is occasional, but where sound recording is going to be a regular activity it is worthwhile for it to have its own studio. The first essential is for this to have extremely good sound insulation separating it acoustically from the rest of the building. Approach to it should be through sound lobbies with acoustic seals round doors and sound absorbents on the walls.

The ventilation system must be as near silent as possible. The recording equipment should be in a control room separated from the studio by a double-glazed sound-insulating window. There is little point in suggesting sizes for recording studios, as these will depend entirely upon the scale of use which a company proposes. If the proposals are ambitious and likely to be elaborate, expert advice is essential.

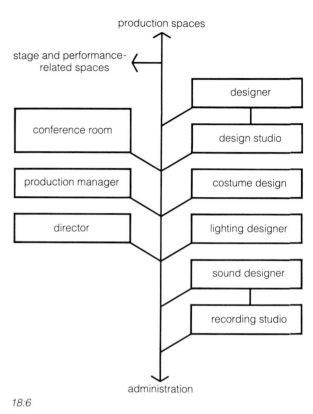

18:6

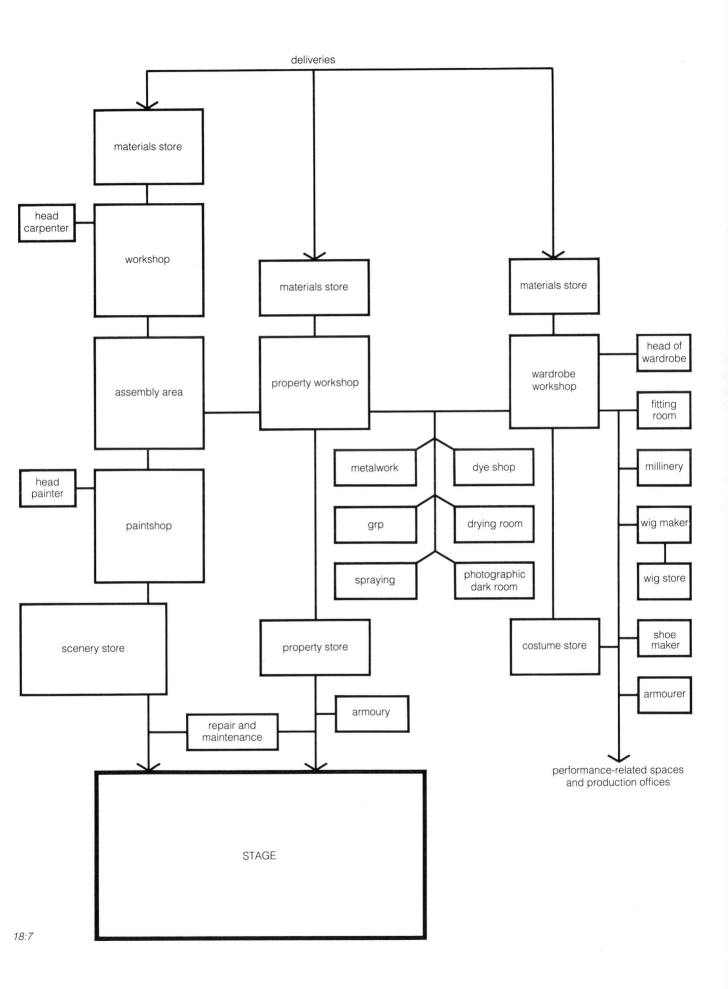

deliveries

materials store

head carpenter

workshop

assembly area

head painter

paintshop

scenery store

materials store

property workshop

metalwork

dye shop

grp

drying room

spraying

photographic dark room

property store

armoury

repair and maintenance

materials store

wardrobe workshop

head of wardrobe

fitting room

millinery

wig maker

wig store

costume store

shoe maker

armourer

performance-related spaces and production offices

STAGE

18:7

19

Public areas

Each age dictates the form of building it needs, and one would not expect theatres built for a world subsisting without films, television, motor cars and aeroplanes to be ideal in the late twentieth century. A very different society, with increasing leisure time and a range of staple entertainment on tap in almost every home, needs something of special interest to attract it away from its fireside, or rather teleside, armchairs. Fortunately electronic gadgets are still no substitute for the immediacy of being physically present at the moment of creation, nor can they provide social contacts with other people.

There are times when people go to the opera, theatre or concert hall as much to be seen as to see. In the cinema it is usually only the film premiere which attracts this kind of audience, but for theatre and opera house patrons the social occasion is often as attractive as the performance itself. This motivation is considered unworthy by some serious-minded persons, and it is true that there was a time when the social activity was clearly more important than the quality of the performance. A visit to a place of entertainment emphasised the stratified structure of society, and the building itself stressed the segregation of society into classes. Patrons would dress according to the variously privileged parts of the auditorium for which they had bought seats, and the entrances and foyers serving the different tiers of the auditorium would often not connect one with another. The Second World War finally ended the dress conventions, and informality became the rule: the average audience made a rather drab and colourless, if not shabby, impression. We are unlikely to return to the conventional evening dress of the past, but we can nevertheless expect people to dress up for the theatre from time to time, though not in the uniform of conformity.

There are still special cases where a theatre is

19:1. Foyer of the Wolsey Theatre, Ipswich

the setting for a state occasion; when for example a visiting dignitary is formally entertained to a performance of the opera. If this is included in the brief and VIPs are regularly to form part of the audience, the foyers may have to be designed to cope with additional security precautions, special entrances and anterooms, matters of protocol and accommodation for the security personnel. In the auditorium the traditional "royal box" is one answer to this situation, but it may also be necessary to provide for a number of VIPs who may have to be given seats wider than the average of 520 mm (20 in.), say 750 mm or a metre (30 or 40 in.).

As there is no shortage of "canned" entertainment in the home, one of the distinctive characteristics of a visit to a place of live entertainment should be a sense of occasion, and the public spaces where the audience assembles before a performance must provide a suitable setting for this. Foyers have to meet functional requirements, circulation must be easy and uncongested, but they should also create an atmosphere of anticipation and excitement. In the past this was achieved by buildings being dressed in formal architectural motifs with gilt and crystal decoration, an exact parallel to the evening dress and jewels worn by the audience. As society has changed, so has the attitude to both architecture and dress. The pendulum swung too far in the sixties and seventies, and the reaction to decorative excesses has produced some dull buildings which fail to provide a stimulating setting for the social aspects of attending a live performance.

Success in this respect depends upon the quality of the architecture, for which it is not possible to give a recipe here. The Modern Movement in architecture and the avant-garde of the theatre held the old Victorian and Edwardian theatres in contempt, and as they were often in commercially desirable locations in town centres, most of them have disappeared. They were no longer financially viable and had often acquired a run-down, tarnished image which did little to stimulate any defence by the public. Attitudes have changed in recent years; the virtues and hidden glories of some of these old buildings have been perceived, and there is now a strong lobby for their restoration and refurbishment as working theatres. This subject is dealt with in more detail in Chapter 24. However, the functional purposes of the public areas can be described here.

The foyer provides circulation routes for the audience to the various entry points into the auditorium and access to the cloakrooms and lavatories. In it the audience assembles and takes refreshment before the show and during intervals. The minimum space which should be allowed is 0.5 m² (5 sq. ft) for each seat in the auditorium; this excludes the areas required for lavatories, cloakrooms and vertical circulation. Where theatres have been built on restricted city-centre sites with high land values, there has been pressure to reduce foyer sizes in a way which the public find less and less acceptable in new buildings. In busy towns where there is a profusion of restaurants, pubs and bars, it may not be essential to provide these amenities within the theatre building itself, but in smaller places there may be nowhere to get a meal after the show (or before it, for that matter). Theatregoers expect to find refreshment facilities at the theatre, and even cinemas now provide licensed bars for their patrons. Probably the strongest argument for providing food and drink is that these departments make a profit, whereas the live performance itself almost invariably requires a subsidy.

If the use of the public spaces is to extend beyond the circulation of an audience for particular performances, then the space allowance may have to be increased. Foyers will have places designed for the display of posters, photographs and details of current productions, and it is an easy step to extend this to provide an area where exhibitions can be mounted. This can be open to the rest of the foyer for most exhibitions, but if it is intended to display precious or rare objects it may be necessary to provide a separate gallery where there is a check on the security of the exhibits. The licensing authorities may have additional requirements if a foyer space is to be used for purposes other than as an ancillary area to an auditorium.

Wherever the exhibition space is situated, it will need a flexible system of display lighting which can easily be adapted for a new layout without trailing wires across the floor. This is often done by providing permanent display lighting tracks in the ceiling, walls or columns. Once upon a time, the only information required by a gallery to prepare for hanging a painting would be its dimensions. Exhibits nowadays quite often require electric power to drive them or for internal lighting, and exhibition areas should therefore be liberally provided with electrical points.

The foyer can provide an attractive setting for dancing, but this is one activity it is difficult to provide for while performances are being given in the auditorium. When such functions are held there will again be a demand for power sockets, even an elaborate lighting rig, and it is always good policy to provide a substantial electricity supply and a network of microphone and speaker cables in foyer areas if they are to be truly flexible in use.

Access for the disabled

In Britain various acts have been passed in recent years making it obligatory to provide access to places of entertainment for the disabled, including people in wheelchairs. The Building Regulations (Fourth Amendment), 1985, now require a minimum of six spaces, or one hundredth of the total audience capacity, whichever is the greater, for wheelchairs.

In the past, licensing authorities and fire officers have been less than enthusiastic about wheelchairs in escape routes, and even when the physical provisions in the building have been designed in by the architect there has been reluctance on the part of the local authority to permit their full use. This attitude has been changed by the new Building Regulation, but the problem of wheelchairs possibly blocking escape routes is a real one and should be taken into account when planning the building. Provisions for the disabled are set out in British Standard 5810, Code of Practice for Access for the Disabled to Buildings, 1979.

The essentials are that a person in a wheelchair should be able to enter any of the public parts of the building without having to negotiate any steps. Changes in level can be joined by ramps, providing the slope does not exceed 1 in 12, and providing there is a flat section at the top of the ramp. If the vertical circulation is greater than can be accommodated by a ramp, there must be a lift large enough to take a wheelchair and attendant. In a place of entertainment, corridors and door openings will already be wide enough if they conform to the normal regulations. For the ambulant disabled not confined to wheelchairs, staircases will be sufficiently easy going, and the necessary handrails will have been provided.

In the auditorium itself, it is much more satisfactory to set aside a special area for wheelchairs and their attendants than to expect the disabled to be transferred to ordinary auditorium seats. Degrees of disability vary, and for some this might not be too difficult, but many problems then arise with storing the chair, retrieving it after the performance, and obstructing the movement of the more fortunate fit. It is far better for the disabled to remain in their wheelchairs in a special position with a level floor. Given their own entrance to the auditorium they are not in danger of blocking the circulation of other members of the audience; but this cannot always be done, and if the disabled do share the exits with the rest, the rules of management will probably insist that they and their attendants stay put until the last of the audience has left the auditorium. The management's emergency routine will have to include action to be taken when wheelchairs are present. If a lift is to be used as a means of escape, it will be necessary to provide it with a method of operation independent of the electrical system, probably a manual one.

The disabled must have a lavatory designed specially for their use, with the necessary space for a wheelchair, grab rails, a wash-basin reachable from the seat, and an outward opening door. One such lavatory usable by both sexes is sufficient, as the number of chairbound people attending at one time is unlikely to be very great. A more generous approach is to provide a specially designed cubicle within each group of lavatories, but when the chairbound person is accompanied by someone of the opposite sex an independent lavatory for the disabled is still needed. The licensing authority will probably set a limit to the number of people in

wheelchairs permitted to be present at any one performance. For a very full and detailed description of their requirements the reader is recommended to refer to *Designing for the Disabled* by Selwyn Goldsmith, published by the Royal Institute of British Architects.

Deaf aids

Another common form of disability which spoils many people's enjoyment of an entertainment is deafness. A person with poor hearing who benefits from using a hearing-aid can be helped: the systems have been described in Chapter 13 (Communications). They have in common a microphone or microphones which pick up the sound of the performance (these can be the same as those used for the show relay system to dressing rooms and other backstage spaces). The signal is amplified, and it is the methods of reaching the individual in the audience which differ from then on.

Certain places in the auditorium can be wired to sockets, which can have a headset plugged in. The individual earpieces can be provided with a volume control. The great disadvantage of this system is that unless every seat is wired for sound, which is an expensive business, there will be administrative complications at the box office. If the special seats are held back in case a deaf person turns up, sales may be lost; if they are not, they may all be sold to people who do not need an aid before a deaf person asks for one.

If a small radio transmitter is used, with receivers and earphones available for hire at the box office, the system can be extended to include simultaneous translation and can therefore be accommodated economically in theatres where international conferences are anticipated. The radio signal can be picked up anywhere in the auditorium without elaborate permanent wiring or trailing temporary flexes. The disadvantages in this case are the administration expenses of issuing and collecting the receivers and the problems of maintaining them, bearing in mind the rough treatment they are likely to get. A radio loop may be installed as an intercom for the stage management, and it is possible to extend the system on another broadcast wavelength to include a transmission for radio hearing-aids or on several channels for simultaneous interpretation.

The cheapest method is the induction loop. Most hearing-aids contain an induction coil which will be activated by the field set up about this wire. The system is cheap to install and has the advantage that most people will be able to use their own hearing-aid. A few receivers can be kept at the box office for loan or hire to those not so equipped.

In the UK, permission to use this or a radio system must be obtained from the Department of Trade and Industry at the address given in Chapter 12, p. 106.

Outlook

The question of taking advantage of the outlook from the site is worth discussing in general. The auditorium and stage are entirely inward-looking spaces, sealed from contact with the outside world. The foyers on the other hand may, if the site is a good one, have opportunities of splendid views over parks or city squares, tempting the architect to introduce vast glazed walls. Assuming this can be successfully done, care should be taken to see that the audience is not dazzled by direct sunlight on emerging from the dim light of the auditorium. The glare from too bright a foyer also has the reverse effect of making it more difficult for people to adjust to the gloom as they enter the auditorium. This matter has been referred to when discussing artificial lighting, but not all performances take place after dark, and the effects of daylight in foyers should also be anticipated. At night a large glass wall to the foyer is probably more effective from outside than from inside. Seeing the pattern of artificial light within the building and people moving about from one level to another can be very attractive and a good advertisement. From inside a large uninterrupted dark area of glass can be rather forbidding, especially on a wet and stormy night. In practice the glass acts as a mirror after dark, and the view is mostly of the foyer lights reflected in it.

If the outlook is the most important feature of the foyers then it should be as interesting at night as during the day. When there is not enough street lighting it might be worthwhile floodlighting trees or a building nearby. In any case, even with the finest view it is not imperative to have a wall of glass to appreciate it, and there are many disadvantages of large, badly insulated glazed areas which cause either excessive heat losses or solar gains, and place a heavy load on the heating and ventilating plant. They are also often difficult and expensive to keep clean.

Another way of exploiting good views and a sunny aspect is to provide outside terraces which can be opened up to the foyers. At the Sydney Opera House the effect is particularly splendid; in places where the climate is less kind, the number of days in the year when this would be possible casts doubt on its value.

Entrance

The location of the main public entrance to the theatre depends on site conditions. Needless to say, the position chosen should be a prominent one, easily recognised by strangers making their first visit. There should be a canopy over the entrance to protect those arriving, and it is an advantage to extend this to a porte cochère where people may alight from cars, taxis or coaches under cover. All this area should be brightly illuminated, and there should be a display of publicity material, including posters, photographs and cast lists.

The theatre entrance may have to compete with shop displays, and it is particularly important that it should hold its own with its advertising material at all times of day, not just when it is open for performances in the evening. The main entrance doors should not open directly into the foyer or they will let in draughts or street noises every time they are used. There should be a lobby with double-swing self-closing doors at either end. Some situations may allow this to be enlarged to form a waiting area or a place for the box office.

More than one main entrance for the public should be avoided, as it leads to confusion for visitors and the expense of additional staff, duplication of security and public information.

Foyers

Inside the foyer the routes to the entrances to the various parts and levels of the auditorium should be clear and easily appreciated without too great a reliance on signposting. There will have to be notices, but where the routes arise naturally from the layout of the building, results are more satisfactory.

Entrances to auditorium

Means of escape regulations will determine a minimum number of exits from the auditorium, and from the point of view of the licensing authority there is no reason why more than one of these for each tier should connect with the foyers. On the other hand, circulation can be freer if several entrances to the auditorium are used. Members of the audience do not wish to find that they have unwittingly chosen an exit which takes them right out of the building before they have had a chance to retrieve their coats from the cloakroom, or if all they want is a drink during the interval. Fire separation between alternative means of escape must be maintained, but if at the same time a connection with the foyers can be contrived for each escape route, better use is made of the building.

The disadvantages of having a lot of entrances to the auditorium are the number of stewards needed to check tickets and the possibility of confusion in the public about which entrance they should choose. This is where clear signposting, closely related to an equally clear indication on the ticket, is important. Unified graphic design here serves a practical purpose – though it hardly needs any such justification.

Acoustic separation

All connections between foyer and auditorium should have acoustic treatment in the form of a lobby with doors at each end provided with acoustic sealing strips. Only with these precautions carefully observed can any activity continue in the foyers while a performance is in progress.

Latecomers

The attention of the audience must not be distracted by external noise, which can be kept at bay by careful design and detailing; but their own members can cause worse disturbance by coming late. There was a time when it was alleged that dramatists never put any dialogue or plot that mattered into the first twenty minutes of the play, to allow the more ostentatious latecomers time to arrive and settle down. Nowadays if people are late they are very often not allowed into the auditorium until an interval. There are less severe remedies, such as providing a special place with a viewing window to the auditorium and a relay through a loudspeaker, or installing a closed-circuit television monitor somewhere in the foyer where the show can be watched until there is an opportunity for the transgressors to creep to their seats without disturbing the virtuously punctual.

Public telephones

There should be coin-operated telephones for the public in the foyers. Quieter positions off the main circulation routes should be chosen, and it may be considered necessary to provide them with acoustic cowls or separate kiosks.

Cloakrooms

The cloakrooms and lavatories should also be closely related to visitors' natural routes. They must be placed so that queues which may form do not interfere with the flow of people through the building. The ideal situation is for these facilities to be on such a scale that queues never form, but this is very difficult to achieve with reasonable economy. By the very nature of the use of the building there are bound to be short periods of intense demand and relative idleness the rest of the time. This applies to all the front-of-house facilities: cloakrooms, lavatories, bars and refreshment counters. In the case of the cloakroom, for instance, an audience arrives over a period of fifteen to twenty minutes before a performance, but will expect to retrieve its coats and umbrellas at the end of the show within a fraction of this time. Where cloakrooms are attended there is a limit to the number of coats each attendant can deal with in a given time. For example, if it takes six seconds to retrieve and hand out one coat, each attendant can deal with fifty coats in five minutes and it would take ten attendants to cope with 500 coats in that time; or five attendants would take ten minutes.

These figures are if anything optimistic, and many people are not prepared to wait more than two or three minutes for their coats. In Britain, this is

probably why it is rare for more than one third of an audience to part with their outer garments. Another reason is the unreliability of the heating arrangements in many buildings. As standards of heating and ventilation improve, more people will expect to be able to divest themselves of overcoats, provided they know they are not going to suffer irritating delays in getting their belongings back. Attended systems can only be efficient if enough staff are employed, and this is expensive. Management policy can improve efficiency, for instance by switching the stewards to the cloakroom counter at the end of the performance. The alternative is some form of self-service where each individual is responsible for depositing and retrieving his or her own coat.

In clubs and smaller amateur organisations, security may not be very important, and it may be quite satisfactory for coats to be left unattended on a hook or hanger. This system has been used on quite a big scale outside the British Isles. A coat hanger is allotted to each seat in the auditorium and carries the same number. Buying a ticket entitles one to a particular seat and a particular coat hanger.

The British, it seems, are less trusting, or possibly less trustworthy, and they are not usually prepared to part with their possessions without some assurance of security. This is normally provided by the attendant, but self-service arrangements can be equally secure. One solution is to provide lockers with keys. These can be coin-operated, as at railway stations, or free. Their disadvantage is that they are expensive and space-consuming. Another method is the tethered hanger. This consists of a hanger fixed to a coat rack frame upon which the coat is hung in the usual way. Each hanger has a chain attached to it which is passed through the sleeve of the coat and locked off on a rail in the front of the rack. The special lock is designed to secure an umbrella at the same time. The user withdraws the numbered key and pockets it until he wishes to release his coat. It is a good system so long as people don't take the keys away, either absent-mindedly or maliciously. This system is marketed by Lock Systems Limited under the name of Paralok.

Some licensing authorities have been reluctant to permit self-service cloakroom arrangements because of the danger of fire from matches and smokers' equipment left in pockets. There is also the problem of bomb scares, which are less likely where there is a manual check.

Lavatories

Lavatories for the public are intensively used for short periods before and after performances and during intervals. Minimum numbers of fittings for audiences of given sizes are laid down in BS 6465: Part 1: 1984, but these are minimum provisions and are seldom enough to avoid people having to wait in queues at peak times. Where a more reliable estimate is not available it may be assumed that the total audience will consist of equal numbers of males and females. Minimum provision for male and female staff is regulated by the Shops, Offices and Railway Premises Act.

BS 6465: Part 1: 1984
Scale of provision of sanitary appliances. Tables of minimum requirements: Table 7, Cinemas, theatres and similar buildings used for public entertainment

Appliances	For male public	For female public
WCs	In theatres, concert halls and similar premises: Minimum 1 for up to 250 males, plus 1 for every additional 500 males or part thereof	In theatres, concert halls and similar premises: Minimum 2 for up to 50 females, 3 for 51 to 100 females, plus 1 for every additional 40 females or part thereof
	In cinemas: Minimum 1 for up to 250 males plus 1 for every additional 500 males or part thereof	In cinemas: Minimum 2 for up to 75 females, 3 for 76 to 150 females or part thereof
Urinals	In theatres, concert halls and similar premises: Minimum 2 for up to 100 males, plus 1 for every additional 80 males or part thereof	
	In cinemas: Minimum 2 for up to 200 males, plus 1 for every additional 100 males or part thereof	
Wash-basins	1 per WC and, in addition, 1 per 5 urinals or part thereof	1, plus 1 per 2 WCs
Cleaners' sinks	Adequate provision should be made for cleaning facilities, including at least one cleaners' sink	

If the foyers and refreshment areas extend through more than one level, the lavatories should be distributed so that they are within easy reach of the various parts of the building used by the public. This is usually done by having the main lavatories at the principal foyer level and secondary lavatories at other levels which will serve other entrances to the auditorium or the restaurant or refreshment area. To achieve this the minimum requirements of the British Standard will probably be exceeded.

Women's lavatories should include an area designed as a powder room where make-up can be repaired. It will need mirrors, preferably not over wash-basins, and a wide shelf for make-up, hair brushes, etc. Long mirrors should be provided and the lighting designed so that people standing in front of the mirrors are properly illuminated. Chairs or stools and ashtrays will be needed, and the provision of tissue dispensers should be considered.

In the women's lavatories the disposal of sanitary towels can cause problems. Staff lavatories can be provided with a single incinerator in the wash-basin area, but this is not acceptable in the public lavatories; there should be means of disposal within each WC compartment. Bins or containers may have to be emptied into a central incinerator or disposal unit by the cleaning staff. There are companies which offer a service of providing and emptying purpose-made containers.

If the building is used much during the daytime, space should be allocated for mothers to feed and change babies.

WC compartments need coat hooks and a shelf for handbags. Alternative methods of dispensing lavatory paper should be considered. The wash-basin area should be provided with towel cabinets, and each basin should have a soap dispenser.

The men's lavatories should also be provided with an area equipped with mirrors where hair can be combed, ties straightened and clothes brushed.

Refreshments

The traditional pattern of theatre-going still typical in many places, including the West End of London, does not make heavy demands on the refreshment facilities. The audience arrives in the half-hour before the curtain rises. Some will give themselves time to have a drink at the bar, and during the interval or intervals, there are more chances to visit the bar. Sometimes coffee or tea can be served in the auditorium or the foyer, and usherettes sell ice-cream and chocolates. After the performance nothing more is offered and the building is closed as soon as the audience can be cleared out.

For many new theatres, however, particularly those run by a resident company, this pattern is no longer typical. The building becomes a social centre, a meeting place where people expect to go at any time of the day. Instead of teas served on trays in the auditorium, there is a permanent coffee bar also serving tea, soft drinks, sandwiches, cakes, biscuits and ice-cream.

Audiences can be lured from their seats in intervals if the foyers are attractive enough, if there is room to move about and if the source of refreshments is efficiently organised. The sale of sweets, nuts, ice-cream and cold drinks is too valuable a source of revenue to be neglected, and if customers cannot be persuaded to leave their seats, managements will pursue them into the auditorium.

There is a contrast in the behaviour of theatregoers and average cinemagoers. Separate performances punctuated by intervals are expected in the live theatre, and the audience are accustomed to leaving their seats if for no other reason than to stretch their legs. It is becoming increasingly rare for smoking to be allowed in the auditorium, and this supplies another motive for the more addicted to go into the foyers. In the cinema, however, the continuous performance, with people coming and going all the time, still lingers on in Britain, though now it is more common to be able to book a numbered seat. Without a booked seat people are inhibited from leaving their seats during an intermission for fear that somebody else will come and take possession while they are gone. Even smokers can indulge their habit without moving from their seats in many commercial cinemas in the UK.

The pattern is changing slowly, and there is a tendency towards bars serving refreshments in the foyers, though sales in cinemas are still often made by girls carrying trays. This has its effect on the seating layout. Continental seating in long rows does not make it so easy to reach customers in the middle. This is one more factor which increases the difference between an auditorium designed for live performances, where the close relation between actor and audience is crucial, and one designed for showing films, where most people prefer to be further away from the screen rather than in the front rows.

In the new theatre enterprises, a much greater importance is generally attached to creating an attractive meeting place not restricted solely to those actually attending performances. If the public can be persuaded to enter a theatre by the refreshments and amenities it offers, they can more easily be tempted to buy seats for the shows it puts on. This is in itself good business, but the real aim is to make the building an accepted part of the life of the community. The least that is expected is a coffee bar serving simple snacks, and most new schemes try to include a restaurant where more elaborate meals can be served.

All countries have their own attitude towards the sale of alcoholic drinks, ranging from strict prohibition to complete freedom. In England and Wales the occupier of any premises licensed to be used as a theatre under the 1968 Theatres Act is permitted to sell alcoholic drinks to anyone eligible within the permitted opening hours prevailing locally. In Scotland the current situation is slightly more complicated and some form of licence is usually necessary for theatres except for those operating since before 1903. There are always groups lobbying for either the tightening or relaxation of the licensing laws. Recently the trend has been towards relaxation, and in Britain we may even see the abolition of restricted opening hours.

Bars

The refreshment areas in the foyers are, like the lavatories, subjected to periods of intense activity. There should be plenty of bar space to cater for the likely number of customers, although how many can be served will depend as much upon the staff available as the actual length of counter.

The location of the coffee bars and other bars within the foyer must relate to the public circulation in such a way that routes to and from the auditorium are not impeded by those taking refreshment. Obvious though this may sound, it is too often found that a bar has been installed, apparently as an afterthought, in a position where it jams up the circulation to one of the auditorium entry points.

The bars should be easily accessible for an audience emerging from the auditorium, and in large multi-tier theatres it may be better policy to have several bars distributed so as to cover each level or part of the house. The audience will thus be spread more evenly throughout the building. It is not appropriate to go into great detail here over the fitting out of bars, but there are some fundamental planning considerations that must be borne in mind from the start. For the well-being of both customers and management, the bars must work efficiently in those brief periods of intense activity when the bulk of their trade is done. In an interval, bottled beer is much quicker to serve than draught beer, and this is one of the reasons why it used to be rare to find the latter in a theatre bar. With more relaxed opening hours, draught beer is again commonly provided, and it must have proper cellar arrangements designed in. Each person serving behind the bar should have a till and access to a set of bottles with optic measures. The back of the bar is as important as the counter itself; island bars set in the middle of the foyer, for instance, are at once at a disadvantage unless there is some vertical storage unit in the middle. Underneath the counter is bound to be untidy, and unless there is some sort of barrier in the middle the back of the other side of the counter will be too obvious to customers. The back of the counter can also be revealed by too much mirror on the wall behind a bar. An island calls for more staff if it is to cover all points of the compass. If it does not it will lead to frustration for its customers at peak periods of demand.

Security and licensing conditions will require that the alcoholic drinks be locked up. This can be done in various ways with shutters or grilles covering the back of the bar or coming down on the counter. Without them, the only alternative may be to stock the bar before opening it and laboriously remove full and partly full bottles to a store after it closes. Another expedient is to have a mobile bar on trolleys which can be wheeled back into store and locked up after it has served its purpose. There will in any case have to be a store from which to replenish the bars. Security there is particularly important, because spirits and tobacco carry such high excise duty that the money value of the stock is very great.

The delivery, storage and distribution of supplies to the bars must be taken into account. Crates of bottles are heavy and it should be possible to avoid staff having to carry them up and down stairs.

Each bar should have a small washing-up sink with hot water and mains drinking water. Most public health authorities will insist on a basin for hand washing in addition to the sink. Serving tea and coffee is a much longer process than serving cold drinks, soft or alcoholic. Instead of just a glass, there is a cup, a saucer, a spoon, and the complication of some preferring with or without milk and some with or without sugar. The tea or coffee must be at the right temperature, and if it has been kept too long its flavour deteriorates. However, the demand is there, and it would be unwise for any management to ignore it. From this point of view, the economic advantage of vending machines is attractive, and if the quality of their products can be made acceptable they will become more and more common in public places. The process of brewing up tea or coffee is an exacting one, and machines which rely on powdered substitutes do not yet produce results which can be compared with beverages prepared in the traditional manner. A machine vending alcoholic drinks, on the other hand, would be quite simple mechanically, and there is no reason why there should be any detectable difference from a drink dispensed by hand. Clearly the objections are legal rather than mechanical.

Bars need storage space for bottles and glasses, cooling shelves, and ice-making machines, and it may be worthwhile, or in some places mandatory, to have a machine for washing up glasses. Where tea, coffee and snacks are served, the equipment needed to do the job efficiently can become elaborate and the electrical loads considerable. Storage of crockery and cutlery is needed; display cases and hot cabinets for food begin to fill up the counter, and the washing-up problem is more than can be adequately dealt with in a small bar sink. In this case there should be another room opening off the back of the counter where preparation of simple snacks and washing up can be done. If communications within the buidling permit, it may be possible for this preparation and washing up to be done centrally in the restaurant kitchen.

The restaurant

The restaurant has become established as an essential ingredient of most new theatres. Many people like to have a restaurant meal to complete the evening's outing, and unless the theatre is right in the centre of the entertainment district of a big city, there will not be much choice of places to go. Even with competition close by, an attractive restaurant forming part of a theatre has advantages over its rivals. From the management point of view, it has a regular potential clientele, and from the customers' angle the convenience of being on the spot. The opportunity of exploiting the theatrical connection of the restaurant should not be missed, though there are problems involved in deciding how close this connection should be. Running the restaurant and the theatre alongside and in the same building has practical difficulties which must not be ignored. The time of opening can be arranged to coincide as far as possible, but if meals are served after the last performance the management will want to be able to shut up the rest of the building so that some staff can go home. Although it may be visually more attractive to make the dining area part of the foyer, the difficulties of running a restaurant which cannot be physically separated from the rest of the building should be realised. It is not sufficient to assume that the foyer can have the dual use of circulation and dining area unless it is very large. Diners will not appreciate being swamped by the interval crowd, though they may enjoy being able to see the throng moving about from a vantage-point in the restaurant. If there are good views from the site, the restaurant is one of the most suitable places from which to appreciate them.

The policy of the management on running the restaurant will affect its planning and should be decided at an early stage. The usual pattern of use is for some people to have their meal in the hour before the show, others in the hour after it. This is an important limitation, and it is not possible to serve and enjoy an elaborate meal in such a relatively short time. The menu should, therefore, be designed to cope with this kind of demand, and other customers not attending a performance may have to conform to these limitations. On a bigger scale, it may be possible to have separate dining rooms or suites which can be let for private functions.

The question of waiter service or self-service will arise. Smaller restaurants, where the main demand is for fairly quick meals before and after a show, are probably better with a cafeteria-type service. The public is now accustomed to this system for meals of a very good standard, and there is no reason why it should be considered cheap or second-rate. In order to make proper use of the investment in the restaurant, its kitchens and furnishings, and to provide full employment for the staff, it is desirable to open at lunch-time as well as in the evenings. The lunch-time customer will not usually be combining his visit with going to a performance, except when there is a matinee. His or her motives will be different, and the menu will not necessarily be the same as in the evening. The theatre can gain much in publicity if it can establish its restaurant as a popular rendezvous.

The equipment and planning of the kitchen to serve the restaurant are a subject outside the scope of this book, but there are certain basic planning problems which must be considered in the early stage of a design. Deliveries of supplies will be frequent, and there must be space to store them and mechanical aids to distribute them if the kitchen is remote from the unloading point. Raw food, cooked food and waste materials must be strictly segregated from each other. The disposal of empties, old packing materials and kitchen garbage can be an even greater problem. If the local authority rubbish collection is efficient and frequent, there may be no trouble, but where there is a visit only once a week and if for some reason a collection is missed, then the garbage may begin to rot and breed flies. One safeguard is to get rid of most waste food, vegetable peelings and materials likely to decay through a waste disposal unit powerful enough to cope with the load; a domestic type would be useless.

The cooking equipment can be heavy and will use a lot of power. Services in the kitchen will be complicated, with probably both gas and electricity required at many different points, and the same applies to both hot and cold water supplies and drainage. Ventilation must be efficient, and the vitiated air laden with grease and cooking smells must be filtered and carried away where it will not be a nuisance in the building or to any adjoining owners.

The kitchen staff must be provided with a staff room and lavatories and coat storage for both males and females. The catering manager will need an office, and a large establishment may need space for more administrative staff. Only a brief outline of the problems can be given here, and it is advisable to seek expert advice before the final details are decided.

The box office

The simplest box office is the kind still used by many cinemas. The seats are not bookable, and the cashier's task is to take money, give change and dispense tickets from an automatic machine. There may be more than one price, but that is the only complication. The one important quality appreciated by both public and management is speed of operation.

Where seats can be reserved and bought in advance, which is the custom for most live performances, the procedure is more complicated. The box office will be selling tickets at several different prices for performances of different plays, recitals,

concerts, etc. The staff will have to deal with telephone reservations, postal applications, agency bookings and personal callers. They will also have to sell tickets "at the door" in the hour before the show begins. This is when the box office staff are under the greatest pressure, and for this reason there should be at least two windows, one labelled "Advance Bookings", and one "This Performance" (or the equivalents), in all but the tiniest undertakings.

New box offices are most likely to be computerised, and old ones are steadily being fitted with computer terminals to bring them up to date; but before describing them in detail it is worthwhile looking at the functioning of the manual system.

Each performance has a seating plan and a book or books of tickets representing each seat. The performance, the date and the prices are marked or printed on each, and as the tickets are sold, the seats are marked off the plan. To work efficiently, the box office clerk should have space screened from the public to handle the book of plans easily and select the corresponding book of tickets quickly without being overlooked.

It is this need for readily accessible racks for tickets which led to the orthodox ticket window or guichet. The pigeon holes for the books of tickets were ranged on either side of the opening through which the ticket buyers had to stoop and peer. This was convenient for the staff in the box office, but it made most members of the public feel at a disadvantage. It seemed too easy for the clerk to hide, to be evasive, to adopt a defensive position behind a weapon slit. These were, no doubt, irrational suspicions, but the fact remains that box offices often still have a reputation for rudeness fostered and amplified by memories of the guichet. Even railways are abandoning it in new stations.

The alternative is a counter such as is found in a travel agency. It can be open, or if it is exposed to cold draughts in a lobby or too much noise in a foyer, it can be glazed in, with openings for taking money and handing out tickets and for speaking. One of the reasons for the guichet was to prevent the public leaning over the counter and looking at the clerk's book of plans. These are management records, and customers should choose their seats from a prominently displayed seating plan giving a more graphic representation of the auditorium. If it is not protected by glass the counter should be wide enough to prevent anyone leaning over and grabbing and to discourage people from interfering with the work of the box office staff. Where the counter is in a vulnerable position close to the street, thieves may be tempted to try a snatch. Security is then an important factor, but the risk is less when the box office is in the centre of the foyer. The house manager should, in any case, transfer cash to the safe frequently to avoid leaving too much in the till.

The most convenient location for the box office is somewhere near the entrance to the theatre so that

19:2. Public spaces

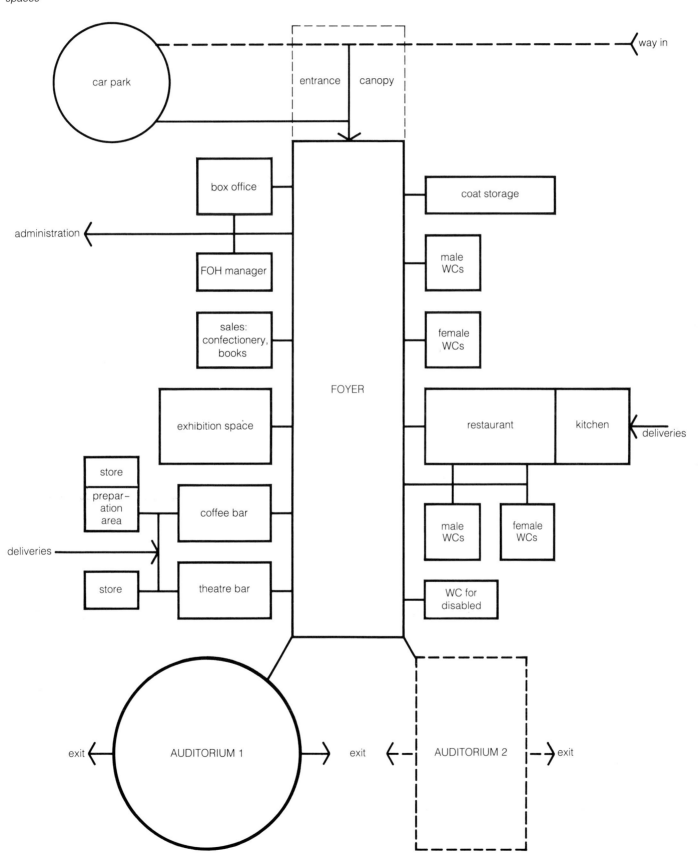

it is on the route which visitors must pass. This is desirable when tickets are being sold just before a performance, but is less important for advanced bookings. Some larger organisations have a box office quite remote from the rest of the public areas. Where the policy is to keep the foyers open during the day, and to encourage people to patronise the coffee bar, it may be preferred to site the advance booking office in this area combined with a sales counter for books and magazines. The object is to make the buying of tickets as painless a process as possible.

At times, queues will form at the box office, wherever it is sited. As a sign of a demand for seats they are welcome, but if their occurrence has not been foreseen in planning the circulation of the public they can cause bottlenecks and irritation.

The box office operation is essentially one of storage and retrieval of information. These tasks, formerly carried out by a rather laborious hand process, can be handled much more efficiently by a computer, as in the comparable case of airline bookings. Theatres benefit from the advances made in computers designed for other uses, and schemes for dealing with theatre tickets are being introduced at a rapidly increasing rate. The computer hardware to handle the problem has become relatively cheap – even commonplace. The spread of the computerised box office has been retarded by the typical growing pains of any new system where a number of rival organisations are trying to introduce their own versions of the necessary equipment. There are several firms who have adapted computer hardware and written the programme software to handle booking and issuing tickets from a number of terminals, some on both sides of the Atlantic.

The main advantage is not in the saving of manpower in the box office, which is hardly significant, but in increasing the sales of tickets by making it easier for the public to buy from a wider number of sales points. The ticket agencies have traditionally levied a surcharge on their sales, but there are signs that this is changing, so that it will be possible to buy tickets at the same price wherever a terminal is installed. The system should be more efficient because the seats available and sold are instantly recorded in a central databank to which each terminal has access. The up-to-the-minute state of booking is known, and the haphazard method of allocating blocks of seating to the box office and to agencies is no longer necessary. The old box office will not be eliminated entirely and will be required, for example, to sell tickets in the hour before the show. However, a machine which would project the auditorium plan of any theatre one wished, indicating for any particular performance what seats were available and at what price, is quite feasible. It would then print out tickets for the seats chosen in return for a glimpse of a credit card and store all the information instantaneously. Bank cash-points perform a similar task and have become a familiar feature of our high streets. We may before long see such methods used to sell tickets to the public for all kinds of activities, including sporting events.

20

Administration

Theatre and the performing arts seem to need more and more administrative input to keep up with, and survive in, an increasingly bureaucratic society and to meet that society's increasing expectations.

The management of the activities of an organisation, its administration, has responsibility for controlling a whole range of tasks which have to be carried out by every organisation, whatever its size. In small companies one person may have to look after several jobs which in a larger organisation are split into separate departments. The larger the organisation, the more complicated these become; the more sub-divided and specialised the administration, the more staff are employed and the more space they need. This is usually underestimated, and it is rare enough for a theatre to be built with sufficient accommodation for its administration when it opens, let alone with provision for future expansion.

Location of offices within the building

The administration needs to be in contact with both front-of-house and backstage areas. There are offices which are better related to the departments they control, and however neat it may seem to centralise all the administrative functions in one part of the building, it is not often practicable to do so.

Detail design of offices

The requirements for the offices of theatre-type buildings do not differ from those of other types, and, as the subject has been dealt with at length in other publications, it is not proposed to discuss it in detail here. There are, however, a few points which should be borne in mind when drawing up the brief and planning the layout. Secretarial staff need as much space as their managers to accommodate their equipment and files; offices can be smaller if meeting rooms are provided; kitchen, lockers, showers and lavatories should be on a generous scale, particularly as live entertainment takes place at unsocial hours.

To determine the extent of the office accommodation, it is necessary to study the administrative structure of the organisation which will use the building and anticipate as far as possible areas of future development.

The managerial functions that have to be performed are as follows.

A: Government

Most theatres will have a governing body, be it a board of directors, trustees or a committee of a larger institution, such as a local authority or a university. They will usually be unpaid and elected or appointed to represent local interests. They will meet from time to time, but, having appointed an artistic directorate, they will ideally leave the policy and management to their appointees. It will be a matter of local judgement as to how the somewhat artificial difference between the artistic and the commercial responsibility is divided between an organisation's executives. The governing body will need a boardroom, supported by a secretariat, and an archive may be necessary.

B: Artistic directorate

It is likely that the chief, or joint chief, executive of a theatre will be responsible for providing the creative drive in pursuit of the theatre's policy. There may be several associate and assistant directors with responsibility for various aspects of its activities, all requiring office accommodation, meeting space, secretarial support and archive space.

B1. *Drama*

(a) *Literary management:* The reading, selection and editing of plays, the preparation of scripts and the maintenance of a library.

(b) *Casting:* The selection of performers and the placing of contracts for them. A separate interview space should be provided, and a dedicated waiting space is desirable.

B2. *Music*

(a) *Directorate:* Policy on the musical directorate depends on the organisation's output. An opera or ballet house will naturally place great emphasis on musical direction, whereas a drama house, even with a large company, will probably have a lesser need. A music room with piano and equipment for reproducing recorded sound will be essential, as may be a music library and facilities for a librarian. Space will need to be available for those who may also be engaged on the staff of the theatre to direct productions or assist in their preparation.

(b) *Music staff:* Conductors, rehearsal pianists, coaches and, in an opera house, repetiteurs and prompters have some paper work and should be able to do it in their dressing or changing rooms. Office space may also be required for orchestra management near the orchestra's changing rooms.

B3. *Dance*

In a dance house the artistic direction is likely to flow from dancers or choreographers. These will need to be supported by a team of dance staff to rehearse dancers in their performances. Provision might also be required for medical and paramedical staff to care for dancers' physical well-being.

B4. *Visitors*

(a) *Guest artists:* It is a reasonable assumption

that most theatres will occasionally engage guests to direct productions, and provision for this should include space to accommodate guest designers, conductors, authors and composers. Visiting teams might also include choreographers, lighting designers and sound designers.

(b) *Visiting staff:* The need to accommodate visiting staff or personnel will vary according to the policy under which the building operates. A theatre acting as a receiving house only may need to accommodate a substantial number of visiting staff, particularly if the incoming productions are large. A small theatre relying entirely on its own product may not need to house more than a guest director and designer, and the music director and choreographer of the Christmas show. An opera house used for an annual festival may have a small nucleus of staff for much of the year, substantially expanded when the season goes into rehearsal, and again when the season opens to the public. A multi-purpose building may need to duplicate some of its resident staff to cope with the variety of activities and then take in visiting staff as well. It is essential that full account of these activities is taken during the preparation of the brief and the development of the design. Inadequate provision for administration can lead to wasteful practices.

B5. *Production departments*

(a) *Designers:* The design of scenery, costumes and properties will need studio space for drawing, painting, model making and the showing of film, slides and video. Lighting designers may additionally need a photographic dark room. Sound designers should be based in the specialised production facilities covered elsewhere (Chapter 12).

(b) *Scenery and property workshops:* The management of workshops for production purposes will need a drawing office within or adjacent to the workshops.

(c) *Costume making:* The management of the production wardrobes is likely to need office space to administer the purchasing of materials and the allocation of work, but the various sub-departments of the wardrobe – male and female cutting and sewing; dyeing and painting; wigs; shoes; millinery, accessories and armour – should not need their own separate offices. The wardrobes and workshops may have to cope with frequent and bulky deliveries, and the reception and handling of these will have a profound influence on the planning of the building.

(d) *Lighting technical:* Space to lay out lighting plots and playscripts and to carry out the paper work associated with the electrical department should be provided in or near the electrician's workshop and in the lighting control room. Access to daylight, with efficient blackout blinds, is desirable.

(e) *Sound technical:* The sound department will need a system for storing and cataloguing tapes and discs.

B6. *Stage management*

At the appropriate time, productions are transferred either from the making departments (the theatre's own workshops), from outside contractors or from other theatres to the stage, and therefore become the responsibility of the performance organisation to operate. In larger theatres the stage departments are traditionally broken into a series of separate technical skills. In a small house the same services may be supplied from a group of general technical staff.

The departments are:

The Stage: responsible for the scenery and stage machinery.

Electrics: responsible for the operation of lighting equipment and special effects.

Properties: responsible for the furnishings of the set and for the performers' hand props.

Sound: responsible for the operation of sound equipment for effects and amplification.

Maintenance wardrobe: responsible for the organisation and cleaning and repair of costumes and the dressing of performers.

Wigs: responsible for the maintenance of wigs.

Each of these functions is likely to need office accommodation for the management of plans and budgets, the engagement, briefing and disciplining of staff (including temporary, part-time and casual staff), and for the storage of records. The subject is treated in more detail above in Chapter 17 on the performance organisation.

B7. *Performance company and stage management*

There is normally a small management team which works closely with, and is part of, the creative group which assembles the performance. The job of company manager, who has an overseeing role in all matters affecting the company of performers, may be merged with that of stage manager in a small organisation. In larger ones it is likely to be a self-contained post and will need offices. The stage management usually works in teams of four or five, and a large operation may employ several teams to manage its repertoire. Each will need the use of an office, preferably strategically placed between rehearsal spaces, dressing rooms and the stage or stages. Offices should be generously sized to cope with plans, the collation of scripts and the wealth of impedimenta normally associated with a performance. Fresh air and daylight are essential, as are changing, lavatory and kitchen facilities. In a large building it may be necessary to site a satellite office close to each stage, particularly for the periods immediately before the opening of a new production. A number of other staff who work closely with performers, such as music and dance staff, are closely associated with the stage manager, and consideration should be given to providing accommodation for these in the same area.

B8. *Transport*

Even comparatively small performing organisations find they need their own transport for the collection and delivery of goods. A small theatre, producing a dozen plays a year, will quickly accumulate stocks of scenery, furniture, costumes and other equipment which may have value in the future. In large theatres these stocks can be both a major asset and a liability, and since space is usually scarce within the building external storage is hired or purchased. An organisation with major touring commitments may have to make a policy decision between contracting out transportation and owning its own fleet. Provision should be made for transport and stores management, bearing in mind that these assets might be hired out to others when not required by the organisation.

C: Administrative machinery

Various titles are used to describe the executive who may be responsible to, or with, the artistic director for the administrative drive in pursuit of the theatre's policy: "administrator", "general manager", "managing director" and "administrative director" are all used. In a small organisation the two roles may be merged, but here it is useful to consider them as separate. A number of activities for which the administrator will be responsible will justify analysis in their own right, but the administrator may well take responsibility for a number of functions which will require supporting staff and therefore accommodation:

C1. *Personnel*

(a) *Personnel – staff relations:* In addition to the appropriate office space, meeting and interview rooms may be needed, together with secure archive space. Provision for computers may be needed. Training space may be appropriate for a large organisation.

(b) *Legal and contractual:* A building which relies on others to provide a large part of its activities may need to issue many hundreds of contracts in the course of a year.

C2. *Accounts*

(a) *Management accounting:* The preparation and co-ordination of detailed budgets; the control of

expenditure against budget; the aggregation and distribution of financial information from income and expenditure centres; the preparation of monthly, quarterly and annual financial results.

(b) *Financial control:* The day-by-day control of the income and expenditure of the operation; the collection of debts and the payment of creditors; the control of cash and credit instruments; the maintenance of accounts; the conduct of bank accounts; the payment of wages.

A high level of security will be needed for these offices. The insurance companies will set out their requirements for the storage and handling of cash, and the provision of alarms for cash and personnel. Provision will need to be made for computerisation, and for the storage of considerable quantities of paper to meet statutory requirements for the retention of records.

C3. *Box office*

The box office itself (see Chapter 19) is the physical space in which tickets are sold to the general public in person, by post and on the telephone. It may need to be supported by management offices, cash counting space, computer room, staff interviewing and training rooms, and by locker, toilet and kitchen facilities of its own.

C4. *House management*

It is traditional for the house manager to be responsible for: welcoming the public to the building and for their well-being while they are there; the daily maintenance and security of the building; the upholding of the statutory obligations that govern places of public entertainment; and the management of the administration functions.

(a) *Front-of-house staff:* The size of the building, the variety of its activities and the hours it is open to the public will determine the numbers of staff required to operate the building for the public. Statutory requirements will dictate the presence of a duty manager, normally drawn from the house manager's team, and a staff of full-time or part-time stewards. In some multi-purpose buildings the house manager may also be responsible for operating such facilities as the concert platform, conference rooms and display spaces. In most theatres the equivalent of these facilities will be managed by others, unless they are within the public foyers. The house manager's offices need to be close to the public areas of the building.

(b) *Stage-door reception of staff:* The stage-door keeper can have an important role in looking after the interests of the backstage personnel, the cast and technicians, and in monitoring the comings and goings of visitors and staff to the working areas of the theatre. This job is described in more detail in Chapter 16.

(c) *Cleaning:* All parts of the building used by the public will need to be cleaned regularly, not only every day but at times during the day. In addition to the sweeping, polishing, washing down, and collection of rubbish, most buildings will need specialist cleaning and maintenance of surfaces and equipment; glass cleaning; floor stripping and resurfacing; the deep cleaning of catering equipment; the periodic stripping and lacquering of brightwork; the disposal of sanitary towels; the treatment of infestation by pests. Offices will be required for supervising staff, stores, both central and local, for equipment and cleaning materials, and lavatory, changing, and kitchen facilities for staff. The local provision of hot and cold water and drainage is important, as is the convenient storage of access equipment.

(d) *Security:* The extent of these services will vary according to the size, value and complexity of the building; the value of its contents; the frequency of visits by VIPs; and the likely amount of cash stored on the premises. A large complex may need a resident team of security guards and firemen. They will need a strategically sited control point and may be equipped with fire-detection and alarm systems and sophisticated apparatus for surveillance and monitoring of plant failure, lift failure, intruders and emergencies. The routes used by the security personnel patrolling the premises should be considered. A large building will almost certainly need a two-way radio network to provide base and person-to-person communication. Alternatively, radio paging facilities may be provided. Since these functions are likely to be required on a twenty-four-hour basis, they will need office and rest room arrangements. Workshops and stores for fire-fighting equipment and portable barriers may have to be provided. Expert advice should be sought on the mastering of locks, and on the storage of the means of securing the statutory exits from the building. There is often a clash of opinions between the licensing authority, which is concerned lest there be any danger of the means of escape being locked while the public are on the premises, and the security department, whose job it is to keep out unwelcome visitors.

(e) *Traffic and car parking:* Management will have to take charge of roads and car parking on its own site, and it may also have to concern itself with security of its parking areas.

(f) *First aid:* In a small organisation, first aid may be provided for the staff and for the public by trained nominated members. In Britain this is often handled by one of the voluntary organisations, such as the Red Cross or St John's Ambulance Brigade. In a larger operation it may be expected that full-time nursing staff will be provided, probably with some voluntary support at busy times. All will require a separate and fully equipped first-aid room or rooms, including treatment cubicles and lavatory facilities. Statutory obligations will need to be met in respect of local first-aid boxes.

(g) *Maintenance of equipment and engineering services:* The engineering requirement of a building for performance purposes will vary enormously. It will be determined by the sophistication of the environmental services, the size of the building, the nature of the activities, the extent to which the building is in constant use, and, to some extent, the amount of forethought put into the design. It is a reasonable proposition that a single-auditorium theatre, with modest public and production facilities, may only require staff to operate boilers and ventilation plant, change lamps in those areas not maintained by the theatre technical staff, and attend to minor breakdowns such as drain blockages. These tasks will add up to a two-man job at most, probably reporting to the house manager and requiring a small office, workshop and store. At the other extreme might be a major arts centre housing theatres, gallery, extensive foyers, catering facilities and underground car parks. Such a project might well require a maintenance staff of forty, supported by secretarial, clerical and storekeeping staff. The activities may be broken down as follows.

(i) *Engineering management:* The organisation and control of the activity will need an office, drawing facilities and storage for large volumes of as-fitted drawings and manuals.

(ii) *Environmental engineering:* Workshops will be needed for those engaged on maintaining heating, cooling, ventilation, electrical services, water and waste, and control systems. These operations are not necessarily compatible and will probably require separate workshops.

(iii) *Building maintenance:* Whilst major maintenance and renewal in any building is likely to be carried out by outside contractors, the management will be responsible for the daily maintenance of finishes, furniture, fixtures and fittings and running repairs to the fabric of the building.

(iv) *External maintenance:* In addition to the maintenance of the external structure included within the previous section, external works may include gardens and paving, ornamental water and roads. Staff and storage may be needed for mowing equipment, mechanical sweepers, a boat, watering equipment and road-marking machinery.

(v) *Visiting contractors:* In a large building it is advisable to make provision for offices, stores, workshops, lavatory, shower, rest room, and an open-air compound for building equipment and materials. Even if finance does not permit the provision of permanent facilities, it will be prudent to identify a space, accessible to the street for deliveries, reasonably accessible to all parts of the building and capable of enclosure, so that temporary facilities can be created. It will be essential for such a space to have water, waste and electrical power laid on.

(vi) *Stores:* Building maintenance is likely to have a heavy stores requirement, even in a small building. In addition to central storage, it may be advisable to have local stores, so that, for example, a large foyer using many hundreds of light fittings has a local lamp store, to simplify the process of lamp replacement. Such a store, which might also house the appropriate access equipment, must be well secured.

(vii) *Support facilities:* Thought should be given to the management, supervisory and staff accommodation, bearing in mind that large budgets may be involved, that preventative maintenance systems may need considerable management, and that engineering staff, particularly those working shifts, may be performing dirty, difficult and dangerous tasks.

(h) *Provision of office services:* The house manager will be expected to provide the administration with the resources to manage itself: telephone and other telecommunications; reception and stage doors; copying and printing; messenger and postal services; the provision and maintenance of office equipment and furniture; the storage and distribution of office consumables. All these activities will need space devoted to them, and discussion should take place as to the degree of centralisation that is necessary, and the standard of service expected. It is, for example, economic to create a single entrance for all staff and visitors to the private areas of the building, since it is essential that such a position be manned at all open times. This is usually the stage door. In a small building such an entrance could also provide a focus for deliveries of smaller items, the sorting of post and the provision of telephone and copying services.

C5. *Publicity and marketing*

Places of public entertainment need to develop a productive relationship with the general public in order to sell tickets for performances. Office space may be required for the following functions.

(a) *Graphics studio:* The design, production and distribution of printed material, which may include brochures, texts, leaflets, posters, programmes, menus and temporary signs. Also included may be all the internal paperwork of the organisation, such as letter-headings, control forms, visiting cards and similar ephemera. If it is the policy of an organisation to carry out these functions in house, there should be space for a design studio and a print shop on site.

(b) *Public relations:* The design and administration of publicity material reproduced by the media. Allied to this may be the development of a mailing list for the distribution of publicity material. Whether or not distribution is carried out by a contractor or in house is a matter of policy. Media and public relations will be handled by specialists accustomed to dealing with the needs of the media. Interview and hospitality space (close to the auditorium and foyers) may be desirable.

(c) *Display:* A large building may need staff devoted to setting up foyer publicity, to putting up posters, distributing leaflets within the building, reconfigurating signs and information boards, and reprogramming video text equipment. Considerable storage may be needed.

C6. *Catering*

The matter of catering is discussed above in Chapter 19 on public areas. Catering requirements will vary according to the size of the operation, and may range from the simple bar to full-scale restaurants, banqueting facilities and canteens for those working in the building. The administration of the catering will depend on the size and diversity of the operation and to some extent on whether it is managed in house or contracted out. It is wise to assume the former, since that option is not then prejudiced at any time during the life of the building. The administrative functions that might need housing are:

(a) *General management:* The provision of duty catering management, financial services, personnel, recruitment and training services and purchasing.

(b) *Kitchen management:* Offices for the head chef and for control staff.

(c) *Essential services:* The control of the movement of goods, overseeing the equipment and facilities; liaising with the service departments of the building; controlling stocks of equipment and furniture.

(d) *Goods in:* The administration of the arrival of foodstuffs, liquor, consumables and equipment, and their entry into the control system and their placing into storage. The storage and dispersal of waste and returnable empties will also need management.

(e) *Unit management:* A large and diverse catering operation will need an office for the manager of each unit – restaurants, bars, coffee shop, canteen, banqueting etc.

(f) *Support facilities:* The matter of stores, lavatory accommodation, showers and lockers for staff are a matter for specialist guidance, since they stem from the general catering philosophy.

C7. *Lettings for conferences and private functions*

This can be an important part of the activities of the organisation and a principal source of revenue. In

20:1. Admin-
istration

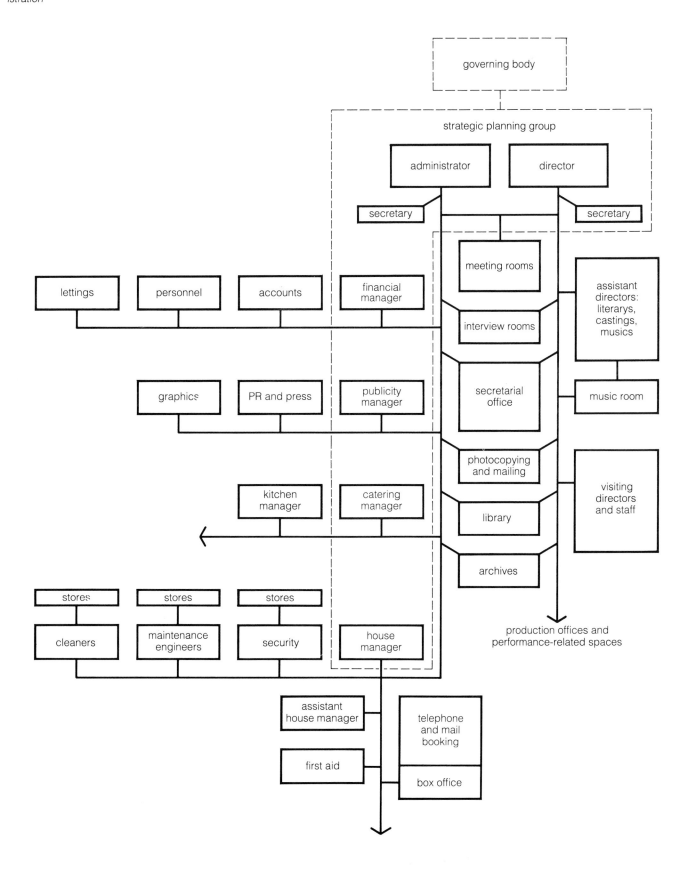

such cases, offices are needed to handle the bookings and to control the arrangements for each hiring.

C8. *Sales to public*

The public has come to expect to find shopping opportunities in places of public entertainment. Since there is profit to be made from this, sales counters should be provided on a suitable scale to sell a range of goods such as confectionery, books, records, posters, and postcards. The shop or kiosk will need supporting store rooms and office accommodation. Merchandising may also include the sale of ice-cream and programmes in the foyers and auditorium, as well as occasional temporary points to sell material associated with a particular event. Storage and distribution points for these items as well as secure facilities for cash counting must be provided. Special attention needs to be paid to the services connections required for ice-cream conservators and for cash registers.

D: Planning

Provision may need to be made for managers to run all or any of: education programmes; exhibitions; foyer activities; conferences; tours out of the theatre; tours into the theatre; associated festivals.

D1. *Planning programme of total output*

A complex operation will require someone to maintain a continuous overview to ensure that different activities do not clash and that the human and physical resources are available when required. Computers may be used to support this function.

D2. *Financial forecasts*

The calculation of the financial consequences of the artistic and administrative policies of plans; the preparation of bids for grant and sponsorship support; the extrapolation of current trends in business; and the evaluation of proposals for new projects.

D3. *Sponsorship*

The growing expectation that performing arts organisations will look to commercial, private, corporate and charitable sources for funding is leading to an expanding specialisation in this field. Office accommodation may need to be supported by hospitality space.

D4. *Development programme*

A large building may need to conduct a rolling plan for the development, alteration and refurbishment of its facilities.

21

Electrical and mechanical services

The designs of both electrical and mechanical services for a theatre are complicated tasks which cannot be dealt with as an afterthought. Design criteria for electrical distribution, heating and ventilating are exacting, and the systems must all be integrated with the main functions of the building. Safety must be combined with flexibility and convenience. Consulting engineers for both services should join the design team at the start of the development of a scheme.

Within this chapter, wiring methods and techniques for the various specialised stage systems such as lighting, sound and communications are considered along with general electrical distribution.

Electrical regulations

Electrical installations in a theatre are usually subject to certain regulations and codes. In the United Kingdom, it is normal to specify compliance with the current edition of the *Regulations for Electrical Installations of the Institution of Electrical Engineers* (IEE). At present the fifteenth edition applies and this is likely to prevail for a number of years, having been introduced in 1981.

In addition, the fire insurance company, the electricity supply authority and the theatre licensing authority may impose their own constraints, and health and safety legislation may also apply. Where additional requirements are imposed, they are often aimed at reducing the risk of audience panic which might result from, for example, smoke caused by overheated wiring.

Electrical supply

A main electrical switchroom should be provided on the perimeter of the building and close to the stage. The incoming supply to the theatre will be terminated in the switchroom, which will contain the main distribution switchboard with provision for cable ducts to connect to the various sub-distribution centres for stage lighting, stage engineering, heating and ventilation plant and general power and lighting. In the United Kingdom, the incoming supply will be provided at 240/415V, 50Hz, from an electricity authority sub-station located nearby. If no convenient sub-station is available it may be necessary to provide one within the site to the requirements of the electricity authority.

Preliminary estimates of total load must be made at an early stage of the design in order to determine the demand on the sub-station and to establish the switchroom dimensions.

Supply capacity

The largest single component of the total electrical load is likely to be the stage-lighting installation, although where a central air-conditioning system is specified, its power supply can become the dominant load.

The total power of connected stage lighting seldom exceeds 75% of the total installed dimmer capacity, and a further diversity factor can sometimes be allowed beyond this.

The design engineer should take into account that when the stage lighting is in use, the main auditorium and stage working light systems will be dimmed and operating at their performance loads, which represent only a small percentage of their total installed capacity. Therefore a diversity factor can be considered between stage lighting and the ancillary lighting services.

General lighting and small power loads throughout the theatre building can be estimated using conventional principles.

Where television outside broadcasts have to be accommodated, provision should be made for up to two 100 amp single-phase mains supplies, as described in Chapter 11. Touring productions too may have additional power requirements, which have also been mentioned in Chapter 11 under *Stage power* (p. 96). Load calculation is more complicated in a theatre with a substantial content of power-operated lifts and flying systems. Although hydraulic or electrically controlled stage machinery may be run for no more than a few minutes per week, the short-term power consumption can be substantial and must be taken into consideration in the design process.

The worst conditions producing the highest peak load would in theory occur with stage machinery operating during a stage lighting "full-up" on a hot summer's day. The heat load from both the stage lighting and the external environmental heat gains would already be causing the air-conditioning plant to run at maximum capacity. However, as most performances take place in the evenings and as stage machinery is usually run during scene changes under blackout or near blackout conditions, such a combination is unlikely to occur in practice.

The final total load calculation will differ from theatre to theatre according to particular circumstances, but in practice, the electrical designer will be able to allow for significant diversity factors within most load categories, as well as on an overall basis.

Cable containment

It is normal practice to provide ducts or cable trays to carry the multicore power cables interconnecting the switchroom and the sub-distribution centres such as dimmer room and mechanical plant room.

The large quantities of circuits required by stage lighting and ancillary applications such as house-lights, working lights and independents determine that insulated single-core conductors and surface-mounted cable trunking systems be provided

21:1. Electrical intake room. Note the size of the cables

between dimmer and contactor racks, sub-distribution boards and lighting sockets or points. This is in conflict with the common continental practice of using large cable trays with numerous three-core PVC/PVC insulated cables. Stage-lighting trunkings can range in size from 50 mm × 50 mm (2 in. × 2 in.) up to multiple runs of 150 mm × 150 mm (6 in. × 6 in.). Integrating these trunking runs with the building structure and other services needs careful design co-ordination.

Communications, sound and video systems demand the use of considerable quantities of multi-core and screened cables. Here too it is normal to provide a completely separate system of single or multi-compartment trunking. Where cabling for a number of such systems needs to be run together, three-compartment trunking can be used, divided into:

— microphone cables, low-level audio cables,

video cables and broadcast reception aerials;
— loudspeaker cables (from amplifier outputs), communications cables, screened signalling cables for paging or communications control, feed to RF (radio frequency) transmission aerials;
— technical mains power associated with the sound and video systems, cue light cables and any cables associated with special stage manager's controls, such as telephone ringers, pyrotechnics etc.

Use of steel trunking for both power and signal cabling systems has the significant advantage of reducing interference and cross-talk. But, as far as possible, power and signal trunkings should not run side by side unless they are at least 2 m (6 ft 6 in.) apart. Crossings between the different trunking systems should be made at right angles.

Sound and communications wiring

The cable infrastructure is the key element in the success of sound and communications system design. If the cabling installation is adequate in both quality and quantity, then the systems will be able to meet the majority of demands simply and efficiently.

The systems will require a number of types of special cables. These will need to be grouped into various independent trunking and conduit runs, as described above under *Cable containment*. Sound and communications cabling must not be mixed with the general wiring of the building, and particularly not with that of the stage-lighting power system.

Microphones and low-level audio cables are usually known by the collective title of "audio tie lines". As well as microphones and input lines feeding into the main jackfield, there will also be the output lines returning to the amplifiers in their various locations. Video lines and broadcast reception downfeeds can also be placed in this section. These lines use identical cabling which must be robust braided or foil screened twisted pair cable. The audio signal will, in voltage terms, be amplified by a factor of up to 10,000 before reaching the audiences, so it is important to ensure that all cables are installed and protected from interference. They should be terminated and tested by a specialist installer.

Final connections to the main sound mixer should preferably be by multipole connectors; this is essential if there is an auditorium mixing position.

The audio cabling infrastructure is not dependent on the particular equipment that will be used. If the cabling is adequate the system will be flexible enough to cope with changes of equipment, artistic programmes and even changes to the shape of the building.

Stage-lighting wiring

Sizes of conductors and trunkings should be calculated so as to comply with IEE Wiring Regulations. Voltage drop limits and ambient temperature conditions must also be taken into account. In certain cases with long circuit cable runs, it may be deemed acceptable to exceed the normal voltage drop requirements in order to avoid use of excessively large conductors with consequential increases in trunking dimensions.

Stage and ancillary lighting installations will also involve control cabling interconnecting the lighting control desk, dimmer racks, remote control outlets and lighting control sections of facilities panels. Provided that control operation uses steady stage DC or pulsed digital signals, lighting control cabling may, on occasions, be grouped with sound and communications wiring.

Phase balance

Stage-lighting effects and methods differ widely, and the design should allow for the three phases occasionally to be 100% out of balance without adverse effect. Previous IEE Regulations have required 2 m (6 ft 6 in.) separation between sockets connected to different phases, and, recognising that extension cables will be widely used, theatres have often been divided into large single-phase zones, typically:

— Over stage   Phase 1
— Stage level   Phase 2
— Front-of-house   Phase 3

The current IEE Regulations omit this requirement, so now the easiest and most economical way to try to spread loads equally across the phases is to connect sockets and dimmers in rotation. However, some proprietary dimmer equipment designs require that a group of six or more adjacent dimmers be connected to the same phase, and many theatre technicians believe that removal of the 2 m (6 ft 6 in.) separation is an unnecessary reduction in safety standards. Each new installation must therefore be worked out in detail to reach an economical and acceptable solution. If single-phase zones are considered desirable, it is then necessary to ensure that all supplies in the area are co-phased, whether they be stage lighting, ancillary lighting or general domestic services.

Heat loads of stage lighting

The stage-lighting load presents a considerable problem to the mechanical services engineer. In sizing ventilation plant or chiller plant for the stage and auditorium, the first tendency is usually to assume that the full lighting and auditorium lighting loads will be in use together, creating a major source of heat. But this should never happen in practice. As mentioned previously, most of the dimmers will only be part-loaded, and some will not be used at all. Additionally, lighting cues cause a flow between different lighting states during the course of a performance, so that the average load is considerably less than the short-term "full-up" load, and dimmers set at intermediate levels reduce the power to the lamps in use. Of the electrical energy dissipated at the lanterns, part will be converted to light, but the major proportion will be released in the form of heat, which will need to be removed efficiently by the ventilation system. Estimating the probable average and maximum heat outputs requires the experience of a theatre consultant and agreement with the mechanical services engineer and user. If the figures assumed in the design calculations are exceeded, the audience will suffer discomfort.

Heat is also released at the dimmers. Efficiency

of more than 98% should be expected from good dimmer designs and from this the amount of heat expected to be generated in the dimmer room can be assessed in relation to the maximum load in the theatre. Although seldom greater than 10 kW, it is important that this load is recognised and removed when necessary, so that the maximum operating temperature of the dimmer equipment is not exceeded.

Ventilation in the control room is important not only to prevent overheating of the equipment but also to provide comfortable and therefore efficient working conditions for the technicians.

Occasionally both dimmer and control rooms will have to be cooled during rehearsals, when, in the absence of an audience, the main auditorium ventilation plant may not be running.

All stage areas should have a generous provision of ring main power sockets for tools and cleaning equipment. Sockets intended for stage lighting or sound equipment are not suitable for this purpose.

Additionally, power supplies may be needed for the temporary lighting, sound and stage machinery equipment installed by touring productions. 60 amp TPN should be a minimum for the on-stage temporary supply. In a large theatre, full-scale touring lighting rigs for pop concerts can require 400 amp TPN or more. Connection arrangements must be both convenient and safe, with locks and interlocks to prevent casual use and access to live parts. Use of the BS 4343 range of connectors is to be encouraged but with direct connection to switch output terminals or bus-bars as an option. Local fuses should be easily changed to match the capacity of temporary wiring. Generous provision for earth connections is essential.

Safety lighting and management lighting

All parts of a theatre or similar building to which the public have access, and all main escape routes for staff from backstage and elsewhere, must be adequately lit from two independent sources of supply at all times when the building is open to the public.

The licensing authority is responsible for determining the requirements, and in fact most authorities still follow BS CP 1007: 1955, Maintained Lighting for Cinemas, compliance with which will normally be deemed to fulfil the statutory and other requirements. BS 5266: Part 1: 1975, Code of Practice for the Emergency Lighting of Premises Other Than Cinemas and Certain Other Specified Premises Used for Entertainment, is also important and has been adopted by some authorities.

These codes of practice deal with the maintained lighting, which in the absence of daylight is intended for use during the whole time the public is on the premises. Maintained lighting comprises

both management lighting fed from the mains and the safety lighting fed from some source independent of the mains. Two electric service cables from the supply are not normally accepted as "independent". Generally speaking, the safety lighting must be fed from a battery, normally charged from the mains, except for very large premises, where it might be worth considering a diesel generating set. Even then, a battery is likely to be required to cover the interval while the diesel starts up.

Inside the auditorium the management lighting will be the minimum required to enable the staff to see their way about and perform their essential task of controlling and assisting the audience. The amount of light required will vary with circumstances but in theatres can usually be provided by a few low-wattage downlighters near exits and at gangway intersections connected to a dimmer that cannot fade fully out in normal use. Outside the auditorium the management lighting will normally be the whole of the lighting, although in some buildings part of the foyer lighting is switched off as an economy measure once the show has started. The safety lighting must be sufficient to enable the public and staff to leave in safety even after total failure of the mains supply.

The standard safety lighting in the auditorium required by the code of practice is between 0.01 and 0.025 lux, depending on circumstances and provided that the light is adequately distributed. Measures must be taken to ensure that nosings of treads, the perimeter of blocks of seats and changes in the direction of gangways are treated in such a way that they stand out from their surroundings. Certain critical areas may require a higher illumination, but sharp changes of intensity should be avoided. A higher standard of safety lighting, in excess of 1 lux, is required outside the auditorium.

Internally illuminated exit notices must be provided to mark the escape routes from both auditorium and backstage; these should be fed from both sources of supply. There is a British Standard (BS 2560: 1954) for exit signs for cinemas, theatres and places of public entertainment, which goes into a great many unnecessary details of construction and lays down even the style of the lettering. Those provisions which are relevant are that the lettering should be not less than 125 mm (5 in.) high and so designed that there is sufficient contrast between the lettering and surround to make the word EXIT clearly legible even when the internal lighting is not on. The exit notices have to be illuminated continuously whenever the public is admitted to the building.

The rest of the maintained lighting in the auditorium may be turned off for short periods when required by the action of the play, provided that some responsible person in, or in immediate contact with, the auditorium has control of the switches whenever this lighting is turned off. The wiring of safety lighting must be completely separated from all other wiring, except that, as in exit notices, one lighting fitting may contain lamps fed from both mains and safety systems, provided that the fitting is properly constructed and is of fire-resisting materials.

In recent years self-luminous exit signs have begun to be more widely used. They depend on phosphors which are excited to luminescence by radiation from radio-active materials. Radiation from the sign is negligible and there is no danger to health. They require no wiring and once screwed in position need no futher attention. In time there will be a slight diminution in brightness, but this will not be appreciable for many years. Although they are initially more expensive than the orthodox box signs, the savings on wiring two systems may redress the balance, and the complete elimination of maintenance cost in replacing bulbs and the cost of electric power is a further advantage. These signs are quite satisfactory from a front viewpoint but are less obvious from an oblique view, and they are not accepted by many authorities.

Battery rooms for safety lighting

The battery room should be located where it will be easily accessible and yet not so close to the intake position that it is liable to be affected by fire or explosion in the mains voltage apparatus. The plan area of the battery room should be approximately 0.15 m² (1½ ft²) for every 100 W of safety lighting provided, with a minimum of 2 m² (21 ft²). No single dimension should be less than 1 m (3 ft 3 in.), with a minimum height of 2.2 m (7 ft 3 in.).

The battery room should have good natural ventilation to the open air independent of any other ventilated spaces. Batteries give off gases which in certain conditions can be explosive, or in others can be poisonous. If forced ventilation is unavoidable the fan motor should be outside the air stream.

The battery room should be of substantial non-combustible construction, have a fire resistance of one hour and the doors should be of half-hour resistance and kept locked. Except in the case of small buildings with a self-contained metal cabinet housing both "sealed" type batteries and charging plant, the battery room should not be used for any other purpose.

The walls and floor should be of acid-resistant materials and easily washable; a gully for hosing down is an advantage. Inside the room or nearby, there should be a porcelain or earthenware (not steel) sink and cold water supply. The battery room should contain space for racking for carboys of distilled water in addition to that for the batteries themselves. Battery racks are normally provided by the manufacturers, but if made up by a contractor they should be of a substantial timber construction and the shelves covered with lead sheet, ceramic plates or other acid-resisting material.

Except in the case of the self-contained units described above, the charging plant should not be in the battery room, but in an adjacent room.

Heating, ventilation and air conditioning

The term "air conditioning" is often used loosely by the layman to cover any ordinary form of mechanical ventilation, especially if it has some element of cooling. True air conditioning means that the air is filtered to remove particles and odours, and its moisture content (humidity) and temperature are controlled. It means having the equipment to handle all conditions of temperature and humidity which may reasonably be expected. For instance in sticky summer weather to extract moisture from the air it has to be cooled by a form of refrigeration until the desired humidity level is reached. It is then too cold for comfort and so must be reheated before it is fed back into the building. In winter low relative humidity has its drawbacks and may have to be compensated for by humidifiers.

In hot weather it is high humidity which causes the most discomfort. High temperatures are much easier to tolerate if the body's natural cooling system is able to work. If the air is already loaded with moisture the body's perspiration does not evaporate quickly enough to keep it cool. The heat given off by human beings is partly radiant but it is also in the form of latent heat in the moisture they exude into the atmosphere. If on the other hand the air is too dry in winter, discomfort of a different kind in the form of sore throats is experienced.

One way to combat the stuffiness of high humidity without actually removing any moisture from the air is to supply a lot more air. It is possible to cool down quite quickly if one sits in a draught, especially if one can control the draught individually. This is the system used in aircraft, where passengers can adjust an individual air nozzle above their heads, but it is not a practical proposition for a seated audience.

Noisy, draughty systems are not acceptable, but some authorities insist on so much air per person that it is difficult to avoid either noise or draughts without an elaborate and expensive system. To keep the noise down to, say, 25 NR, the air velocity has to be kept low, and to supply the large volume of air demanded the supply ducting has to be very large in cross-sectional area. Threading this into the building and providing the extra space to house it is an expense that is often ignored in the cost calculations.

Even when these expedients have been applied, the ventilation system is more likely to give rise to complaints than any other part of the building. In the first year of its life the staff will respond to the grouses of the public about draughts by adjusting the dampers until the complaining dwindles away and a state of equilibrium is reached. By this time the amount of air delivered will be about half the design quantity and half the capacity of the plant which has been paid for.

This unsatisfactory compromise is perpetuated in Britain by respect for the old GLC regulation which called for 8 litres per second (17 cubic feet per minute) per person, regardless of whether smoking was permitted in the auditorium. This could be reduced by 50% with air conditioning, provided the relative humidity was restricted to not more than 55%. The American Society of Heating, Refrigeration and Air-Conditioning Engineers, on the other hand, recommends a series of figures which for an auditorium are far less than those of the GLC. If the money saved on a smaller air-handling plant were to be spent on full air conditioning with good control and energy management, it would not only provide more comfortable conditions but would probably be economically advantageous.

In the United Kingdom, the decision on whether to specify a full air-conditioning system or merely heating and ventilation can be a marginal and difficult one. Although calculation and reference to design manuals may indicate that full air conditioning is necessary, budget constraints may take precedence, particularly when a degree of audience discomfort due to the lack of such equipment can be expected on only a very few days each year. Elsewhere, in areas experiencing intense continuous daytime sunshine, such as parts of the Middle East, the decision is a simple one, there being no realistic alternative to a full air-conditioning system.

Heating and ventilating design brief

The mechanical services design engineer requires a detailed design brief providing information on the following aspects:

—   location, orientation, latitude, altitude and local climate conditions at the site of the theatre building
—   construction details, level of insulation, area of glazing and external surface dimensions
—   daily use pattern and occupancy
—   requirements of local legislation such as temperature and minimum ventilation rate per person
—   whether or not smoking will be permitted in the auditorium
—   lighting heat loads to be removed (this information should be provided by the manufacturers of the lighting equipment)

These details will be the basis for calculations to establish heat gains or losses attributable to the building fabric. Taken together with the heat gains from audience and lighting, internal design conditions can be established including fresh-air requirements.

Internal design criteria

Generally accepted comfort conditions are those that maintain suitable levels of temperature, humidity and air velocity. To avoid the two extremes of sensation, from air stagnation which causes stuffiness to draughts causing general discomfort, Table 21:1 can be used as a guide to room air velocity.

Table 21:1				
	Air temperature		Air velocity	
	°C	°F	metres/sec.	ft/sec.
Winter heating	19	66	0.10–0.13	0.3–0.4
	20	68	0.10–0.15	0.3–0.5
	21	70	0.15–0.20	0.5–0.7
Summer cooling	22	72	0.20–0.25	0.7–0.8
	23	73	0.25–0.30	0.8–0.9
	24	75	0.30–0.35	0.9–1

Air distribution should be designed to avoid directing air at the back of the neck and to limit temperature differences between head and foot level to a minimum, preferably not more than 1.5° C (2.7° F).

Generally relative humidity (RH) should lie between 40% and 60%. The GLC regulations stipulated a maximum of 55% under full air conditioning with a 50/50 mixing of fresh air and recirculated air. Hence a reasonable design value of 50% RH ± 5% could be used.

Acceptable internal temperature varies with local climatic conditions; for instance, people living in a hot climate become acclimatised and will accept higher temperatures as being comfortable. Whereas in Britain an inside temperature of 22° C (72° F) with 50% RH would be reasonable in summer, for a tropical climate (35° C (95° F) DB; 26.5° C (80° F) WB external) a temperature of 25.5° C (78° F) at 50% RH would be acceptable. Winter design conditions also vary throughout the world. In the United States 24° C (75° F) would be expected, while 22° C (72° F) would be acceptable in Britain in similar conditions.

Local codes of practice should be consulted; for example, the GLC stated that for theatres provision is to be made such that a minimum temperature of 13° C (55° F) is to be maintained in the unoccupied building when the outside temperature is 0° C (32° F).

Temperature of other areas should also be considered from an economic standpoint; for instance, foyers are sometimes intensively occupied only for short periods and could be heated or cooled to a transitional level between the external temperature and auditorium temperature.

Assessment of heating and cooling loads

Local climate conditions, and in particular the extremes thereof, will be the starting point in load calculations. The form of construction of theatre building must be taken into account. Changes of external temperature will take much longer to affect a heavy and well-insulated structure than a lightweight or extensively glazed building. Lower construction costs may therefore result in considerably more expensive heating and ventilating systems.

In hot climates, sun shading can cause substantial reductions to the heat gains, and this factor should be considered by the architects at the earliest stage in deciding the siting and orientation of the building.

Inside the building, heat gains from the audience are significant and must be taken into account in the design calculations. For a mixed theatre audience, a suitable design figure is 100 W average heat output per audience member.

Stage and other lighting equipment produces considerable heat loads, as described earlier in this chapter, and close co-ordination is needed between the mechanical and electrical design engineers in determining the levels to be allowed in the heat gain calculations.

Stratification

Auditoria usually have high ceilings, so that warm air floats to the top in a process of stratification. Higher temperatures are perfectly acceptable at well above audience head level. Heat gains from stage lighting will be approximately one third in the form of convection and two thirds radiation. The convected component can be removed by ventilation and need not be included in the heat gain calculations, but the radiant content must be allowed for fully. Heat gains from the building fabric, on the other hand, will be two thirds convected and only one third radiated. This being the case, the convected heat gains from the roof and walls, say, 1.5 m (5 ft) above the air outlets can be discounted in the calculations. Stratification can only be allowed for when the supply air is introduced at relatively low levels so that it does not mix with the hotter upper air strata. Introducing the air at high level, as is often done, means that the convection gains have to be taken into the reckoning. This places a greater load on the plant unless a separate exhaust system is introduced over the lighting bridges, in either case adding to the cost of the installation.

Pre-cooling and pre-heating

Where air-conditioning systems are to be provided, the use of pre-cooling techniques can reduce equipment size when considering a peak short-duration load. This is achieved by pre-cooling the air mass within the auditorium to several degrees below the design temperature while it is unoccupied before a performance when there are no fresh air or audience loads. The temperature gradually rises as the audience arrives and during the performance so that the design

temperature is attained towards the end of the show. A minimum pre-cooling time of one hour is required with a short performance time of not more than two hours. It should be noted that in these circumstance the audience may feel rather too cool upon arrival, and this may not be acceptable.

Similarly, pre-heating is normally employed in temperate climates during winter to raise the auditorium to design conditions with the heat given off by the audience and lighting being sufficient to offset fabric loss and a large portion of the ventilation loss thereafter. Hence only minimum heating of the fresh air is required during the perfomance. Under summer conditions, with the absence of fabric losses and the possible addition of fabric and solar gains, the temperatures can rise quite high and cause discomfort. If this rise cannot be limited to, say, 6° C (43° F) by ventilation alone, then cooling will be required.

Natural ventilation

In the United Kingdom, theatres traditionally relied on natural ventilation, with air being inducted at low level and exhausted through the roof of the auditorium. There can be problems in air distribution, in that audience members in the centre seats receive little fresh air, while those at the sides complain of draughts – in other words, air distribution can be erratic. The Factories Act provides some guidance for minimum ventilation rates – 5 litres per second (10 cubic feet per minute) per person – but there are no standard summer natural ventilation rates. These should be higher to cope with higher ambient temperatures, and ten air changes per hour is often taken as a minimum. It is difficult to offset heat gains and outside and inside temperature variations by purely natural ventilation, and this may be comfortably achieved only with mechanical ventilation. Affected as it is by fluctuating wind velocity and outside temperature, natural ventilation cannot be guaranteed to provide consistently the fresh-air requirements laid down in local regulations such as those of the GLC. The fact that it is difficult to produce a calculation which will satisfy a local authority that natural ventilation will work is probably one of the main reasons why it is not often attempted at present.

In theory at least, it is only possible to have complete control of the amount of fresh air introduced into a building by using a mechanical system.

The great advantage of natural ventilation is that it makes use of the forces of nature that are present in any case, and in these days of energy conservation we ought once again to be looking for methods of controlling our environment which do not require more and more heavy plant to defy the natural order of things. There is a great deal of energy in warm air which has the power to suck in cooler air from outside a building by what is called the stack effect. External wind pressures may be much more powerful than this hot air rising within the building, but there are ways of adjusting the fresh air intake to compensate for this. Instead of forcing air to move in a direction opposite to that in which it would naturally go, and providing plant and burning extra fuel to make it do so, we should make use of this potential energy, let the air flow as it wants, and nudge it in the direction we want.

It is possible to ventilate a small auditorium of, say, 200 seats in a temperate climate in a moderately open location purely by natural ventilation, avoiding the expense of installing, running and maintaining fans and ducting and without the risk of noise. Larger projects and less favourable climates will of course call for mechanically ventilated systems, but these too should be designed to augment the natural flow rather than oppose it.

Comparison of recommended air supply rates

The following comparisons show the variance in the standards for fresh-air supply rates laid down by some authoritative bodies.

1. *Chartered Institution of Building Service Engineers* (CIBSE), Guide B2:
   Table B2–2, *Mechanical ventilation*, states 6 to 10 air changes per hour, but refers to GLC regulation of 8 litres per second (17 cubic ft per minute) per person.
   Table B2–4, *Air-conditioned spaces*, states 8 litres per second and refers to local bye-laws.

2. *British Standards* 5720 and 5925: 1980, codes of practice for mechanical and natural ventilation respectively, recommend 8 litres per second (17 cubic ft per minute) for theatres with "some smoking", though they do not refer specifically to auditoria. They also refer to local bye-laws.

3. *American Society of Heating, Refrigeration and Air-Conditioning Engineers* (ASHRAE), Standard 62–73:

4. *GLC Technical Regulations.* This document stipulates a minimum fresh-air supply per occupant of 8 litres per second (17 cubic ft per minute). If the air is suitably warmed and cleaned, it may consist of 75% outside air and 25% recirculated air. If the air is fully conditioned and limited to a maximum relative humidity of 55%, the supply can be 50% outside air and 50% recirculated air.

The locally adopted codes will have a profound effect on the design of the ventilation system. As smoking is now rarely permitted in auditoria in the United Kingdom it would be no hardship to ban it altogether. In these circumstances there is a case for reassessing the rates of fresh-air supply and bringing them closer to the American standards.

Air distribution – auditorium

As in temperate climates heating is generally only needed for warming up the auditorium before the audience enters, the main requirement during occupancy is clean cool air.

Bearing in mind the critical reservations already made in this chapter, a standard method of supplying this air remains through ceiling diffusers. The cool air tends to absorb heat from the lighting and rising heat generated by the audience above the seating area. Direct exhaust above lighting bridges removes some of the heat generated by the stage-lighting lanterns mounted on the bridges, and should be adopted where practicable. Ceiling diffusers being remote from the audience, air noise from them is less of a problem.

Return air registers in this case are situated under seats or in risers and at low level around the hall. The maximum acceptable velocity of air from underseat registers to avoid uncomfortable draughts is 1.4 metres per second (4.6 ft/sec.).

Use of a distribution system whereby the supply air diffusers are selected for the highest velocity consistent with low noise levels can result in insuffi-

Area	Minimum		Recommended	
	litres/sec.	ft³/min.	litres/sec.	ft³/min.
Foyers and lobbies	10	21	12.5–15	27–32
Auditorium (No-smoking)	2.5	5	2.5–5	5–10
Auditorium (Smoking permitted)	5	10	5–10	10–21
Stage	5	10	6–7.5	13–16
Working areas	5	10	6–7.5	13–16

If adequate temperature regulation is provided and filtration restricts air particle content to 6 mg/m³ (0.17 mg/ft³), the outdoor air may be reduced to 33% of the listed quantity. Further reduction to 15% is possible with extra odour/gas removal equipment, but in no case should outdoor air supply be less than 2.5 litres per second (5 cubic ft per minute) per person.

The auditorium figures above may also be reduced if the facility is used for a short time and if the air can be flushed out between performances.

cient throw to parts of the auditorium. Hence the return air flow should be designed to pull the air down over the audience, so avoiding dead spots. The object is to introduce the cold air at high level in a blanket which is drawn down by the return air system.

An alternative is to use jet-type diffusers having throws of 15–40 m (50–130 ft), either ceiling or side wall-mounted. They should be able to cover most theatre configurations. This type of air distribution does give more of a feeling of freshness by inducing a more positive air movement throughout the auditorium. However, there is a danger of raising the noise levels. If jet-type diffusers are to be used, the design engineer should consult fully with the diffuser manufacturer when selecting the equipment.

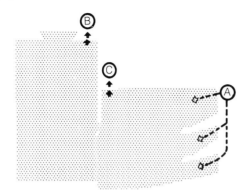

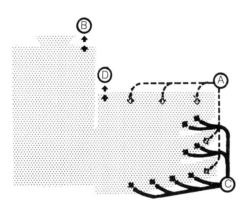

21:2. Diagrams illustrating displacement ventilation systems based on GLC requirements.

1 (above). Simple plenum system with one inlet fan and independent stage and auditorium extract fans:
 A = inlet fan
 B = stage extract fan (capacity 40% of total)
 C = auditorium extract fan (capacity 60% of total)
 Total capacity of extracts to equal 75% of input
 Usual order of starting: B, A, C
 (Where convenient, the stage extract for B and the auditorium extract for C can be combined into one extract fan common to both.)

2 (below). Downward system with inlet fan and independent stage and auditorium extract fans:
 A = inlet fan
 B = stage extract fan (capacity 40% of total)
 C = auditorium extract fan (capacity 60% of total)
 D = auditorium emergency extract fan (capacity 60% of total)
 Total capacity of extracts to equal 75% of input
 Extract from the auditorium in normal circumstances is by ducts under the seating. The stage extract discharges directly to the open air. On lowering the safety curtain or operation of emergency controls, the normal extract from the auditorium stops and the emergency auditorium extract fan starts.
 Usual order of starting: B, A, C

Note: *A single fan may combine the duties of fans C and D, changeover dampers being arranged in the ductwork so that in normal circumstances air is extracted from below the seating. In an emergency, this is shut off and the extract duct above the proscenium arch is opened. Order of starting would then be: B, A, (C and D)*

Other methods

In small and medium-size theatres it is possible to use alternative methods of distribution, such as upward distribution from floor outlets. However, the limitations of velocity and low permissible temperature differentials – 3° C (5° F) – apply if draughts are to be avoided. Another form is crossflow distribution, but throw and noise are limiting factors.

System design

Because of their large volume coupled with high fresh-air requirements, auditoria are normally designed to have all-air systems usually using low-pressure single-zone units. Owing to practical limitations in equipment size and space, an auditorium will normally be served by a number of units. Auditorium air handling units should ideally be equipped with the facility to automatically use up to 100% outside air when economic to do so and to be remotely adjustable from 100% fresh air to virtually 100% recirculated air to cater for reduced loads during rehearsals and for pre-cooling and flushing if desired. Heat reclaim should also be considered; up to 70% of the energy in the exhaust air can be reclaimed by air-to-air heat exchangers of various types.

The ductwork system should be low-velocity, self-balancing preferably without dampers, acoustically lined and ending with air termination devices specifically selected to provide the required distribution with a minimum of noise. Ductwork outlet velocities range from 5.0 m/s (16 ft/sec.) down to 2.5 m/s (8 ft/sec.) in noise-sensitive areas, such as under balconies. Full co-ordination is required with the architect and structural engineer to ensure that large ducts are accommodated in the ceiling space without obstructing access ladders and walkways. This is often not the case; in more than one example, walkways above the auditorium false ceiling have been reduced to crawlways.

Air distribution – stage

The stage area presents a particularly difficult problem in its volume, configuration, and usually greater external exposure to the elements. The only form of heating on the stage of most existing theatres in Britain is either recessed wall-mounted radiators or natural convectors. Air distribution systems on the stage, whether for heating or cooling, are difficult to design because scenery is an unknown quantity and often varies during the performance. It is also generally of lightweight construction and can be shaken even by relatively gentle air flows.

If a warm-air or air-conditioned system is to be installed, then the air should be supplied at very low velocities – 2.5 m/s (8 ft/sec.) – at the low side or back of the stage, but finding room for ductwork in these positions is difficult. One method is to suspend the ductwork below the stage side galleries and rear crossover gallery (where provided) and to discharge towards the stage centre.

The floor plays such a crucial role in the theatrical use of the stage that return air grilles and ducting in the stage floor are not usually a practical proposition; nor can they compete with the stack effect of the fly tower. However, provision for return air from the stage area should be included where possible. It can be discharged through ductwork mounted below the loading gallery, with the exhaust air taken from the top of the fly tower together with exhaust air from the auditorium lighting bridges.

In winter conditions provision should be made for heating the stage sufficiently before the performance to avoid a column of cold air collecting in the fly tower and flowing over the stalls in an icy draught when the curtain is raised.

Another problem is billowing of the stage curtain from the stack effect in the fly tower, caused by heat from the lighting and temperature differential between stage and auditorium. It can be reduced to a minimum with good air-flow temperature distribution and careful balancing.

Foyer ventilation

Foyers are subject to heavy peak demands during interval times and at the start and finish of the show, when for twenty to thirty minutes they can be densely populated with smokers. Such areas are normally served by separate equipment. The ventilation units should have adjustable exhaust and recirculation facilities with perhaps two-speed operation. ASHRAE Standard 62–73 recommends 12.5 to 15 litres per second (27–32 cubic ft per minute) per person of fresh air, while the CIBSE Guide recommends 18 litres per second (38 ft^3 per minute).

Other areas

Backstage rooms and corridors pose no unusual problems and should be dealt with using conventional systems. A separate ventilation system to serve the orchestra pit may be needed. Some means of removing the heat gains in the dimmer rooms should not be forgotten either.

Controls and energy management

As in so many aspects of theatre design, so with the mechanical services: the system has to be flexible to meet the many different conditions of use of the building. Energy should be used economically, and controls to make this possible should be considered early in the project. They will have to be simple and easily understood so that they can be operated by the theatre staff, who cannot be expected to be highly skilled mechanical engineers.

Consideration should be given to central and local equipment covering any or all of the following:

— warm air heating and humidification
— cooling and heating with changeover; this may also involve humidification control
— control of air dampers between 100% fresh air and 100% recirculated air
— monitoring and operation to permit adjustments during a performance

Filtration

Generally filtration systems for auditoria have been minimal, with ASHRAE Standard 52–76 recommending filters of 30–35% efficiency. With the advent of smoking bans in public buildings and theatres, as well as energy conservation, this should be reconsidered.

An air-conditioned theatre, for instance, having smoking zones served by a number of units would have an obvious air recirculation problem. Under such circumstances filters with 80% efficiency or higher would be required to remove tobacco smoke effectively. Cleaner air also has the advantage of providing better protection to the finishes and decorations generally.

Systems with floor supply and exhaust air diffusers and registers become dirt collectors and impose severe strains on filters and cooling coils. This can be eased by incorporating a low-velocity settling chamber to intercept some of the dust.

The theatre staff must be instructed in a regular routine of cleaning and replacing filters, which, if neglected, can put the whole ventilation system out of action.

Table 21:2	Noise levels		
Application	Desired NR level	Acceptable NR level	Maximum NR level
Theatre and concert	20	25	30
Conference and cinema	30	35	40

Consultation at design stage with an experienced acoustics engineer is recommended. To achieve NR 20 within the space requires that the noise levels from mechanical equipment and the noise coming into the space from outside or adjacent spaces must not exceed NR 15.

In practice this means locating the mechanical equipment away from the auditorium, preferably on a separate independent structure. Transmission of noise and vibration can be reduced by mounting pipes and ducts on acoustic spring isolator supports and equipment having isolation joints and pads.

If the mechanical equipment rooms are close to the auditorium it may be necessary to float the rooms on isolators.

22

Arts centres and studio theatres

The term "arts centre" is not a very precise one; it is applied to a range of hybrid enterprises which may include performing arts, exhibitions and educational activities such as classes in the arts and crafts.

Theatres up to the first half of this century were built very much for their primary purpose, and in Britain they had little space to spare for any other activities. The buildings were efficiently and functionally designed to cope with the coming and going of an audience every evening, sometimes twice in an evening, and for two matinees a week. Outside those hours they were closed to the public, as are most London West End theatres today.

Customs have changed, and since the Second World War, particularly where there is a resident company, the trend has been to keep theatres open all day, inviting the public to take their refreshment in the foyers, to look at exhibitions and to be entertained informally. If the programme includes music and film shows, the organisation sometimes likes to claim that it is an arts centre.

The other genesis of the arts centre begins with a place where painting, sculpture and crafts are practised and exhibited. By expanding to include serving refreshments to the public, encouraging the use of the premises for social contacts, and then adding a performance space, it can call itself an arts centre.

Some arts centres are purely professional (for example the Barbican in London), but most are community-based and include both amateur and professional artists and performers. Unless it originated as a theatre, the performance space is likely to be of the drama-studio type, adaptable, fairly small, say two or three hundred seats, and without much concession to comfort. An austere character with all the works showing is all part of the image of the studio theatre. It should turn out very similar whether it is the second auditorium of a theatre or the performance space added on to an exhibition or educational building. It is unlikely to be equipped with a fly tower or the machinery developed for the proscenium theatre, but it will still need space to store, manoeuvre and suspend scenery, stage-lighting and sound systems.

Such performance spaces come in all shapes and sizes, often influenced by having to be fitted into existing buildings. They will need most of the ancillary accommodation described in this book, albeit on a commensurate scale to the brief: dressing rooms; stage management and staff, technical rooms for lighting and sound systems, storage space for scenery, maintenance wardrobe, lavatories and washing facilities. Being part of an arts centre or one of a group of other activities, foyers, bars and refreshments are assumed to be already available. In a place where there is a continual programme of arts activities it is particularly important to check that there is complete sound insulation between the performance space and other parts of the building and complete independence of the stage organisation from any of the other activities which may coincide with a performance.

Our concern in this book is with the requirements for stage and auditoria, not the whole range of possible arts activities which can and do take place in arts centres. Detailed information can be found elsewhere on the design of painters' and sculptors' studios, workshops for potters, printers, cabinet-makers, etc. The list can be a very long one and may include sports and games and a library.

The great advantage of an arts centre is that it provides a meeting place for people interested in many different aspects of the arts. However, these multifarious activities are not always compatible. For instance, potters and sculptors covered with clay and plaster do not necessarily mix happily with those who have come to see a play. Finishes for the clean areas are not necessarily suitable for the dirty ones.

Smaller theatres

In this category we are considering auditoria with fewer than 300 seats. There is a wide variety and they have many names:

Fringe theatre

This is not so much a type of building as a theatrical movement. Independent groups without the resources to hire a full-scale theatre find makeshift premises where they can show their work to a limited public. The work is often new and of a high standard, and the movement is a seed-bed for talent which frequently moves on to the mainstream theatre. The premises they occupy, typically in the upstairs rooms of public houses, are usually appalling and unlicensable by the authorities. The company has to be dedicated to work in such atrocious conditions.

Some of the groups eventually manage to find the support and the cash to build themselves properly equipped theatres.

Studio theatre

This is often the name given to the second or third auditorium of a theatre complex. The main house puts on the shows it considers have a wide popular appeal, while the studio stages the less orthodox or "experimental" work. A lively company will want to pursue a wider range of work than can be produced in one 450-to-900-seat house, and this is a matter which should be discussed at the briefing stage. With the budget inevitably restricted, it is an easy way out to omit the studio. Sometimes it is slipped in as a rehearsal room, or at any rate what was originally called a rehearsal room on the plans becomes the studio. This is a poor way of achieving a second auditorium, because a rehearsal room should be designed to be used in connection with the main stage and the dressing rooms, and need not have any direct access to the front-of-house. A studio, on the other hand, is better approached from the foyers, where the audience can use the amenities of the main public areas.

When there is a performance in both or either of the auditoria the team involved in each must be independent of the other. Clashes of use of technical areas could disturb the smooth running of either show.

Adaptable/flexible/experimental theatres

These terms can be appropriate to larger theatres but are more often applied to smaller-capacity studios where the adaptability can be handled fairly simply. The question of adaptability has been discussed in Chapter 2.

There was a time when the drama theorists rejected the concept of an auditorium in any architectural sense and asked to be provided with a box of tricks with which they could invent their own theatre starting from scratch for each production. The interior had to be black and neutral, and all the equipment for seating, for the stage, for lighting and sound had to be adjustable, mobile, flexible, adaptable etc. Such an ideal is an immensely seductive challenge to a designer's ingenuity, and much time and money has been spent on attempts to devise infinitely variable systems. It soon becomes apparent in use that every system has its limitations, and in the elaborately mechanised versions these are often more tiresome than the familiar limitations of a permanent auditorium layout. Directors have enough to think about without having to rebuild the auditorium for every production. The constituent of the experience of drama which suffered most from the black-box theory was the audience. It was more suited to the self-indulgent theatre groups who would really have preferred to do without any audience at all. They seemed to be more interested in group therapy than group theatre.

There are a number of criteria to be met in a successful studio theatre depending upon the activities for which it is to be used and the policy of the company using it.

Height

A low ceiling is one of the most inhibiting features of a performance space. For sightlines it will be necessary to build up seating; for dancers there must be height enough to leap or to lift a partner; for lighting there must be room to suspend lanterns etc. The minimum practical requirement is a double-height room with enough space for a gallery with sufficient headroom above and below it. If space and the budget allow, it is valuable to have a basement under the main floor with the possibility of providing entrances from below or stage traps as on an orthodox stage. Similarly an additional

gallery for technicians with access to the grid overhead is better than having to rig lanterns and scenic pieces to the grid from ladders or access towers.

Floor

The floor is the most important element in the practical working of the studio theatre. If it is used permanently as a miniature proscenium theatre or end stage, it will need a raked or stepped floor for the seating and probably a raised stage. There may be some flexibility in the front of the stage to form some kind of orchestra pit, but the problems are the same as for a larger auditorium scaled down. If the intention is to serve a wider range of activities, then it will probably be better to have a flat floor upon which it is possible to move seating and acting area about. This can be done manually, but there are various useful mechanical methods, of which the most common is "bleacher seating", developed initially for sports halls and gymnasia. The name derives from the open-air benches in sports arenas where spectators were bleached by the sun. They are banks of retractable seating which fold up into a stack taking up little more floor space than a single row of seats. They can be spartan backless benches like the original bleachers, but it is now more usual to have upholstered folding chairs for a more comfortable installation.

They are mechanically most effective when they are in simple rectangular blocks of, say, 150 seats. It is possible to make them wedge-shaped in plan so that they can be made to form a seating layout focused on a stage area, but it is a rather clumsy arrangement, and for this purpose it is probably better to have the shaped seating blocks on tailor-made rostra.

A practical point that should be watched is the way the supporting wheels run on the floor and where they rest when they are carrying the considerable load of an audience. The floor structure and finish must be strong enough to stand up to the additional stress and wear.

Sightlines

When bleachers are used on a flat floor and there is no raised stage there is a tendency to distance the actors from the audience. This happens when the stage is at the same level as the front row of seats, whose occupants mask the bottom half of a performer who gets too close to them. For the whole of him to be seen by all the spectators he must be about 3 m (10 ft) at least from the front row. If the stage is raised to form a stage riser, he can easily be seen over the heads of the front row. However, raising the stage in a flat-floored hall is usually inconvenient because the platform has to be assembled, which takes time and effort, and everything used on the stage has to be lifted up on to it. It is much simpler if the stage remains at the normal flat-floor level coinciding with all the access points to it. The problem can be solved by forming a trough at the edge of the acting area into which the first two or three rows of seats can be put. This creates a stage riser and has the added advantage of reducing the number of bleachers or seating on rostra that are required. This matter has been discussed in Chapter 3 (Sightlines).

Storage

The paraphernalia of flexibility makes great demands on storage space. To clear the floor of chairs, platforms and rostra, let alone scenery and stage properties, requires large stores, or the floor space of the main hall will be cluttered with stacks of temporarily unwanted apparatus. One solution is to use a large platform lift to take the equipment to space under the floor in a basement. If this lift has another use, for instance to form an orchestra pit, it may be easier to justify it economically.

Circulation and access

In a flexible studio theatre the acting area could theoretically be put anywhere within the space, and it follows that performers and spectators must have possible access points all round. An actor normally needs to be able to reach his entrance unseen by an audience, and if there is no space for circulation outside the auditorium it may have to be created within it by curtains or temporary partitions.

Incidentally a rectangular hall offers more opportunities for variety of staging than a square one with all sides equal. It is better to have the choice of putting the acting area on either the long or the short side.

Seating

A theatre company putting on a regular programme of public performances will probably need reasonably comfortable upholstered seating even if some of it is on mobile rostra. Harder plastic shells may be acceptable if public performances are infrequent or the audience are fellow students or pupils at a school or college.

Lighting

It must be possible to exclude all external light, but it is still desirable to be able to have daylight in the auditorium for some purposes.

Rehearsals need not be conducted in artificial light in the early stages of a production; stage lighting will be introduced only quite late in the process. If the space is to be used for a range of purposes, daylight will clearly be a positive advantage in many of them. It is only dress rehearsals and performances or film and slide projection which must have a complete blackout, and even some performances such as music recitals can tolerate

daylight. If the building is used purely for drama presentation or as a cinema, there is a case for the total exclusion of outside light, but if it lays claim to be a multi-purpose hall it will be at a severe disadvantage without daylight.

A stage-lighting system is probably best handled by installing a grid over the entire area from which lanterns can be suspended where needed. Ideally the grid should be accessible from lighting galleries above it or integrated with it. The control of the stage lighting can be in a separate control room, as described elsewhere in this book, but a small portable control desk which can be plugged in at various points in the studio allows much greater flexibility of use and is probably more appropriate.

Sound

The importance of insulating a performance space against noise from outside has already been emphasised. There should not be any problems with acoustics for the human voice in an auditorium which holds no more than two or three hundred seats.

For a stage sound system it is probably best to have a mobile control desk, as for the lighting, but it will need a secure store or small room to pack it away.

23

Conference facilities

There has been a steadily expanding demand over the last twenty-five years for conference facilities and growing competition to satisfy that demand. The very large conference centres, usually adjuncts to exhibition halls, have special requirements which are best purpose-designed, but many smaller meetings can be successfully catered for by theatres and arts centres without compromising their primary use. In some ways a theatre with a well-equipped stage can provide a better service than a typical conference auditorium, for instance for the launch of a new product such as a motor car with a dramatic presentation using the resources of the stage machinery, lighting and sound.

Conferences and conventions, a term with a more American significance, are good business because they *are* business and benefit from the tax advantage of business expenses against which their costs can be claimed. They are often as much entertainment and celebration as they are work or the serious exchange of information. International conferences usually have connections with tourism and benefit the country in which they are held in both direct and indirect ways.

Types and sizes

In terms of frequency there are far more small gatherings of up to fifty people than large conventions with hundreds attending. Their purpose may be, for example, the training of staff in some new technique or system, or it may be a seminar at which ideas and experiences are shared, or a meeting of shareholders or a group with a common professional interest. These are the kind of gatherings for which the organisation or firm arranging them cannot use its own premises and has to look for somewhere to hire for the purpose.

These smaller conferences and meetings can often be accommodated by hotels or in the secondary spaces of purpose-built conference centres. Theatres and arts centres can also handle such gatherings with minimum disruption to the normal programme if the dual use of an area such as a rehearsal room or restaurant can be arranged.

For medium-size conferences of 200–500 participants, where it is important for speakers to be clearly seen and heard and for films and other audiovisual aids to be presented, it becomes increasingly advantageous to have a properly designed and equipped auditorium. This is the range where theatres and arts centres can compete on favourable terms with fully-fledged conference centres.

This chapter is therefore primarily concerned with providing the outline information that can enable a theatre or arts centre to offer conference and convention facilities in the main auditorium as a supplement to normal activities. From an economic point of view it can be a particular advantage for them to be able to offer such services using minimum numbers of administrative and technical personnel during the closed season or holiday shutdown period.

The larger gatherings, where a thousand or more may participate, need a great deal of back-up and may be too great a strain on an organisation which does not regularly provide for such a number. Once these larger conferences exceed the seating availability of conventional theatres, they can be accommodated only by the few large purpose-built conference auditoria with suitably vast capacities. Specialist publications are available on the subject, and the design of such centres is outside the scope of this book. The temptation to use the very large auditoria evolved from conference requirements for theatrical performances, for which they are most unsatisfactory, should be resisted.

Support facilities

Many conferences and meetings, smaller ones included, run for more than one day and may involve a national or international gathering of participants. It is therefore essential that a suitable number and quality of hotel rooms together with restaurant or banqueting facilities are available in the immediate vicinity of the conference venue.

The larger conferences, particularly the international ones, will only select venues where sufficient hotel accommodation is available. This gives the big cities an advantage and it has also boosted the flagging fortunes of seaside and other resort towns where there is much under-used hotel accommodation outside the traditional holiday season. The event may also be dependent upon transport being laid on. Quite often airlines are involved in special charter flights, and coaches may have to be provided to ferry the delegates about.

Trade fairs are frequently associated with conferences, and in this case the proximity of the exhibition halls is all-important. Where the main purpose is educational, universities and schools are usually best equipped, and their premises can be used out of term-time.

Besides needing transport, hotel accommodation and meals, the conference delegates will also require good communications by post, telephone, telex, facsimile, copying and possibly other secretarial services. For business conferences the venue which can provide these facilities has an advantage over the less well equipped.

Whether such investments in space, equipment and staff are economically viable depends upon the frequency with which they will be used. For the smaller theatre or arts centre with a mixed programme, it is difficult to justify elaborate conference provisions, but it is still possible to engage outside contractors to provide the services required if there is a suitable space in which they can operate.

Seating layouts

At the medium or larger conference in a theatre, procedures will often require participants to move between their seats in the auditorium and a speaker's lectern or podium on the stage.

Theatres are not always designed with direct access from auditorium to stage, and to avoid the necessity of going outside the hall, steps should be provided either permanently or temporarily for an easy route to the platform. The need for freer movement within the seating area suggests wider spacing of seats and rows than would normally be expected in a layout designed only for a theatre audience. Continental seating in very long rows is more likely to interfere with freedom of movement than seating in smaller blocks with intermediate aisles.

Sometimes there is a requirement for writing tables for each conference participant. University lecture theatres are well equipped in this way, but it is not so easy to make such provision in an auditorium normally used for theatrical performances. There are chairs which can be fitted with a clip-on table or have a fold-down table at the back, as in an airline seat, but these have other shortcomings when used as theatre seats.

Conference microphone systems

There are two fundamentally different conference formats, each having a completely different set of requirements and problems. The first takes the form of an enlarged committee meeting or even a parliamentary body. In these circumstances every member must be able to address the meeting from his seat, which should be provided with either an individual microphone or, at worst, one between two adjacent seats. Each speaker should be able to see and be seen by the complete gathering without the discomfort of too much twisting and turning of heads. Conferences of this kind at the simpler levels are best handled by seating members around an oval table or an arrangement of rectangular tables in a similar form. Such facilities are frequently offered by hotels or by the smaller rooms of a purpose-built conference centre. With greater numbers, a specially designed meeting chamber becomes essential. Models for this can be found among the world's parliament buildings and council chambers, provided they are examined with a critical eye. Not all are well designed, and some seating configurations are quite unsuitable.

In the second principal format, those present are basically divided into a small panel of experts or eminent persons and an audience. One or more of the former may make speeches, while the latter's participation is restricted to questions or comments from a limited number of its members. It is for this kind of conference that a traditional stage and auditorium arrangement are ideally suited, the panel of speakers being seated at a table on the stage with the audience using all or part of the auditorium.

An essential requirement of all but the smallest conferences is microphone access for all participants. The special problems that this poses have been recognised by a number of manufacturers, such as Philips, Netherlands, and DIS Congress, Denmark, who produce purpose-built systems including delegate panels and microphone management controls. A typical delegate's panel will be fitted with a gooseneck microphone, a "request-to-speak" pushbutton and a "permission-to-speak" or "microphone-alive" indicator. The chairman's panel will be more elaborate and will have a take-control or override pushbutton.

Most purpose-built conference centres use a conventional theatre seating arrangement for their main hall. There are some examples in which every seat or pair of seats in the auditorium is provided with an individual microphone panel, usually built into the armrests. Some designs have been introduced where every second row is used for seating and the row in between is adapted to provide desks.

Conference systems with large numbers of microphones require a sophisticated control and management system. At the very simplest level this comprises a control panel with one pushbutton per delegate microphone panel. A request-to-speak action by a delegate could cause the corresponding pushbutton on the control panel to illuminate. Selection of that button by the conference chairman or operator would switch on the delegate's microphone and a microphone-alive indicator on his panel. In recent years conference microphone systems have become more and more elaborate as the latest microprocessor technology has been applied. Chairman or operator controls of larger systems now comprise a keyboard, VDU and sometimes a printer. Master panels of medium-range systems are provided with illuminated displays to identify the seat numbers of delegates who have requested to speak. Systems can generally be operated in manual or automatic mode; in the former the chairman selects the next speaker while in the latter there is automatic microphone selection and queueing on the basis of FIFO – first in, first out.

Delegate identification at the control panel or VDU is by the individual panel number which in turn corresponds to a seat number. If delegates are given pre-assigned seat numbers, then with microprocessor systems their names can be entered against seat numbers before the conference starts using the alpha-numeric keyboard. In this way, the delegate's name as well as seat number appears on the chairman's VDU when he makes a request to speak.

All this technology sounds splendid in theory but faced with a non-technical chairman it can very easily break down. In the few minutes he is on the platform before the conference starts, he probably has a lot to think about without learning how to use an unfamiliar switchboard studded with coloured lights.

Simultaneous translation

In conferences with an international audience, it is essential to be able to provide simultaneous translation facilities. The interpreters sit in soundproof booths with a view of the speaker, listening to the speech on headphones. The translation is spoken into a microphone and broadcast on a frequency chosen for that particular language. Each delegate has headphones and a receiver which can be tuned to the channel broadcasting the chosen language. The floor language – that spoken by the speaker – is broadcast over the auditorium sound reinforcement system.

Planning requirements for translators' booths are covered in Chapter 15 (Control rooms).

There are three principal types of simultaneous interpretation system:

1. Inductive loop, using magnetic field transmission generated by a conductor looped around the auditorium either above the false ceiling or under the floor. Specialist advice is necessary in positioning the loop cable.

2. Infra-red, using modulated light signals which are radiated from a number of sources.

3. Hard-wired, using cabling installed in underfloor trunking and connected to panels in the armrest or back of each seat.

The inductive loop and infra-red types use lightweight battery-powered delegate receivers with plug-in leads to headphones. Large numbers of delegates mean large numbers of portable receivers, which in turn means large numbers of staff to hand out and collect the receivers at the beginning and end of each conference session. The exercise must be handled in a disciplined way if losses of receivers and headsets are to be kept within acceptable limits. There is a certain analogy with the headsets for airline in-flight entertainment systems. Generally an infra-red system is more costly than an inductive loop, but it has security advantages in that auditorium walls form a screen which prevents eavesdropping from outside.

Wired systems involve greater overall capital cost when trunking, cabling and chair modification costs are taken into account. However, in a heavily used conference centre they are cheaper to operate, as less front-of-house staff are needed and there are no disposable or rechargeable batteries to be considered. It makes good economic sense to install a hard-wired type of simultaneous interpretation system in an auditorium in which all chairs are in any case to be fitted with delegate microphone panels.

Voting systems

Conference systems employing individual delegate panels can easily be extended to provide voting facilities. Each panel is fitted with three additional pushbuttons offering the choice of YES, NO and ABSTAIN. It is normal practice to provide one or more alpha-numeric display panels in conjunction with a voting system. With a microprocessor-controlled conference system, counting of votes is achieved virtually instantaneously, and the chairman's panel includes a button which can be pressed to release the voting totals on to the display panel.

Delegate identification

Yet another advanced facility of a microprocessor-based conference system is a delegate badge reader. At registration, each delegate is presented with an embossed or magnetically encoded credit-card-type badge, and when he takes his place in the conference hall, he inserts his card into a slot in the seat's conference panel. Operation of his request-to-speak button causes the delegate's name to be displayed on the conference chairman or technical operator's VDU. The badge reader system can also incorporate individual hotel-type message-awaiting indicators.

Lectern

A further important piece of special equipment where lectures and illustrated talks are given is a lectern. In addition to a place for a script, a light to illuminate it, a jug of water and a glass, there would be a microphone, possibly of a lapel-fixing type, controls for the dimming of the lights in the hall, for remote operation of the slide and video projectors, and a hand-operated light pointer. The lectern may even include a teleprompter screen.

The lectern may be provided under the furniture sub-contract, as its appearance will need to match tables and chairs placed on the stage and generally to fit in with the auditorium decor. The lectern microphone and control panel, however, would form part of the audiovisual sub-contract. An integral, motorised lectern-raise-and-lower device is a worthwhile facility, as some speakers will be tall and others short, and it gives speakers the choice of sitting or standing to deliver their message.

Projection systems

Audiovisual aids are vital accessories to a conference or presentation. Theatres or arts centres intending to offer conference usage during closed-season or holiday periods should seriously consider the installation of projection facilities for film (16 mm and 35 mm), slides and video. These systems are fully described in Chapter 14 (Film projection).

24

Restoration of old theatres

The surge in the provision of new theatres in Britain during the sixties and seventies, mostly to house or rehouse the repertory companies, has subsided now that demand has been largely satisfied. During this time the old Victorian and Edwardian city theatres were unfashionable and neglected, and many of them disappeared before their merits were once again recognised. It has now been realised that they are well suited to provide a base for provincial or touring operatic, dance and theatre companies and that they are worth preserving for their own sake, as many of them are buildings of great character and interest.

In many parts of the world there are theatres of similar quality in need of rescue. In countries like Britain, where they were built for commercial reasons to meet a current demand, they have been lost in greater numbers than in most of the European states, where the theatres and opera houses were, and remain, important elements of the city in their own right alongside the town hall, the civic library, the cathedral, the castle and the gaol. They have a monumental status never accorded to even the most famous theatres in Britain.

In the forty years before the First World War there was a boom in theatre building before the cinema took over as the great entertainer of the masses. In contrast to the restless experiments of our recent past, there was then a standard form: the proscenium or picture-frame theatre. Within the limitations of this form, theatres were competently and often very skilfully planned. The architects who designed them had plenty of experience to learn from, and their buildings worked in a practical way. In Britain, Frank Matcham, the doyen of them all, is variously reputed to have built, or substantially altered, 100 to 200, and many of the other architects who designed theatres, and later cinemas, learned their skills in his office.

Matcham's buildings have now reached a dangerous age, and although many have already disappeared or are threatened with extinction, others such as the Coliseum and the Palladium in London still play an important role in the theatre world. The many opera houses and playhouses with which Matcham and his contemporaries embellished the cities and towns of the British Isles are now 75 to 100 years old or more, and the fabric of such buildings is usually in need of extensive repair. Leases are coming to an end and commercial pressures are strong. Unfortunately theatres are one of the many types of building that no longer provide a profitable return on the large investment involved. They are protected to a certain extent by the town planning regulations, which will not permit a live-theatre use to be changed. But this can lead to a stalemate while the owners and local government (often the same) squabble among themselves, and the building begins to deteriorate — sometimes until it is beyond redemption.

When these old theatres were first built there was no competition from cinema or television, and many of them had large seating capacities. A fair proportion of the audience was up in "the gods", with uncomfortable benches and a distant view of the stage. These under-privileged seats are seldom used today but the capacity is still large without them, and there remain forms of entertainment for which they are suitable. Opera, for instance, has steadily increased in popularity in recent years, and the artistic standards of the British companies have never been higher. However, all attempts to build a new full-scale opera house in the United Kingdom have foundered; even in its never-had-it-so-good years, this country was too parsimonious to invest in such a project. The National Theatre was intended to have a National Opera House as its companion on the South Bank, but that has been forgotten long ago; and the saga of the Edinburgh Opera House went on for years before finally coming to a rancorous end.

In some places the gap has been filled by refurbishing the big old theatres to provide a venue for the national opera and ballet companies and for large-scale musicals. The Coliseum (1904) houses the English National Opera in London, and the Grand Theatre in Leeds (1878) – a remarkable building – is the home of its sister company, Opera North. Scottish Opera is staged in the attractively restored Kings Theatre in Glasgow (1904). The Grand Opera House, Belfast (1895), and the Buxton Opera House (1903), both by Matcham, have been refurbished and are embarking on new careers. The Theatre Royal, Nottingham (1865), has been lavishly refurbished; improvements have been made in the Birmingham Hippodrome (1899); the Palace, Manchester (1891; auditorium 1915), has recently reopened; and the New Theatre Royal, Portsmouth (1880, by Phipps, extensively altered by Matcham in 1900), is being restored.

Some of the smaller Victorian and Edwardian theatres can also be adapted satisfactorily for use by repertory companies, as at the Harrogate Theatre (1900); but in general the regional theatre companies are the ones that have been rehoused in new buildings.

Assuming general repairs to the fabric are carried out as in refurbishing any old building, the particular problems of theatres are as follows.

The auditorium

Many of these were expertly designed and need to be treated with respect. The first task will be to remove unsightly additions such as loudspeakers, lighting bars and advertising projectors. Positions for stage lighting will have to be found front-of-house, and it will be difficult if not impossible to hide them completely. Modern theatres take account (or should do so) of the necessity for lighting positions at the sides and in the ceiling of the auditorium, but in the old theatres these are the places where the decorations which create the atmosphere are concentrated. Domes in the ceiling and moulded balcony fronts to circles and boxes should not be disfigured with crude lighting bars tacked on at random. One method of avoiding this problem is to put the lighting positions in the roof space and devise a trap door or sliding panel which remains closed until the house lights dim and the performance begins. This is not so simple with the essential side positions, but it is sometimes possible to incorporate the lighting within the boxes.

24:1. The auditorium of the London Old Vic (1818), reopened in 1984 after restoration by Renton Howard Wood Levin – the latest in a series of alterations (1871, 1879, 1928, 1950, 1963)

If the gallery is still in its original state, with steep rows and benches without arms, it is now unlikely to be acceptable to the public or to the licensing authority. The back part of the gallery is a useful place to locate the lighting and sound control rooms, and there is often plenty of space which becomes available for other uses. However, it is not advisable to do away with audience at gallery level entirely: the balustrade is probably an integral part

of the design, and the presence of faces at that level is important for the atmosphere of the auditorium. The front few rows usually have a good view of the stage and if provided with proper seats are a saleable proposition.

There is a temptation to extend the forestage in line with current fashion; however, sightlines should first be checked, since if they are designed for the edge of the existing stage the results will not be satisfactory. The same applies to a proposal to replace a raked stage floor with a flat one: the lowering of the back of the stage which this entails may spoil the view from the back of the stalls.

Orchestra pit

The big old theatres were seldom designed to accommodate an opera orchestra of, say, sixty or seventy players (or, for Wagner, over 100), and if the building aspires to take tours from the Royal Opera House or the English National Opera a new pit will have to be constructed. Part of this can go

under the stage but inevitably some of the stalls seating will be lost for these performances. At other times there would be a disastrous gap unless some provision is made for removing the pit and replacing it with seating. This sort of adjustment can be made manually, but an elevator or series of elevators is better.

Structure

Columns supporting tiers can be an irritating obstruction to the view of the stage, and the question of their removal may arise. Most things can be done, at a price, but if the budget is restricted there may be higher priorities. Columns were unobjectionable when they supported shallow tiers of boxes and formed part of the architecture, but when the tiers began to get deeper they become bulky props to hold up the much heavier construction and no longer appeared integrated with the architecture. Removing heavy structural columns is a major engineering operation and can be costly.

The stage

Often the stage space is restricted and, if the site and the budget allow, it is worth considering building an entirely new stage and fly tower. This was done at the Bristol Old Vic, where the charming auditorium, originally built in 1766, has been restored and grafted on to a completely new stage and dressing-room block.

A few theatres still have wooden grids, and if alterations are to be made to a stage with one of these it is essential – and the fire authorities will insist – that it is replaced by a steel grid. A counterweight system should be installed with some hemp sets to provide additional suspension. A single-purchase system is best, but if there is not a sufficient height of uninterrupted wall it may be necessary to have double-purchase lines. Sometimes the slope of the fly tower roof makes it difficult to fit in counterweights at all; unless it can be altered and raised, some other method may have to be found, such as powered winches, or it may be necessary to revert to purely hemp lines. The loading has to be checked to find whether the old structure is capable of bearing the new stresses imposed upon it.

Lighting control in old theatres is often in the perch position at the side of the stage, one floor up behind the proscenium. It has for many years been the practice for the lighting control board to be put out front where the operator can monitor the stage picture directly. Possible positions have already been discussed; usually it is put in a soundproof room at the back of the auditorium, but there have been successful installations where it has been located in one of the boxes or the orchestra pit.

Front-of-house

In theatres built before the First World War, the hierarchical nature of society was reflected in the subdivision of the theatre into stalls, pit, dress circle, upper circle and gallery. "Dress circle" meant what it said – the audience in that part of the house and in the boxes and front stalls would be wearing evening dress. They would not expect to jostle shoulder to shoulder with the pit or gallery customers, and the foyers were planned so that they would not have to. Usually there was a separate entrance for each part of the house, with the main entrance only for the "nobs". At the side was the gallery entrance with a tiny paybox tucked into a corner at the foot of a long bare staircase. The pit would also have its own entrance and paybox, and, once inside, each section of the audience would have its own lavatories and its own bar.

This segregation is one of the reasons why the foyers often seem disproportionately small in relation to the size of the auditorium: there was only meant to be enough space in them for the people who dressed. One of the architect's problems when renovating old theatres is to find ways of routing the whole audience, whatever part of the house they are going to, through the main entrance and foyers. The old access stairs will probably still be needed as means of escape, but people normally expect to return the same way as they came in.

Foyers are far more important than they were fifty years ago as a meeting place and for serving snacks, tea, coffee and drinks; if there is room on the site and enough in the budget to expand them, the restored theatre stands a better chance of success. One example is the Theatre Royal, Bristol, where it was possible to take an adjoining building, the Coopers Hall, and make it a grand entrance foyer. At the Nottingham Theatre Royal foyers were rebuilt with considerable additions.

Heating and ventilating

Old theatres relied on natural ventilation, usually making use of the chimney effect of hot air rising and finding its way out through a ventilating lantern in the dome over the auditorium. Air to replace it was drawn in sometimes through ducts from the walls or from above the roof, and sometimes through windows in the auditorium which could be opened. The trouble with this system was that unless the air coming in was warmed at its point of entry, cold draughts occurred and led to complaints from the audience. The management reaction would be to stop up all the sources of draught and later, when they received complaints of stuffiness, to add extract fans which brought back the draughts.

The modern answer has been to introduce warm-air systems or, one stage further, air conditioning. However, the physical problems of finding room for the plant and threading in the ducting in an old building are not easy to solve and can be very expensive. To supply the volume of air required by regulations at an acceptable noise level, large cross-sectional areas of duct have to be installed without ruining the decorative panelling and plasterwork. And even if these difficulties are overcome, it is extremely unlikely that the audience will find conditions to their liking.

Theatres are great consumers of energy, especially for stage lighting, and methods of fuel conservation should be investigated. Natural ventilation systems, where power is not used to force air into directions in which it would not normally flow and where the heat given off by lighting and the audience themselves is at least in part reclaimed, must be devised. At the moment one of the chief obstacles to a reassessment of theatre heating and ventilation is the amount of air demanded by local authority regulations, a matter which has been discussed at greater length in Chapter 21 (Electrical and mechanical services).

25

Economics

A book on theatre planning would not be complete without some general discussion of the economics of theatre building. The word "economics" is used in an attempt to divert the passions which can be induced by arguments about cost. The whole question of costs is often so shrouded in mystery that it is difficult to discover the real truth.

When the cost of a project is announced the figures are usually coloured by political expediency. In a generally puritan country such as Britain, every effort is made to conceal the true cost for fear of righteous outcries against extravagance, but in some other places the citizens are proud to know that no expense has been spared in making their theatre or opera house worthy of their own city or nation.

Cost comparisons

While we need to have some standard of comparison by which to assess theatre costs, quoting sums of money which are alleged to have been expended on a particular building is a very misleading method. It is always difficult to find out what is or is not included in the calculation. For instance, has the cost of purchasing the site been included, or should it be given a notional value? How much equipment has been included and how much furniture and furnishings?

It is apparently indelicate for architects, engineers and other consultants to include their fees, though, from the promoter's point of view, these are bound to form a substantial proportion of the cost (probably around 17%).

There are many variables which affect the cost of any kind of building in a stable economy, and in an inflationary situation comparisons which are not precisely contemporary rapidly become meaningless.

Economic factors are, nonetheless, vitally important; but to avoid adding to the confusion, figures and amounts in money are not mentioned in this book. There are economic implications in every aspect of theatre planning, from the kind and scope of production it is intended to present to the capital and running cost of labour-saving machinery. Both artistic and economic factors are involved in every decision that has to be made.

At the present time, the clients' original motivation is most likely to be artistic, using the word in the broad sense to include social and educational purposes. It may to a lesser extent be commercial, but as there are many other investments which will produce much higher and safer returns, commercial motivation is unlikely to be very strong. An exception is when, in order to carry out a large commercial redevelopment, the developer is required by the authorities, goaded perhaps by the strength of public opinion, to replace an existing theatre, or when the promise of a theatre is offered as a sweetener in a big town-centre scheme.

Theatres are not physical necessities like housing, schools or hospitals. When they are built it is not by an Act of Parliament but by an act of faith: faith that they will contribute to the quality of living. They offer various degrees of participation in a creative process, from appreciation of a professional performance to taking part in an amateur one. On a simple level they provide a leisure activity competing with other forms of entertainment, but on another level it is the opportunity they give people to exercise creative talents which gives them their particular social value.

The type of building which emerges from the consideration of these artistic and economic factors will probably come within the categories discussed in Chapter 1, but these do not exhaust the possible forms a project can take. It may end up quite a different shape or size from the promoter's original idea. Sometimes artistic ambitions shrink when faced with economic realities, but the opposite process is not uncommon. Small projects intended, for example, for amateurs or as rehearsal rooms begin to grow as more potential uses and users appear. The expanding brief leads to demands for more space and equipment, and the whole scale of a scheme can alter. The original brief may turn out to be misleading and if such developments have not been anticipated the architect may be in difficulties and the building will suffer.

Theatres are likely to be initiated by enthusiasts whose ideas and methods differ widely. The preparation of the architect's brief for a new building, or for the rehabilitation of an old one, is a task with heavy responsibility. Best results are obtained when the architect takes part in the process of assembling the brief. A sponsor operating in the capacity of landlord only, such as a local authority, a development company or a benefactor, may delegate the carrying out of the project to a committee, a trust or a theatre board, which might consist of councillors, local citizens, and members of a theatre company if one exists in the area. Their task would be to get the project under way and decide on general policy.

A body of this nature is well advised not to involve itself with the detailed artistic policy. For this purpose they should appoint an artistic director, theatre consultant or someone to represent the interests of the prospective user. On the other hand the theatre company management or individual visionary may have very clear ideas on artistic direction but no adequate organisation to cope with the financial arrangements for carrying out the task of building.

A cautious sponsor may want some reassurance on the viability of a theatre building. Some kind of social survey may be called for but it should be remembered that theatrical enterprises are not very susceptible to the normal techniques of this kind of investigation. The quality and reputation of both the activity and the building will profoundly influence the demand. A company with a vigorous policy can stimulate demand in a community where little interest is evident from a survey. The location and ease of access by various means of transport indicate the potential catchment, but do not guarantee that the audience will be persuaded to come.

Pilot scheme

Another cautious approach is to have a trial run with a pilot scheme before embarking on a large-scale project. This may be a way to test demand and stimulate and build up the public for theatre, but there are dangers in this approach. A pilot scheme must essentially be cheap, but if it is too obviously makeshift an uncomfortable audience is not likely to be converted to theatre-going. It should at least have a satisfactory audience-to-stage relationship. The success or failure of a small-scale scheme does not necessarily give any indication of the fate of a large-scale one. Each is likely to develop a personality of its own and succeed or fail in its own right.

The quest for cheapness often leads to temporary buildings; but temporary buildings have a habit of becoming very permanent.

Subsidy and self-sufficiency

For brief periods, social and economic factors have made it possible for the live theatre to pay for itself out of charges for admission. We are just emerging from such a period. In the last century the live theatre was the popular mass public entertainment. People prosperous from the proceeds of the industrial revolution could pay for entertainment and found it in the live theatres and music halls. Their taste was not for highbrow intellectual drama; they responded to unashamed sentiment and broad comedy. Theatres and music halls sprang up all over the British Isles, and medium-size towns might easily support five or six. There was no question of subsidy.

This boom was hit by the arrival of the cinema, which grew from a sideshow curiosity at the beginning of this century, to take over as the mass form of entertainment after the First World War. The movies had their heyday between the two world wars, but after 1945 they too yielded first place to television, which is far and away the most widespread and universal purveyor of entertainment that has ever existed. It is difficult to imagine any new medium ever displacing television as the mass popular entertainer. However, the cinema did not kill the theatre any more than television has killed the cinema or the long-playing record has killed the orchestral concert. In one way each innovation has liberated its predecessor. The sheer mass of output required to feed the voracious appetites of a mass public leads to mediocrity in most of the material. Competition for the attention of the majority only encourages the suppliers of this material to seek for the lowest common denominator of public tastes.

When the live theatre was challenged by films it lost its mass audience, but there remained the people for whom the theatre had a meaning, who took a more discriminating interest in it. The theatre patrons became a minority, largely middle-class and better educated than the average. Plays became more sophisticated. Ibsen, Chekhov and Shaw made people feel and think in a different way, and the audience for the drama expected some intellectual stimulation from what it saw and heard. There was a move away from the stereotyped comedy or tragedy with stock characters into more adventurous ideas both in subjects for plays and in staging.

But this change from a mass medium to a more sophisticated minority interest inevitably started the change back to the more normal state of affairs where the performing arts depend upon sponsorship and patronage rather than box-office returns. This process is not yet complete, but it gathers momentum all the time. In London the West End remains a commercial enterprise, but it subsists on wasting assets. At West End prices, it is possible for theatres to make a moderate profit on running expenses, but little or nothing can be set aside for rebuilding. The prospects for the investment of capital for private gain in the building of new theatres are not attractive; almost any other investment would produce a better return. However, in terms of the community as a whole, there is a very considerable dividend on investment in new theatres. It may fairly be said that they add to the quality of life and thereby make the area they serve more attractive to other undertakings. They certainly do much to attract tourist trade.

The memory that theatres were once built for profit dies hard, and the implications of the new situation have not yet sunk in. Nobody now expects libraries and swimming baths to pay for themselves, though their appeal is only to a minority. The need for subsidy is not new, and without it the theatre would wither away to a very minor insignificant activity.

The site

Usually the first essential for getting a project off the ground is the ground itself. The availability of a site is often the catalyst which triggers off the whole scheme. Even if it is not ideal it may have to be accepted for reasons of political expediency. One has only to look at the comparative plans of existing theatres to see how seldom the site is ideal. If it is too cramped it may not be possible to fulfil the requirements of the client's preliminary briefing. Certain critical dimensions are implied by the kind of theatre it is proposed to build, and if these cannot be fitted on the site, either the programme will have to be reduced in scale or another site must be chosen. Some preliminary studies will have to be done to find out what the critical dimensions of a theatre for a particular purpose, holding a particular number of people, will be. For instance, a medium-size proscenium theatre, initiating its own productions and having workshop facilities on the site, would need an area of about 40 m × 50 m (130 ft × 165 ft).

Access to the site

An island site is ideal; access from two sides is essential. Regulations will demand means of escape for the audience to two separate thoroughfares, and the fire brigade will want to get its appliances to all parts of the site. The public requires access for cars, taxis, coaches, buses and, in some instances, boats, monorails, hovercraft and other as yet unimagined means of transport. The staff and artists will have their entrance, preferably on another side of the building. Articulated lorries and pantechnicons must get to the stage to unload and collect scenery and properties. Costumes must be delivered to the wardrobe and dressing-room area, raw materials to the workshop, provisions to the restaurant, supplies to the bars, fuel to the heating plant; and the rubbish has to be removed. Car parking for visitors somewhere in the vicinity is essential. If the area is not well served by public transport, parking spaces for up to one car per two persons in the audience may be required. As the main demand for parking for the theatre will be in the evenings, it may often be possible to make use of car parks used for other purposes during the day, for instance, for offices and shopping.

The policy for new theatres is often to make them a part of the everyday life of the community, not just an evening entertainment. During the day they become a meeting place serving coffee, snacks and sometimes meals, and holding exhibitions and lunchtime entertainments. They can only do this successfully if they are sited in the centre of a busy part of the town. A site outside the town may have a magnificent view and a beautiful setting, but if it can only be reached by car it has little chance of becoming a popular rendezvous at all times of the day.

Large cities often have an entertainment area where theatres are just one of a wide range of diversions offered to the public. There has been a tendency to group the more highbrow activities together in a centre which may earn the description of cultural ghetto if it is remote from the more vulgar entertainments offered by the town. Successful theatres are very likely to have to put up with the restrictions of city sites.

Relationship of functions

All the various component parts of the theatre have been described in some detail. The relation between activities and departments is summarised in Figure 25:1.

The economic framework

Once the kind of theatre and the purpose to which it is to be put have been decided and it is known whether drama, opera, ballet or musicals are to be produced there, and the scale upon which these are to be mounted, and whether it will play in repertory or repertoire, and whether it will originate productions and set them up on the premises, and the number of seats in the auditorium and the standard of amenity for the audience and the standard of provision of all the elements which go to make up a theatre and have been described in this book, have been decided, then it is possible to make some estimate of how much all this will cost.

Usually the largest single expense will be the cost of constructing the building itself, but there are many other costs which must be taken into account.

Capital costs

The site

The site may have to be purchased freehold or leasehold. If it is given or leased at a peppercorn rent this is a form of subsidy equivalent to the market value of the site at the time. Certain works may have to be carried out in order to make the site suitable, such as demolitions and diversion of services, before construction can begin. Landscaping and the provision of car parks may add further expense.

Building

The building contractor must be paid as the work proceeds, and the client has to arrange for the cash to be available. The services, including heating, ventilating and electrical, the plumbing and drainage will be included as in most building contracts, but theatres are very much more complicated than the general run of buildings, and a good deal of specialised stage equipment will form part of the contract. Loose equipment and tools for the stage and workshop will usually have to be purchased separately. Built-in furniture, carpets and curtains can be within the main contract or within a separate furniture and furnishings contract.

Loose chairs and tables may still be wanted for the restaurant and coffee bar, and the offices will have to be provided with chairs, desks, office

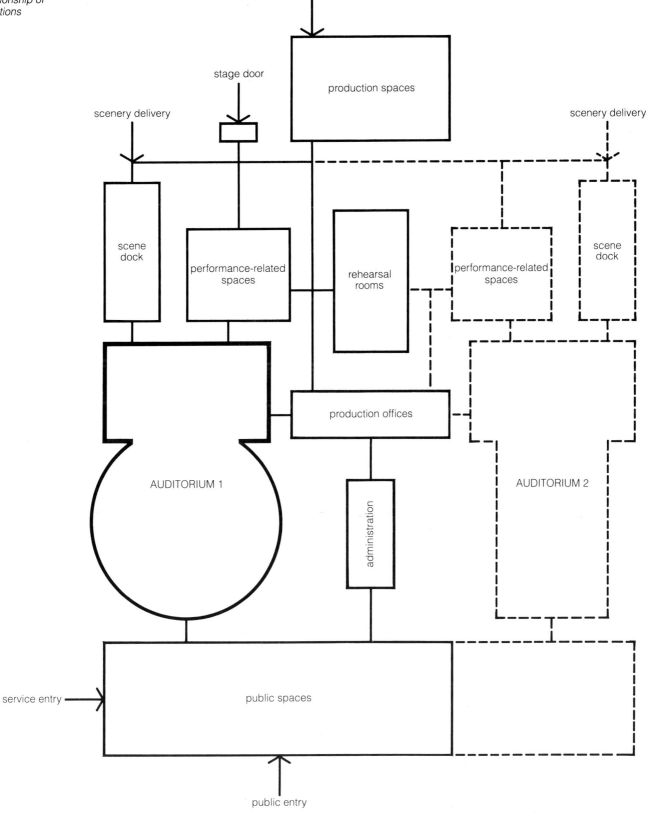

25:1. The relationship of functions

equipment, typewriters and office machines. Heavy catering equipment will probably be built in as part of the main contract, but cooking pots and pans, cutlery, crockery and table linen will still have to be found.

Fees

The complexity of theatre design involves the skill of a wide range of specialists. Professional fees will be a larger proportion of the total cost of the work than for most building projects. Fees will have to be paid for the services of most of the following, according to the scope of the project:

— solicitors; land surveyors; architects; quantity surveyors; structural engineers; heating and ventilating engineers; electrical engineers; theatre consultants; acoustic consultants; interior designers; graphic designers; landscape architects.

Running costs

The client should prepare a draft budget of the expected running costs of the building before any final decisions on the budget for the capital costs are taken. It is very important that this should be done realistically. A large building with sophisticated equipment will be expensive to run, and will need permanent staff of the right calibre and training to look after it efficiently. The lighting and fuel bills will be high; large stages can swallow up a great deal of scenic material. Amateur enterprises should beware of falling into the trap of creating an over-ambitious scheme which they will find a great burden to run with unskilled part-time staff.

Running costs and capital costs are, of course, related. All too often capital costs are cut in a way which has a baleful effect on later running costs. Cheap materials often do not last long and cost a great deal of money to maintain properly or replace. The cost in labour may soon outweigh the saving made in cutting out some mechanical aid.

Unfortunately, problems of the moment are more pressing than those which may arise in the future. Short-term savings are often made in the knowledge that extra running costs will be covered by subsidies or by tax exemptions. The reluctance to invest in the future and the readiness to accept continually rising day-to-day expenses are symptoms of an economic malaise which is not confined to theatre building.

The following is a list of headings under which regular running costs can be classified:

— Interest on loans and repayment of mortgage for the purchase of the site
— Ground rent
— Interest on loan, repayment of mortgage, amortisation of capital on the cost of the building
— Rent
— Building maintenance

— There will be a number of maintenance contracts for the regular inspection and servicing of items of equipment such as the boilers and ventilation plant, the lifts, the kitchen equipment, the stage lighting and sound equipment
— Local authority rates
— Heating and power
— Water and drainage
— Cleaning
— Insurances
— Accounting and legal fees
— Wages and salaries of permanent staff
— Administration costs (including printing, advertising, telephones, office expenses, stationery, postage etc.)
— Actors', directors' and designers' salaries or fees
— Production costs: scenery, lighting, properties, costumes, music and musicians, royalties
— Taxation of profits (very often a theatre company is a registered charity which, being non-profit-making, will not be obliged to pay tax)

Sources of capital finance

There are many possible sources of finance available for the building of theatres and it is most likely that several of them will be tapped in each individual case. They include:

— Private gifts, legacies and endowments
— Loans from banks, building societies, insurance companies, local authorities or private individuals
— Grants from local authorities paid for out of local taxation
— Grants from national sources out of general taxation (for instance in Britain the Arts Council's now defunct "Housing the Arts" fund, the Ministry of Education's grants, the University Grants Committee and the British Film Institute)
— Charitable trusts and foundations with interests in the arts
— A fund-raising appeal in which the public is asked to contribute towards a fund with private gifts, subscriptions and covenants, the appeal being accompanied by fund-raising activities of many kinds such as garden parties, sweepstakes, dances, dinners and charity performances

Commerce and industry will sometimes lend support, but unless there is some tax advantage in doing so this is unlikely to be substantial. Sponsoring productions as part of an advertising budget is more attractive to industry than contributing to the capital costs of a building. In some places lotteries and gambling have yielded vast sums for the arts; Sydney Opera House was financed out of lotteries, and in Hong Kong the Jockey Club has paid for a lavish new Academy for the Performing Arts out of its monopoly of racecourse betting.

Substantial capital sums can only be found out of

taxation either directly, from government funds or through a government-funded agency such as the Arts Council of Great Britain, or indirectly, by allowing companies or individuals to set off expenditure on the arts against taxation. The whole situation could be changed overnight by new government legislation.

- Commerce and industry
- Private gifts and subscriptions
- Fund-raising activities

Continuous sources of income

Once the building opens the continuous sources of revenue can be classified as follows:

1. *Sources direct from the activities of the theatre*

- Box-office receipts
- Sale of refreshments and bar profits, which may be either direct or from concessionaires
- Restaurant profits
- Sale of programmes and advertising in them by outside firms
- Kiosk sales of books, records, etc.
- Club members' subscriptions
- Revenue from transfer of successful productions
- Film and television rights
- Hiring out of costumes or scenery to outside groups or companies
- Hiring out the premises to outside organisations for private functions
- Running conferences and trade shows
- Outside broadcasting by television companies (of snooker, for instance)

2. *Indirect sources connected with the particular theatre*

If the theatre is part of a much larger building complex, which may include, for instance, shops and offices, the revenue from these may be collected by the theatre, though it is more likely that the landlord may offset a reduced rent from the theatre against income from these other sources.

Touring companies using the theatre may themselves be subsidised.

There have also been hidden subsidies, such as the readiness of actors to accept low wages which did not bear comparison with other occupations. Actors' pay and conditions are now showing signs of improvement, and this situation may not exist for very much longer. However, the unemployment rate among actors is still very high.

3. *Revenue from sources outside the theatre*

- The local authority may choose to support a theatre with a revenue grant
- Local-authority education grants (for instance for plays put on in connection with school examinations)
- Arts Council revenue grants
- Charities and foundations

26

Comparison of theatres

Having examined the practical requirements of the various departments which go to make up a theatre and considered what is expected of the site, it is interesting to see what has actually been done by comparing plans and longitudinal sections to the same scale of a number of theatres.

In the first edition of this book there was a table comparing the vital statistics of a range of different theatres and a diagram showing the steepest lines of sight and the distance of the furthest seat from the stage. The point of the exercise was to illustrate the proportion of the building used for the auditorium in comparison with the other components of the plan and to show the effect of stacking the audience in tiers.

It is no longer necessary to compile this information into tables to illustrate these points, but it is still valuable to be able to compare the plans of theatres old and new. Many of these examples appeared in the first edition, but we have added a number which have been built since that was published.

All the plans in the book, including those in Chapter 2, have been drawn to the same scale (1:1000). There is clearly not enough room to provide drawings of every relevant level; each has been drawn to show the auditorium and main distribution of the accommodation around it. This has meant some telescoping of the plans, but it should still be possible to picture the layout by reference to the accompanying sections. It is not possible to do justice to these buildings at such a small scale and with such brevity; readers who would like more complete details should consult back numbers of the *Architects' Journal*, the *Architectural Review*, *Tabs* or *Sightline*, where most of the newer ones have been published, or reference books for those of historical interest. Books with particularly good drawings of theatres are Richard and Helen Leacroft's *Theatre and Playhouse* and Richard Leacroft's *The Development of the English Playhouse*, which have cut-away axonometric drawings of admirable clarity of many of the key historical theatres, and George C. Izenour's *Theater Design*.

26:1. The Piccadilly Theatre, London (1928). Architects: Bertie Crewe and E. A. Stone; seats 1144

26:2. The Aldwych Theatre, London (1905). Architect: W. G. R. Sprague; seats 1030

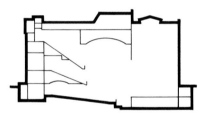

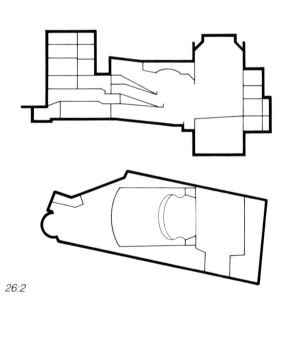

26:2

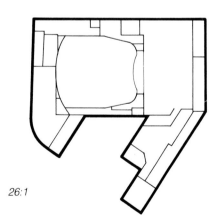

26:1

26:3. Wyndhams Theatre, London (1899). Architect: W. G. R. Sprague; seats 765

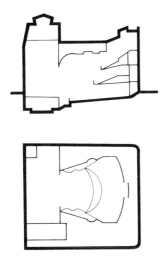

The only common factor in all these diverse buildings is the individual theatregoer in an auditorium seat. Sightlines and audibility restrict the maximum dimensions, and standards of comfort restrict the number who can be accommodated within the space defined by these dimensions.

In the last century, it was acceptable to cram many more people into an auditorium than would be tolerated now. For instance, when the Grand Theatre, Leeds, opened in 1878, it had a seating capacity of 2600, with standing room for a further 200. The same auditorium now seats a maximum of 1558. Recent theatres in Germany and the United States have sometimes spread the audience so thinly that the characteristic concentrated atmosphere of a closely packed audience is entirely dissipated, and it becomes very difficult for live players to make any dramatic contact with the audience.

The floor area per seat in the auditorium does vary from theatre to theatre and from era to era, but still there is more in common between auditoria of similar seating capacity than there is in any other

26:4. The Old Vic, London (1818). Designed by Rudolph Cabanel; altered many times since, most recently in 1984 by Renton Howard Wood Levin

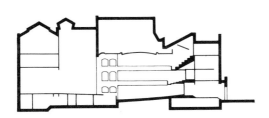

26:5. Thorndike Theatre, Leatherhead (1969). Architect: Roderick Ham; seats 520 in a single-tier theatre. Acted as a prototype for several others

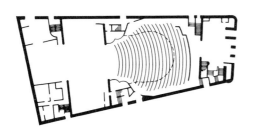

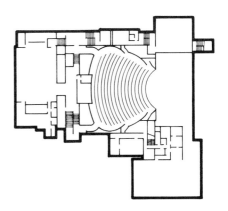

 26:4

26:5

26:6. Eden Court Theatre, Inverness (1975). Architects: Law and Dunbar-Naismith; a return to multi-tier seating

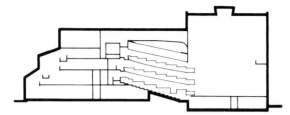

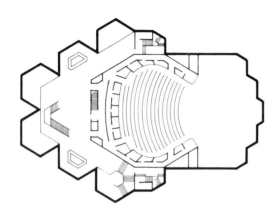

department of the theatre building. Compare, for example, London's Royal Opera House, Covent Garden, even after the extensions which are now being planned, with the Opéra National, Paris (Figures 26:7 and 26:8). They each have a traditional horseshoe-shaped auditorium with very similar seating capacities. Not surprisingly, the shape and size of the auditoria are almost identical, but in every other respect the difference in scale of the two buildings is enormous. In Paris, the auditorium is completely submerged in a vast baroque building on the scale of a cathedral rather than a theatre. In fact the plan dimensions correspond remarkably closely with those of Amiens Cathedral, including transepts.

While the auditorium floor area per seat does not vary widely, the site area taken up by the auditorium as a whole depends upon how many tiers there are. One of the main reasons for introducing seating on several levels is to get as many people as possible within seeing and hearing distance of the stage. At the same time it is a method of squeezing more accommodation on to a restricted site.

In terms of providing the maximum number of seats on a small site the achievement of the architects of some of the West End theatres is remarkable. By ingenious planning the amount of dead space is reduced to an absolute minimum. Typically the entrance is arranged at approximately front circle level and the space under the circle tier is used for foyers and public spaces. But however cunningly economic the planning, the auditorium can only occupy a greater proportion of

the site at the expense of the stage or public areas or both.

Before the advent of the National Theatre on the South Bank, even our largest London theatres – Covent Garden, Drury Lane and the Coliseum – did not occupy island sites. One of the few in London which does is the Palace Theatre (Figure 26:11), built as an opera house and now used for musicals, but the shape and size of the main elements of the theatre were obviously dictated by the tight boundaries of the site. The problem in London has been to provide an auditorium and enough seats to enable the theatre to pay its way on a site which, because of the high land value, is invariably restricted and frequently of irregular shape.

Unlike most other European nations, Britain has no tradition of civic theatre. Virtually all the theatres built up to the time of the Second World War were commercial ventures. Since the war public perception of the arts as a community responsibility has grown, and it has become politically acceptable, though often grudgingly so, for most new theatres to have a measure of civic or national support, even if they cannot be classed as civic theatres in the German sense. The stringent economic curbs remain, and many schemes only get under way because there is an old building which it is possible to convert, or even because a new one designed for another purpose happens to be available, as at Leeds Playhouse in 1970. This was a temporary arrangement which is now being replaced by a new repertory theatre of a design won in an architectural competition.

The horseshoe-shaped auditorium with several tiers facing a proscenium stage was the traditional theatre plan in the nineteenth and early twentieth centuries. For a scenically dominated theatre, sightlines were not very good from many of the seats, and it was to satisfy Wagner's requirements for the focus of all seats to be the conductor that the fan-shaped auditorium was introduced at the Bayreuth Opera House in 1876. The plans in Chapter 2 (p. 15) show how the stalls are stepped with two shallow tiers at the rear, all with excellent sightlines. However, the house was designed not just for opera, but a particular kind of German grand opera which, in Wagner's view, was to be a personal experience for each individual present at a performance. He had no desire for the flow of the music drama to be interrupted by a corporate audience response, and the auditorium seating layout was designed to avoid this as far as possible.

The flow of a film can only be interrupted by a mechanical breakdown, and, sightlines being the most important factor, the fan was a very suitable shape for the cinema auditorium, for which, with the addition of a deep balcony, it became standard. But the Bayreuth influence spread further, and the fan shape with deep balconies was applied to many theatres whose principal use was for drama, and some of its shortcomings became apparent. A

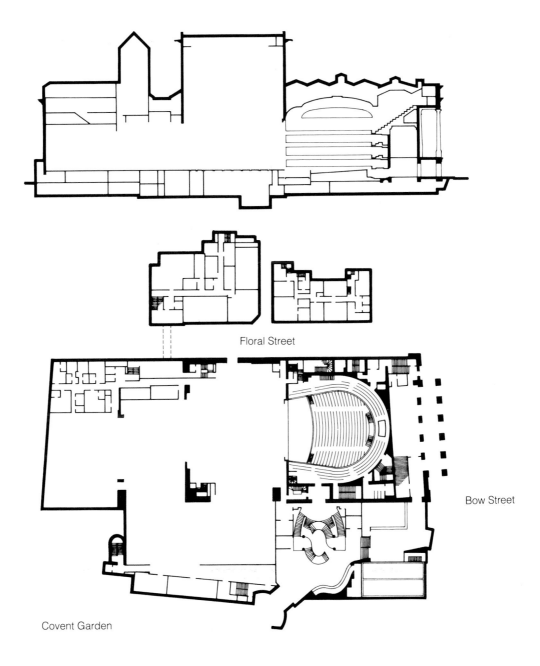

26:7. The Royal Opera House, Covent Garden, London (1858). Architect: Sir Edward Barry; seats 2158. Used by both opera and ballet companies. The drawings show the enlargements and additions proposed in 1986, designed by Jeremy Dixon and Bill Jack

Floral Street

Bow Street

Covent Garden

26:8. The Opéra
National, Paris
(1874). Architect:
Charles Garnier;
seats 2150

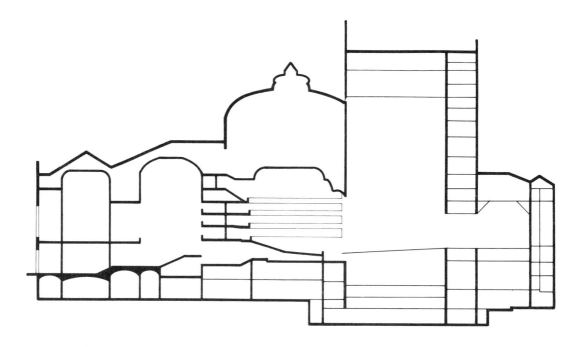

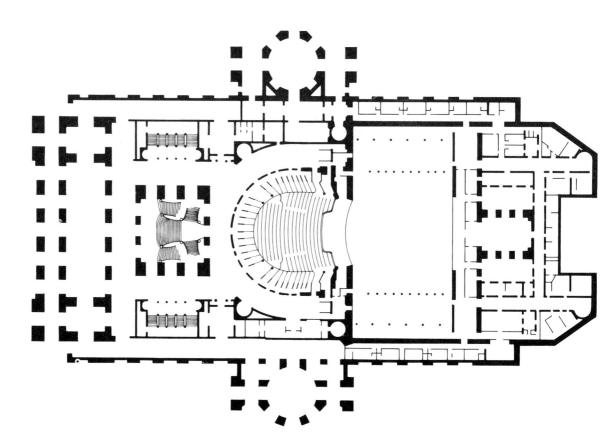

26:9. The Coliseum, London (1904). Architect: Frank Matcham; seats 2340. Now the home of the English National Opera; and example of ingenious planning within a difficult site

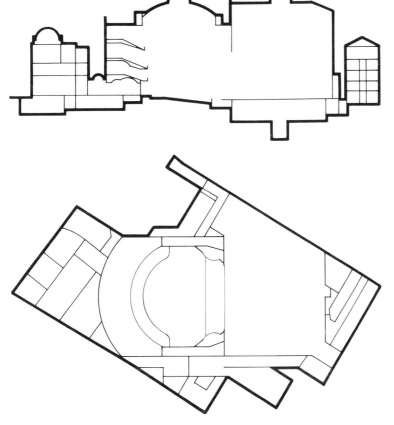

26:11. The Palace Theatre, London (1891). Architects: T. E. Collcutt and G. H. Holloway; seats 1462 for musicals

26:10. The Auditorium Building, Chicago, USA (1889). Designed by Louis Sullivan when Frank Lloyd Wright worked in his office. One of the first theatres to be lit by electricity and to have a form of air conditioning. The proportion of auditorium to site area is high

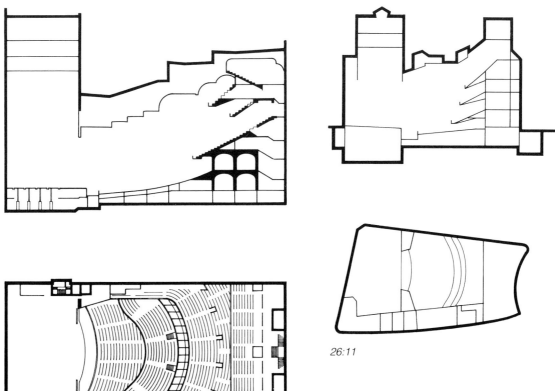

26:11

26:10

deep gallery tends to divide the audience into two and make it more difficult for the players to get a unified audience reaction. The diverging side walls give an effect of false perspective which exaggerates the distance from the stage. In an auditorium with boxes or balconies lining the side walls, it is unquestionable that the sightlines from seats in these positions are not so geometrically excellent as those enclosed within a fan. This is the principal argument in favour of the fan form, but the experience of attending a live performance is neither entirely visual nor entirely aural, and auditorium shapes are also chosen to improve the sense of audience participation. Bringing spectators round to the side of the auditorium helps to emphasise the acting area as a part of a combined audience and performance space and avoids the directional and distancing effect of a true fan shape. Attempts have been made to get the best of both worlds by placing an essentially fan-shaped seating arrangement within a curved or circular-shaped auditorium.

In this century there has been a revival of interest in open stage forms, and they are now common enough for the qualification "experimental" to be dropped. The blame for their slow development has sometimes been placed upon fire regulations, and while it must be conceded that these did delay the building of open stages on any large scale, it does not follow that the picture-frame theatre was invented for the convenience of the safety curtain. Already by 1880, some twenty years before the first regulations were issued, there were theatres with a picture-frame moulding carried right round the proscenium opening, including along the edge of the stage floor. A number of disastrous theatre fires occurred at the end of the last century which led to the widespread adoption of fire regulations and in particular to the familiar and almost universal safety curtain in a proscenium wall. The regulations were framed to meet an ad hoc situation which had developed as a natural historical process. Inevitably they tend to perpetuate the situation which they were designed to regulate.

The auditoria of the various theatres have common factors which can be compared wherever they are situated, but when it comes to other departments there is a division on national lines. The contrast between the Royal Opera House, Covent Garden, London, and the Opéra National in Paris has already been pointed out, but comparison of a British theatre with any of the German theatres will show similar striking differences. In Germany there is an operatic tradition of vast heavily mechanised stages, and an industry has grown up to provide them. Whether such elaborate and expensive installations are necessary for the health and survival of the drama is questionable, but at the other extreme the lack of working stage space, wing space, scene docks, workshops, storage space, and ancillary accommodation in many British theatres is a handicap and can be an expensive burden to bear. It is less onerous for West End theatres, designed for long runs, than for theatres used for repertory or productions in repertoire; but as this more flexible pattern of use becomes more common, the demand for more space and equipment will become stronger.

26:12. The theatre at Leiden, Netherlands, restored by Onno Greiner (reopened 1976). All theatres in Holland are touring theatres

26:13. The Wilde Theatre, Bracknell (1984). Architect: Levitt Bernstein; courtyard theatre seating 350–400

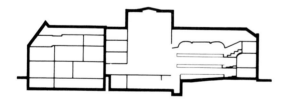

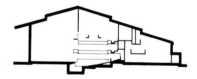

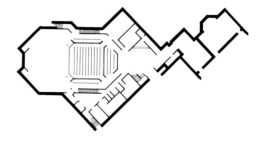

26:13

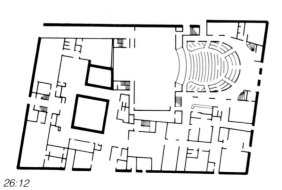

26:12

26:14. St Gallen, Switzerland (1968). Architect: Claude Paillard; seats 855

26:15. Sackville Theatre, Sevenoaks School (1983). Architect: Roderick Ham; drama studio seating 200–300. Used for teaching and drama

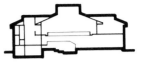

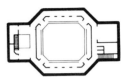

26:15

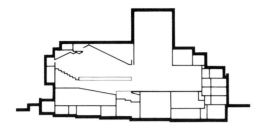

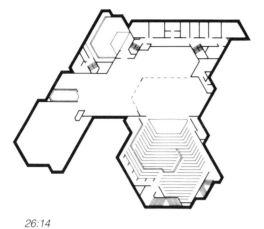

26:14

26:16. Christ's Hospital School, Horsham (1974). Architects: Howell Killick Partridge & Amis; seats 400–600. Used for teaching and a mixed programme

26:17. Wolsey Theatre, Ipswich (1979). Architect: Roderick Ham; open stage theatre seating 440, with permanent repertory company

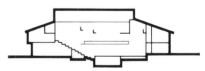

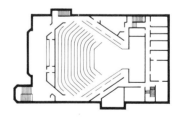

26:17

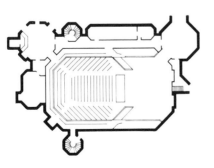

26:16

26:18. The National Theatre, South Bank, London (1976). Architect: Sir Denys Lasdun. The Olivier Theatre (wide fan) seats 1160; the Lyttelton Theatre (proscenium theatre) seats 895; the Cottesloe Theatre (studio theatre) seats 200–600

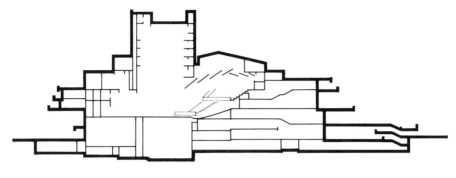

Section through Olivier auditorium

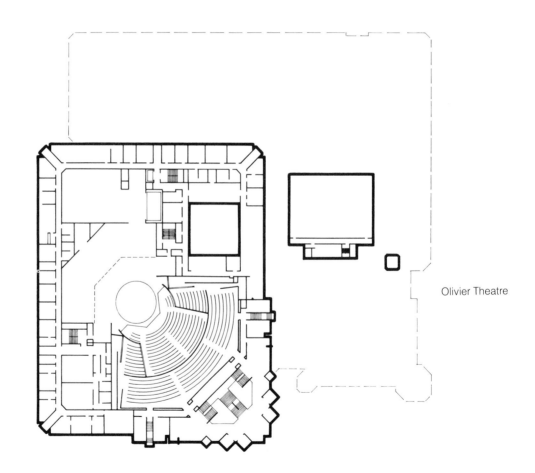

Olivier Theatre

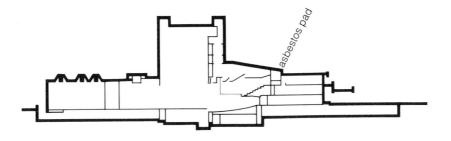

Section through Lyttelton auditorium

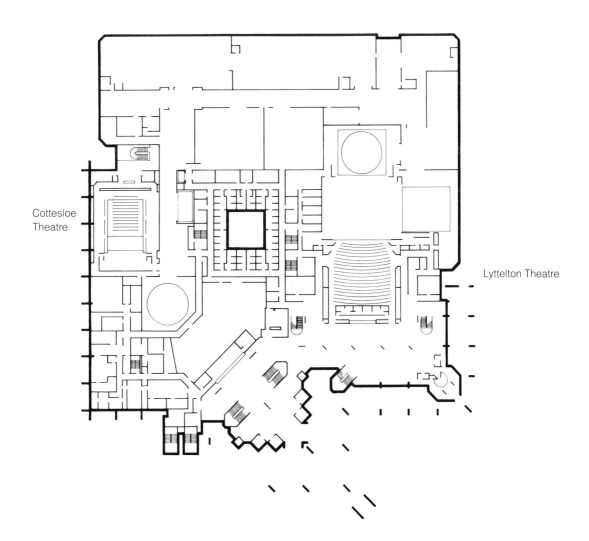

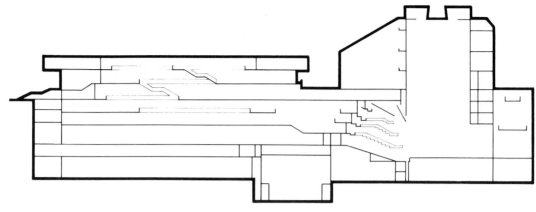

26:19. The Barbican Centre, London (1981–2). Architects: Chamberlin Powell & Bon. The theatre seats 1166; the concert hall seats 2026

Section through theatre

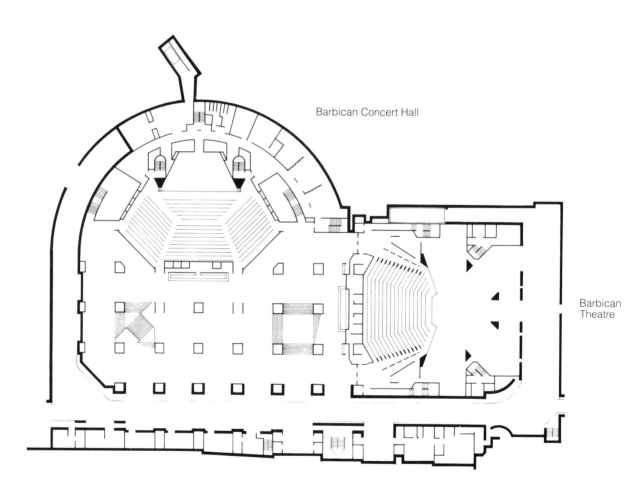

Barbican Concert Hall

Barbican Theatre

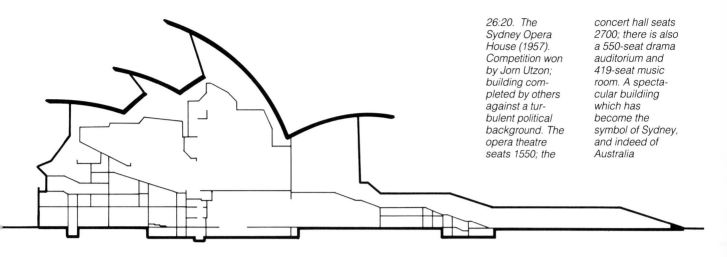

26:20. The
Sydney Opera
House (1957).
Competition won
by Jorn Utzon;
building com-
pleted by others
against a tur-
bulent political
background. The
opera theatre
seats 1550; the
concert hall seats
2700; there is also
a 550-seat drama
auditorium and
419-seat music
room. A specta-
cular buildiing
which has
become the
symbol of Sydney,
and indeed of
Australia

Section through theatre

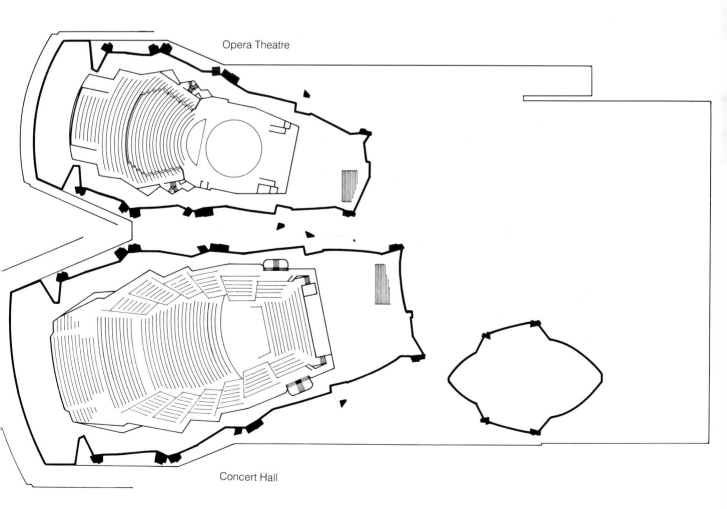

Opera Theatre

Concert Hall

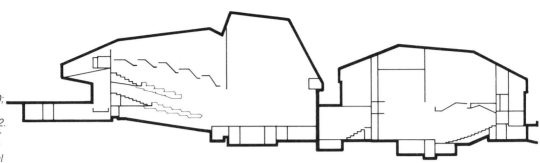

26:21. The Adelaide Festival Theatre, South Australia (1973–4). Architect: Colin Hassell. The drama theatre seats 700; the opera auditorium seats 1992. Less spectacular than Sydney, but far more practical

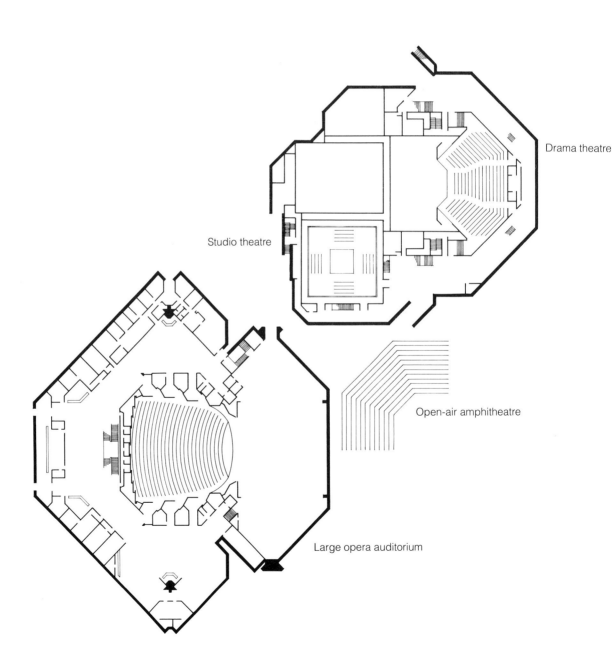

Drama theatre

Studio theatre

Open-air amphitheatre

Large opera auditorium

26:22. The Calgary Centre for Performing Arts, Alberta, Canada (1985). Architects: Raines Finlayson Barrett & Partners with Theatre Projects. Concert hall seats 2000; drama theatre seats 550; opera theatre seats 1550

Section through drama theatre

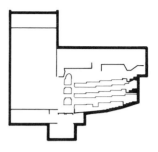

Section through opera auditorium

Concert hall   Drama theatre

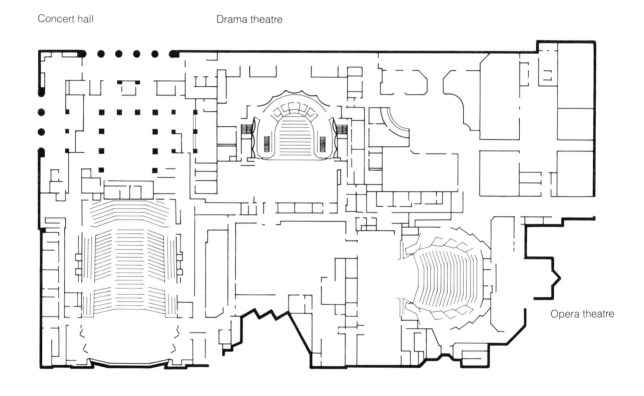

Opera theatre

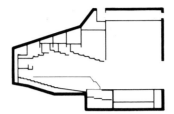

26:23. The
Stadttheater,
Ingolstadt, West
Germany (1966).
Architect: Hardt
Waltherr Hamer;
the smaller
theatre auditorium
seats 734

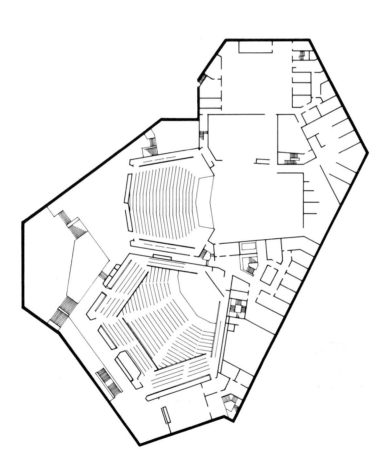

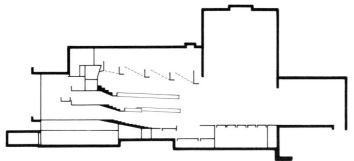

26:24. Het Musiektheater, Amsterdam (1986). Architects. Wilhelm Holzbauer and Cees Dam; seats 1614–1689

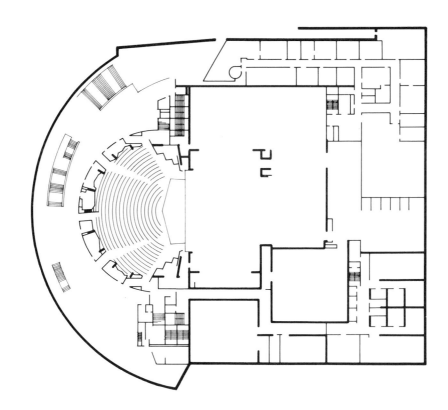

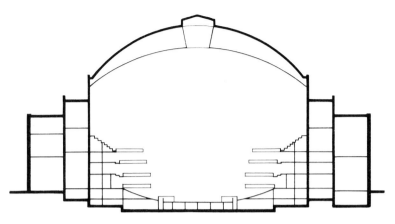

26:25. The Royal Albert Hall, London (1871). Architect: Captain Francis Fowke; seats 4800–6500 for concerts and various uses such as sports and exhibitions

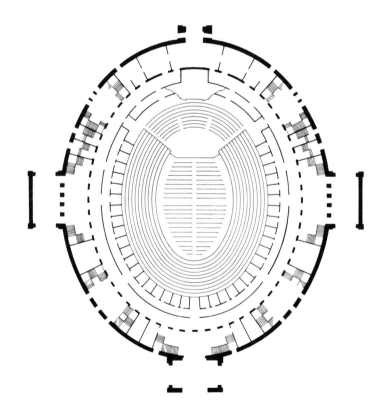

26:26. The Maltings Concert Hall, Snape, Suffolk. Converted (1967) by Arup Associates; used for concerts and recitals

26:28. The Queen Elizabeth Hall and the Purcell Room, South Bank, London (1967). Architects: GLC, Hubert Bennet, Blyth & Engleback. The Queen Elizabeth Hall (concert hall) seats 1094; the Purcell Room (recital room) seats 368

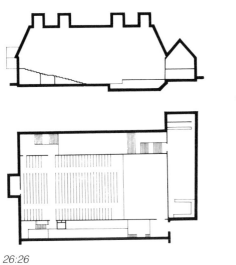

26:26

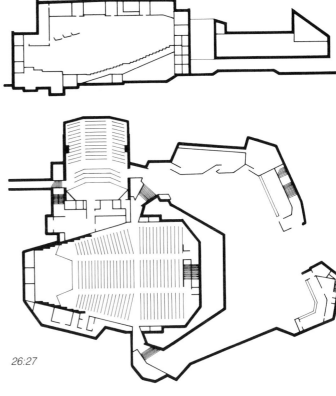

26:27

26:27. The Royal Festival Hall, South Bank, London (1951). Architects: Robert Matthew, Leslie Martin, Peter Moro; seats 2895

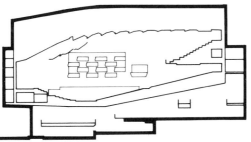

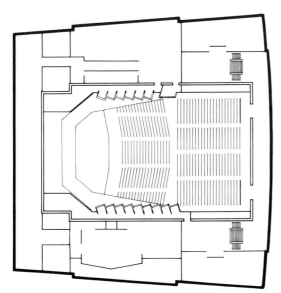

26:28

26:29. The Theatre Royal, Nottingham (1865; architect: C. J. Phipps), with the Royal Concert Hall (1982; architects: Renton Howard Wood Levin; seats 2500; used for concerts and conferences)

26:30. St David's Hall, Cardiff (1922). Architects: Seymour Harris Partnership with Carr and Angier; seats 1950; used for concerts and conferences

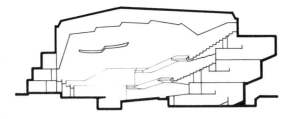

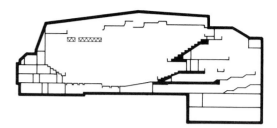

Section through Royal Concert Hall

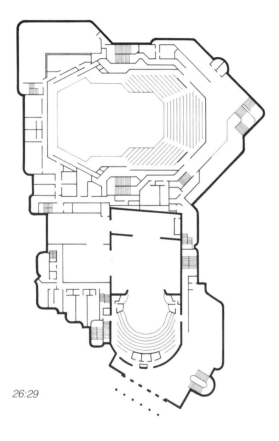

26:29

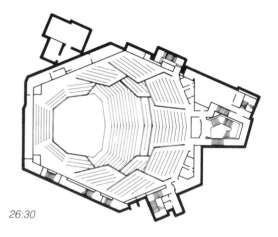

26:30

Glossary of stage terms

This glossary does not attempt to be exhaustive. Both British and American terms are included, which should make it easier to study theatre literature in both countries.

Above   *See Upstage.*

Act drop   Painted cloth or curtain that may be lowered at the end of each act. *See also Cloth and Drop.*

Acting area   Those portions of a stage in which any action of a performance takes place.

Amphitheatre   Stepped banks of seating surrounding an arena. Also used to describe one of the tiers of a multi-level auditorium.

Apron   The extension of a stage projecting outwards into the auditorium: in certain types of theatre the apron may be quite large. *See also Forestage.*

Arena   One of the terms used to describe types of open stage. As it derives from the sand-strewn combat area in a Roman amphitheatre, it should be a term for 360° encirclement; but it has been used to describe thrust stages.

Backdrop (backcloth)   *See Drop and Wing set.*

Backing   Scenery used behind, and limiting the view of the audience through, an opening (e.g. doorway or window) in a set. *See also Masking.*

Band room   Musicians' changing room.

Band shell   Movable sound reflector placed behind a group of musicians on a stage or in the open air to improve acoustics.

Bar   A tube, pipe or barrel for holding spotlights.

Barre   A horizontal rail, usually of wood, used by ballet dancers when practising.

Barrel   Length of metal pipe, suspended on a set of lines, to which scenery may be attached by means of snatch lines instead of being tied directly to the suspension lines. It is a standard part in a unit of the counterweight system. Also called pipe batten.

Batten (lighting batten)   Length of metal troughing carrying lamps, suspended above and lighting the acting area. Now obsolete.

Batten (scenery batten)   Length of rigid material, usually wood, used in scenery construction generally; also a length of timber carrying and stiffening a hanging cloth.

Bastard prompt   The prompt side is always on the actor's left. The other side of the stage is called the OP side (opposite prompt). If the stage manager's control desk and therefore the prompt corner happens to be on the OP side it is called a bastard prompt.

Belay pin   *See Pin.*

Below   *See Downstage.*

Bleachers (bleacher seating)   Stepped seating blocks which can be retracted for storage and to clear a flat floor.

Block   *See Loftblock.*

Boat (boat truck)   *See Wagon.*

Bobbin (sliding bobbin)   Cylindrical carrier for the suspension and movement of draw curtains on a horizontal track.

Book-flat   Pair of flats hinged together and set like a book upon its edges. Also called twofold.

Book-wing   Wing constructed and set in a manner similar to a book-flat.

Border   Abbreviated drop or pelmet used to mask the line of sight over a setting and to hide the flys, lighting battens, etc. (Sometimes painted to represent overhead foliage etc.)

Box set   Setting comprising a series of canvas flats arranged in a more or less continuous line around the three sides of the acting area away from the audience. Normally used for interior scenes. May be provided with a ceiling piece over.

Brace   Piece of wood used diagonally in the frame of a flat to strengthen it.

Brace (extending brace)   *See Stage brace.*

Brace (French brace)   *See French brace.*

Brace-weight   Slotted iron weight, normally rectangular, which can be set on the foot-iron of a brace to hold it in position (in lieu of a stage screw) for speed in setting and striking.

Bracing eye (brace cleat)   Small metal plate attached to the frame of a flat, for attachment of a stage brace. Simple screw eyes are also used for this purpose.

Brail (brail line)   Line used to pull and retain any piece of hanging scenery or property from the position it would occupy if left hanging free.

Break-up   Scene or part of a scene, or a property, constructed to collapse or disintegrate as part of the action of a performance.

Bridge   1. A gallery bridging across the stage or auditorium used for lighting equipment.
2. A lift (q.v.) in the stage floor extending across the stage opening.

Bridle   A short length of cable or chain used to distribute the stress on a barrel at a suspension point.

Built-up ground   *See Rocks.*

Canvas (canvasing)   The fabric used to form a cloth or to cover a flat etc.

Call   Warning to be ready for a part of a performance. Once the job of the callboy, now done over the show relay system controlled at a "call board".

Carpenter   In touring theatres the resident stage manager is often called the "stage carpenter".

Carpet cut   Series of flaps in the stage floor which can be closed upon the downstage edge of a stage cloth to hold it in position.

Ceiling (ceiling piece)   Large canvas-covered frame hung on two or three sets of lines and used to close in the top of an interior set.

Ceiling plate   Metal plate with a ring, used in bolting together and flying a ceiling frame.

Cill iron   *See Sill iron.*

Clearing stick   *See Longarm.*

Cleat   Wooden or metal fitment round which a line may be turned and/or made fast. *See also Fly-rail cleat, Throw-line cleat, Tie-off cleat.*

Clew   Trip (q.v.).

Cloth   Any hanging painted cloth. *See also Cut-cloth, Drop, Stage cloth.*

Collapse   *See Break-up.*

Contour curtain   A curtain which is pulled up by cords or cables in swagged folds. The opening can be adjusted by pulling each cord to a different height. *See also Festoon tabs.*

Corner plate (corner block)   Small triangular piece of plywood used to reinforce joints in the frames of scenery.

Counterweights (counterweight system)   Mechanical system for flying scenery in which the weight of the pieces of scenery is balanced by adjustable weights in a cradle running up and down in guides in a frame normally at the side of the stage.

Cradle   *See Counterweights.*

Crossover   A passageway behind the stage for actors or technicians to cross from one side to the other.

Cue   The signal for an action by an actor or a technician during a performance. Actors' cues are mostly verbal, but for technicians they may be given verbally over the intercom by the stage manager or visually by a cue light.

Curtain line   The imaginary line across the stage immediately behind the proscenium which marks the position of the house tabs when closed. The term is sometimes used to describe the line of descent of the safety curtain, but this is normally downstage of the true curtain line. *See also Setting line.*

Curtain set   A setting comprising either curtains only or mainly curtains with a small amount of painted scenery in the form of an insert or a set piece. The curtains may be any combination of tabs, surround, legs, borders or gauze cloths.

Curtain track   Rails from which draw tabs are hung and along which the runners or bobbins travel when the curtains are moved; the track may be fixed or flown.

Cut   Any long opening in the floor of a stage. *See also Carpet cut.*

Cut-cloth   A cloth which has a part cut out to reveal another cloth set behind; the cut-out portion is often filled with gauze.

Cyclorama   Plain, curved, stretched cloth or rigid structure used as a background to a setting, giving an illusion of infinity. *See also Surround.*

Dead   The predetermined level to which a suspended scenic piece is raised or lowered to take up its correct position in the setting. *See also Trim.*

Dips   Stage dips or dip traps are small traps in the stage containing stage-lighting outlets and electrical cables.

Dock   The scene dock is a store for scenery next to the stage. Scenery is unloaded and taken through the "dock door" into the stage area.

Door stop   Metal plate screwed to the edge of a flat or other piece to provide positive location for the edge of another flat.

Dope   Priming (q.v.).

Double-purchase   A system of blocks and suspension ropes which gears the movement of a counterweight to half that of the scenery it is supporting.

Downstage   Portions of a stage nearest the audience. (To *move downstage* means to move towards the audience; to *move below* a person or object means to move on the side nearest the audience.)

Draperies (drapes)   Any unspecified fabric hanging in folds as a scene or part of a scene, especially curtaining fabrics such as woollens, velvets, etc. *See also Curtain set.*

Draw tabs (curtains)   Curtains suspended from sliding or rolling carriers running in an overhead track and opened by being drawn to the sides.

Drencher   A perforated sparge pipe which in the event of a fire will spray water on the back of the safety curtain.

Dresser   Personal assistant to a star performer or to someone with an elaborate costume.

Drop   Large sheet of canvas battened at top and bottom, hung on a set of lines. The term is also used sometimes to describe a curtain hung on lines and lowered vertically. *See also Act drop.*

Drop holder   Metal fitting for attaching a drop direct to a suspension line. Also called top batten clip.

Elevator   *See Lift.*

False proscenium (show portal)   Arrangement of scenery forming an arch immediately behind the proscenium opening. *See also Teaser and Tormentor.*

Festoon tabs (curtains)   Curtains fixed at the top and raised (opened) by drawing the bottom upwards towards the top and/or sides. *See also Contour curtain.*

Fire curtain   *See Safety curtain.*

Fire-proofed (flame-proofed)   Treated with a flame-inhibiting substance so as to reduce the danger of ignition. (NB. Fire-proofing does not render a material non-combustible.)

Fit-up   Arrangement of constructional units which can be put together and taken apart in a relatively short time and which can be transported from place to place and set up to form a stage etc. in premises not equipped for the performance of stage plays.

Fixing iron   Metal plate with a fixed ring (as distinct from a flying iron, which has a hinged ring), used for scenery suspension.

Flat   A unit section of flat scenery, in the form of a tall screen of canvas stretched upon a wooden frame. *See also Book-flat, Threefold, French flat.*

Flipper   Small piece of flat scenery hinged to a larger piece of flat scenery.

Floats (footlights)   Row of lamps on front edge of stage at floor level and in front of main (house) curtain, used principally to neutralise shadows cast by overhead lighting. Seldom installed in new buildings, though still used in opera houses.

Flown Suspended on lines, as distinct from standing on the stage floor or hanging from fixed rails etc.

Fly Lift above the level of the stage floor by means of sets of lines run from the grid. The term *flys* is also used as an abbreviation for fly gallery.

Fly gallery (flying gallery) A gallery extending along a side wall of the stage, some distance above the stage floor, from which ropes used in flying scenery are operated. Also known as a *fly floor*. The fly galleries are usually referred to collectively as the *flys*.

Flying iron Metal plate with a hinged ring used for scenery suspension.

Fly loft *See Hanging loft.*

Flyman Stage-hand employed on a fly gallery.

Fly rail Heavy rail along the onstage side of a fly gallery, equipped with cleats to which the ropes can be made fast. Also called pin rail.

Fly-rail cleat Metal fitting secured to a fly rail, to which a rope can be easily made fast.

Flys *See Fly gallery.* Sometimes spelled *flies.*

FOH *See Front of house.*

Folding rostrum *See Rostrum.*

Follow spot A high-intensity spotlight controlled and directed by an operator, used to follow, for example, a performer in a variety act.

Foot-iron Metal bracket used with a stage screw or brace-weight to secure scenery or a stage brace in position. *See also Spring foot-iron.*

Footlights *See Floats.*

Forestage Portion of the stage floor in front of the curtain line. *See also Apron.*

Frame *See Paint frame.*

Framed cloth Scenic cloth battened all round.

French brace Triangular frame hinged to the back of a piece of standing scenery and folded flat for storage. Also called jack.

French flat Arrangement of several flats battened together and flown as one unit on a set of lines.

Front cloth Sometimes a painted cloth is brought down near to the house curtain for a front scene to be played on the forestage. This front cloth usually masks scene changes behind it.

Front of house (FOH) Areas of a theatre on the audience side of the proscenium wall or stage area are called FOH.

Gauze (gauze cloth) Flat curtain of fine mesh mosquito netting or similar fabric, either painted or unpainted, which when lit solely from the front appears to be opaque, but when lit from behind becomes transparent. It is used for a transformation scene or other illusions. A fabric known as "shark's tooth" is also used for this purpose.

Get in (and out) The process of delivering and taking scenery and props in and out of a theatre.

Glue size A preparation used in priming and paint for scenery.

Grave trap An oblong trap, usually downstage centre; originally the "ghost trap".

Grid (gridiron) Framework of steel or wooden beams over the stage used to support the sets of lines employed in flying scenery.

Grid pulley *See Loftblock.*

Ground plan Plan of a stage on which is marked the position of the scenery in a setting (including borders, hanging pieces and sometimes lighting equipment).

Groundrow Low topped piece of flat scenery, profiled and painted to represent ground foliage, a bank of earth, a distant mountain range, etc., designed to stand up independently on the stage, used to mask cyclorama lighting units.

Grummet Metal fitting resembling a saddle, for attaching a throw-line to a piece of scenery. Also called lashline eye.

Handling ropes Ropes actually manipulated in flying scenery, as distinct from suspension ropes or cables (counterweight system). Also called hauling line. *See also Hemps.*

Hanging iron (hanger iron) Metal fitting, formed into a square hook at one end, used in flying flats and other framed pieces.

Hanging loft The space above a stage in which scenery can be flown out of sight of the audience. Also called fly tower, fly loft or stage loft.

Hauling line *See Handling ropes.*

Haystack lantern *See Lantern.*

Head block *See Lead block.*

Hemps The term is usually employed to signify lines used for flying scenery which are made from vegetable fibre as distinct from the steel wire ropes used in the counterweight system. Hemp lines are hauled up manually and tied off on a cleat or pin on the fly rail. A *hemp house* is a stage equipped with these hand-operated "hemp sets" and no counterweights. *See Pin-rail system.*

House tabs (curtain) The main curtains between stage and audience, normally placed immediately behind the proscenium (they may be either draw tabs or festoon tabs, and they may be flown).

Inset Small scene set within a larger one.

Iron (iron curtain) *See Safety curtain.*

Jack French brace (q.v.).

Jigger Narrow section set between and hinged to two of the flats forming a threefold so as to allow both of the outer flats to fold painted side inwards onto the centre flat. This section may also be referred to as a tumbler (q.v.).

Jog Narrow flat, usually substantially less than half the width of a standard flat, used to form short return to a major surface and thus increase the illusion of solidity. *See also Reveal (thickness).*

Keystone Small piece of plywood in the wedge shape of an architectural keystone, used to reinforce joints in scenery.

Lantern *Stage lantern* or *haystack lantern* is the term given to the automatic smoke vent over the stage. "Lanterns" are also stage-lighting units, though the recommended word is now *luminaires*.

Lash cleat   Throw-line cleat (q.v.).
Lashline   Throw-line (q.v.).
Lashline eye   Grummet (q.v.).
Lead block (head block)   Device comprising three or more sheaves set together either in a line or parallel to each other on a common shaft and attached to the grid directly above the fly rail. The lines from the three or more loftblocks in a set are brought together at the lead block and pass on down to the fly-rail cleat in a hemp set or to the weight cradle in a counterweight set.
Leg   Vertical length of unframed canvas or other fabric used in place of a wing. *See also Curtain set.*
Lift   Section of stage floor that can be raised or lowered or tilted to provide differing levels of acting area, or to enable changes of setting to be made in the stage basement. Also known as a *bridge* or in North America as an *elevator.*
Lighting batten   *See Batten.*
Limes   Name derived from an early form of lighting, hence "limelight". Now occasionally used to describe front-of-house positions for follow spots.
Lines   *See Set of lines, also Brail, Spot line and Throw-line.*
Loading gallery   Narrow gallery above the fly gallery, used for storing the weights and loading them on the cradles when balancing scenery in the counterweight system.
Locking rail   In a counterweight system the handling rope passes through a rope lock attached to a locking rail which runs the length of the counterweight wall frame.
Loftblock (grid pulley)   Sheave in a metal frame bolted to the grid and used to pass a suspension line; there is one block for each line in a set. *See also Set of lines.*
Longarm (clearing stick)   Long piece of wood or other lightweight material, fitted with a short crosspiece at the upper end, used for freeing scenery, lines etc. when accidentally caught up or fouled.
Louvred ceiling   Arrangement of ceiling pieces, each hung on two sets of lines with the downstage edge higher than the upstage edge, so as to form a ceiling with gaps through which light may be projected.
Luminaire   An illuminating engineer's term for a stage-lighting unit or lantern.
Masking (masking piece)   A piece of scenery, not necessarily painted, used to cut off from the view of the spectators any part of the stage space which should not be seen. *See also Backing and Permanent masking.*
Offstage   Any position on the stage floor out of sight of the audience.
Onstage   Any position on the stage within the acting area.
OP (opposite prompt)   The side of the stage opposite the prompt side: traditionally stage right is actors' right. When the prompt corner, occupied by

the prompter, is on this side of the stage, it is sometimes known as a "bastard prompt".
Pack   All the pieces required for a particular scene when stacked together in the correct order for setting.
Packing rail (stacking rail)   A rail, usually of steel tube, projecting from stage or store wall against which flats are stacked.
Paint bridge   A platform or wide cradle the width of the paint frame which can be hauled up and down, usually mechanically, so that all parts of a cloth can be reached.
Paint frame   The frame to which backcloths, flats etc. are fixed for painting in a vertical position.
Panorama hinge   A hinge formed by two interlinked rings each attached to a metal plate.
Pass door   A door connecting the front of house with the backstage area.
Pelmet clip and socket   Picture-frame hook and socket (q.v.).
Perch   Position above stage level on the stage side of the proscenium wall either side of the opening.
Periaktoi   A triangular-plan-shaped scenic device orginating in the classical Greek theatre. Each surface can be painted with a different subject, colour or texture, so that revolving periaktoi can change a scene.
Permanent masking   Show portal, or teaser and tormentors, or similar arrangements of masking pieces which remain in place throughout a performance, regardless of scene changes.
Picture-frame hook and socket   Two-piece metal fitting used to hang one unit of scenery, or a stage property, on another unit. Also called pelmet clip and socket.
Piece   Any unit of scenery, but more especially a major item.
Pin   Belaying pin, used for making fast hemp lines. *See also Fly-rail cleat.*
Pin hinge   A hinge with removable pin, used so that the two halves may be easily separated.
Pin rail   Fly rail (q.v.).
Pin-rail system   A system for flying scenery in which the suspension lines are taken over loftblocks and lead blocks and then brought straight down to the pin rail (fly rail); there are no counterweights or other means of sustaining the load of the scenery when the lines are free of the pins (cleats).
Pipe batten   Barrel (q.v.).
Platform   *See Rostrum.*
Portal   Unit of permanent masking set between the show portal and the backdrop or cyclorama. In America the term is also used to signify the proscenium opening.
Practical   Capable of being used for its apparent function, as distinct from being merely decorative, e.g. a hinged door, a switch that actually controls a light, etc.

Priming Mixture of glue size and whiting in solution, used as a primer in scene painting. Also called dope.

Profile Plywood or other thin material covered with canvas or scrim, used for forming non-straight edges to wings, groundrows etc.

Prompt corner The stage manager's control point.

Prompt box The traditional position for the prompter in opera is in a box let into the front of the stage.

Prompt side (PS) Traditionally stage left, i.e. actors' left, regardless of the position of the prompter.

Properties (props) Objects, such as furniture, pictures, carpets, flowers, books, implements, weapons, etc., used in a performance.

Proscenium (pros) The theoretical "fourth wall" of a stage, comprising the proscenium opening and its surrounding treatments. *See also False proscenium.*

Proscenium doors Doors on either side of the stage leading on to a forestage in front of the house curtain or act drop.

Proscenium opening (proscenium arch) The opening through which spectators view the stage.

PS *See Prompt side.*

Pulley *See Loftblock.*

Rail Horizontal member of the frame of a flat. *See also Fly rail and Toggle rail.*

Rake A sloped floor of auditorium or stage.

Raking piece Length of wood tapered for placing under a scenic piece so that it will set level on a raked stage floor.

Ramp Inclined rostrum, normally sloping up from the stage floor.

Return The narrower of two flats cleated, hinged or otherwise fixed together at an angle. *See also Jog.*

Reveal (thickness) Piece of timber or other material attached to the edge of an opening (e.g. a doorway) to give the effect of depth or thickness.

Revolve Circular table forming a permanent part of the stage floor or standing upon it, on which scenery can be set for quick changing of scene or for creating various effects. Sometimes the revolve is formed of two or three rings and a centre, capable of independent or simultaneous movement, differing speeds and opposite directions. It can be turned through 360° either manually or by motor.

Rig Set-up scenery on stage. *Rigging* is a collective term for the suspension equipment.

Riser The vertical front of a raised stage where it faces the auditorium is the *stage riser*.

Rocks Rostrum of irregular form, to simulate uneven terrain. If not to be stood or walked upon, the piece comprises only a canvas or other lightweight material covering a wooden framework.

Roller Where there is no flying space over the stage a backdrop can be rolled and is then called a roller or roll drop. Roller safety curtains are permitted in some circumstances.

Rope lock The handling rope of a counterweight set passes through a "rope lock" which when locked prevents any further movement.

Rope sheave *See Loftblock.*

Rostrum Platform placed on the stage floor to create changes of level where required. A large rostrum is usually constructed in sections with loose tops and folding frames, but some small ones are rigid. A sloping rostrum is known as a ramp.

Runner Length of stage flooring that can be drawn off sideways leaving a long narrow opening (cut) through which a cloth or flat may be raised.

Saddle iron *See Sill iron.*

Safety curtain (fire curtain; iron) Screen or shutter comprising a steel framework faced with sheet steel and mineral fibre fabric, mounted immediately behind the proscenium opening and fitted with a mechanism for raising it clear of the top of the proscenium arch and with a quick-release device to allow it to descend by gravity in the event of fire on the stage.

Sandbag Bag of canvas with strap and ring, filled with sand and used for weighting purposes.

Scene pack A set of flats etc. which form a particular set.

Scenery paint Paint composed of glue size and powder colour in water, sometimes with whiting added to give body, used for painting scenery (p.v.a. emulsion paint can also be used for this purpose).

Scrim Coarse woven hessian, or similar material, used in scenery construction.

Set Arrangement of scenery units which together represent a single location. The term is also used as a verb to mean to put up or assemble scenery for use (e.g. to *set a stage*).

Set of lines Unit group of suspension lines hanging from the grid for the attachment and flying of scenery; there are usually three or four lines in a set. *See also Counterweights and Pin-rail system.*

Set piece Built-up unit of scenery, complete in itself, often three-dimensional, and capable of standing free on the stage floor.

Setting line The imaginary line across the stage in front of which scenery cannot be hidden by the house curtain. *See also Curtain line.*

Sheave Grooved wheel (pulley) over which a line may be passed.

Shot-bag Similar to a sandbag but smaller and filed with lead-shot.

Show portal *See False proscenium.*

Sill iron (saddle iron) Narrow strip of metal, often half-round, used to brace the bottom of a door flat across the doorway opening.

Single-purchase A suspension system where there is no gearing of pulleys. The counterweight and its travel will be the same as that of the object which is suspended.

Size   *See Glue size.*

Sky cloth   Unit of scenery used to convey the impression of open sky. *See also Cyclorama.*

Spot block   Pulley fixed to the grid specially for a spot line.

Spot line   Single suspension line specially rigged from the grid to fly a piece of scenery or stage property which cannot be handled by the regular lines.

Spring foot-iron   Form of spring hinge screwed to the bottom of a piece of scenery or a French brace, for securing to the floor, self-closing out of the way when not in use.

Stacking rail   *See Packing rail.*

Stage brace   Adjustable device comprising two lengths of wood sliding one along the other and held fast by clamps; used to prop scenery from behind. *See also French brace.*

Stage cloth   Large piece of canvas, used to cover the stage floor, often painted to represent paving etc.

Stage lantern   *See Lantern.*

Stage left   Actors' left. *See Prompt side.*

Stage loft   *See Hanging loft.*

Stage right   Actors' right. *See OP.*

Stage screw   Large tapered wood screw with a ring handle, used to secure a foot-iron to the stage floor.

Star (star trap)   *See Trap.*

Steps (treads)   Light portable stairway, normally in unit sections for easy handling.

Stile   Side or upright member in the frame of a flat.

Strike   Take apart and remove from the acting area a set of scenery after it has been used, usually at the end of an act.

Surround (curtains)   Set of legs (ordinary pleated curtains) hung from a curved or angled bar to form the sides and background to an acting area. *See also Curtain set.*

Swag   Looped-up curtain, border or leg.

Swivel arm   Device for suspending a leg so that the angle of the leg in relation to the proscenium can be varied.

Tableau curtains (tabs)   Either the house tabs (q.v.) or similar curtains which can be opened to reveal a scene. *See Draw tabs, Festoon tabs, also Curtain set.*

Tail   The length of flex from a stage-lighting unit.

Teaser   Border hung between the tormentors, just behind the proscenium opening. *See also Permanent masking.*

Threefold   An arrangement of three flats hinged together.

Throw-line   Length of cord attached by a grummet to a piece of scenery and used to secure the piece to an adjacent piece.

Throw-line cleat   Metal fitting attached to a flat or other piece, round which the throw-line is passed when securing adjacent pieces together.

Thunder sheet   A sheet of metal, usually steel, suspended somewhere on the stage area, which when shaken gives a sound effect of thunder.

Tie-off cleat   Metal fitting around which a throw-line is made fast.

Toggle rail   Movable horizontal member in the frame of a flat, between the top rail and the bottom rail.

Top batten clip   Drop holder (q.v.).

Tormentor   Substantial wing, not necessarily painted, placed immediately behind the pro-scenium opening, to mask the offstage edges of the setting etc. *See also Permanent masking.*

Track (curtain track)   Rails from which curtains are hung and along which they may move.

Trap   An opening in the stage floor. Special-purpose traps are grave traps, dip traps, star traps.

Treads   *See Steps.*

Trim   Level off a piece of suspended scenery at the right height for use during a performance.

Trim chain   Short length of chain used in attaching the top batten of a cloth to a barrel.

Trip   Raise the bottom of a drop or other piece of suspended scenery, using an auxiliary set of lines, so as to make it occupy a space approximately half its height; tripping is resorted to on stages where there is not sufficient height above the stage floor to get the unit out of sight by taking it straight up with one set of lines only.

Truck   *See Wagon.*

Tumbler   Batten or roller fixed to the bottom edge of a cloth, about which the cloth can be rolled upwards when not in use.

Twofold   Book-flat (q.v.).

Upstage   The portions of the stage furthest from the audience. (To *move upstage* means to move away from the audience; to *move above* a person or object means to move on the side furthest from the audience.)

Velarium   Ceiling cloth, not stretched or battened out, but hanging as a canopy.

Vomitory   An entrance through a block of seating as distinct from through the surrounding wall.

Wagon (truck)   Low trolley, either running in tracks or free-moving, on which scenery etc. can be mounted for horizontal linear movements of settings.

Winch   Mechanism, either hand-operated or motorised, for opening and closing curtains etc.

Wing   Two or three flats hinged together and used at the side of the stage to mask offstage space.

Wings   Offstage spaces to left and right of the acting area.

Wing set (backcloth-and-wing set)   Setting comprising backcloth (or cyclorama) and pairs of wings with borders above. Sometimes cut cloths are used in the place of wings and borders (e.g. for a woodland scene).

Bibliography

ABTT Information Sheet No. 5: *Safety Check Lists for Theatre Managements*

Aloi, R., *Teatri e Auditori* (*Theatres and Auditoriums*), Milan, 1972, Hoepli

American Theater Planning Board Inc., *Theater Check List*, Middletown, Connecticut, 1969, Wesleyan University Press

Athanasopoulos, Christos G., *Contemporary Theater: Evolution and Design*, 1983

Baur-Heinhold, Margarete, *Baroque Theatre*, London, 1967, Thames & Hudson (1st German edition 1966)

Bentham, Frederick, *The Art of Stage Lighting*, London, 3rd edition 1980, A. and C. Black

Bentham, Frederick, *New Theatres in Britain*, London, 1970, Rank Strand Electric Ltd

Burris-Meyer, H., and E. C. Cole, *Theatres and Auditoriums*, New York, 1964, Reinhold; 2nd edition 1975, London, Chapman & Hall

Collison, David, *Stage Sound*, London, 1976, Studio Vista

Cremer, L., and H. A. Müller, *Principles and Applications of Room Acoustics*, 1978; Vol. 1, translated by Theodore Schultz, London, 1982, Applied Science Publishers

Elsom, John, *Theatre Outside London*, London, 1971, Macmillan

Forsyth, Michael, *Auditoria Designing for the Performing Arts*, London, 1987, Batsford

Forsyth, Michael, *Buildings for Music – The Architect, the Musician and the Listener from the 17th Century to the Present Date*, 1985, Cambridge University Press

Gascoigne, Bamber, *World Theatre*, London, 1968, Ebury Press

Gillette, A. S., *Stage Scenery, its construction and rigging*

Giteau, Cécile, *Dictionnaire des Arts du Spectacle*, Paris, Dunod

Glasstone, Victor, *Victorian and Edwardian Theatres*, London, 1975, Thames & Hudson

Graubner, Gerhard, *Theater-Aufgabe und Planung*, Munich, 1968, Callway

Greater London Council, *Places of Public Entertainment: Technical Regulations*, Publication 378, London, 1971, GLC

Greater London Council, *Play Safe – A guide to standards in halls used for occasional stage presentations*, London, 1968, GLC

Greater London Council, *Code of Practice: Means of Escape in Case of Fire*, Publication 7168, London, 1974, GLC

Hartnoll, Phyllis (ed.), *Oxford Companion to the Theatre* (4th edition), London, 1983, Oxford University Press

Home Office, *Manual of Safety Requirements in Theatres and Other Places of Public Entertainment*, London, 1934, HM Stationery Office

Izenour, George C., *Theater Design*, London, 1977, McGraw-Hill

Joseph, Stephen, *Theatre in the Round*, London, 1967, Barrie & Rockliff

Joseph, Stephen, *The Story of the Playhouse in England*, London, 1967, Barrie & Rockliff

Joseph, Stephen, *New Theatre Forms*, London, 1968, Pitman

Leacroft, Richard and Helen, *Theatre and Playhouse*, London, 1984, Methuen

Leacroft, Richard, *The Development of the English Playhouse*, London, 1973, Eyre-Methuen

Lord, Peter, and Duncan Templeton, *The Architecture of Sound: Designing Places of Assembly*, London, 1986, Architectural Press

Lord, Peter, and Duncan Templeton, *Detailing for Acoustics* (2nd edition), London, 1986, Architectural Press

Mackintosh, Iain, Michael Sell and Victor Glasstone, *Curtains!!! or New Life for Old Theatres*, 1982, London, John Offord (Publications) Ltd

Meyer, Jurgen, *Acoustics and the Performance of Music*, Verlag das Musikinstrument, Frankfurt-am-Main

Mielziner, Jo, *The Shapes of our Theatre*, New York, Potter

Miller, James Hull, *Designing Small Theatres*, 1982

Mullin, Donald C., *The Development of the Playhouse*, Berkeley and Los Angeles, 1970, University of California Press

Nicoll, Allardyce, *The Development of Theatre*, London, 1958, Harrap

Parkin, P. H., and H. R. Humphreys, *Acoustics, Noise and Buildings* (4th edition), London, 1979, Faber & Faber

Pearson, A., *Arts for Everyone: Guidance on Provision for Disabled People*, 1985, Carnegie UK Trust and Centre for the Handicapped

Pilbrow, Richard, *Stage Lighting*, London, 2nd edition, 1979, Studio Vista

Reid, Francis, *The Staging Handbook*, London, 1978, Pitman

Reid, Francis, *Stagelighting Handbook*, London, 2nd edition, 1982, A. and C. Black

Reid, Francis, *Theatre Administration*, London, 1983, A. & C. Black

Sachs, Edwin O., and E. A. E. Woodrow, *Modern Opera Houses and Theatres: London 1896–1898*, NJ, 1968, Arno Press

Schubert, Hannelore, *The Modern Theatre*, London, 1971, Pall Mall Press (first German edition 1971)

Silverman, Maxwell, and Ned A. Bowman, *Contemporary Theatre Architecture* (includes extensive bibliography), 1965, New York Public Library

Simpson, Robert, *Effective Audio-Visual – A User's Handbook*, London, 1987, Focal Press

Southern, Richard, *The Georgian Playhouse*, 1948, London, Pleiades Books Ltd

Southern, Richard, *The Open Stage*, London, 1953, Faber & Faber

Southern, Richard, *The Seven Ages of the Theatre*, London, 1962, Faber & Faber

Sweeting, Elizabeth, *Theatre Administration*, London, 1969, Pitman

"Tabs" Publications, *Stage Planning 1971*,
  London, Rank Strand Electric Ltd
Talaske, R. H., E. A. Wetherill and W. J.
  Cavanaugh, *Halls for Music Performance: Two
  Decades of Experience 1962–1982*, New York,
  1982, American Institute of Physics for the
  Acoustical Society of America
Thomson, Peter, and Gamini Salgado, *The Every-
  man Companion to the Theatre*, London, 1985,
  J. M. Dent & Sons
Tidworth, Simon, *Theatres, an Architectural and
  Cultural History*, London, 1973, Pall Mall Press
Walne, Graham, *Sound for Theatres – A Basic
  Manual*, London, 1981, John Offord
Warre, Michael, *Designing and Making Scenery*,
  London, 1967, Studio Vista

Periodicals

ABTT Newsletter, Association of British Theatre
  Technicians, London
Acta Scaenographica, Praha 2, Vinohradska 2
AS Actualité de la Scénographie, Les Éditions de
  Vincennes, France
Bühnentechnische Rundschau, Berlin
Cue, Twynham Publishing Ltd, England
Sightline, Association of British Theatre Tech-
  nicians, London
Tabs Quarterly, Rank Strand Electric (now discon-
  tinued)
Theatre Crafts, Rodale Press Inc., Emmaus, Pa,
  USA
*Theatre Design and Technology, Journal of the
  U.S. Institute of Theatre Technology*, New York

Index